D1300182

Soft Canons

Edited by

Karen L. Kilcup

Soft Canons

American

Women

Writers and

Masculine

Tradition

University of Iowa Press

Iowa City

University of Iowa Press,
Iowa City 52242
Copyright © 1999 by the
University of Iowa Press
All rights reserved
Printed in the United States of America
Design by Richard Hendel
http://www.uiowa.edu/~uipress
No part of this book may be reproduced
or used in any form or by any means,
electronic or mechanical, including
photocopying and recording, without
permission in writing from the publisher.
All reasonable steps have been taken to
contact copyright holders of material used
in this book. The publisher would be
pleased to make suitable arrangements with
any whom it has not been possible to reach.
Printed on acid-free paper

Library of Congress
Cataloging-in-Publication Data
Soft canons: American women writers
and masculine tradition / edited by
Karen L. Kilcup.
p. cm.
Includes bibliographical references and
index.
ISBN 0-87745-688-7, ISBN 0-87745-689-5
(paper)
1. American literature—Women
authors—History and criticism.
2. American literature—Male authors—
History and criticism. 3. Women and
literature—United States—History.
4. Influence (Literary, artistic, etc.).
5. Authorship—Sex differences.
6. Masculinity in literature. 7. Canon
(Literature). 8. Men in literature.
I. Kilcup, Karen L.
PS147.S67 1999
810.9'9287—dc21 99-29209

99 00 01 02 03 C 5 4 3 2 1
99 00 01 02 03 P 5 4 3 2 1

For my father

RICHARD S. KILCUP

(1931–1997)

Contents

Acknowledgments

Completing this project has been a great pleasure; many thanks to the contributors for not only their excellent essays but also their patience and timeliness. I am grateful to the University of Hull in in England, my home institution in 1995, for financial assistance when I formed the International Nineteenth-Century American Writers Research Group, whose members are well-represented here. I want to thank Susanne Opfermann for the opportunity to give a keynote address at a conference on nineteenth-century American women writers at the Johann Wolfgang Goethe-Universität in Frankfurt on materials related to the introduction of this volume, and I appreciate the many thoughtful comments of the conference participants on my remarks. I believe it is important for scholars in the United States to reach beyond national boundaries and construct dialogues and alliances with international scholars as the field of nineteenth-century American women's writing and the broader study of nineteenth-century American literature mature. The University of North Carolina at Greensboro has provided generous support in the form of a Regular Faculty Research Grant and in the shape of such excellent research assistants as Kelly Richardson and Anna Elkins. I appreciate the helpful suggestions of my colleague Christian Moraru. Thanks again to Jim Evans, my department head, and Walter Beale, the dean of the College of Arts and Sciences, for their continuing support. I am also grateful for the support and vision of my editor, Holly Carver, and assistance of the editorial staff at the University of Iowa Press, including my excellent copyeditor, Carolyn Brown; they have eased the production process with their efficiency. As always, this book could not have been completed without the patience, generosity, and humor of my husband, Chris.

Appearing here with some revisions, Judie Newman's "Was Tom White? Stowe's *Dred* and Twain's *Pudd'nhead Wilson*" is reprinted by permission from *Slavery and Abolition*, vol. 20. Published by Frank Cass Publishers, 900 Eastern Ave., Ilford, Essex IG2 7HH, England. Copyright © Frank Cass and Co. Ltd., 1999. Grateful acknowledgement is made for permission to reprint.

Soft Canons

The Conversation of "The Whole Family": Gender, Politics, and Aesthetics in Literary Tradition

KAREN L. KILCUP

In 1849 tireless anthologist and literary guru Rufus Griswold separated his bestselling *The Poets and Poetry of America* into two collections. The first, with the same title, contained only male poets. The second, *The Female Poets of America*, expanded the selection of increasingly popular women writers. The implications of this division were clear: male poets represented "real" poetry, while their female counterparts occupied a separate category—what Robert Frost would later call "sentimental sweet singer[s]"—appealing largely to a female audience.[1] If from one angle Griswold's gesture celebrated the achievements of his female contemporaries—and if Griswold worked personally to advance the reputations of many women poets—from another perspective this separate publication emblematized and helped inaugurate the bifurcated consideration of American male and female writers, of "masculine" and "feminine" traditions, that is still very much with us. A central goal of *Soft Canons* is to explore connections, discuss mutual influences, and propose theories of difference or alliance, attempting to bring together these separate spheres of criticism and to create a more richly textured account of American literary history.[2]

At this point one might well ask, what *are* masculine and feminine literary traditions? These terms are of course constantly in flux, negotiating with ideas of canon and criticism that, as I will outline below, have themselves changed dramatically over time. Moreover, although such traditions may have had a degree of internal coherence (with varying degrees of self-awareness) at the

moment of their elaboration, they are also created and transformed retrospectively by readers who tell different stories of
their development. To speak of them as actual facts rather than
virtual events in some sense falsifies them. We also need to recognize that both writers and critics were involved (sometimes differently) in the creation of literary traditions and that literary criticism identified itself as a "discipline" only in the opening decades
of the twentieth century, when the evaluation of literary texts
moved from the broader ("popular") culture into the academy.[3]
In addition, what was masculine to one generation would sometimes prove feminine to another: the gendered quality of literary
production varied, depending on the position of the critic and his
or her historical moment. Finally, "aesthetics" and "politics" have
been intricately connected in American literary history.

I wish to suggest here that literary criticism has not only severed feminine and masculine traditions, it has done so in a way
that has made a genuine reintegration of the canon more difficult.
By often conceptualizing women's writing *in opposition* to male
writing, this scholarship, some of it feminist, has opened a gap
that is difficult to bridge.[4] In some sense, the impetus for discussions about the canon in recent years has emerged from an ongoing debate about the appropriate situation of "the aesthetic"
(often, in a political move, identified with the masculine or the
male) and "the political" (often identified with the feminine or the
female) in American literary tradition.[5] Another important goal of
Soft Canons, then, is to work toward a model of criticism that
closes these fractures. Critics' oppositional stance may in fact
emerge from the structure and protocols of literary criticism itself, and, in particular, "the use of argument as the preferred
mode for discussion." The adversarial strategy demands that we
distinguish ourselves from our predecessors, that we clear our
own intellectual space, "establishing credibility or cognitive authority";[6] such a strategy almost determines an adversarial rather
than a dialogical stance. At the same time, as I point out in more
specific terms below, it may be necessary for a group attempting
to identify its tradition at least initially to demarcate an aesthetic
and/or cultural terrain in distinction from the "mainstream" in
order to achieve an acknowledged presence in literary history. We
need to ask, however, how long such a separate identity is useful,
for opposing the "mainstream" necessarily reiterates its centrality.

The essays in *Soft Canons* suggest that it may be more beneficial at this moment of cultural fragmentation in the United States to inquire into the conversations between, and even the meshing of, "traditions"—here principally masculine and feminine, but also black and white, straight and gay, Western and Eastern—while continuing to value the particularity of each.[7]

The distinction between male and female authors' work—and an awareness of the constructed tension between aesthetics and politics—has inflected American literature from the time of Anne Bradstreet's pronouncement in "The Prologue" that "carping tongues" would consign her hand to the "needle," not the "pen," and that she was radically circumscribed by gender expectations: "If what I do prove well, it won't advance, / They'll say it's stol'n, or else it was by chance." In the nineteenth century, at virtually the same moment in American literary history that Griswold performed his radical surgery on poetic tradition, Nathaniel Hawthorne was complaining privately (though now famously) to his friend and publisher William D. Ticknor about the "damned mob of scribbling women," whom he claimed dominated the literary marketplace, in effect recreating segregated literary traditions.[8] Several years before Hawthorne's grousing, Margaret Fuller had reviewed the terrain of "American literature" in curiously bifurcated—and, where female poets were concerned, wholly elliptical—terms. Fuller's critical overview of American prose includes the historians William Hickling Prescott and George Bancroft along with Emerson and Cooper; she touches upon the contributions of Catharine Maria Sedgwick and Caroline Kirkland in one very brief paragraph and devotes only a single sentence to Lydia Maria Child and Anne Stephens. Poets include Bryant, Fitz-Greene Halleck, Richard Henry Dana, Longfellow, Lowell, and others, but exclude entirely the huge, and hugely popular, contingent of women represented in Griswold's anthology: Elizabeth Oakes Smith, Lydia Sigourney, and Frances Sargent Osgood among them.[9] In some sense, Fuller performed a criticism that regarded masculine and feminine—here, *literally* male and female—traditions in tandem but not necessarily in dialogue.

The path to the current segregation between these traditions was, however, a circuitous one. Writers, as opposed to critics or reviewers, often seemed to interact briskly and profitably. In the late nineteenth century, for example, William Dean Howells presided over the development of a realistic fiction that attempted to correct the emotional excesses of ostensibly feminine senti-mental literature, but his movement included female as well as male writers: Sarah Orne Jewett, Mary Wilkins Freeman, and Alice Brown among them. Even in antebellum America, review-ers, as Nina Baym suggests, were both male and female, and their "opinions [did] not divide along gender lines."[10]

Although other anthologists and critics did not necessarily fol-low Griswold's lead in this approach, literary culture as a whole would become increasingly bifurcated, culminating in modernist critics' "disappearing" (popular) women writers from the canon, often on the basis of their inadequate aesthetic merit and/or their overinvestment in political and, hence, nonuniversal concerns.[11] This disappearance was perhaps most evident and most hostile in the case of poetry — not surprisingly, since the most influential early modernist critics were T. S. Eliot and Ezra Pound. The dis-tinctions and oppositions that were made at the turn of the cen-tury and into the twentieth century emerged in a variety of loca-tions: for example, in anthologist Edmund Clarence Stedman's jittery assertion in his *American Anthology* (1901) that "the work of [women's] brother poets is not emasculate, and will not be while grace and tenderness fail to make men coward, and beauty re-mains the flower of strength"; in an essay in the elite *Century Mag-azine* by poet-critic Helen Gray Cone claiming that "sentimental-ism has infected both continents [America and England]" and disparaging "the flocks of quasi-swan singers"; in a later, famous essay by poet-critic Louise Bogan in which she observed that "women . . . contributed in a large measure to the general leveling, dilution, and sentimentalization of verse, as well as of prose, dur-ing the nineteenth century."[12] Female writers like Bogan and Marianne Moore would be admitted to an increasingly masculin-ized and aestheticized literary field only on the condition that they wrote unemotional, detached, and intellectual poetry: that they wrote "like men" and contributed to masculine literary tradition.[13]

Yet many modern critics, like Van Wyck Brooks, however much they might condescend to some women writers, neverthe-less discussed them alongside their male counterparts: Catharine Maria Sedgwick and Lydia Maria Child on the same page with Emerson and Hawthorne, for example. Brooks devoted substan-tial attention to Margaret Fuller and Harriet Beecher Stowe well before the recent renaissance of interest in these writers.[14] He also acknowledged that the years after the Civil War were dominated by women writers: "The 'glorious phalanx of old maids' that rejoiced the heart of Theodore Parker was to dominate New England for an age to come, the age of the 'strong-minded women' that might have been called the age of the weak-minded men."[15] Though it was explicitly limited to white, New England writers, Brooks's account offers one example of an attempt to envision an holistic American literary tradition. With the development of a modernist aesthetic criticism opposed to Brooks's historical approach, this kind of linking between men and women writers would virtually disappear; the new paradigm was F. O. Matthiessen's powerful *American Renaissance*, which, with its narrow assumptions about the aesthetic, managed to reduce an eclectic and polyvocal period to a tiny group of writers, with Emily Dickinson noteworthy by her absence. Joanne Dobson has pointed out the limitation of this still-current definition of the American Renaissance, observing that "the 1850s saw a variegated literary arena in which realism contended with romanticism, popular sentimentalism influenced private thinking and public policy at least as much as did high-minded cultural analysis, and the writing of women achieved a visibility equal to that of the writing of men."[16] In spite of these realities, American literary tradition became synonymous with male — white male — writing.

With the arrival of feminist and minority perspectives in the critical domain beginning in the mid-to-late 1960s, writing by women, men and women of color, gays and lesbians, and other excluded groups began to be the subject of investigations, but it was necessary to establish these traditions *as* traditions, to explore the minoritized writing by itself, to make claims for its aesthetic as well as cultural significance.[17] During the 1970s and 1980s these perspectives helped to generate a flood of recovered and new work, from the authentication of *Incidents in the Life of a Slave Girl* by Jean Fagan Yellin to the recognition of Toni Morrison with the Nobel Prize for Literature. The appearance of *The Heath Anthology of American Literature* in 1990 — a project conceived and inaugurated, Paul Lauter tells us, in 1968 — marked a turning point in the reintegration of the canon, and yet literary criticism itself has been slow to react to this reintegration and to develop a synthetic and nonoppositional view of nineteenth-century American writing.

Studies such as David S. Reynolds's *Beneath the American Renaissance* and Suzanne Clark's *Sentimental Modernism* begin to suggest the fruitfulness of a comparative approach across gender.[18] As Dobson observes, "A truly revisionary history of nineteenth-century America will work toward dismantling hierarchical assumptions that privilege masculine experience over feminine, elite literature over popular, and the culturally dissenting over the culturally embedded" (165).[19] Attempting to heal the bifurcation in language that is embedded even in affirmative and proactive accounts like Dobson's, this revisionary history must, as *Soft Canons* does, include a consideration of male and female writers together: of their mutual influences, their alliances and alienations, and their construction of the terms of literature.

It is important to pause to acknowledge the direct influences and personal relationships that existed between many of these writers: Hawthorne may have been critical as well as complimentary when he affirmed of Fanny Fern that "the woman writes as if the devil was in her" (17:307), but like many of his counterparts in the nineteenth and early twentieth centuries, he had close relationships, whether competitive, affiliative, or supportive, with women writers.[20] Well-known associations include those between Whittier and Lucy Larcom, Frances Sargent Osgood and Edgar Allan Poe, Henry James and Constance Fenimore Woolson, and, of course, Emily Dickinson and Thomas Wentworth Higginson. As Shirley Marchalonis has observed, such literary friendships have been repeatedly been oversimplified: "either [the male] was the mentor who taught her to write and used his influence to have her work published, or else she was in love with him." She adds, "In either case, critical interpretation has made her the inferior being. . . ." Moreover, scholarship has frequently ignored the role of women as mentors for male artists.[21] Some of the essays in *Soft Canons* expand our understanding of such relationships, while others outline the poignant absence of such relationships where they were perhaps most urgently needed.

Perhaps no text better emblematizes the relationship between male and female writers than the "collaborative" novel, *The Whole Family*, which serves as both an instance of and metaphor for cross-gender conversation in American literary history in the opening moments of the twentieth century.[22] In some sense, *The*

Whole Family illuminates the complex relationship between aesthetics and politics, and highlights the alienation between feminine and masculine literary traditions, that would come to dominate criticism in the next sixty-odd years. The novel was conceived in 1906 by William Dean Howells, who suggested the project to Elizabeth Jordan, then editor of *Harper's Bazar*. Howells sought to assemble a group of eleven other distinguished authors who would each month contribute a new chapter to be published serially in Jordan's magazine and later collected into a book. He proposed that the book would depict an ordinary American family whose "Young Girl" had just become engaged to be married, and he projected that each contributor would write from the point of view of a family member or friend.[23] Jordan, who agreed to act as editor, hoped to showcase regular contributors to the Harper's group of magazines and "to bring together the greatest, grandest, most gorgeous group of authors ever collaborating on a literary production."[24] Yet the pair's plans for the "Harper's family of writers" encountered unexpected difficulties. Some contributors wanted to be paid more than the project promised; others could not fit it into their timetable; some agreed to participate and then later bowed out; others, considered very important to the project (such as Mark Twain), declined altogether.[25]

The difficulties attending the novel's inauguration were dwarfed, however, by its actualization. The "conversation" of the "whole family" of American authors fractured sharply along gendered lines: Mary Wilkins Freeman, by then a fading if still admired figure, managed to interrogate the trajectory of the domestic romance toward inevitable marriage by creating "The Maiden Aunt" as an attractive — even erotic — "other woman" who intervenes between the young engaged couple. According to Alfred Bendixen, although Freeman "had a great deal of respect and admiration for Howells . . . apparently his remarks on women in the first chapter, particularly his treatment of the old-maid aunt, irritated her. Freeman felt that Howells's conception of the aunt was based on outdated values that condemned a single woman in her thirties to an eternal and dowdy spinsterhood" (xxii). In a letter to Jordan defending her chapter, Freeman highlighted the many single women for whom "their single state is a deliberate choice on their part, and men are at their feet. Single women have caught up with, and passed, old bachelors in the last half of the century.

I don't think Mr. Howells recognizes this. He is thinking of the time when women of thirty put on caps, and renounced the world. That was because they married at fifteen and sixteen, and at thirty had about a dozen children. Now they simply do not do it" (quoted in Jordan, 266). It is worth noting that Freeman herself had been single until she was forty-nine, and Jordan was at the time single and in her early forties.

Freeman's Aunt Elizabeth embodies not only sexual freedom but also freedom of speech; she tells us, "I have never cared an iota whether I was considered an old maid or not," and she complains of the narrowness of small-town life: "Here I am estimated according to what people think I am, rather than what I actually am" (30, 31). That Elizabeth's complaint extends beyond the boundaries of an individual character is evident in her later pronouncement: "men know so little of women" (38). Not surprisingly, Freeman's chapter provoked a brouhaha among the members of the "family"; Henry van Dyke was among Freeman's critics, writing to Jordan, "Heavens! What a catastrophe! Who would have thought that the maiden aunt would go mad in the second chapter? Poor lady. Red hair and a pink bow and boys in beau-knots all over the costume. What *will* Mr. Howells say?" (quoted in Bendixen, xxiii). According to Jordan, "The gentle and lovable William Dean Howells sent me a letter that almost scorched the paper it was written on" (264). The dissent sparked by Freeman's chapter opened a Pandora's box of problems: "the plot increasingly focused on family misunderstandings and family rivalries, which were mirrored by the artistic rivalries of the authors. The writing of the novel became as much a contest as a collaboration, with each author trying hard to impose his vision on the entire work" (Bendixen, xxvi). As Dale M. Bauer has observed, "The spinster delays the conventional marriage plot and thereby forces us to confront the alternative plots for women offered" in the novel.[26]

Both the text and the "pretext" of *The Whole Family* provide us with a valuable window into the cultural (as well as literary) atmosphere that had evolved by the turn of the century, indicating one version of the relation of masculine to feminine tradition as the writers themselves regarded it.[27] If Freeman alarmed her famous contemporaries, her chapter was in some sense meant to alarm. In fact, it offered to men like Howells and James (and many of their more conventional female counterparts) nothing less than a wake-up call and a battle cry. For Freeman and others, such as Sarah Orne Jewett, Rose Terry Cooke, Pauline Elizabeth Hopkins, and Alice Dunbar-Nelson, the image of woman as both erotic and autonomous was hardly a new insight. Freeman highlighted the role of the woman writer as a determined and sometimes self-aware outsider in the "home" of the American domestic text; that is, her intervention into the drama of *The Whole Family* problematized the history of men's representation of women, making a marginal and stereotypical character (the "maiden aunt") central to that family history. Sexualizing the ostensibly nonsexual, beautifying the ostensibly aging, and giving voice to the putatively silent, Freeman exposed the ways in which gender authorized a buried story, as she revivified the strong presence of women both inside and outside American literary history. This story attempted to require women — both as writers and characters, as participants in their own texts — to costume themselves in convention, while at the same time it produced surreal and comic effects in the work of many of its male creators. In effect, Freeman exposed the political foundation of ostensibly aesthetic matters.

Masculine tradition dictated that women writers should not transgress beyond certain imaginative boundaries structured by "the home."[28] Following Kate Chopin's *The Awakening*, which depicted adulterous sexual desire, Freeman's portrait of Aunt Elizabeth deconstructed the stereotype of the virgin old maid while it directly challenged Howells, the man who in some sense embodied the tradition.[29] Not surprisingly, power and control are fundamental concerns in *The Whole Family*'s narrative of gender, and the masculine tradition would not be able to "keep the women contributors in their 'place'" (Crowley, 112). Howells's ostensibly bland opening chapter touched on a number of sensitive spots for Freeman and her contemporaries. One was the matter of coeducation; the dialogue of Howells's father with his neighbor, Ned Temple, suggests anxiety about the subject, affirming, "When you think of the sort of hit-or-miss affairs most marriages are that young people make after a few parties and picnics, coeducation as a preliminary to domestic happiness doesn't seem a bad notion" (6). A man of influence and authority in the community who "held the leading law firm in the hollow of his hand," Talbert can afford, literally, to make such judgments. Howells dug himself in deeper with Freeman, however, in his portrait of "Aunt Elizabeth." Ned Temple, the editor-neighbor with whom Freeman would construct an earlier love affair for Aunt Elizabeth, muses that "My wife inferred from the generation to which [Talbert] belonged that [Elizabeth] had long been a lady of that age when ladies begin to be spoken of as maiden" (19). The irony here is that seeing only her role as "Aunt Elizabeth," he, like many others, misses that individual's existence as "Lily Talbert," as Lily herself acknowledges.

To be fair to Howells, he eventually allows the patriarch Talbert to articulate a philosophy of equal education for men and women, but even in this "The Father" proves objectionable: "You see, I've always had the idea that women, beginning with little girls and ending with grandmothers, ought to be brought up as nearly like their brothers as can be — that is, if they are to be the wives of other women's brothers. It doesn't so much matter how an old maid is brought up, but you can't have her destiny in view, though I believe if an old maid could be brought up more like an old bachelor she would be more comfortable to herself, anyway" (23; see Bauer, 110; Perosa, 108–109). To the creator of "A New England Nun," "Louisa," and other strong and relatively contented single women, such a philosophy must have seemed like giving with one hand and taking back with the other. Freeman was not the only one to object to Howells's chapter, for Elizabeth Stuart Phelps would pick up on his hint of a bossy older daughter (12–13) and Edith Wyatt on his suggestion of an opinionated, hypochondriac grandmother (15–16) to create other portraits of dissenting women. Far from being "realistic" depictions of women, Howells's portraits, they suggested, were outdated, even sentimental: paradoxically, in the critical context developing at the time, feminine.

Freeman's criticism of masculine literary tradition for its attempt to confine women writers' subject matter to the domestic and for its warped creation of women and the homes they inhabit permeates her chapter. Howells's mansard-roofed house embodies for Freeman the limitations of his art, as well as of his politics; Elizabeth observes: "I have always had a theory that inanimate things exert more of an influence over people than they dreamed, and a mansard-roof, to my mind, belongs to a period which was most unsophisticated and fatuous, not merely concerning aesthetics, but simple comfort. Those bedrooms under the mansardroof are miracles not only of ugliness, but discomfort, and there is no attic. I think that a house without a good roomy attic is like a man without brains" (32). The creator of such an antediluvian, ugly, and uncomfortable "home" could scarcely have missed the analogy. To crown the lesson, Elizabeth-cum-Freeman affirms, "today an old-maid aunt is as much of an anomaly as a spinningwheel, that she has ceased to exist, that she is prehistoric, that even grandmothers have almost disappeared from off the face of the earth" (33). No wonder Howells's letter to Jordan nearly caught fire.

As these passages reveal, the distance between what we would call "aesthetics" and "politics" is very small indeed, and Freeman is (infuriatingly) conscious of her position in the gender wars of the period.[30] Women's clothing, another aesthetic signifier, becomes another declaration of independence for Aunt Elizabeth. The members of the family — not just the fictional family, but the traditionalists such as Howells and the women who assume a subservient position in his literary "family" — "all unanimously consider that I should dress always in black silk, and a bonnet with a neat little tuft of middle-aged violets, and black ribbons tied under my chin." Elizabeth's confessed "sense of humor," however, elaborates another, shockingly erotic and exposed aesthetic: "I know I am wicked to put on that pink gown and hat, but I shall do it" (45). "The Mother" speaks for the whole family: "Ada really looked more disturbed than I have ever seen her. If I had been Godiva, going for my sacrificial ride through the town, it could not have been much worse. She made her eyes round and big, and asked, in a voice which was really agitated, 'Are you going out in that dress, Aunt Elizabeth?'" (45 – 46). Sexual licentiousness, outspokenness, and a self-determined bodily aesthetic threaten the harmony of the American "family," both literal and literary.

I highlight "American" deliberately here, for it seems that the only way to restore harmony in *The Whole Family* is for some family members to leave the country and go to Europe, just as Henry James expatriated one version of the novel itself at the end of the nineteenth century.[31] Not surprisingly, although Mary Stewart Cutting intimated this departure in "The Daughter-in-Law," James provided the major impetus for this movement abroad, offering a way out of the domestic crisis in his long-winded chapter on "The Married Son," who represents the artist trapped by commitments to the family business. In indirect support of Howells, James's character affirms, "I think we should really all ban together, for once in our lives, in an unnatural alliance to get rid of Eliza" (164; see Perosa, 112). To this end, *The Whole Family* not only departs from America and its strong women, it concludes, ironically and rather schizophrenically, with a gesture toward marriage more typical of the traditional nineteenth-century domestic novel than of the "modern" novel. In the final chapter — written by Henry van Dyke, another strong supporter of Howells in the affairs of *The Whole Family* — "The Friend of the Family" observes, with no tangible irony: "Everything has turned out just as it should, like a romance in an old-fashioned ladies magazine" (303).[32] And he is ultimately right, with the glaring exception of Aunt Elizabeth, who, having joined a New York partnership as a clairvoyant, nevertheless hovers over the closing image of Peggy, "the brave little girl, her red hair like an aureole, waving her flag of victory and peace" (315). Although van Dyke declares "victory," it is a Pyrrhic one at best, since one version of feminine literary tradition determines the ending.

Masculine and feminine literary traditions as embodied in *The Whole Family* converge, however, in the contributors' elision of the central and troubling issue of race in American culture. Racial difference remains nearly unremarked in the novel, surfacing only in the elusive presence of a cook with a fondness for children, Sallie, who is referred to elsewhere as "the darky" (92, 106, 240, 244). Sallie's occupation highlights not only the dominance in "literary tradition" of white perspectives on the American family and American culture more broadly, it also suggests the convergence of racial matters with those of social class. Unlike race, this issue emerges over and over, from the neighbor's observations about the wealth of "The Father," to the snide remarks of "The Married Daughter" about Aunt Elizabeth's New York friend, Mrs. Chataway, whom Maria assumes is not a "lady" but the keeper of a "boarding-house" (192), to the representation of Mrs. Chataway as a "Magnetic Healer and Mediumistic Divulger" (290). Class and money concerns are opposed to matters of aesthetics in the novel: compared with his sister, Maria, and her husband, Tom, who form "a pattern of success" (152), "The Married

Son," Charles Edwards, is a "loser" by virtue of his "artistic temperament": "We artists are at the best children of despair — a certain divine despair" (168). Part of the reason for the row in the family of artists was Howells's desire, no doubt shared by some of the participants, to construct a novel that would be not only creatively but also commercially successful — though not necessarily by means of a sensational chapter like Freeman's (Crowley, 108, 110; Bauer, 108).[33] The commercialism depicted in the novel and esteemed by some of its contributors parallels American economic and cultural imperialism in the turn-of-the-century world order. At the same time, *The Whole Family* represents (in both senses, and however ambivalently) a gendered nationalism that will trouble many contemporary readers. On her European tour, Peggy will gain sophistication while exporting the white middle-class feminine ideal, at least as Alice Brown and Henry van Dyke constructed it in the concluding chapters.

In the final analysis, *The Whole Family* clearly did *not* speak for "the whole family" of American authors; one cannot imagine Pauline Hopkins, for example, omitting an exploration of racial politics had she been asked to contribute a chapter. But the text's conflicted production and its final form were representative of the radical split between (white) masculine and feminine traditions that occurred in the opening years of the twentieth century. The essentially conservative thrust of the novel (both this novel in particular and the romantic novel more generally), with its values of family, hard work, and success, is overturned by the emergence of the "new woman," free from household chores and free to explore her own desires. Nevertheless, this figure is both in and out of "the family"; as Bauer observes of Elizabeth, "She throws off the concept of dependence for an 'in-dependence,' a relation to the family that allows her to work within its structure . . . without being forced into silence. To be a spinster, then, is not to be an outsider but to work within the family to alter it" (109). Alter it she does, and not always for the best: suggesting that confrontation with masculine endorsed values engenders disruption, Elizabeth's freedom fosters a conflict among the women in the family, just as Freeman's freedom in her character's creation sponsors an altercation between her and the two women who were "deeply indebted to Howells's literary authority," Alice Brown and Edith Wyatt (Crowley, 111). As Bauer so aptly points out, however, "The ideology of the family serves to keep everyone in line and at home"; "the men in the family" are also "tamed" and "repressed" (117). Standards, both behavioral and literary, constrain both men and women. At the same time, such standards were elaborated in different ways in African American literary tradition, which both invoked and questioned women's independence.[34]

In terms that are extremely useful for the present occasion, Bauer observes, "Who controls representation controls social power" (120). As the preceding discussion suggests, at the heart of *The Whole Family*, and at the center of gendered literary traditions, is the matrix of connections and tensions between the aesthetic and the political, broadly conceived. *Soft Canons* interrogates the critical opposition between these terms, and, in the process, the notion that "good" writing must be "universal" or culturally detached. In focusing on matters of influence and confluence — not merely opposition — between male and female writers, *Soft Canons* draws attention to several overlapping areas of concern. As the conflicts and silences of *The Whole Family* suggest, matters of representation and authority are central to the many permutations of masculine and feminine literary traditions. Many contributors to *Soft Canons* necessarily focus on the intersections and interactions of gender, sexuality, race, and class as these identities inflect authorship and reading, both in the writers' era and in our own. Enhanced by the "outsiders' eyes" of its distinguished European contributors, *Soft Canons* also extends current debates about literary nationalism, interrogating the role of gender and other identities in the framing of "American" and self-consciously "unAmerican" literature.[35]

The essays in the first section, "Gendered Genealogies," address directly the matter of influence, which, they indicate, is multidirectional. For example, Susanne Opfermann's study of the "Indian" novels of Child, Cooper, and Sedgwick explores the "intertextual dialogue" among the writers on matters of national identity, power, and cultural hierarchy. Opfermann argues that the issue of interracial love (or hate) offered the authors and their readers "a dramatic metaphor of cultural contact/conflict and allowed them to address questions of difference (cultural, religious, gender) involving questions of hierarchy and power that were central to their own era." As M. Giulia Fabi demonstrates, such literary genealogies occur not only across gender but also across race. Literary critics who take for granted the precedence (in many senses of the term) of European American literature may find their narratives of development unsettled or even overturned by recent recovery work, which suggests that we need to be cautious in conceptualizing "who revised whom."

Judie Newman's restoration of the lines of connection between Harriet Beecher Stowe's neglected novel, *Dred: A Tale of the Great Dismal Swamp*, and Mark Twain's *Pudd'nhead Wilson* emphasizes the close similarities between these seemingly disparate works. Newman highlights how both authors interrogate the long-term consequences of sympathetic audience identification in effecting actual social change, fostering readers' self-awareness and self-skepticism. Working with genealogy from another angle — the effects of gender within the African American tradition — Stephen Matterson's discussion of Douglass's and Jacobs's slave narratives interrogates their respectively "masculine" and "feminine" stances. Matterson argues that while Douglass inadvertently seeks an assimilationist stance, Jacobs retains a measure of African identity unavailable to her better-known male counterpart. Finally, he suggests, each constructs gendered as well as racialized versions of "American identity."

The second section, "Genre Matters," highlights some of the formal concerns touched upon in the first. Both women writers and writers of color have frequently been accused of writing "merely" political (and insufficiently artful) texts; hence, another crucial concern of *Soft Canons* is the connection between the aesthetic project, its formal representations and transgressions, and a gendered "American" self. As R. J. Ellis makes clear, the aesthetic complexity of African American writing is abundantly evident in the polyphonic genre mixing of such "novels" as Harriet Wilson's *Our Nig* and William Wells Brown's *Clotel*. The two novels' generic shape-shifting must be read, Ellis suggests, within gendered historical and social contexts, with Wilson's emphasis on "the private politics of the body" and Brown's on the "body politic." Addressing the sometimes limited perspectives from which Charlotte Perkins Gilman's *The Yellow Wallpaper* has been read, Gabriele Rippl reconsiders the story in terms of sexual poetics rather than sexual politics. Rippl argues that while Poe's work provides an important "pretext" for Gilman's, Gilman revises a masculine-authored aesthetic to imagine feminine ("arabesque") forms of both reading and writing.

In the past several years there has been a resurgence of interest in regionalism as an aesthetic strategy that was in the modern period diminished and retrospectively feminized by an urban, male, intellectual elite, as well as a political strategy linked with national concerns.[36] Aranzazu Usandizaga's comparison of George Washington Cable and Sarah Barnwell Elliott underscores the writers' revisionary commitment to a "local color" aesthetic. Exploring their representations of women in the light of the emerging New Woman, she demonstrates how both writers unpack the myths of pre–Civil War Southern culture, critiquing the continuing presence of Southern racism and achieving a balance between romanticism and realism, nostalgia and practicality, that enabled them to mediate across the literary and cultural divide of the twentieth century.

In *The Whole Family* Elizabeth's and Peggy's beautiful bodies, as well as the Father's ice pitchers, highlight the commodification of the aesthetic. As several contributors to the third section, "Developing Dialogues," explore, the "aesthetic" is hardly ever "pure," for the relationship between the gendered and/or sexualized body, American capitalist culture, and "art" lies at the heart of literary culture. Janet Beer investigates how questions of consumerism and consummation are fundamentally invested in gender power relations, arguing that the notoriety of Dreiser's *Sister Carrie* and Chopin's *The Awakening* emerged in part because of their (differently inflected) representation of a female desire that at some level intimated Americans' anxiety about the roles of women at the turn of the century. Working in an adjacent vein, Claire Preston investigates money-novel protagonists, mapping out the proximity between desire and consumption and their transformations through gender. Wharton's Undine Spragg embodies the essence of capitalist consumption; because she cannot participate in the manufacture of goods, she in some sense manufactures herself through the things that she purchases, in contrast to Dreiser's Cowperwood, who is confined to intellectual and detached notions of money.

Invested in the debate surrounding Bret Harte's and Mary Hallock Foote's "mining their Western experience for ready cash,"

Janet Floyd's essay reflects on West and East, on makers and marketers of literal and literary "ore," where the writers elaborate allied but ultimately different experiences of the Western "frontier," experiences based in part on gender and in part on complex regional affiliations. Beer, Preston, and Floyd's concern with the negotiation between economics and gender in the late nineteenth and early twentieth centuries reemerges in Alison Easton's sensitive comparison of Hawthorne and Fanny Fern. Bringing together representatives of putatively masculine romanticism and feminine sentimentalism, Easton argues that, with all their obvious differences, the writers engage with "related aspects of the same social order," sharing a hatred of "'humbug': the hypocrisy and duplicities of the middle class."

Synthesizing many of the concerns articulated throughout *Soft Canons*, the final section, "Transforming Traditions," also circles back to literary genealogy, acknowledging that such genealogies are often as noteworthy for what is left out as for what is made explicit, and for their absence as for their presence. Redrawing the boundaries of the aesthetic, Ralph Poole interrogates the connection between sexuality and textuality in the context of haunting and haunted lesbian revisions of Poe's poetics. Using as a starting point Poe's famous dictum that the death of a beautiful woman is the most poetical subject, Poole asks: What if the death is that of a lesbian? He argues that Rose Terry Cooke and Elizabeth Stuart Phelps transform Poe's work into a complex kind of "ghost writing." Ghostwriting a dialogue between W. E. B. Du Bois and pioneering black feminist intellectual Anna Julia Cooper, Hanna Wallinger explores the unidirectionality of their relationship. Ironically, both educators acknowledged the crucial role of African American women in the project of racial advancement, but the gender norms of their historical moment ensured a prominence and access for Du Bois that Cooper, even as an educated, middle-class person, could never achieve.

As Lindsay Traub's essay on Emerson and Margaret Fuller also underscores, masculine and feminine traditions sometimes elide or repress each other. Traub explores the motivations behind Emerson's revision of his intense and intellectually intimate relationship with Fuller as he worked toward publication of her memoirs with James Freeman Clarke and William Henry Channing, and she demonstrates how he transformed a powerful public writer into merely an unusual private woman: he was ultimately unable to read — or write — Fuller as Woman Thinking. Finally, Susan Manning's study of Dickinson and William James illuminates the poet's anticipation of James's confounding concern: how consciousness can be mediated (or, just as importantly, not mediated) by language. In constructing an implicit dialogue between Dickinson and James, Manning provides both an inverse literary genealogy and a depoliticized, philosophic view of the aesthetic.

Dickinson, of course, exemplifies the paradoxes of domesticity, ranging far abroad imaginatively while remaining, famously, in her father's house. As Amy Kaplan reminds us, "*domestic* has a double meaning that not only links the familial household to the nation but also imagines both in opposition to everything outside the geographic and conceptual border of the home" ("Manifest Domesticity," 581). Extending women's writing beyond the domestic pale, the essays in this collection explore conscious and unconscious dialogues between male and female writers — figured in *The Whole Family* — that, however dissonant at times, fundamentally shape the period. Recognizing that masculine literary tradition may include marginalized male writers as well as canonized female writers, the collection engages in canon criticism that, while it may not reunite "the whole family" of American authors, establishes the basis for a continuing conversation among its many members.

NOTES

1. Robert Frost to Susan Hayes Ward, 10 February 1912, in *Selected Letters of Robert Frost*, ed. Lawrance Thompson (New York: Holt, Rinehart and Winston, 1964). Ironically, Frost's reference was to himself; he marked his own participation in a long tradition of "feminine" writing by both male and female poets. See Karen L. Kilcup, *Robert Frost and Feminine Literary Tradition* (Ann Arbor: University of Michigan Press, 1998). Rufus Griswold, ed., *The Female Poets of America* (Philadelphia: Carey and Hart, 1849); Griswold, *The Poets and Poetry of America*, 9th ed. (Philadelphia: Carey and Hart, 1848).

2. The metaphor of "soft canons" is of course intended to invoke the canon criticism of scholars like Paul Lauter, Barbara Herrnstein Smith, and John Guillory, but it also resonates in a more complex variety of other ways, as the remarks that follow and the contributors' essays suggest. See

Lauter, *Canons and Contexts* (New York: Oxford University Press, 1991); Smith, *Contingencies of Value: Alternative Perspectives for Critical Theory* (Cambridge: Harvard University Press, 1988); Guillory, *Cultural Capital: The Problem of Literary Canon Formation* (Chicago: University of Chicago Press, 1993).

3. Gail MacDonald, *Learning to Be Modern: Pound, Eliot, and the American University* (New York: Oxford University Press, 1993).

4. Judith Fetterley, "'Not in the Least American': Nineteenth-Century Literary Regionalism as UnAmerican Literature," in *Nineteenth-Century American Women Writers: A Critical Reader*, ed. Karen L. Kilcup (Malden, Mass.: Blackwell, 1998), 15–32.

5. For a discussion of literary value, see, for example, Susan K. Harris, *Nineteenth-Century American Women's Novels: Interpretative Strategies* (New York: Cambridge University Press, 1990). It is, of course, as easy to identify the political (i.e., public realm) with the masculine and the aesthetic (embodied in the beautiful woman in the private realm) with the feminine. For a more complete history and analysis of these shifting affiliations, see, for example, Cathy N. Davidson, "Preface: Separate Spheres No More," *American Literature* 70.3 (1998): 443–463; Lawrence Buell, "Circling the Spheres: A Dialogue," *American Literature* 70.3 (1998): 465–490; Amy Kaplan, "Manifest Domesticity," *American Literature* 70.3 (1998): 581–606.

6. Olivia Frey, "Beyond Literary Darwinism: Women's Voices and Critical Discourse," in *The Intimate Critique: Autobiographical Literary Criticism*, ed. Diane P. Freedman et al. (Durham, N.C.: Duke University Press, 1993), 43, 47; see also Jane Tompkins, "Me and My Shadow," in Freedman et al., 23–40.

7. For a discussion of some of these false binaries, see, for example, Werner Sollors, ed., *The Invention of Ethnicity* (New York: Oxford University Press, 1989); Sollors, *Multilingual America: Transnationalism, Ethnicity, and the Languages of American Literature* (New York: New York University Press, 1998); Henry B. Wonham, ed., *Criticism and the Color Line: Desegregating American Literary Studies* (New Brunswick, N.J.: Rutgers University Press, 1996); Toni Morrison, *Playing in the Dark: Whiteness and the Literary Imagination* (Cambridge: Harvard University Press, 1992).

8. Nathaniel Hawthorne, *The Letters, 1853–1856*, vol. 17 of *The Centenary Edition of the Works of Nathaniel Hawthorne*, ed. William Charvat et al. (Columbus: Ohio State University Press, 1987), 304. Hawthorne's reputed hostility toward women writers has been overstated at times. In addition to Alison Easton's essay in this volume, see James D. Wallace, "Hawthorne and the Scribbling Women Revisited," *American Literature* 62.2 (1990): 201–222.

9. Margaret Fuller, "American Literature; Its Position in the Present Time, and Prospects for the Future," in *Papers on Literature and Art* (New York: Wiley & Putnam, 1846). Paula Bennett's recovery work suggests the presence of numerous well-known poets at the cultural moment of Fuller's essay, and it seems odd that Fuller would obscure them in her account of American literature. See Paula Bennett, ed., *Nineteenth-Century American Women Poets: An Anthology* (Malden, Mass.: Blackwell, 1998); Bennett, "'The Descent of the Angel': Interrogating Domestic Ideology in American Women's Poetry, 1858–1890," *American Literary History* 7.4 (1995): 591–610.

10. Nina Baym, *Novels, Readers, and Reviewers: Responses to Fiction in Antebellum America* (Ithaca: Cornell University Press, 1984), 21.

11. See Suzanne Clark, *Sentimental Modernism: Women Writers and the Revolution of the Word* (Bloomington: Indiana University Press, 1991); Andreas Huyssen, *After the Great Divide: Modernism, Mass Culture, Postmodernism* (Bloomington: Indiana University Press, 1986). Ironically, as Bennett and others have argued, many male writers wrote in the sentimental tradition; indeed, the work of male poets has been erased as vigorously as that of their female counterparts (introduction to *Nineteenth-Century American Women Poets*). A defining issue for putative feminine tradition was not gender, then, but the display of emotion. See Ann Douglas, *The Feminization of American Culture* (New York: Discus-Avon, 1977); Jane Tompkins, *Sensational Designs: The Cultural Work of American Fiction 1790–1860* (New York: Oxford University Press, 1985).

12. Edmund Clarence Stedman, *An American Anthology, 1787–1900* (Boston: Houghton Mifflin, 1900), xxix; Helen Gray Cone, "Woman in American Literature," *Century Magazine* 40.6 (1890): 922; Louise Bogan, *Achievement in American Poetry* (Chicago: Henry Regnery, 1951), 20.

13. Timothy Morris, *Becoming Canonical in American Poetry* (Urbana: University of Illinois Press, 1995), 21.

14. Van Wyck Brooks, *The Flowering of New England, 1815–1865* (New York: Dutton, 1936), 188–189, 228–251; Brooks, *New England: Indian Summer, 1865–1915* (New York: Dutton, 1940), 80–100.

15. Brooks, *New England*, 99–100. Even Brooks could not resist the implication that this transformation, based in the movement of the United States toward an intensely commercial and adventurist ethic, was a negative one (101).

16. F. O. Matthiessen, *American Renaissance: Art and Expression in the Age of Emerson and Whitman* (New York: Oxford University Press, 1946); Joanne Dobson, "The American Renaissance Reenvisioned," in *The (Other) Ameri-*

can Traditions: Nineteenth-Century Women Writers, ed. Joyce W. Warren (New Brunswick, N.J.: Rutgers University Press, 1993), 226–243.

17. Scholarship concerning women writers, for example, is well developed, thanks to such critics as Nina Baym, Judith Fetterley, Marjorie Pryse, Elizabeth Ammons, Frances Smith Foster, Paula Bennett, Cheryl Walker, LaVonne Ruoff, Carla Peterson, Hazel Carby, and many more. In *Sensational Designs*, Tompkins proposed an important new paradigm for the study of nineteenth-century American literature ("cultural work") that has with few exceptions been applied either to female writers alone or to male and female writers in isolation from each other. One exception is David Reynolds's *Beneath the American Renaissance*, which nevertheless focuses more on the ("major") male figures (and Emily Dickinson) than on the "popular" and female-authored literature in which he contextualizes these figures. Baym, *Woman's Fiction: A Guide to Novels by and about Women in America, 1820–1870* (Ithaca: Cornell University Press, 1978); Baym, "Reinventing Lydia Sigourney," in Warren, 54–72; Fetterley, "'Not in the Least American,'" in Kilcup, 15–32; Fetterley, ed. *Provisions: A Reader from Nineteenth-Century American Women* (Bloomington: Indiana University Press, 1985); Fetterley and Pryse, eds., *American Women Regionalists, 1850–1910* (New York: Norton, 1992); Foster, ed., *A Brighter Coming Day: A Frances Ellen Watkins Harper Reader* (New York: Feminist Press, 1990); Foster, *Written by Herself: Literary Production by African American Women, 1746–1892* (Bloomington: Indiana University Press, 1993); Peterson, *"Doers of the Word": African American Speakers and Writers in the North (1830–1880)* (New York: Oxford University Press, 1995); Walker, *The Nightingale's Burden: Women Poets and American Culture before 1900* (Bloomington: Indiana University Press, 1982); Ammons, *Conflicting Stories: American Women Writers at the Turn into the Twentieth Century* (New York: Oxford University Press, 1991); Ruoff, *American Indian Literatures* (New York: Modern Language Association, 1990); Ruoff, ed., *Wynema: A Child of the Forest* (Lincoln: University of Nebraska Press, 1997); Carby, *Reconstructing Womanhood: The Emergence of the Afro-American Woman Novelist* (New York: Oxford University Press, 1987); Reynolds, *Beneath the American Renaissance: The Subversive Imagination in the Age of Emerson and Melville* (Cambridge: Harvard University Press, 1989).

18. Paul Lauter et al., "Preface to the First Edition," *The Heath Anthology of American Literature*, 1st ed. (Lexington, Mass.: D. C. Heath, 1990); 3d ed. (Boston: Houghton Mifflin, 1998). Many valuable collections on nineteenth-century American women's writing, such as Warren's *The (Other) American Traditions* and Shirley Samuels's *The Culture of Sentiment: Race, Gender, and Sentimentality in Nineteenth-Century America* (New York:

Oxford University Press, 1992), begin to touch upon male-female connections; my *Nineteenth-Century American Women Writers: A Critical Reader* includes several pieces that briefly situate women's writing in relation to male writing: Cheryl Walker's "Nineteenth-Century American Women Poets Revisited" (231–244), Melody Graulich's "Western Biodiversity: Rereading Nineteenth-Century American Women's Writing" (47–61), Tiffany Ana Lopez' "'A Tolerance for Contradictions': The Short Stories of Maria Cristina Mena" (62–80), and Annette Kolodny's "Inventing a Feminist Discourse: Rhetoric and Resistance in Margaret Fuller's *Woman in the Nineteenth Century*" (206–230). An important analogous project is Wonham's *Criticism and the Color Line*. See also Laura Skandera-Trombley, *Mark Twain in the Company of Women* (Philadelphia: University of Pennsylvania Press, 1994); Karen L. Kilcup, "'Quite Unclassifiable': Crossing Genres, Crossing Genders in Twain and Greene," in *New Directions in American Humor Studies*, ed. David E. E. Sloane (Birmingham: University of Alabama Press, 1998); Gregg Camfield, *Sentimental Twain* (Philadelphia: University of Pennsylvania Press, 1994) and *Necessary Madness: The Humor of Domesticity in Nineteenth-Century American Literature* (New York: Oxford University Press, 1997).

19. I would take issue with Dobson's assumption here that "mainstream" or "canonical" literature is necessarily "culturally dissenting."

20. See Melinda Ponder and John L. Idol, *Hawthorne and Women: Engendering and Expanding the Hawthorne Tradition* (Amherst: University of Massachusetts Press, 1999).

21. Shirley Marchalonis, introduction to *Patrons and Protégées: Gender, Friendship, and Writing in Nineteenth-Century America* (New Brunswick, N.J.: Rutgers University Press, 1988), xi–xii, xvi; see Ann Edwards Boutelle, "'A Crescent that Shall Orb into a Sun': The Art and Friendship of Celia Thaxter and Childe Hassam," *over here* 17.2 (1997): 115–138.

22. John W. Crowley calls the novel "a compendium of the literary codes, conventions, and practices in force at the historical moment of its composition" (107). Crowley, "Whole Famdamily," *New England Quarterly* 60.1 (1987): 106–113.

23. W. D. Howells, *Selected Letters, Volume 5: 1902–1911*, ed. William C. Fisher and Christoph K. Lohmann (Boston: Twayne, 1983), 179–181.

24. Elizabeth Jordan, *Three Rousing Cheers* (New York: D. Appleton, 1938), 258; see 258–280. As Alfred Bendixen observes, Jordan's account is "lively, but not completely accurate" (xxxviii n. 1). My discussion relies on Bendixen's excellent and engaging reconstruction. Bendixen, introduction

to *The Whole Family*, ed. Alfred Bendixen (New York: Ungar, 1987). Citations from the novel are from this edition.

25. The writers included (in this order): Howells, Mary E. Wilkins Freeman, Mary Heaton Vorse, Mary Stewart Cutting, Elizabeth Jordan, John Kendrick Bangs, Henry James, Elizabeth Stuart Phelps, Edith Wyatt, Mary Raymond Shipman Andrews, Alice Brown, and Henry van Dyke.

26. Dale M. Bauer, "The Politics of Collaboration in *The Whole Family*," in *Old Maids to Radical Spinsters: Unmarried Women in the Twentieth-Century Novel*, ed. Laura L. Doan (Urbana: University of Illinois Press, 1991), 107.

27. See Sergio Perosa, *Henry James and the Experimental Novel* (Charlottesville: University of Virginia Press, 1978), 129 n. 24.

28. For a positive view of women's affiliation with "home," see, for example, Ann Romines, *The Home Plot: Women, Writing, and Domestic Ritual* (Amherst: University of Massachusetts Press, 1992). The risks of transgressing boundaries were high. See Joyce W. Warren, "Fracturing Gender: Women's Economic Independence," in *Nineteenth-Century American Women Writers: A Critical Reader*, ed. Kilcup, 146–163.

29. As I suggest below, Howells by this time was also a representative, for many modern writers, of an effeminate tradition based in the women's domestic novel of the nineteenth century; naturalist writers such as Crane and Norris and Western writers such as Harte (not to mention Twain) were responding to the "femininity" they perceived in the realist tradition advanced by Howells.

30. Sandra M. Gilbert and Susan Gubar, *No Man's Land: The Place of the Woman Writer in the Twentieth Century*, 3 vols. (New Haven: Yale University Press, 1988, 1989, 1994).

31. Perosa regards James as the master writer and the other contributors to *The Whole Family* as bumblers (110); he also comments approvingly on James's scheme to take Peggy and the artistic couple, Charles Edward and Lorraine, to Europe (126–127). The novel, and American literature more broadly, would continue its expatriation with Hemingway, Stein, Barnes, and their poetic "cousins" T. S. Eliot, Ezra Pound, and even — though only for a time — Robert Frost.

32. Van Dyke's chapter reads like a (comic) defense of Howells, in that he identifies Howells with "The Father," Talbert. Van Dyke defends the "architecture" and "aesthetic" of Howells's house and his character (296). In an interesting movement to define the terms of literary tradition, Henry James called Freeman's depiction of Aunt Elizabeth "subjectively sentimental," and he criticized the public for "that so completely lack-lustre

domestic sentimentality" that he saw inflecting the novel (quoted in Perosa, 113, 116).

33. If one opposition in "literary tradition" has been constructed between aesthetics and politics, another important one has been created between "art" and "profit." Many women writers of the nineteenth century, including Sigourney, Fern, Freeman, and Harper, began writing for the income, not for the sake of art.

34. For a discussion of black women's and men's different domestic relations, and the effect of these differences on literary traditions, see Jennifer Campbell, "'The Great Something Else': Women's Search for Meaningful Work in Sarah Orne Jewett's *The Country of the Pointed Firs* and Frances E. W. Harper's *Trial and Triumph*," *Colby Quarterly* 34.2 (1998): 83–98.

35. Amy Kaplan, "Nation, Region, and Empire," in *Columbia Literary History of the American Novel*, ed. Emory Elliott (New York: Columbia University Press, 1991), 240–266; see Fetterley, "'Not in the Least American.'"

36. On the regionalism debate, see David Jordan, ed., *Regionalism Reconsidered: New Approaches to the Field* (New York: Garland, 1994); James M. Cox, "Regionalism: A Diminished Thing," in *Columbia Literary History of the United States*, 761–784; Susan Gillman, "Regionalism and Nationalism in Jewett's *Country of the Pointed Firs*," in *New Essays on* The Country of the Pointed Firs, ed. June Howard (New York: Cambridge University Press, 1994), 101–117; Fetterley and Pryse, introduction to *American Women Regionalists*.

Gendered Genealogies

Lydia Maria Child, James Fenimore Cooper, and Catharine Maria Sedgwick: A Dialogue on Race, Culture, and Gender

SUSANNE OPFERMANN

According to Roy Harvey Pearce, James Fenimore Cooper "set the pattern for writers who would treat of the Indian."[1] Although the importance of Cooper's mythopoetical rendering of an American frontier experience that helped shape a discourse of national identity remains clear, such phrasing tends to obscure the dialogic nature of the early republic's fictional discourse on "Indians"[2] and to de-emphasize its gendered aspects. In fact, some of Cooper's authorial decisions may owe more to women competitors in the field of the historical novel than to his own imagination. Looking at Lydia Maria Child's treatment of miscegenation in her novel *Hobomok* (1824), Carolyn Karcher sees Cooper's handling of the topic in *The Last of the Mohicans* (1826) as his answer to a perceived challenge, and she suggests that in *Hope Leslie* (1827) Catharine Maria Sedgwick amplified the possibilities that Child had opened up. Again, Cooper reacted and "authoritatively revised Sedgwick's plot" in *The Wept of Wish-ton-Wish* (1829).[3] In effect, literary traditions that were subsequently designated masculine and feminine were intimately connected.

Karcher's claim of a gendered authorial power struggle and an intertextual dialogue centered on the theme of intercultural contact and racial intermarriage in these novels merits further discussion. Let us briefly, and in chronological order, review the authors' positions. In Child's *Hobomok*, set in the 1630s, the heroine, in a fit of despondency after she has learned that her true love has died at sea, marries the Indian Hobomok according to Indian custom. Three years later, her first love, Charles Brown, returns; Hobomok nobly gives her up and withdraws. She then marries Brown, who adopts her son from her union with Hobomok. This child goes to Harvard and later completes his studies in England; finally, "his father was seldom spoken of; and by degrees his Indian appellation was silently omitted."[4] Child's model of intercultural exchange and, specifically, of Indian assimilation to Anglo-Saxon culture is absolutely refused by Cooper in *The Last of the Mohicans*, in which the noble Indian Uncas as well as the ignoble Magua both covet Cora, Colonel Munro's daughter, who, it turns out, is herself of mixed English and African descent. All three characters are killed, however, before any love entanglement can develop; even the hinted-at union of Uncas and Cora in some afterlife is denied by Hawkeye, who "shook his head, like one who knew the error of their simple creed."[5]

Cooper's novel is set in 1757. When Sedgwick took up the topic of interracial marriage in *Hope Leslie*, she returned to an earlier period, the seventeenth century. As a child, Faith, the heroine's younger sister, is taken captive by Indians, later converting to Catholicism and marrying one of her captors, Oneco, the son of an Indian chief. When she is forcibly returned to her English family, we learn she has completely forgotten her mother tongue. Moreover, she explicitly prefers her Indian family and feels trapped with her English relatives. Her husband frees her and both escape back to the remnants of their Indian tribe. Cooper's *The Wept of Wish-ton-Wish* is likewise set in the seventeenth century and parallels closely some of the plot elements of Sedgwick's novel. In Cooper's novel, Ruth Heathcote is captured by Indians when she is six years old. She, too, forgets her cultural heritage and her native tongue and becomes the wife of Conanchet, a Narragansett chief, with whom she has a child. When Ruth, whose Indian name is Narrah-mattah, is returned to her English parents, she is clearly unhappy and runs away. In the end Conanchet and Narrah-mattah die. Just before her death, however, Narrah-mattah's Indian history is revoked: she mentally regresses to her childhood years before her Indian sojourn — which she seems to have completely forgotten — recognizes her mother, remembers her first language, and dies in her mother's arms. Only Whittal Ring, another white captive who has turned Indian, remains a mental "borderer" (thus, the British title of Cooper's novel) between cultures, but he is mentally retarded. Although the last chapter brings the story up to the present, summarizes the fate of the remaining characters, and takes us to the gravestones commemorating the dead, Cooper never again mentions the mixed-blood baby. At variance with Karcher, who maintains that "the dismissal of intermarriage from the history and literature of white America could hardly have been more definitive" (Karcher, 36), I would say that Cooper has created a textual ghost, an uncanny heritage, that haunts the text and its readers.

The intertextual connection between these four novels seems obvious; the question that needs to be addressed is, What is the significance of their common topic? Perhaps this question can be approached when we have answered another: Did Cooper indeed purposefully revise the concepts of his female colleagues, and if so, why? Did they even know of each other's ideas? Cooper, for instance, flatly denied that he had ever read *Hope Leslie*.[6] A closer look at the relations between these authors suggests some answers.

As was then customary, all four novels were published anonymously. However, Cooper and Sedgwick were well known, and their authorship was an open secret because they were identified on the respective title pages through previous works (e.g., "by the author of *Redwood*"). Reviewers mentioned their names as a matter of course. *Hobomok*, on the other hand, was Child's first novel. She was just twenty-two years old at the time of publication and virtually unknown; the first reviewer for the *North American Review* assumed a male author.[7] But the secret was out quickly and Child was delighted: "Praises and invitations have poured in upon me, beyond my utmost hopes" (see Karcher, 38). Early in 1825, she had secured for herself admission to one of Boston's exclusive literary salons as the latest protégée of George Ticknor, distinguished Harvard professor and literary kingmaker (Karcher, 39 ff.). Although we are uncertain whether Child and Cooper ever met, it is more than likely that Cooper had learned about *Hobomok* and its author, since gossip from the Boston literary circles usually spread to New York City, where Cooper lived at the time. Moreover, in her preface Child modestly bows to Cooper and acknowledges his mastery in the field. When she later reviewed *The Wept of Wish-ton-Wish* for the *Massachusetts Weekly Journal* in November 1829, she displayed more self-confidence, judging it "far short" of his previous novels and particularly criticizing his female characters (see Karcher, 118). Child's connection to Sedgwick is more direct; the writers corresponded during the 1820s and into the 1830s and commented favorably on each other's work. In her letters to Sedgwick, Child expressed much admiration for the older woman's writings, most of all for *Hope Leslie*, which Sedgwick had sent her immediately on publication. In 1832 Child dedicated *The Coronal*, a collection of her tales, to Sedgwick.[8]

Cooper and the Sedgwicks had initially been on friendly terms in the 1820s. In 1822 Cooper had written a laudatory review of Sedgwick's first novel, *A New England Tale* (1822). The poet William Cullen Bryant reports that he first met Cooper at the house of Catharine Sedgwick's brothers in New York City. Henry Sedgwick was a member of the "Bread and Cheese Club," a social club that Cooper had founded in 1824 in New York City.[9] Relations between Cooper and the Sedgwicks, however, soon became strained; Cooper had borrowed money from Robert Sedgwick that he was unable to repay on time. A series of lawsuits ensued, the last of which Cooper won in late February 1826. In June of the same year Cooper and his family sailed for Europe, where they remained until 1833. It is understandable that the Sedgwicks and the Coopers were never again particularly fond of each other, but this did not keep Catharine Sedgwick from reading Cooper's novels, including *The Last of the Mohicans* and, immediately following its publication, *The Prairie* (1827).[10]

For his part, although he was in France, Cooper had ample time to hear of and read *Hope Leslie* after its American publication in July 1827 and its London appearance in November. Reviews on both sides of the Atlantic were full of praise. While in Europe, Cooper would also have been congratulated as the author of a novel that was actually written by Catharine Sedgwick: *Redwood*, Sedgwick's second novel, came out in Italian in 1827 and the title page read, "romanzo americano del Sig. Cooper."[11] It is highly unlikely that Cooper, given his competitive and contentious personality, would not have been reading the works of a fellow writer who had quickly risen to fame in his home country and was hailed as one of America's leading novelists. It would have been just as unlikely, however, for him to admit openly to plagiarism. The case seemed clear to Hugh Swinton Legaré, who reviewed *The Wept of Wish-ton-Wish* in 1830. Pointing out a number of plot parallels between the interracial love stories of *Wept* and *Hope Leslie*, he affirmed: "the former has so much the air of a copy, that we think in fairness the author of the latter should have been honoured by the dedication. Mr. Cooper has not materially altered the story as told in Hope Leslie, except by a tragical conclusion" (219). Certainly, neither the similarities nor the differences between the two novels are accidental.

In view of these historical details it seems safe to assume that Child, Cooper, and Sedgwick had read and reacted to each other's texts. However, the significance of their exchanges resides beyond mere plot reversals: on the symbolic level these authors differ in more important ways. I will argue that, although stimulated by each other's texts, Child, Cooper, and Sedgwick used the topic of interracial relations for quite different reasons, reasons that underscore the complex interactions between aesthetics and politics that, as Karen Kilcup suggests in the preceding essay, occur across the nineteenth century. Both women employed it for a critique of gendered structures of power, although this is by no means their only interest. Cooper, however, is concerned with legitimizing existing power relations and their distribution of property. All three also had a common goal; like many others of their time, they took part in the discursive construction of an American national identity that was foremost on the cultural agenda in the 1820s. The topic of interracial relations was central to this undertaking because it was by excluding the savage Other that "American" society historically defined itself.[12]

"A Perfect Eden": *Hobomok*'s Native Revisionings

As she later explained, Child derived inspiration for the depiction of interracial relations from *Yamoyden*, an 1820 poem about King Philip's War by James Eastburn and Charles Robert Sands. The poem, which she often quotes in chapter epigraphs, provided her with basic plot elements. But Child's goal was not just to highlight and dramatize a chapter of colonial history with the story of an interracial marriage. Neither was it, as Karcher claims, "a radical revision of the patriarchal script" that culminates in the overthrow of patriarchal authority (Karcher, 31). The antipatriarchal criticism is there, to be sure, but there are also countertendencies. Like most of her colleagues, male and female, Child conformed to what Sacvan Bercovitch has called "the ritual of consensus," the mythic construction of America's greatness and the steady promise of its progress.[13] The historical novel as a genre contributed to the symbolic construction of America; Child's *Hobomok* is no exception. Thus, it is by no means ironic when her narrator opens the first chapter exclaiming proudly:

> I never view the thriving villages of New England, which speak so forcibly to the heart, of happiness and prosperity, without feeling a glow of national pride, as I say, "this is my own, my native land." A long train of associations are connected with her picturesque rivers, as they repose in their peaceful loveliness, the broad and sparkling mirror of the heavens,— and with the cultivated environs of her busy cities, which seem every where blushing into a perfect Eden of fruit and flowers. The remembrance of what we have been, comes rushing to the heart in powerful and happy contrast. . . . Two centuries only have elapsed, since our most beautiful villages reposed in the undisturbed grandeur of nature. (5)

Similar passages recur in *Hobomok* as well as in most other historical novels of the time. In *Hobomok*'s case they contribute a double-voiced quality to the narrative. While the text celebrates the achievements of the forefathers — who enable both the present prosperity of the United States and its glorious future — it simultaneously criticizes the authority of literal and symbolic fathers. The narrative strategy echoes this double-voicedness: Child uses two first-person narrators, both male, and starts her novel twice over. The preface presents a fiction of male authorization in which a first-person narrator declares that his friend Frederic had written this novel and requested his opinion; he had recommended publication. In the first chapter, however, we encounter the well-known device of an ancestor's manuscript that another narrator claims to have found. This second first-person narrator authorizes himself when he tells the reader that he has taken "the liberty of substituting my own expressions for his antiquated and almost unintelligible style" (7) and later even claims that he only extracted materials for his own story (16).

This story emphasizes the dark side of the forefathers, who appear harsh, ill-humored, doctrinaire, emotionally cold, and full of misogyny. Mary Conant, not Hobomok, is the central character of this tale of a daughter who successfully takes vengeance on her father. Mr. Conant's doctrinaire Calvinist stubbornness, which makes him forbid Mary's marriage to the man she loves, Charles Brown, because he is an Episcopalian, earns him an even less acceptable son-in-law, the Indian Hobomok, and a "semi-savage" grandchild (review of *Hobomok*, *North American Review*, 263). In the end Mr. Conant has to make peace with Charles Brown and bless his daughter's marriage. Child relies on the principle of repetition to drive her point home; the text affirms the selection of Mary's friend, Sally Oldham, who chooses her husband independently. And Mary's mother, who also married against her father's wishes, is equally justified because in the end her father had to reconcile himself to his daughter's choice, too. Thus, the text articulates the wish both for a woman's freedom and for a reconciliation with, and acceptance by, the father, as well as the "fathers."

The theme of interracial marriage is subservient to this message. Child's awareness of the political implications of the Indian question was still undeveloped when she wrote *Hobomok*. She displays significant ambivalence about the affiliation, since Mary Conant marries Hobomok only in a fit of severe depression "that almost amounted to insanity" (120). It is clear that Mary does not really love him. The marriage also "civilizes" Hobomok to the extent that "he seems almost like an Englishman" (137), as interracial contact becomes cultural genocide. The offspring of Mary and Hobomok is completely assimilated into Anglo-Saxon culture; his Indian heritage is simply forgotten.[14] Nevertheless, Child's text is daring, since it clearly violates genre conventions. According to the sentimental tradition, Mary should have died because she is a "fallen" woman. Her "marriage" to Hobomok is neither sanctioned by English law nor by the church; her child is therefore illegitimate. *Yamoyden* upheld the sentimental pattern and had the Indian-white couple die in the end, whereas Child's heroine not only lives but remarries and lives happily afterwards. No wonder that two assessments in the *North American Review*, although they were not unfavorable, criticized this series of events as "unnatural" and "revolting," and judged the story to be "in very bad taste."[15]

"A Price Has Been Paid": Racial Crossings in Cooper

Turning to Cooper, we find, not surprisingly, that a feminist critique of an authoritarian power system — even an ambivalent critique like Child's — is not on his agenda. In *The Last of the Mohicans* he employs elements of the sentimental tradition to paint an idealized picture of father-daughter love (see the description of Colonel Munro and his daughters that opens chapter 16) in order to endanger (but not invalidate) this idyll with his plot. White women function in a quite conventional way: morally superior beings, they are the objects of desire for Indians as well as white men, and they represent innocence threatened by violence. *The Last of the Mohicans* is unusual insofar as one of the white women, Cora, turns out not to be white after all, but of mixed African and English descent. As the offspring of an interracial marriage, Cora thus personifies the consequences of such unions, a fact that helps shed some light on a topic that features so prominently in the novel. Symbolically speaking, interracial marriage results in sterility. Cora is not marriageable once her father has revealed her ancestry. Major Haywood — quite conventionally opting for the fair sister, Alice — claims to be above racial prejudice, but the narrator corrects him by insisting that the officer's aversion to racial impurity is "as deeply rooted as if it had been ingrafted in his nature" (188). Cora herself acknowledges, "the curse of my ancestors has fallen heavily on their child" (362). Uncas, in contrast, does not seem to object to Cora's ancestry and, like Hobomok, is ennobled and "civilized" by his love for her. But there is no indication that Cora returns his feelings; in the end Hawkeye makes it quite clear that there is no future for an interracial union, not even in another world. Cooper's point, repeated in *The Wept of Wish-ton-Wish*, is that interracial marriage is a dead end.

At a symbolic level, too, the text emphasizes that the blending of races will not be fruitful. Hawkeye, notwithstanding his tireless insistence that he is "a man without a cross," symbolically does belong to two races and cultures. He is a link between Indians and whites, he possesses both white and red "gifts," he mediates between both ethnic groups. But he has no descendants and is thus "sterile." Just like his Indian friends and enemies, he is doomed to make way for civilization. In *The Wept of Wish-ton-Wish*, Submission, the regicide, who says of himself, "[t]hough of white blood and of Christian origin, I can almost say that my heart is Indian" (437), similarly links both cultures and moves between them — and for all the good he does remains similarly sterile, a solitary figure belonging to the past. Nevertheless, Hawkeye and Submission are clearly positive characters — and so is Cora, albeit, as a woman, she figures less prominently than these men. Thus, one cannot conclude that Cooper flatly discredits interracial union; he does so only when it produces offspring. Why?

Cooper "is continually given to a double strategy of revealing and concealing";[16] the way he handles the topic of interracial union, therefore, may serve other goals besides emphasizing the value of racial purity at a time when it was widely believed that "amalgamation" would bring out the most negative features of each "race." In his *Notions of the Americans* (1828) Cooper's narrating Bachelor does not seem threatened by this idea at all and even argues that "as there is little reluctance to mingle the white and red blood, . . . I think an amalgamation of the two races would in time occur."[17] We can resolve Cooper's inconsistency when we consider the function these books fulfilled for their author. Aimed at a European audience, *Notions* was written to correct English critics of American society, whereas the novels addressed an American audience in the first place and were concerned with legitimizing his ideas about American society over and against competing versions by other Americans. Psychological reasons have to be taken into account as well. According to Robert Clark, Cooper used his fiction to ease personal anxieties and to invent solutions for intractable real-life problems: what is at stake in the Leatherstocking series (and other novels) are Cooper's guilt feelings over his family's possession of Indian land.[18] These novels attempt to rewrite the real history of Indian-white relations by transforming it into a mythic "history" that reduces the complexity of the past and offers a reassuring fantasy of legitimate ownership and historical justice.

Starting with *The Pioneers* and continuing in *The Last of the Mohicans*, Cooper removes the blemishes from his family's history and establishes the justice of their (and his) claim to Indian land and its expropriation from the original owners, the Mohawks. For that end his plots distort historical and contemporary facts, although he must have known, for instance, that the Mohawks had fought for the British and not for the French, as they do in *The Last of the Mohicans*. When Cooper in his historical novels maintains that amalgamation of red and white had never been a viable way, neither in the eighteenth century, the period context for most of the Leatherstocking series, nor in the seventeenth century, when the events of *The Wept of Wish-ton-Wish* transpire, he is also saying that the land, his land, could not have been acquired by interracial marriage. This had long been a legitimate and peaceful way of obtaining property, at least in the European tradition, and *The Pioneers* provides a case in point that "international" British and American marriage can solidify property claims.[19] In Cooper, who married into one of the leading families himself, the topic of marriage tends to be entangled with questions of property and inheritance. Alliances between whites and Indians would have established Indian hereditary claims to land that had already been taken away from Indians. Since Cooper's concern is to justify the white man's possession of the land, it would have been counterproductive to strengthen the legitimacy of Native American claims by bringing them in accordance with English law. It would, furthermore, have weakened the traditional justification for expropriation: namely, that American Indians did not make proper use of and improve the land, whereas white Christians did. Cooper could therefore be expected to object even to Child's model of total assimilation because it did nothing to obliterate hereditary titles.

If anxiety about property rights is indeed the deeper reason that Cooper was so determined to preclude the union of Uncas and Cora in *The Last of the Mohicans*, it is not hard to understand why Sedgwick's *Hope Leslie* would have disturbed him. Sedgwick makes clear that — in the historical conflict between Puritans and Native Americans — truth, justice, and moral righteousness cannot simply be attributed to one side; what is more, she insinuates that the Indians have been dealt with unfairly. In her preface she lauds the Puritans for their character and their intelligent and extensive historical records but then suggests that they presented a biased view of their Indian antagonists: Indian behavior "will be viewed by an impartial observer, in a light very different from that in which they were regarded by our ancestors. In our histories, it was perhaps natural that they should be represented as 'surly dogs,' who preferred to die rather than live, from no other motives than a stupid or malignant obstinacy. Their own historians or poets, if they had such, would as naturally, and with more justice, have extolled their high-souled courage and patriotism."[20] But if, indeed, an impartial observer cannot simply agree with the Puritan appraisal of Native Americans, then the justification for the dispossession of Native Americans and their removal and extinction become questionable as well.

The legitimacy of possession predominates in *The Wept of Wish-ton-Wish*. As in *The Last of the Mohicans*, Cooper repeats his plot line twice for emphasis: twice Wish-ton-Wish is attacked by Indians; twice the attack seems unprovoked and is only later explained. During the first attack little Ruth asks her mother why the Indians "'seek to do us harm? Have we ever done evil to them?'" The mother denies this with the conventional argument that God had given the right of ownership of the land to those who cultivate and improve it, and she goes on to say, "I hope that what we enjoy, we enjoy rightfully; and yet it seemeth that the savage is ready to deny our claims" (183). Much later, we are informed that "for these lands, a price has been paid" (356); Wish-ton-Wish had been purchased by the Heathcote family.[21] Thus, the first Indian attack seems to lack even the justification of the dispossessed. Only later do we find out that the Indians indeed had a motive: they wanted to free Conanchet, their future chief.

Turning to the question of the legitimacy of interracial union, it is obvious that *Hope Leslie* occupies some common ground with *The Last of the Mohicans*.[22] It may well have raised the specters that Cooper had tried to lay to rest. Particularly Sedgwick's revisioning of Cooper's ending through the inclusion of a successful interracial marriage could have teased him into answering with the marriage plot of *The Wept of Wish-ton-Wish*. He closely follows Sedgwick's lead with the marriage between Ruth Heathcote and Conanchet but attaches a tragic ending to this couple's tale, which fits in with his earlier fictional argument against intermarriage. So eager is he to make this point that he overdoes it. Cooper has Conanchet himself, the loving Indian husband, send his wife back to her white family ("The Great Spirit was angry when they grew together" [452]); he has Ruth/Narra-mattah resist the separation so that Conanchet must extend his pleading; finally, he even makes Conanchet express the wish that Ruth/Narra-mattah forget her life with him: "Let thy mind be like a wide clearing. . . . let it forget the dream it dreamt among the trees. 'Tis the will of Manitou. . . . Let Narra-mattah forget her chief" (460). And then Cooper has this wish come true: in the end Narra-mattah reverts to Ruth, who no longer recognizes her former husband but, looking at his face, finds that "an evil Spirit besets me" (470). Finally, in his energetic attempts to restore his perspective, Cooper overlooks Ruth's and Conanchet's child — clearly a slip that underscores his eagerness to repress it.[23]

As often in Cooper, the scene is not without ambivalence. Conanchet's death is the death of a tragic hero. As Ulla Haselstein points out, he dies guiltlessly guilty. It is the Puritans who sentence him to death, but they leave the actual killing to an Indian, specifying only that the victim must not be tortured. Conanchet's rebellion against the law of history is necessarily futile: his opposition to the superior civilization fails. In the end he recognizes his defeat by accepting his death; three times, he refuses shady offers to save his life.[24] Cooper scholarship customarily reads this as the workings of the law of historical progress, but Haselstein suggests another reading. With his farewell words to Narra-mattah ("thy people speak strange traditions. They say that one just man died for all colors. . . . If this be true, he will look for his woman and boy in the happy hunting-ground, and they will come to him" [460]), Conanchet calls up Christian religion and is thus presented as a figure of reconciliation even though he adheres to his own culture. Those Puritans responsible for his death are heavily satirized; the Heathcotes, who were not involved in his conviction and are not present at his execution, gather in sorrow around the dead Conanchet and thus present a model for the reader. As Haselstein rightly argues, the achievement of this scene lies in the fact that historical guilt toward the original owners of the continent is simultaneously admitted and obliterated through the redeeming self-sacrifice of Conanchet (192). Thus, Cooper employs the interracial union to clarify (or obscure) possessory interests.

Like Magawisca, Sedgwick's Indian heroine, Cooper's Conanchet becomes a cultural mediator and translator: a speaker of both languages, he orchestrates the reunion of a mother and daughter who at first do not know each other. When Ruth finally recognizes her daughter — who in turn recognizes her mother's voice — the text proves the bond between mother and child to be indissoluble. It naturalizes cultural identity as a core that cannot be transcended or relinquished, however much outward appearance may change. Conanchet, who withstood all attempts at conversion during his captivity with the Heathcotes, exemplifies this essential identity. Thus, Conanchet represents an insurmountable natural difference between cultures, again paralleling Magawisca, who also finally rejects cultural coexistence ("the Indian and the white man can no more mingle, and become one, than day and night" [330]). In both novels the Indians, as well as transitional figures such as Leatherstocking and Submission, are glorified as victims; they are given dignity but at the same time they are defeated and lost to history's upward movement.[25] The principal difference between the texts is that in Cooper the inherent superiority of civilization, like the inherent superiority of the male sex, is never questioned, whereas Sedgwick's text entertains serious doubts in both respects.

"So Near to Her by Nature, So Far Removed by Habit and Education": Cultural Differences in Sedgwick

Sedgwick's portrayal of intercultural contact and conflict elucidates a problematics of difference and hierarchy that exists between cultures and races (Indian and white) as well as within white society's gendered power structure. In a series of repetitions and mirrorings that comment on each other, her narrative searches for (and fails to locate) a lawful, moral basis for these hierarchies; no superior institution justifies cultural, racial, or gender supremacy.

Sedgwick focuses on the Puritan community. In the historical conflict between Puritans and Indians, the Puritans have maintained their notion of superiority by denying the Indians' different perspective. That there is a difference becomes obvious, for example, in the order in which historical conflicts are narrated. It is noteworthy that the novel begins in England, where the Puritans themselves are pursued and driven from the land. Their wish for religious self-determination is justified; but, however just their principles, their practice soon becomes less so: in America heresies arise, power is sometimes perverted, and one can see "those,

who had sacrificed whatever man holds dearest to religious freedom, imposing those shackles on others from which they had just
released themselves at such a price" (16). Therefore, the Puritan
William Fletcher moves his family to the wilderness. While he is
absent, Indians attack the dwelling and brutally kill the peaceful
and defenseless inmates. One Indian takes Mrs. Fletcher's baby,
"tossed him wildly around his head, and dashed him on the door-
stone" (65). From a Puritan perspective this behavior confirms
the savage nature of the Indians who are said to be "ruthless,
vengeful" (72), and "wolfish" (21). But the Puritan point of view
is subverted because this massacre is preceded by a scene in which
Magawisca tells how the Puritans annihilated her tribe, the Pequods. Magawisca was an eyewitness to the events and together
with her brother Oneco was taken captive. Her report makes clear
that the Puritan attack, too, was a massacre of women and children (47–53). Authorial comment shows the effect of the different versions on Fletcher's son Everell, who had heard the tale before, "but in the language of the enemies and conquerors of the
Pequods; and from Magawisca's lips they took on a new form and
hue" (53). Because the Indian attack on the Fletcher home immediately follows Magawisca's narrative, readers can see it as an act
of vengeance that is not unmotivated; furthermore, to some extent the Pequod chief is morally justified because he wants to free
his children.

Thus, Sedgwick presents the conflict in terms of such nineteenth-century moral categories as the destruction of home and
family and the murder of women and children. Indians as well as
Puritans, notwithstanding their differences, act with similar cruelty; neither of the two cultures is inherently superior. Sedgwick
extends this principle of equality in affirmative terms by portraying selflessly heroic deeds by women on both sides. After the massacre of the Fletcher family Magawisca prevents the execution of
Everell — whom her father had sentenced to death in order to
avenge the Puritans' murder of his son — by throwing herself in
the way of the descending tomahawk. Although she saves Everell,
she loses her arm, a mutilation signifying the loss of power that
is a consequence of cultural conflict. Fittingly, this is exemplified
by the Indian side, which suffered much greater losses in the historical conflict — both sides sacrificed individuals, but the Indians also lost their way of life and their land. Though disabled,

Magawisca retains her power to love and remains capable of interpreting and translating her culture. Magawisca's magnanimous act is mirrored on a lesser scale by the white heroine, Hope Leslie, who later saves Magawisca's life by liberating her from prison. Hope does not have to risk life and limb, but both women give life to the other culture.

Intercultural contact in the novel always follows one of two principles. On the one hand, there is the principle of hierarchy that aims to conquer and subdue the Other under one's own law. Hierarchy results in the extinction of difference, the final negation of the Other, as the two massacres exemplify. The second principle, on the other hand, is life-giving and life-saving, based on mutual help, and could be termed an ethic of kindness. This ethic includes tolerance for the Other and is exemplified by the heroines' acts. While the first principle is associated with male authority, the second is affiliated with female responsibility.[26] Like Child, though with more sophistication, Sedgwick articulates a feminist critique of authoritarian, gendered power relations; in this sense she helps create a feminine tradition that both interacts with and rejects its masculine counterpart. The novel also dramatizes why intercultural exchanges tend to be problematical: predominantly ethnocentric, characters perceive the Other according to preconceived cultural notions. Thus, the Puritans fall victim to their own prejudices. The text does not exempt the heroine; in a remarkable scene we are shown Hope Leslie's limited vision. Immediately after Magawisca has saved Everell's life, there is a hiatus; the narrative continues seven years later. Hope writes a letter to Everell, who is now a student in England. She describes a painting that she has just finished: "The scene is a forest glade — a boy is sleeping under a birch tree, near a thicket of hazel bushes, and from their deepest shadow peeps a gaunt wolf in the act of springing on him, while just emerging from the depths of the wood, in the back ground, appears a man with a musket levelled at the animal" (95).

Clearly, this painting represents a version of Everell's rescue. But in Hope's rendering the participants in the drama have become unequivocal. The young white man is portrayed as a sleeping boy, which twice marks him as innocent; the Indian who wants vengeance for his son is reduced to a wild animal, and the Indian woman who sacrifices her arm and saves the white victim has been turned into a white man carrying a firearm. This version shifts the events to a Puritan perspective: it eliminates Indians as human beings altogether and presents the conflict of different cultures as the confrontation of nature versus culture in which only white men act. The picture, as Digby, the Fletchers' servant, says, "will be a kind of history for Mr. Everell's children, when we, and the forest too, are laid low" (96)—when the land is cleared and settled. The painting thus translates a morally complex situation, in which danger as well as deliverance originate from the Indian "enemy," into one that corresponds to the Puritan world view and its distribution of good and evil; it even corresponds to the Puritan notion of gender roles because it casts a man in the role of savior. Hope Leslie's painting not only shows the limitations of her perspective but further points to the bias inherent in historical records. The fact that it is the heroine who produces this biased version calls for an explanation.[27] Hope has given the picture as a gift to her beloved foster father William Fletcher. Her remark that "love can paint as well as fear" (96) can be read as a comment on her picture: to reduce the Other to the animal level and deny her/his human qualities may originate in fear of the Other, but it may also be a result of love to those who share one's cultural traditions. Since love produces loyalty, the daughter's version may originate in her love for the father (and the law of the father).

Cultural conditioning is not easily overcome, because it does affect social realities. However, *Hope Leslie* is remarkable because it questions cultural norms and the processes by which they are generated. Sedgwick suggests that cultural difference does not necessarily imply a difference in value. This notion was unusual in the nineteenth century and in contradiction to the law of history that guaranteed the legitimacy of white ascendancy. Metaphorically, the sisters who belong to different cultures convey the concept of equality *and* difference: Hope, the Puritan sister; Faith, the Indianized sister who has converted to Catholicism; and Magawisca, the Indian who has become their sister-in-law, since Faith has married Magawisca's brother Oneco. In a masterful scene Sedgwick has Hope and Faith meet after years of separation. Since Faith no longer speaks English, the sisters have to rely on Magawisca as interpreter. Hope has been most eagerly looking forward to this meeting and is overjoyed, but when she sees her sister's "savage attire" she is shocked: "Her heart died within her; a sickening feeling came over her, an unthought of revolting of *nature*" and she pulls back, "but when she felt her sister's touch, the energies of *nature* awoke, she threw her arms around her. . . . Hope knew not how to address one so near to her by *nature*, so far removed by habit and education" (227, 228; emphasis added). Nature itself becomes problematical here: Hope's nature rebels against Faith as an Indian, but the forces of nature make her embrace her sister after all. To Hope the concepts of sister and Indian are irreconcilable and yet Faith is both — this is Sedgwick's illuminating metaphor for the difference of cultures that may still be of equal value.[28]

The point recurs when the scene is developed further. Hope tries to pull Faith over to her side but all her attempts fail. Faith is not willing to let her appearance be covered by a cloak, she is not to be bought by diamonds (Hope offers her rings) and she does not share Hope's version of her history. When Hope reminds her of the time when she was taken captive and asks Magawisca to ask Faith "if she remembers the day when the wild Indians sprung upon the family at Bethel, like wolves upon a fold of lambs? — If she remembers when Mrs. Fletcher and her innocent little ones were murdered and she stolen away?" Magawisca replies, "she remembers it well, for then it was that Oneco saved her life" (229). What Hope considers her captivity, Faith regards as her liberation. Closely bound to their respective cultural perspectives, these two assessments are mutually exclusive. However, neither version is "correct," for Sedgwick uses the theme of interracial contact to suggest that there may be equality in difference. A similar line of argument is developed with respect to gender relations. The willingness to tolerate the Other and not negate her/his Otherness necessitates the recognition that one's own human perspective may be limited, that one may be wrong, and that there can be no *one* right view. The answer to the question of whether America's situation is hopeless or whether there will be solutions such as Hope Leslie often finds is delegated to readers.

Questions of race, gender, and culture are thematically central to an American discourse of national identity because they affect the societal distribution of power. They were as contentious points in the 1820s as they are today. In their novels Child, Cooper, and Sedgwick were stimulated by each other to present partially competing versions of the past while at the same time addressing issues of the present. Although all three upheld the "American consensus," the driving force of their arguments diverged. Child's novel voices an antipatriarchal criticism tempered by her wish for reconciliation and acceptance. Cooper aims at explaining and legitimizing white possession, white civilization, and male supremacy but is countered by the surplus of his own argument, so to speak. Sedgwick shares Child's criticism of the gendered power structure but moves beyond that to question the basis of other hierarchies.

Thus, the early American discourse of national identity cannot be considered a purely masculine tradition. Neither do I want to claim it as a feminine literary tradition. Both men and women contributed to it, and their writings converge in the theme of America's greatness. What has been disregarded for too long is the gendered nature of this discourse. Unless we pay attention to the ways these texts handle issues of gender and power, on the level of plot and symbolism as well as on the level of narration, we miss an important quality of early American fiction. Similarly, a literary canon that is blind to matters of gender will see only part of the picture. What we need now are comparative analyses on a national and an international level, for only then may we perceive and begin to understand the configurations of "the whole family" of American literary tradition.[29]

NOTES

1. Roy Harvey Pearce, *Savagism and Civilization: A Study of the Indian and the American Mind*, rev. ed. (Baltimore: Johns Hopkins University Press, 1965), 197.

2. Recognizing the problematics of such terminology, I use the term "Indians" to differentiate white authors' fictional constructions from Native American individuals.

3. Carolyn Karcher, *The First Woman in the Republic: A Cultural Biography of Lydia Maria Child* (Durham, N.C.: Duke University Press, 1994), 36. All second references to this and other sources are cited in the text. For two (limited and, in my view, problematic) comparative views of these novels, see Domhnall Mitchell, "'Acts of Intercourse': Miscegenation in Three Nineteenth-Century American Novels," *American Studies in Scandinavia* 27.2 (1995): 126–141, and Stephen Carl Arch, "Romancing the Puritans: American Historical Fiction in the 1820s," *ESQ* 39 (1993): 107–132. James D. Wallace criticizes the use of the term "miscegenation" in relation to Cooper's novels as ahistorical because it was only invented in the 1860s.

Wallace, "Race and Captivity in Cooper's *The Wept of Wish-ton-Wish*," *American Literary History* 7.2 (1995): 191.

4. Lydia Maria Child, *Hobomok and Other Writings on Indians*, ed. Carolyn L. Karcher (New Brunswick, N.J.: Rutgers University Press, 1986), 150.

5. James Fenimore Cooper, *The Last of the Mohicans* (1826; reprint, New York: New American Library, 1962), 407.

6. Emma Willard, founder of the Troy Female Seminary, repeatedly visited the Coopers in Paris in 1830 and wrote to her sister: "One day I told him [Cooper] the report, with regard to his having borrowed the plot of 'Wish-ton-Wish' from Miss Sedgwick's 'Hope Leslie.' He said, that he had never read 'Hope Leslie' in his life nor had he heard of the subject of it at the time of writing the book." Willard, *Journal and Letters from France and Great Britain* (Troy, N.Y.: N. Tuttle, 1833), 90. Willard seemed unconvinced. Thanks to Barbara Buchenau, who told me of this letter, and Deborah Schneider, who ransacked Harvard's Widener Library for a copy of Willard's book. In a lengthy anonymous review, Charleston gentleman Hugh Swinton Legaré raised the charge of plagiarism. Review of *The Wept of Wish-ton-Wish* in the *Southern Review* 5 (Feb. 1830): 207–226.

7. Review of *Hobomok*, *North American Review* 19 (July 1824): 262.

8. See the correspondence between Child and Sedgwick contained in the Catharine Maria Sedgwick Papers, Massachusetts Historical Society, Boston. The relationship cooled when Child became an ardent abolitionist.

9. William Cullen Bryant, "Reminiscences of Miss Sedgwick," in *Life and Letters of Catharine M. Sedgwick*, ed. Mary Dewey (New York: Harper, 1871), 441; see 437–446. On Henry Sedgwick, see Robert Spiller, *Fenimore Cooper: Critic of His Times* (New York: Russel and Russel, 1963), 85.

10. Sedgwick mentions both novels in a letter dated June 1827. The Catharine Maria Sedgwick Papers II, box 1, folder 7.

11. Rolando Anzilotti, "Un' Amica Americana del Sismondi: Catharine Maria Sedgwick (con 19 lettere inedite)," *Studi e Recerche di Letteratura Americana* (Firenze: La Nuova Italia, 1968), 60; see 51–119.

12. Other texts contributed to this thematic field. Two in particular deserve mention because they present interracial marriage in a positive light: James Eastburn and Robert Charles Sands, *Yamoyden: A Tale of the Wars of King Philip, in Six Cantos* (New York: James Eastburn, 1820), and James Seaver, ed., *A Narrative of the Life of Mrs. Mary Jemison* (New York: Corinth Books, 1968). In literature as well as in life, then, there were models for unions between whites and Indians.

For one discussion of historical and literary debates on "the Indian problem" and its relation to American national identity at this time, see

Lucy Maddox, *Remorals: Nineteenth-Century American Literature and the Politics of Indian Affairs* (New York: Oxford University Press, 1991).

13. Sacvan Bercovitch, *The Rites of Assent: Transformations in the Symbolic Construction of America* (New York: Routledge, 1993), 49.

14. It would be unfair to judge Child only by the stance she took when she was twenty-two years old; she later became an active campaigner for the rights of Native Americans and champion of cultural pluralism.

15. Review of *Hobomok*, 263; [Jared Sparks], "Review of Ten Novels," *North American Review* 21 (July 1825): 87.

16. Helmbrecht Breinig, "'Turn your mind on the ways of the inner country': Cooper and the Question of Westward Expansion," in *Westward Expansion in America (1803–1860)*, ed. Wolfgang Binder (Erlangen: Palm & Enke, 1987), 49.

17. Cooper, *Notions of the Americans: Picked Up by a Travelling Bachelor*, ed. Gary Williams (1828; reprint, Albany: State University of New York Press, 1991), 490.

18. Robert Clark, *History and Myth in American Fiction 1823–1852* (New York: St. Martin's, 1984), 93.

19. See James Fenimore Cooper, *The Pioneers* (1823; reprint, New York: New American Library, 1964), and *The Wept of Wish-ton-Wish* (1829; reprint, New York: Hurd and Houghton, 1867).

20. Catharine Maria Sedgwick, *Hope Leslie; or, Early Times in the Massachusetts*, ed. Mary Kelley (1827; reprint, New Brunswick, N.J.: Rutgers University Press, 1987), 6.

21. *How* the land came into possession of the Heathcotes is never explained — whether by direct contract with its Indian owners or through the activities of a white salesman of frontier lands, which is how Cooper's father made most of his fortune. In any case, the fortifications of Wishton-Wish are elaborate; several defense rings protect the innermost tower that serves as a last place of refuge. The setting suggests a dwelling in enemy country.

22. See Edward Halsey Foster, *Catharine Maria Sedgwick* (New York: Twayne, 1974), 91–93.

23. Conanchet does make a move to put his child in the care of a white man. He places his son in the arms of Dudley (459), but in the next chapter we find Ruth in a state of shock at the feet of her dead husband and the child lying "unheeded at her side" (462). This is the last time the child is mentioned. James Wallace misses this point and misinterprets *Wept* as Cooper's argument for "the glories of amalgamation" (Wallace, 207).

24. Ulla Haselstein, "Poetik der Gabe: Kulturberührung im Literarischen Text," unpublished manuscript, 189.

25. Mitchell finds no basic difference between the novels of Child, Cooper, and Sedgwick and so-called Indian-hating novels such as Robert Montgomery Bird's *Nick of the Woods* (1837), because in the end they all deny a peaceful community of both cultures.

26. For a more extensive discussion, see Susanne Opfermann, *Diskurs, Geschlecht und Literatur: Amerikanische Autorinnen des 19. Jahrhunderts* (Stuttgart: Metzler, 1996), 189–222.

27. Christopher Castiglia comments on the painting but fails to account for the interesting fact that it is done by the heroine; see Castiglia, *Bound and Determined: Captivity, Culture-crossing, and White Womanhood from Mary Rowlandson to Patty Hearst* (Chicago: University of Chicago Press, 1996), 175. Hope both subverts and supports her cultural order. Sedgwick systematically uses names to create expectations but also to disappoint them; thus, the name Hope Leslie personifies hope as well as hopelessness. See Opfermann, *Diskurs*, 205 ff.

28. For a different reading, see Judith Fetterley, "'My Sister! My Sister!': The Rhetoric of Catharine Sedgwick's *Hope Leslie*," *American Literature* 70.3 (1998): 491–516, esp. 507.

29. Margaret R. Higonnet, "Comparative Reading: Catharine M. Sedgwick's *Hope Leslie*," *Legacy* 15.1 (1998): 21.

Reconstructing Literary Genealogies: Frances E. W. Harper's and William Dean Howells's Race Novels

M. GIULIA FABI

[Figures of] the "mulatto/a" . . . [tell] us little or nothing about the subject buried beneath them, but quite a great deal more concerning the cultural and psychic reflexes that invent and invoke them: . . . A semantic marker, already fully occupied by a content and an expectation, America's "tragic mulatto" exists for others.
—*Hortense Spillers*[1]

Critic Frances Smith Foster's recent and groundbreaking rediscovery of three early serialized novels by the well-known writer and abolitionist Frances E. W. Harper has effectively opened up new vistas on the history of African American literature, as well as of American fiction as a whole. In fact, the striking thematic and formal continuities between one of these rediscovered texts, *Minnie's Sacrifice* (1869), and the later and better-known *Iola Leroy* (1892) have an impact on the critical evaluation not only of Harper's literary strategies and goals but also of William Dean Howells's one and only "race novel," *An Imperative Duty* (1891), a text that presents remarkable similarities to *Iola Leroy*, and, chronologically, represents its direct antecedent. The rediscovery of *Minnie's Sacrifice* thus compels scholars to problematize who revised whom in American literary history by providing a broader literary historical context for a comparative analysis of Harper's and Howells's competing novelistic representations of the politics of race, color, gender, and class in turn-of-the-century America.

Although there seems to be no currently available evidence

that Harper and Howells knew each other or wrote about each other's work, their parallel revisions of the popular literary trope of the (tragic) mulatta are to be read as part of the process of *reciprocal* artistic invention that links black and white writers of the nineteenth century. Indeed, the continuities and differences existing between the literary uses of the trope of passing in the three aforementioned works by Harper and Howells effectively complicate our understanding of interracial literary genealogies and problematize the long-standing notion that early African American writers' works are "other-directed" revisions of mainstream texts or, to quote Frances Foster, that they "should be read as attempts — weak and inadequate, but given their situation, rather heroic — to imitate the literary productions of Euro-Americans."[2]

For these reasons, and in order to foreground the critical and epistemological impact of contemporary challenges to the literary canon, in my analysis I have chosen to follow not the chronological order in which the three novels under examination were published but rather the chronology of their re/discovery by critics. Moving beyond traditional notions of univocal white-on-black literary influences will serve to highlight the artistic sophistication and deliberate experimentation with literary genres that characterize nineteenth-century African American fiction, and, more specifically, Harper's adoption of popular narrative strategies characteristic of the slave narrative and of the utopian genre. The proposed comparative approach will also help recover the complexity of *An Imperative Duty* by foregrounding how Howells courageously deconstructed prevailing "biological" notions of race in ways that are not dissimilar from Harper's. Harper's and Howells's unorthodox approaches may indeed account for the less than enthusiastic reception with which the mainstream press greeted their race novels at the time of their publication, as I will illustrate through a closing examination of reviews of *An Imperative Duty* and *Iola Leroy* that appeared in the *Nation* in 1892 and 1893, respectively.

It seems as if there might be circumstances in which it was one's right to live a lie.
—*Howells,* An Imperative Duty[3]

In 1869, the same year that Harper serialized *Minnie's Sacrifice* in the African American journal the *Christian Recorder*, Howells published in the *Atlantic Monthly* a review of Anna E. Dickinson's *What Answer?*— a book that, to quote Howells, presented "the question of intermarriage with the negroes" through a heroine who looks white but "turns out the daughter of a mulatto gentleman."[4] In evaluating Dickinson's hero's decision to marry the all-but-white heroine, Howells notes that in the case "of a beautiful young girl" who was "endowed with every personal, pecuniary and mental gift, the sacrifice of marrying her, even at the cost of all ties of kindred, and many ties of friendship, is greatly mitigated" (134). The "sacrifice required" would have been more credible if she had been "*black to the sense as to the eye,* and her father some poor but respectable whitewasher or barber" (135, emphasis added).

Both the content and the light, even humorous, tone of Howells's critique anticipate the dominant mood of *An Imperative Duty,* as the author explodes the tragic mulatto stereotype by deconstructing the traditionally pseudobiological notion of race into such sociocultural components as class, caste, beauty, education, and the impact of skin color. In Howells's review, however, the oppositional potential of such deconstruction (one that characterizes the origins of African American fiction and accounts for the popularity of the theme of passing in nineteenth-century black novels)[5] is quickly neutralized by his coterminous relocation of the issue of race within the private sphere of individual conscience: "Let every one conquer his own prejudices . . . *if he finds himself called upon to do so,*— and the prejudices of others will take care of themselves, as pounds do when pence are well looked to" (135, emphasis added). And as the reality of prejudice becomes individualized, the societal issue of intermarriage is denied any broad present relevance by being catapulted into a distant future: "We should not . . . be saying . . . that a mixture of the races is desirable. We reserve our opinion on this point for publication in the January 'Atlantic' of 2869, when the question will be, perhaps, practically presented" (135).

More than twenty years later, the ambivalent approach to blackness that characterizes this review, in its dual attempt to undermine racial stereotypes through humor and to contain the effects of such critique by confining the issue within the bounds of individual conscience, will also dominate in *An Imperative Duty*, a short novel that, as critics have noted, represents the culmination of Howells's thinking on the important contemporary issues of race and segregation.[6] In *An Imperative Duty*, the author's dual impulse to explore and exorcise issues of race emerges, not only in the consistently and conspicuously light tone with which he treats a controversial contemporary issue such as miscegenation, but especially in the close textual connection he establishes between the fictional representation of blackness and the critical battle in favor of realism.[7] In the novel, in fact, the related notions of the "tragic mulatto" and of atavism are voiced mostly by his female characters and are treated as romantic and melodramatic notions "not founded in human nature."[8]

Howells thus develops and polarizes the contrast between (racial) romanticism and (literary) realism along gender lines, by opposing the "hysterical" disposition of Mrs. Meredith and, to a lesser degree, of her niece Rhoda, to the "scientifically" analytical attitude of Dr. Olney, the "specialist in nervous diseases" who will eventually marry Rhoda though he knows her to be the daughter of an octoroon (53, 3, 11). Indeed, the female protagonists of the novel raise stereotypical expectations of the tragic mulatto plot that Howells then explodes one by one, either through direct interventions of the narrator or by commenting on events from Dr. Olney's professionally "sardonic" point of view (56, 107). In his "undeniably progressive,"[9] steady avoidance of sensationalism and melodrama, Howells takes issue with the literary and cultural assumptions of an audience that he sees as feminized[10] and that he treats with the same tone of "resolute cheerfulness" that his male protagonist reserves for his "shrill-nerved" female patients (32, 132).

The novel's opening emphasis on Dr. Olney's cultural alienation (as he has just returned from a five-year sojourn in Italy), on the immigrant's situation of cultural in-betweenness, and on the "mixed humanity" (5) that populates Boston evokes — also in light of the connection between Italians and African Americans Howells builds throughout the novel (8, 26, 27, 50) — the metaphor of a "mulatto" culture before the literally mulatta protagonist enters the scene. In Rhoda's case, the cultural mixing and resulting confusion is "only a little greater than in most others" (149), as her situation is placed on a continuum with the other expériences of displacement that open the novel (especially since Dr. Olney and the narrator discard theories of atavism).[11] In a period of mounting segregationist theories and practices (it is worth noticing that the "separate but equal" doctrine was sanctioned by the Supreme Court in the 1896 case that involved the civil rights of an octoroon, Homer A. Plessy), Howells builds on the initial images of a mulatto American culture and dissects race both *qualitatively*, by foregrounding such sociocultural components as class, culture, beauty, and the interpretation of skin color, and *quantitatively*, by insisting that Rhoda is "not . . . very black" (139).

Significantly, Howells's quantitative reductio ad absurdum of biological racial notions anticipates the emblematic paradox that is at the heart of Mark Twain's *Puddn'head Wilson*, i.e., the possibility of disposing of one half a dog.[12] As Olney tells Rhoda in his attempt to convince her to marry him, "All that I shall ask of you are the fifteen-sixteenths or so of you that belong to my race by heredity; and I will cheerfully consent to your giving our colored connections their one-sixteenth" (143).[13] And in Howells's case, such paradox serves to prevent, rather than to foreshadow (as in Twain's novel), the tragic fate of the passer(s), since Olney's reasoning succeeds in convincing Rhoda to accept his proposal. This dissection of race culminates in Olney's disruptive statement that race may, in Rhoda's particular case, be a matter of "consent" (143): because Howells has already discarded the "probabilities" of atavism (88), traditional notions of descent invoking the "taint" of one drop of black blood lose immediacy by contrast with Olney's own commonsensical computations on the prevailing proportion of white blood in Rhoda's veins.

Yet within the economy of the novel Howells's potentially disruptive deconstruction of race is mostly limited to minimizing the controversial quality of the closing consummated interracial union by demonstrating that, both qualitatively and quantitatively, Rhoda is not really, or at least not very, black. She does not look colored, she is beautiful, educated, and privileged, and by all these sociocultural signifiers she is effectively different and separated from "*them*" (144). In fact, she is lamentably nonblack, and Olney will live to regret "that the sunny-natured antetypes of her mother's race had not endowed her with more of the heaven-born cheerfulness with which it meets contumely and injustice" (149). At the same time, in spite of the discovery of her ancestry and the resulting potential threat to her social status, Rhoda never changes her subject position as a privileged white woman. Though psychologically shocking, her discovery (which occurs in a hotel room and within the novel itself never exceeds the boundaries of confidential conversations) has no negative practical consequences: Rhoda decides to reject Mr. Bloomingdale, but she never loved him anyway; and while she does lose her money, this occurs before the discovery and for reasons that have nothing to do with it (80, 112–113). On the contrary, the revelation of her mixed ancestry and Rhoda's consequent, short-lived resolve to leave in search of her mother's family speed up her happy union with Olney, the man she really loves and, incidentally, also the one who knows her secret.

As Rhoda holds on to her subject position as privileged white lady, her point of view on race as a mark of inferiority is never really challenged. Even her visit to the black church reveals nothing more than her estrangement from and disgust for blacks. Although she is supposed to be in the presence of "the best colored society," her perceptions are filled with grotesque, animalistic images, and she indulges in an "imperious attitude" that testifies to the racial and class hierarchies to which she is accustomed (91, 89). More important, like Olney (and Howells) she emphasizes the negative impact of visible racial differences. In the black church, in a "frenzy of abhorrence," Rhoda does "not venture to look around . . . she was afraid that the sight of their faces would harden her heart against them . . . and she kept her eyes shut, listening to their pathetic voices" (95).

Undoubtedly, Howells thought that his description of Rhoda's mental processes was far more realistic than any quick conversion to duty à la Matt Crim would have been,[14] and many contemporary critics would agree with him on that point (Andrews, 156; Banta, viii, xi; Amacher, 217, 223; Bennett, 105). However, to the extent that Howells's strategy to undermine the romantic stereotype of the tragic mulatto is to question the *degree* of Rhoda's blackness, his deconstruction of race fails to problematize negative or even condescendingly positive notions of blackness that compare "the remote taint of [Rhoda's] servile and savage origin" to the "grace of a limp, the occult, indefinable lovableness of a deformity" (133). Rhoda's conviction that the revelation of her ancestry has "murder[ed]" her does not undergo any revision, nor does it seem to be questioned by Olney or by the narrator, and passing thus remains the happiest of all possible endings (88). Any reevaluation of blackness gets set aside because, thanks to secrecy, the only consequence of her aunt's attempted "murder" is Rhoda's recurrent sense of guilt for having to lie, rather than for the content of the lie.

Ultimately, the fact of Rhoda's "blackness" emerges as a mere technicality that seems to have no context and no reality except in her overexcited psychology or in the blatant prejudice of such obvious (female) villains as Mr. Bloomingdale's mother and sisters. Because Howells's dissection of race to ensure a relatively happy ending for his mulatta heroine leaves intact traditional stereotypes of *visibly* black African Americans who are blessed by "natural gayety and lightness of heart," it is not surprising that for Rhoda blacks continue to be interchangeable, because unknown, entities who possess either "no discernible features" or "sad, repulsive visages" (91, 92, 93). Thus, in his attempt to avoid racial melodrama, Howells ends up performing a wholesale cancellation of black culture.

Such cancellation has a strong impact on the level of characterization, where the absence of any viable black community and Howells's collapsing the representation of race with his realistic critical agenda dramatically flatten the depth of the heroine. Having inserted her within a pathologically melodramatic and sentimental framework of "dutiolatry," "hypochondria of the soul," "aimless . . . self-sacrifice," and shrill nerves, Rhoda's proclaimed but remarkably short-lived desire to "go down there and help [the freedmen]" can easily be dismissed as a "whimsical suggestion," much like her equally short-lived intention to go live with the nameless mulatta she meets during her excursion in the black part of town (132, 149, 142, 106). The cancellation of black culture thus comes to coincide with the elimination of female autonomous decision making, and Rhoda's heroism is reduced to the confession of her secret to Olney, who already knows it anyway (135). Similarly, the complex issues of passing and of the racial hierarchy it implies are disposed of by Olney's verbal assurance to Rhoda that he would be willing to reveal her secret *if* that were necessary to convince her that he is not ashamed of her heritage. Thus, as Rhoda is saved from becoming the victim of her aunt's imperative duty, Olney takes center stage as the hero of "imperative logic" who "rescue[s] her from her own thoughts of herself" (12, 148).

The novel's ending leaves provocatively open the controversial issue of passing, though Howells reduces the disruptiveness of his closure by relocating the interracial couple in Italy. Howells is careful — as in his 1869 review of *What Answer?*— not to glorify mixed marriages, and he allots no more "than the common share of happiness" to his protagonists (148). From the relative safety of Rome, and of an as-yet-childless union, Olney (and Howells) can wishfully speculate that it is not race but class and caste that Americans despise, a closing comment that once again courageously emphasizes the constructedness of the notion of race, but also paradoxically reproposes the representational erasure of black culture.

Doctor, I did not choose my lot in life, but I have no other alternative than to accept it. The intense horror and agony I felt when I was first told the story are over. Thoughts and purposes have come to me in the shadow I should never have learned in the sunshine.
—Harper, Iola Leroy[15]

If Olney saves Rhoda from herself, Howells may well be said to have saved both of them from the "unwholesome vapors" of romantic fiction and, we might add, also from the narrative dynamics of Harper's fiction (Howells, quoted in Simpson, 74). The title heroine of *Iola Leroy*, in fact, spends most of her time doing what Rhoda is saved from, i.e., living the psychological, societal, and cultural implications of the discovery of her mixed ancestry. In her determined search for her lost mother (and, metonymically, for her lost race), Iola, unlike Rhoda, slowly negotiates a crucial shift from a white to a black subject position.

The many significant differences between Harper's and Howells's stories of privileged and beautiful heroines who discover themselves to be "all but white" derive from Harper's emphasis on the historical context, on the group (rather than solely individual) dynamics of race relations, and, most important, on the existence of a distinctive black culture. Unlike *An Imperative Duty, Iola Leroy* is a historical novel of slavery and reconstruction, a generic choice that enables Harper to organize her plot around the immediate consequences of Iola's family history. After the death of Iola's aristocratic white father, it becomes known that Iola herself is legally black and she is sold as a slave. Soon thereafter, the Civil War breaks out and she is rescued by Northern troops. As the issue of race thus exceeds the boundaries of individual psychology and confidential conversations, and as Iola experiences "outrages . . . which might well crimson the cheek of honest womanhood with shame" (115), the supposedly scientific attitude of a doctor will no longer suffice to minimize the impact of a proscribed genealogy or the violence of the racial subordination Iola has personally, though briefly, experienced.

It is meaningful, in this regard, that Harper should decide to interrupt the chronological linearity of her narrative, right after Dr. Gresham's marriage proposal and before Iola's reply, to devote four chapters (chaps. 9–12) to a flashback into Iola's family history. Jumping back to "nearly twenty years before the war" (61), Harper recounts Iola's father's marriage with one of his slaves, the social marginalization they experience even though the legal marriage is kept a secret and the wife "passes" for her own husband's mistress, the continuing differences between the spouses on issues of race and slavery, the utter lack of legal protection the family faces after the death of the white patriarch, and finally Iola's profound agony at the revelation of her origins. Significantly, the four-chapter-long flashback ends with the death of Gracie, Iola's youngest sister, who does not survive the shock of the revelation.

After such an interruption, when Harper returns to the present of narration and to the love scene between Dr. Gresham and Iola, Iola's reaction to the marriage proposal "from one of that race who had been so lately associated in her mind with horror, aversion, and disgust" no longer seems as whimsical as in Rhoda's case (111). Unlike Olney's, Dr. Gresham's strategy to insist that Iola's complexion is "as fair as" (116) his own is as ineffective as his marriage offer is unsuccessful, since Iola, after testing her suitor's perplexed attitude toward the possibility of begetting *visibly* mixed children, refuses the compromise of continuing to pass for white and opts instead for her mother's race.

Harper's consistent focus on Iola's point of view (rather than Dr. Gresham's) and on her singular privilege to choose her racial affiliation enables the author to recuperate at once both the issue of the distinctiveness of black culture and the possibility of female heroism. Indeed, within the economy of the novel, the representation of post-Emancipation black culture is contingent upon Iola's courage and decision-making power.[16] On the one hand, by emphasizing Iola's *duty* to choose to be either black or white (since there is no societal middle ground between the races) Harper rewrites contemporary discourses and transforms race from a biological reality into a construct that she then, like Howells, fragments into its various sociocultural components. On the other hand, unlike Howells, by portraying Iola's acceptance of her black ancestry and her subsequent experiences as a member of the African American community, Harper succeeds in moving beyond the tragic mulatta trope, not by erasing the representation of blackness, but by *re*constructing black cultural distinctiveness on different grounds: the specific history of African Americans, the culture of resistance that resulted from the experience of slavery, their truer religious faith, and the group solidarity and self-help philosophy that continue to characterize the black community in the postslavery period. Iola's repeated statement of preference for the more humanistic values of black culture and her choice of belonging to the African American community succeed, on a narrative level, in transforming blackness from a visible, ostensibly unambiguous signifier of inferiority and oppression (as it is for Rhoda) into a force for cultural change, a grand social mission to construct a new, more egalitarian civilization.

In *Iola Leroy* the protagonist's reaction to the revelation of her blackness, though not fatal as in her sister Gracie's case nor as detailed as in Rhoda's, is neither easy nor painless. It is "a fiery ordeal of suffering" that changes Iola's personality, undermines her health, and exposes her to the risk of madness (195, 200, 105–106, 274). It is an ordeal that Harper recounts over and over again (97–108, 113–115, 273, 194) in order to avoid the easy linearity of the traditional "riches to rags" and "rags to riches" plots.[17] Harper represents Iola's shift to a black subject position as a process of acquiring a knowledge of the black community and black history that goes beyond the derogatory or condescending stereotypes with which Iola herself grew up and which she never had any interest in problematizing before the revelation of her own mixed ancestry.

In turn, the process of Iola's acquisition of knowledge gives greater fictional visibility and relevance to the black communities she encounters, communities that for the heroine acquire a vitality and a complexity that contrast sharply both with Rhoda's initial, condescending "love" (*Imperative Duty*, 25) for nameless black waiters and with the nightmarish quality of her experience in the black church. On the level of literary representation, in fact, Iola's choice of blackness opens up the possibility of literary heroism and of a new fictional role (above and beyond contemporary stereotypes) for the many unmistakably black characters who surround the heroine, characters who cannot choose their racial affiliation because of their *un*ambiguous skin color, but who can freely and heroically decide to devote their lives to the advancement of their race.[18]

As Iola moves beyond Rhoda's "hysterical weakness" (*Imperative Duty*, 129) toward heroic decision making, so too does Harper's novel move beyond the potential pitfalls of aimless self-sacrifice, as well as beyond Howells's realism, toward the inspirational uses of the utopian.[19] Iola travels beyond the privileges of whiteness into the realities of blackness, and her increasingly sophisticated knowledge of African American culture eventually culminates in the articulation of the social, economic, legal, and Christian principles upon which a utopian, egalitarian social order should be based.

Harper's utopian project involves both the private and the public sphere, as it grows by a process of expansion. At first Harper acknowledges the birth of new black women, like Iola and Miss Delany, whose independent sense of self is strengthened by an understanding of the politics and jeopardies of race and gender.[20] Then she connects self-empowerment to self-fulfillment by conceptualizing "utopian relations" of equality between black women and black men who "do not engage in the patriarchal exchange of women."[21] Finally, Harper's utopia achieves societal three-dimensionality when — after having portrayed the violent reality of segregation, which she epitomizes in the burning of Iola's school and in the lynchings her characters often discuss — she envisions the cooperation of these new individuals and family units in the creation of a new South that will be a land of freedom for all. At the end of the novel, Iola's initial, seemingly penalizing choice of blackness is rewarded with "love and happiness" as she falls in love with and agrees to marry Dr. Latimer, an ex-passer like herself, with whom she goes south to share a "life of high and holy worth" (271).

Though similarly open-ended, the closure of *Iola Leroy* contrasts sharply with the spatiotemporally well-defined situation of personal, albeit melancholic, security that Rhoda enjoys as a permanent passer in Italy. The final vision of Harper's novel is one of utopian bliss within a conspicuously vague geographical and historical context, and it retains a dual valence. On the one hand, it emerges as a moment of imaginatively enforced respite, when both the author and her genteel heroine entertain the anticipatory vision of a successful struggle for social change. On the other, the author leaves us only "on the threshold of a new era," an era that Harper and her first readers knew had yet to be realized (271). Through the sustained open-endedness of her novel, Harper effectively injects a sense of estrangement into the extratextual reality of the audience, in the attempt to pass on the impetus to fulfill the "concrete" utopian vision she has projected.[22]

He still remained in the South, for Minnie's grave had made the South to him a sacred place, a place in which to labor and to wait until . . . freedom and justice, like glorified angels, should reign triumphant where violence and slavery had held their fearful carnival of shame and crime for ages. . . . And he was blessed in his labors of love and faith.
—Harper, Minnie's Sacrifice *(90)*

Twenty-three years earlier, in *Minnie's Sacrifice*, Harper followed a little longer the lives of her ideal couple in the South, and the tragic outcome is stunningly revealing for us today. The rediscovery of *Minnie's Sacrifice*, in fact, both clarifies the literary origins of *Iola Leroy* and (in light of the different audiences the author was targeting) also reveals Harper's strategic appropriation and deployment of the conventions of popular literary modes, in this case the slave narrative.[23] The story of Minnie and Louis, the social-worker protagonists of *Minnie's Sacrifice*, is very similar to that of *Iola Leroy*. They are unwitting passers who find out about their African American familial roots on the eve of the Civil War. In the post-Emancipation period, after having reunited with their long-lost relatives, they marry and move south to uplift the freed-men. There, where "violence and murder were rampant," Minnie, unlike Iola, will meet her untimely death (85).

As in her later novel, in *Minnie's Sacrifice* Harper describes and reiterates her protagonists' shock at the revelation of their mixed ancestry and details their shift from a white to a black subject po-sition. In Louis's case, Harper signals such a shift not only through clear references to the biblical story of Moses (see Foster, intro-duction, xxx) but also by inserting him within the (non)fictional dynamics of the slave narrative. After learning the secret of his birth, Louis, who had joined the Confederate Army, decides in-stead that he cannot "raise [his] hand against [his] mother's race" and leaves to go north (60). Pursued by his former allies, and risk-ing death as a deserter, Louis escapes, like a runaway slave, by "guiding himself northward at night by the light of the stars and a little pocket compass . . . and avoiding the public roads during the day" (62). He eventually succeeds in reaching the North thanks to an underground railroad managed by recognizably black slaves. Just as Iola's singular success in surviving enslavement unscathed enough to qualify as heroine is preceded by her sister Gracie's death,[24] so is Louis's successful escape contrasted with the pre-ceding, tragic story of Moses. In contrast to her Moses-like pro-tagonist, the runaway slave *named* Moses makes it to the North only to die there, Harper's fictional reminder that instances of in-dividual success were exceptions to the collective situation of overwhelming oppression experienced by the slaves.

Though *Minnie's Sacrifice* anticipates many crucial aspects of *Iola Leroy* and is at times even quoted verbatim in the later novel, the different generic choices and the contrast between the tragic clo-sure of *Minnie's Sacrifice* and the happy — or rather, utopian — ending of *Iola Leroy* illuminate the interaction between Harper's art and historical reality. In *Minnie's Sacrifice*, only four years after the end of the Civil War, Harper is already at work rewriting his-tory through an epic of slavery and Reconstruction that, in con-trast to the "growing . . . fungus crop of sentiment about slavery" (Cady, 77), foregrounds the point of view of the slaves and the freedmen. As in the case of *Iola Leroy*, *Minnie's Sacrifice* implicates the reader in an extratextual reflection that is crucial for the inter-pretation of Harper's generic choices. In fact, in order to augment the effectiveness of her earlier novel, Harper increases the distance of her black first readers from her extremely recent historical material by consistently using the past tense in ways that expand the small chronological gap between the present of narration and the past of the events narrated.

This process of distancing becomes important when we try to recover the inspirational function of the tragic ending of *Minnie's Sacrifice*. Minnie and Louis's narrative life beyond the happy marriage sees the disruption of traditional narrative expectations of heterosexual bliss. While Louis voices very openly his forebodings about the difficulties of Reconstruction in terms that are indeed prophetic of the institutionalization of segregation a few years later, the author realizes such forebodings in the plot, as Minnie loses her life for the cause she has embraced. As a result of this (meta)narrative juxtaposition and of the novel's remote time frame, Minnie's untimely death emerges as the inspirational celebration of the exemplary (and far from aimless) immolation of a heroine whose martyrdom is pushed back into the past and acquires mythical status: her deeds have already become part of the community's lore a few hours after her death (88–89). And Harper herself, in the closing address to the reader, emphasizes more outspokenly than in *Iola Leroy* the revisionist goals of her writing strategies: "While some of the authors of the present day have been weaving their stories about white men marrying beautiful quadroon girls, who, in so doing were lost to us socially, I conceived of one of that same class to whom I gave a higher, holier destiny; a life of lofty self-sacrifice and beautiful self-consecration, finished at the post of duty, and rounded off with the fiery crown of martyrdom, a circlet which ever changes into a diadem of glory" (91).

In light of Harper's later variations on the same theme, the rediscovery of *Minnie's Sacrifice* effectively compels us to problematize the chronological genealogy of literary descent that would indicate *Iola Leroy* as a revision of *An Imperative Duty*. The connections between these three novels are, instead, to be inserted and reinterpreted within a broader process of *reciprocal* cross-fertilization between competing representations of the politics and paradoxes of race and color that are fictionally embodied in the mulatta.

I am beginning to suspect that the public as a rule does not care for books in which the principal characters are colored people, or written with a striking sympathy with that race as contrasted to the white race.

—Charles Chesnutt[25]

Contemporary mainstream reviewers registered the defiance of dominant ideological assumptions and literary tropes that, in spite of their many differences, characterizes the representation of the mulatta and the structural open-endedness of both *Iola Leroy* and *An Imperative Duty.*[26] On February 25, 1892, the *Nation* published a review of *An Imperative Duty* and seven other books in an essay entitled "More Novels."[27] In this short review *An Imperative Duty* is described as "a situation involving two rather difficult problems of conduct" and readers are warned that, in terms of the "solutions" Howells proposes, "the wisdom of a general application would be doubtful." The reviewer comments on how Mrs. Meredith's decision to reveal the truth to Rhoda "is at least debatable" and corroborates this point by noticing how Howells himself shows that the causes of her decision are to be found in "the lash of a hypochondrial conscience, applied to hysterical nerves." The reviewer then critiques Olney's decision to marry Rhoda by noticing that "it is certain that such marriages increase the war between temperament and character which he [Howells] declares to be 'the fruitful cause of misery in the world,'" and proposes to "regard some of Olney's utterances as mere lover's extravagance" rather than as something for which Howells should be held "responsible." Having thus focused on neutralizing the most controversial *thematic* aspects of *An Imperative Duty*, the writer compounds the respectfully dismissive tone of the review by adding three lines of generic praise for the "lucidity, force, and grace which give to all Mr. Howells's stories a rare distinction."

Almost exactly a year later, on February 23, 1893, the *Nation* published a review of four texts, entitled "Recent Fiction," that discusses *Iola Leroy* briefly.[28] This piece is complimentary in ways that would assure the oblivion of the book, to paraphrase critic Mary Helen Washington's evaluation of the reception of Gwendolyn Brooks's *Maud Martha*.[29] The reviewer in fact praises Harper's novel only for its documentary value and summarizes it as follows: "'Iola Leroy' tells again the shameful story [of slavery], and brings the scene through the war days into the time of higher education and professional callings for the colored people" (146–147). As history replaces fiction, so does Harper's own life replace the adventures of her characters: "The book derives added interest from being written from an inside point of view by one of the race, *long known as an ardent worker in the cause of her people*" (147, emphasis added).

In both reviews, polemical and documentary concerns inform the evaluation of the texts in ways that effectively underplay their complexity and overlook their *literary* re-visions of the trope of the tragic mulatta, the very trope that resurfaces aggressively in the first reviewer's extraliterary objections to the (fictional) marriage between Olney and Rhoda and, by implication, to *any such* (nonfictional) marriage. As critic Martha Banta has insightfully noted with respect to *An Imperative Duty*, "the literary values of the story were too often tested on grounds of supposed emotional or social realism" (Banta, introduction, xi); this observation also resonates for *Iola Leroy*. In both cases, Howells's and Harper's revisionary (albeit very different) approaches to the literary trope of the (tragic) mulatta have been subjected to extraliterary criteria of evaluation that effectively ignore the aesthetic quality of the texts, thereby coterminously facilitating their critical dismissal as works of "minor" literary value. With the benefit of hindsight and a few decades of critical challenges to the canon, we can see beyond these parallel (though by no means identical) processes of critical marginalization to the intricate interracial genealogies of nineteenth-century American fiction.

NOTES

1. Hortense J. Spillers, "Notes on an Alternative Model — Neither/Nor," in *The Difference Within: Feminism and Critical Theory*, ed. Elizabeth Meese and Alice Parker (Philadelphia: John Benjamins, 1989), 166–167.

2. Deborah E. McDowell, *"The Changing Same": Black Women's Literature, Criticism, and Theory* (Bloomington: Indiana University Press, 1995), 206; Frances Smith Foster, introduction to *Minnie's Sacrifice, Sowing and Reaping, Trial and Triumph: Three Rediscovered Novels by Frances E. W. Harper*, ed. Frances Smith Foster (Boston: Beacon Press, 1994), xxiii. All second and subsequent references to these and other sources are cited in the text.

3. William Dean Howells, *An Imperative Duty* (1891; reprint, New York: Harper and Brothers, 1893), 54.

4. William Dean Howells, review of *What Answer?* by Anna E. Dickinson, *Atlantic Monthly* 23 (January 1869): 134.

5. See M. Giulia Fabi, "The 'Unguarded Expressions of the Feelings of the Negroes': Gender, Slave Resistance, and William Wells Brown's Revisions of *Clotel*," *African American Review* 27.4 (1993): 639–654.

6. See Elsa Nettels, "One and Many: Howells's Treatment of Race," *American Literary Realism* 18.1–2 (1985): 72–91; Anne Ward Amacher, "The Genteel Primitivist and the Semi-Tragic Octoroon," *New England Quarterly* 29.2 (1956): 216–227; Martha Banta, introduction to *An Imperative Duty*, by William Dean Howells (Bloomington: Indiana University Press, 1970), iii–xii.

7. On Howells's deliberate lightness of tone, see George N. Bennett, *The Realism of William Dean Howells, 1889–1920* (Nashville: Vanderbilt University Press, 1973), 94–105. On his battle in favor of realism and its connections with *An Imperative Duty*, see Everett Carter, *Howells and the Age of Realism* (Philadelphia: Lippincott, 1954), 59–67, 83–87; Edwin H. Cady, *The Realist at War: The Mature Years of William Dean Howells, 1885–1920* (Syracuse: Syracuse University Press, 1958), 155–163; Kenneth W. Warren, "Possessing the Common Ground: William Dean Howells' *An Imperative Duty*," *American Literary Realism* 20.3 (1988): 25–26; William L. Andrews, *The Literary Career of Charles W. Chesnutt* (Baton Rouge: Louisiana State University Press, 1980), 156–157.

8. William Dean Howells, "Editor's Study" (April 1887; reprinted in *"Editor's Study" by William Dean Howells*, ed. James W. Simpson [Troy, N.Y.: Whitston, 1983]), 76.

9. Henry B. Wonham, "Writing Realism, Policing Consciousness: Howells and the Black Body," *American Literature* 67.4 (1995): 720.

10. See Elise Miller, "The Feminization of American Realist Theory," *American Literary Realism* 23.1 (1990): 20–41.

11. On the connection between Olney, the narrator, and Howells, Banta has noted that Howells had originally planned *An Imperative Duty* as a novel "in autobiographic form" (introduction, iii).

12. Mark Twain, *Pudd'nhead Wilson* (1894; reprint, New York: Penguin, 1981), 59–60.

13. Howells invokes the same quantitative approach to race in his review, "Mr. Charles W. Chesnutt's Stories," *Atlantic Monthly* 85 (1900): 701.

14. See the short story by Miss Matt Crim, "Was It an Exceptional Case?" *Century Magazine* 42.6 (1891): 821–828. It appeared in print before *An Imperative Duty*, with which it shares some similarities of theme. How-

ells defended himself from accusations of plagiarism in a short letter to the *Critic*, 3 October 1891, p. 168.

15. Frances E. W. Harper, *Iola Leroy or Shadows Uplifted* (1892; reprint, Boston: Beacon, 1987), 114.

16. The first four chapters of *Iola Leroy* focus on the internal dynamics of the slave community, and the heroine is mentioned for the first time only in chapter 5. After Emancipation, on the contrary, the representation of black communities in the North and South is largely connected with Iola's own peregrinations.

17. Nina Baym, *Woman's Fiction: A Guide to Novels by and about Women in America, 1820–1870.* (Ithaca: Cornell University Press, 1978), 35.

18. See Marilyn Elkins, "Reading Beyond the Conventions: A Look at Frances E. W. Harper's *Iola Leroy, or Shadows Uplifted*," *American Literary Realism* 22.2 (1990): 44.

19. According to Kenneth Roemer, utopian fiction became particularly popular in the United States precisely during the last two decades of the 1800s. See Kenneth M. Roemer, *The Obsolete Necessity: America in Utopian Writings, 1888–1900* (n.p.: Kent State University Press, 1976), 8.

20. See Frances Smith Foster, *Written by Herself: Literary Production by African American Women, 1746–1892* (Bloomington: Indiana University Press, 1993), 184–185, and Claudia Tate, *Domestic Allegories of Political Desire* (New York: Oxford University Press, 1992), 144–149.

21. Hazel V. Carby, introduction to *Iola Leroy or Shadows Uplifted*, xxiv.

22. Ernst Bloch, *The Utopian Function of Art and Literature*, trans. Jack Zipes and Frank Mecklenburg (Cambridge: MIT Press, 1988), 107.

23. Carla Peterson has noted that "in contrast to [Harper's] *Christian Recorder* fiction, which was read by a primarily black audience, *Iola Leroy* was meant to appeal to a white readership as well." See Peterson, "'Further Liftings of the Veil': Gender, Class, and Labor in Frances E. W. Harper's *Iola Leroy*," in *Listening to Silences: New Essays in Feminist Criticism*, ed. Elaine Hedges and Shelley Fisher Fishkin (New York: Oxford University Press, 1994), 99.

24. In *Conflicting Stories: American Women Writers at the Turn into the Twentieth Century* (New York: Oxford University Press, 1991), Elizabeth Ammons describes Iola Leroy as a rape survivor (31). I share Claudia Tate's conviction, however, that Ammons does not provide enough textual evidence to support her argument (*Domestic Allegories*, 262).

25. Letter to Houghton Mifflin, 30 December 1901, quoted in Andrews, *Literary Career*, 127.

26. On the reception of *An Imperative Duty* and *Iola Leroy*, see, respectively, Banta, introduction, ix–xi, and Carby, introduction, xii–xiv.

27. "More Novels," *Nation*, 25 February 1892, p. 154.

28. "Recent Fiction," *Nation*, 23 February 1893, pp. 146–147.

29. Mary Helen Washington, ed., *Invented Lives: Narratives of Black Women, 1860–1960* (New York: Anchor Press, 1987), 387.

Was Tom White?
Stowe's *Dred* and Twain's *Pudd'nhead Wilson*

JUDIE NEWMAN

Ellen Moers has established a persuasive case for the influence of Stowe's *Uncle Tom's Cabin* on Twain's *Adventures of Huckleberry Finn* without, however, considering Stowe's and Twain's other antislavery novels, respectively, *Dred: A Tale of the Great Dismal Swamp* (1856) and *Pudd'nhead Wilson* (1894). For most literary historians *Dred* remains a novel without descendants, written in such immediate response to particular historical events as to have subsequently perished without trace from the literary canon.[1] *Pudd'nhead Wilson* has been read primarily in relation to Poe's influence on the detective plot.[2] A reading of *Dred* reveals, however, that precise parallels exist between the plots, characterization, and overall strategy of the two novels, suggesting that the woman writer had an important role in engendering the work of her male successor. Stowe's rejection in *Dred* of domestic, sentimental discourse in favor of a concentration upon public legal events provides an essential context for *Pudd'nhead Wilson*, a novel that shares with Stowe's a concern with issues of audience identification. Recent work has tended to foreground Stowe as a primarily sentimental novelist, working to engage the sympathies of her audience. In her "Concluding Remarks" to *Uncle Tom's Cabin* she remarks famously: "There is one thing that every individual can do,— they can see to it that *they feel right.* An atmosphere of sympathetic influence encircles every human being; and the man or woman who *feels* strongly, healthily and justly, on the great interests of humanity, is a constant benefactor to the human race. See, then, to your sympathies in this matter! Are they in harmony with the sympathies of Christ?"[3] In both *Dred* and *Pudd'nhead Wilson*, however, working the feelings of the audience is displayed as a strategy of dubious merit — at best tending to merely temporary good effects, at worst revealing the prerogative of the confidence trickster. Delineating a rival line of influence from *Dred* to *Pudd'nhead Wilson* rather than from Uncle Tom to Huck demonstrates what Twain learned from Stowe and throws light back on Stowe as well.

One major problem needs to be addressed at the outset: there is no hard evidence that Twain read *Dred*. Ellen Moers notes that he certainly read *Oldtown Folks* (1869) and *Sam Lawson's Oldtown Fireside Stories* (1873), and *Uncle Tom's Cabin* was hardly to be avoided, but *Dred* does not feature in the record of his reading.[4] Only Alice C. Crozier has suggested a connection; in 1969 she detected in *Dred* "a situation parallel to the one in Pudd'nhead Wilson" in the central pair of half-brothers, slave and free,[5] a situation that also echoes that of George Washington Cable's Grandissime half-brothers and survives in *Absalom, Absalom!* The general influence of Stowe upon Twain is not, however, in dispute. As Moers indicates, Twain first met Stowe in 1868; they became backyard neighbours in Hartford in 1874; they both contributed regularly to the *Atlantic Monthly*; both supported Henry Ward Beecher in his adultery trial in the mid-1870s; they exchanged books and children's gifts; and they starred as rival literary lions in Hartford, standing side by side to autograph books during the 1883 Hartford fair and leading a costume march at a "Carnival of Authors." Stowe later descended into senility (dying in 1896 at the age of 85), wandering in and out of the houses of her neighbors, including Twain, who was rudely awakened early one morning by Stowe playing the piano in his parlor. Both writers were acutely aware of their audiences and thoroughly professional in their commercial operations. Leslie Fiedler argues that Twain was obsessed by Stowe's success in the marketplace. When *The Innocents Abroad* first appeared, he wrote to Livy, "Nothing like it since *Uncle Tom's Cabin*, I guess," something of an overestimation.[6] He flew into a furious rage when his children reported that he had barely beaten Stowe in a classroom poll on who was America's greatest writer. In his comparison, Fiedler portrays Stowe and Twain as opposites, and gendered opposites at that, the one "celebrating Home and Mother," the other "fantasizing escapes from both." For Fiedler, "if Sam

Clemens is a literary father to us all, Hattie Stowe is our mother — however long some of us may in our macho pride have denigrated and denied her" (242, 243). Gregg Camfield's recent study of Twain also opens with a discussion of the close relationship of Twain to Stowe, but, in opposition to Fiedler, Camfield emphasizes resemblances, portraying Twain as a closet sentimentalist, or at least a writer caught between sentimental leanings and intellectual skepticism.[7] Again, the focus is on *Uncle Tom's Cabin* and *Huckleberry Finn*; Dred does not come into the equation.

In the absence of external evidence, the case for a direct relationship has to hinge upon internal textual evidence. Perhaps because, as Hershel Parker has demonstrated,[8] Twain's novel is an editor's nightmare, constructed out of two stories ("Those Extraordinary Twins" and "Pudd'nhead Wilson") inelegantly sandwiched together, and with a published residue to boot, attention has tended to focus on Twain's intratextual maneuverings rather than on external influences. Indeed, the song and dance that Twain himself made about his problems integrating the two stories has proved something of a blind to the critic.[9] Twain described his relief at the final birth of his novel, notoriously, as that of "a mother who has given birth to a white baby when she was awfully afraid that it was going to be a mulatto,"[10] explicitly presenting himself as a female creator with the threat of an illegitimately produced creation hanging over him. It is also suggestive that the villain of Twain's novel steals from his neighbors by entering their homes disguised as a woman — with his best raids occurring when they are at a performance by his great rivals, the Twins, a popular attraction given to "slambanging" (94) on the piano. On some subliminal level, Twain's rivalry with Stowe and his borrowings from her enter the text.

Less subliminally, much more obvious parallels make the case unassailable. In *Pudd'nhead Wilson*, Pudd'nhead is a young lawyer who is unable to practice after one mistake — a misplaced joke that allows the town to pass its own "verdict" (60) upon him. In *Dred* Edward Clayton is a young lawyer who gives up the law after his first case. Wilson is pitted against Tom Driscoll, who is doubled by a "slave" Other, Valet de Chambre or Chambers (though in reality their roles have been reversed by cradle swapping). Edward Clayton is the opponent of Tom Gordon, who is also doubled by a slave Other, Harry, his half-brother. Harry has previously accompanied his father and master to Europe as his valet (68). The legal emphasis in both novels is relentless. Stowe had prepared for *Dred* with an intensive course of reading in the law. One-third of *The Key to Uncle Tom's Cabin* (1853), which might more properly be described as the key to *Dred*, focuses on judicial records of trials and decisions and on statute law, with Stowe assuring the reader that she has taken advice from various legal experts.[11] The action of *Dred* involves three major trials, a mock trial involving slaves (396), a threatened duel, and accounts of the trials of two insurrectionists. As Earl Briden has established, *Pudd'nhead Wilson* is replete with legal metaphors, characters (lawyers, judges, and justices), a parody trial of slaves, a duel (trial by arms), oaths, bylaws, and a climactic court case, all within the overriding theme of race as "a fiction of law and custom" (64).[12] Twain's opening warranty, in particular, swearing the veracity of the legal matters on the authority of one William Hicks, who had studied law in the South thirty-five years earlier but had left for his health to work in a horse-feed shed in Florence, is a lovely burlesque of Stowe's footnotes, appendices, trial extracts, and continual assertions of legal accuracy. As a lawyer who had to leave the South for his health, Hicks recalls the various confidence men of Twain's novels, or, more seriously, the fate of Edward Clayton, whose advocacy of emancipation removes him from the practice of law and settles him in Canada. The action of *Dred* focuses upon a court case for assault and battery upon a slave (Milly) brought by Clayton; in *Pudd'nhead Wilson* Tom Driscoll (the concealed slave) brings a case for assault upon Luigi. In *Dred* Harry has to be got out of the way to escape Tom's wrath and his wife, Lisette, bought by Nina to keep her out of Tom's clutches; in *Pudd'nhead Wilson* Chambers is bought by Judge Driscoll to save him from Tom Driscoll's plan to sell him down the river.

In both novels snobbery looms large. In *Dred* Tiff boasts repeatedly that the Peytons (his owners) belong to the First Families of Virginia; in *Pudd'nhead Wilson* the FFV are prominently represented in the persons of Judge Driscoll and Pembroke Howard. There are similar rivalries between slaves and similar ritual exchanges of insults (between Tiff and Old Hundred in *Dred*, and Roxy and Jasper in Twain's tale). Both novels include a single strong black woman character: Stowe's Milly (who is hired out and maltreated, rebels when a little slave girl is beaten, and runs away) and Twain's Roxy (sold into slavery and maltreated, rebels when a little slave girl is beaten, and runs away). There are, of course, differences within similarities. Twain uses fingerprinting as the means to bodily identification and confirmation of the slave status quo. Stowe slaughters all her redundant characters with cholera, a bodily condition linked to revolutionary insurrection and the upset of the status quo.[13] Stowe makes much of religion, particularly criticizing the temporary piety arising from revivals, and the support of slavery by the Calvinists (represented by Jekyl); Twain's only religious character is Roxy, who justifies swapping the babies on the grounds of Calvinist determinism and is converted at a revival as a result of which she defers her usual practice of theft — for a few weeks (66).

The resemblances between Tom Gordon and Tom Driscoll go beyond the ne'er-do-well stereotype. Both are partly reared by a childless and ineffectual aunt, and both go in for drink and gambling. Tom Driscoll actually takes to burglary and murder in order to meet his debts. Tom Gordon does the same under the cloak of slavery. Because "his cravings for money" were insatiable, Tom Gordon "had as little care how it was come by, as a high-way robber" (587). When he ambushes Clayton on the road, Clayton describes him as a "cut-throat" (613) who is after his watch and purse. Tom Gordon has Cora (his freed slave half-sister) sold into slavery (Tom Driscoll sells his freed slave mother into slavery), and he murders Hark and gets off scot-free, "protected by the express words of legal decision" (590). In *Pudd'nhead Wilson* infanticide is the engine of the plot. Roxy plans to kill her child to save it from being sold down the river but instead swaps the babies in the cradle. In *Dred* Cora Gordon murders her children to save them from slavery. Both Tom and Cora are sold as slaves after a period of passing as white; both are tried for murder. Tom, sentenced to be hanged, is instead sold down the river as the plot comes full circle. Stowe makes it crystal clear that her heroine, Nina, has an enslaved half-sister in Cora (434, 548–549), "doubling" both her major male and female characters. Twain also multiplies doubles, in the shape of the Italian Twins. In *Pudd'nhead Wilson* Tom is too cowardly to fight a duel and escapes by claiming that his opponent is not a man whom he could meet on the field of honor. His uncle, infuriated, foregrounds the issue of Tom's race: "Do you mean to tell me that blood of my race has suffered a blow and crawled to a court of law about it?" (41).

The vital point in the case of Milly in *Dred* is whether a slave *can* have recourse to the law for protection. Milly is disqualified by her race; as a slave she cannot succeed in an action against the man who is in the place of temporary master. If Tom's slave identity were known, of course, he would be disqualified from the field of honor as well as that of law. In *Dred* Tom Gordon demands that Clayton fight him. Clayton refuses on the grounds that Tom's behavior means that he "falls out of the sphere of gentlemen" (605). Tom therefore ambushes him and beats him up in an incident expressly designed to mimic the case of Charles Sumner, beaten in the chamber of the Senate in 1856, supposedly in reprisal for a slur upon the honor of Senator Butler of South Carolina. In *Pudd'nhead Wilson* Tom's uncle avenges the slur on the family name by fighting a duel with Luigi, later discovers that Luigi is not a gentleman, announces his plan to lie in wait for him and shoot him on sight, and then engineers a political revenge by large-handed use of his purse to buy a mob in the runup to the election (171). As the Sumner reference suggests, personal violence extends into the political. In *Dred* Tom Gordon also has electoral ambitions and is running for Congress (585); he raises a mob against his opponents. Both novels are heavy on scenes of mob violence and include threats of lynching. Twain's "Sons of Liberty" get drunk and burn down their own meeting place (137); Tom Gordon's mob, "insane with whisky" (663), burns down the Clayton schoolhouse. The evils of drink feature prominently in both novels, as do meetings of a political or religious nature (revivalist in Stowe, antitemperance in Twain). In short, the reader is taken firmly into the public arena. Jane Tompkins has argued that the Western develops in oppositional response to the female domestic novel — but it is arguable that *Dred* is already well down that road, with its frontier-style violence, ambushes, and lynch mobs, and its action played out largely on the public stage.[14]

Such parallels are too many to be merely adventitious and too specific to be simply the product of generic resemblances (to the "tragic octoroon" or the antebellum fratricide *topoi*).[15] The "So what?" factor nonetheless applies. So far this argument might well be dismissed as a classic case of literary nit-picking. There are, however, obvious consequences for Twain. Some of the problems readers have had with the question of Tom's innate evil are dissipated if we consider it the product not of his racial inheritance but of his literary descent—from Stowe's white character.[16] It is not so much a case of "Was Huck Black?" as "Was Tom White?" Similarly, Stowe's device of multiple doubles provides a template for Twain, and her evocation of the FFV explains the dominance of the FFV in Twain's Missouri setting. The parallels also potentially undermine Hershel Parker's decisive intervention in debates concerning *Pudd'head Wilson*: many of the peculiar features of the plot are the result not of two muddled Twain novels but of intertextual reference to Stowe.

Intertextuality has been characterized as anachronistic, inviting us to consider, in David Lodge's proverbial phrase, the influence of T. S. Eliot on Shakespeare. Without pressing anachronism to extremes, it is also arguable that the relation between Stowe and Twain throws light back on Stowe, particularly in the device both authors share — that of doubling the audience. Critics have recognized the importance of performance in *Pudd'nhead Wilson* and have agreed on the homogenous quality of Twain's crowds.[17] The community in Dawson's Landing speaks as one, with one voice, and is roundly mocked for its gullibility, obtuseness, and conformity. (The opening incident — the half-a-dog joke — marks the difference between reader and audience decisively.) In *Dred* Stowe also foregrounds audiences; the novel is full of crowd scenes, unlike *Uncle Tom's Cabin*, where they scarcely feature at all. (The earlier novel's chapter titles tend to the individual name; *Dred*'s have a group emphasis: "The Lovers," "The Conspirators," "The Worshippers," "The Clerical Conference," for example.) The audience emphasis undermines the view of Stowe as primarily aiming for sympathetic reader-identification, revealing a writer who eschews sentiment, checks sympathy in the reader by dividing her audiences, and moves the action firmly out of the domestic and into the public sphere. In *Dred* audiences are not homogenous but multiple, with a variety of witness points of view and numerous subgroupings (readers, spectators, jury, and judge in the trial scenes, for example). Audience reaction is frequently a topic for immediate discussion by a subgroup. The legal plot foregrounds the inefficacy of feeling against law[18] and confronts us with audiences on the page from whom we may differ, producing an emphasis on the scenic, scopic, and visual that converts all readers into social witnesses. The various group scenes are designed not to carry the reader away into the excesses of the three-handkerchief novel but to offer a critique of easy sympathy and to ask the reader what he or she actually intends to *do* about slavery. Little is individualized: death in *Dred* is a mass event (in the cholera epidemic); the final slave escape is a group enterprise. Stowe is not Brecht — but her method poses the essential Brechtian question: Do we first change the hearts of men and thus the world, or first change the world in order to change men?

Examples of Stowe's comprehensive dramatization of her own reservations about the operation of audience sympathy are particularly striking in *Dred* in relation to two major elements of the plot: public meetings and deathbed scenes, the one tending to elide into the other. Her tour-de-force dramatization of a camp meeting is representative. An initial hymn pulls the different groups together into "one vast, surging sea of sound" (323) in which "negroes and whites, slaves and freemen, saints and sinners, slave-holders, slave-hunters, slave-traders, ministers, elders and laymen" sing with one breath. Although the meeting is a "Union" one (between Presbyterians and Methodists), divisions swiftly appear; the various preachers are, of course, in hot competition for the audience. Many of those present give themselves up for conversion without resistance, "swayed by the feeling of the hour" (324), though the dinner break intervenes with comic effect. Uncle John is about to surrender to conversion but instead hears the call of dinner and three glasses of wine. Discussion immediately centers upon the desirability of such temporary enthusiasm. Tiff comments that "when de preaching is done dere don't 'pear to be nothing to it" (327). Nina sees little point in sermons or hymns, Clayton declares for feeling and enthusiasm, Anne is visibly shocked. Other groups also discuss the morning's spectacle — at a whiskey booth and in a group of slave hunters. The afternoon sermon stirs up a similar enthusiasm all over again: "The excitement now became general" (338) with a frenzy of conversion on all sides. Feelings run high — only to be checked and brought to a close by the voice of Dred, invisible in the trees, roundly condemning all present for their *actions*. For Stowe, he is clearly designed to represent a silent, invisible witness, God, with whom the reader (also invisible, of course, but with similarly panoramic access to the various scenes at the camp meeting) should be allied. In *The Key*, after reviewing various trials Stowe comments, "Think that Jesus Christ has been present, a silent witness through every such scene of torture and anguish — a silent witness in every such court" (206). Dred is repeatedly associated with the term "witness" and the image of "Jegar Sahadutha," the heap of witness,[19] though the audience is skeptical — some assume that Dred is part of the theatrics, a "plant" by one of the preachers (366) designed to manipulate them. Since the reader knows that he is *not* a plant, our own distrust is disbarred. The doubling of audience can work to prevent uncritical identification — or to make skepticism less defensible.

Importantly, the scene immediately modulates into a deathbed — that of Emily, a member of a coffle of slaves, dying of a fever after a presumed "fate worse than death." The account of Emily's death affects the interstate trader with a moment of remorse and is described to Father Bonnie at length by abolitionist Father Dickson, an eloquent speaker: "The reader will not therefore wonder to hear that father Bonnie, impulsive and easily moved as he was, wept at the account, and was moved at the exhortation. Nor will he be surprised to learn that, two weeks after, father Bonnie drove a brisk bargain with the same trader for three new hands" (347). Father Dickson has just as little effect upon the audience when he relates the death scene to them. For a moment they are swayed: "As he spoke with feeling he awakened feeling in return" (370); but when the sermon is over, "it seemed to melt away as a wave flows back again into the sea. It was far easier to join in a temporary whirlwind of excitement, than to take into consideration troublesome, difficult and expensive reforms" (371). Emily's death is not only quite ineffectual, it is characteristic of *Dred*. Tiff's mistress Sue dies so swiftly and with such little ado that her husband sleeps through it, even though he is in the same bed.

Stowe swiftly checks what pathos there is in the person of Mr. Carson, who voices all the stock reactions of the sentimental reader, but who has already been established as completely inane. Once Carson has finished extolling the virtues of charity, the need to reflect on death, and the delightful "effect" (174) of the funeral, he has managed "to talk away the impression of the whole scene they had witnessed. . . . Nina had forgotten all her sympathy in a tumult of vexation" (175). By modeling one conventional reader response, Carson effectively taboos it. Other death scenes are characterized primarily by loss of feeling and by speed of extinction. While Stowe's Eva dies over two chapters and in final fevered, struggling paroxysms, Nina's death from cholera involves a creeping coldness and loss of sensation (she cannot tell water from spirits). A fugitive slave expires (311) with a vacant stare. Dred himself is wounded and dead within the page. Speed is of the essence as far as the Grim Reaper is concerned. Uncle John does have a terrible death struggle, but Nina (a spectator) remains completely calm, almost as if unmoved by his death. The priority in dealing with the cholera epidemic is disciplined action and resolution. No model is offered to the audience for tears, sobs, or sympathy.

Nina's death is the culminating example. In the first place, killing off the sentimental heroine in the middle of the novel does little for the sentimental reader. And second, the manner of her death — she dies singing — is telling. Although it takes place in a domestic setting, the death is constructed as a performance. Clayton and Nina have recently been present at a minstrel show ("The Troubadour") in which the slaves both perform to their masters and score a number of jokey hits off them, provoking blushes and merriment. (The scene is an odd mixture of catering to an audience and making fun of it.) When Clayton sees Nina for the last time he dreams of the show, which turns in his dream into a funeral and then elides (as he awakes) into the sound of Nina's voice singing outside his door. In her subsequent death scene, it is almost as if she dies as a minstrel on a public stage. The song is "The Hindoo Dancing-Girl's Song": Nina is performing as racial Other.

Nina's death is part and parcel of the progression in the novel from private rituals of courtship to public courts. Here, too, sympathetic demonstration yields to the more powerful claims of restraint. In Clayton's first legal action the audience members know that the law is not on his side but hope that he will win because he is spurred on by love (384), because he "has great power of exciting the feelings," and because "his personal presence was good, his voice melodious, and his elocution fine" (387). As a result of his deeply felt performance, "he carried the whole of his audience with him" (389). When the case reaches the Supreme Court on appeal and Clayton loses, his father announces the verdict with no sign of feeling whatsoever. His tone is "passionless" (450) and his earnestness is described as communicating "more than a thousand passionate appeals." Listening to his father's calm peroration, Clayton for the first time realizes the full horror of slavery. The acts of law expounded in the legal action mean more than any amount of fine feeling. In this trial, Nina's love letter to Clayton has to be enclosed in his law book — shut firmly away (446). Clayton himself realizes the full horror of the verdict only as he watches the horrified reaction to it of Harry, the slave valet, who is accidentally in the audience as a spectator and suddenly realizes how the verdict applies to him (450). As readers we have the two extremes of horrified powerless feeling and cold legal power displayed before us. Stowe's implicit support for the righteousness of action on behalf of abolition, rather than for mere moral suasion, is suggested in her differing treatment of black and of white violence. Judge Clayton's unmoving demeanor is echoed in the behavior of the slaves who have shown evidence of resolute action: Cora Gordon, who describes the murder of her children in court with no show of emotion, and Denmark Vesey, Dred's putative father and insurrectionist, whose trial is recounted in flashback. In contrast to the dignified restraint of Cora, Stowe gives us the extreme example of audiences carried away by contagious sympathy in the scenes in which Tom arouses a mob against Father Dickson. Lynch law is, of course, not law at all but the triumph of popular feeling. In the scenes of mobocracy with which the action closes Stowe tests the essential appeal of sentiment against the crowd — and finds it distinctly wanting. Sympathy becomes suggestibility, contagious excitement, and violence, as the audience becomes the mob.[20]

One scene models a correct relationship between feeling and action, private and public spaces, when Nina is asked to read the Bible to Tiff. Tiff is an extremely naive audience who identifies furiously (he converts Herod into General Eaton, for example). The overly detached critical reader is also satirized, however. We are told that "more cultivated minds" (430) might have asked too many questions to get the Bible story told at all. Nina, however, blending two responses and swayed by Tiff's reactions as much as her own (essentially a double audience), reads herself into conversion. The framed reading scene serves as a model for our own reception, directing us toward a "checks and balances" paradigm of the right relation to sentiment. Other discussions of reading — as immoral in the discussion of Byron (37–38), as a substitute for action (283), or as likely to inflame actions dangerous to the proslavery cause — offer similar opportunities for Stowe to invite us to negotiate the territory between sympathy and detachment.[21] Nina herself is an accomplished exploiter of sentiment; she makes up a sentimental love story to enable her to buy Lisette (205), but the result is to deliver Lisette into Tom's hands on Nina's death. Sentiment does not pay in the long term. As Whitney has indicated, sentiment can enslave — Harry remains with Nina because she is his beloved sister, for example, and thus her heart is "the clasp upon my chain" (199). Lack of feeling carries its own dangers, however — not least for Stowe, whose strategy of checking reader sympathies was so successful that *Dred* never equaled the success of *Uncle Tom's Cabin*.[22]

To sum up, both Twain and Stowe are aware of the dangers of easy audience identification and get between the reader and the event to promote a degree of detachment. Both, however, also warn the reader off from any easy superiority to events — the reader remains firmly in their sights as a potential target. Members of the reading audience are often the sudden victims of the incriminating finger — in Stowe's invisible Dred for example — or find that a scene that appeared to be safely in the realm of spectacle has suddenly revealed a precise application to their own case (as in the scene in which Clayton watches Harry's audience reaction to a verdict that suddenly invalidates all Harry's plans for freedom). It is as if the actors had crossed the footlights into the "house." Twain's Roxy thinks that she is merely a spectator to the duel — but she is close enough to be wounded just the same. No member of an audience is at a safe enough distance to escape. Clayton enjoys the spectacle of the minstrel show — until it is his beloved who is performing. In thematizing the operations of sentiment, Stowe puts the sentimental reader on the page in the shape of Carson and convicts him of idiocy. Twain's town convicts Pudd'nhead Wilson of idiocy at the start, only for the tables to turn at the close when he turns upon the audience at the trial to identify one of its members, Tom, as the guilty party, and to force a reassessment. As one of the citizens puts it:

"And this is the man the likes of us has called a Pudd'nhead for more than twenty years. He has resigned from that position, friends."

"Yes, but it isn't vacant — we're elected." (224)

For Stowe and Twain there is no witness immunity — the reader's position is unstable, translating all too easily from judge and jury to accused.

NOTES

1. See Judie Newman, introduction to *Dred: A Tale of the Great Dismal Swamp*, ed. Judie Newman (Edinburgh: Edinburgh University Press, 1998).

2. Lawrence Howe, "Race, Genealogy, and Genre in Mark Twain's *Pudd'nhead Wilson*," *Nineteenth Century Literature* 46.4 (1992): 495–516.

3. Harriet Beecher Stowe, *Uncle Tom's Cabin* (London: Penguin, 1981), 624, emphasis in original. All second and subsequent references to this and other sources are cited in the text.

4. Ellen Moers, *Harriet Beecher Stowe and American Literature* (Hartford: Stowe-Day Foundation, 1978). For the record of Twain's library, see Alan Gribben, *Mark Twain's Library: A Reconstruction* (Boston: G. K. Hall, 1980).

5. Alice C. Crozier, *The Novels of Harriet Beecher Stowe* (New York: Oxford University Press, 1969), 48.

6. Leslie Fiedler, *What Was Literature? Class, Culture and Mass Society* (New York: Simon and Schuster, 1982), 243.

7. Gregg Camfield, *Sentimental Twain: Samuel Clemens in the Maze of Moral Philosophy* (Philadelphia: University of Pennsylvania Press, 1994).

8. Hershel Parker, *Flawed Texts and Verbal Icons. Literary Authority in American Fiction* (Evanston: Northwestern University Press, 1984), 115–145.

9. Mark Twain, *Pudd'nhead Wilson and Those Extraordinary Twins*, ed. Malcolm Bradbury (London: Penguin, 1969), 229.

10. Evan Carton, "*Pudd'nead Wilson* and the Fiction of Law and Custom," in *American Realism: New Essays*, ed. Eric J. Sundquist (Baltimore: Johns Hopkins University Press, 1982), 82.

11. Harriet Beecher Stowe, *The Key to Uncle Tom's Cabin* (Salem, New Hampshire: Ayer, 1987).

12. Earl F. Briden, "Idiots First, Then Juries: Legal Metaphors in Mark Twain's *Pudd'nhead Wilson*," *Texas Studies in Literature and Language* 20.2 (1978): 169–180.

13. See Charles E. Rosenberg, *The Cholera Years* (Chicago: University of Chicago Press 1962), and Michael Durey, *The Return of the Plague: British Society and the Cholera 1831–2* ([no city], Ireland: Gill and Macmillan, 1979), for an account of the wave of insurrections in the wake of cholera epidemics.

14. Jane Tompkins, *West of Everything: The Inner Life of Westerns* (Oxford: Oxford University Press, 1992).

15. On the tragic octoroon topos, see Adrienne Bond, "Disorder and the Sentimental Model: A Look at *Pudd'nhead Wilson*," *Southern Literary Journal* 13.2 (1981): 59–71. On the antebellum fratricide topos, see George B. Forgie, *Patricide in the House Divided: A Psychological Interpretation of Lincoln and His Age* (New York: Norton, 1979).

16. In the first version of the story, centered upon Siamese twins, Tom *was* white, as Parker demonstrates. He is, of course, only "black" because his mother Roxy is so classified by her one-sixteenth African descent. For a discussion of race in the novel, see Susan Gillman and Forrest G. Robinson, eds., *Mark Twain's Pudd'nhead Wilson: Race, Conflict and Culture* (Durham: Duke University Press, 1990). In the original version the Twins are about to win a lawsuit as a result of popular feeling when a judge very similar in his Roman simplicity to Judge Clayton intervenes on a point of law (though in the outcome feeling triumphs). The parallels suggest that Twain had *Dred* in mind from the outset.

17. See Carton, cited above; Mark D. Coburn, "'Training Is Everything': Communal Opinion and the Individual in *Pudd'nhead Wilson*," *Modern Language Quarterly* 31 (1970): 209–219; Muriel B. Williams, "The Unmasking of Meaning: A Study of the Twins in *Pudd'nhead Wilson*," *Mississippi Quarterly* 33 (1980): 39–53. If we accept Williams's argument, powerfully made, that the Twins are confidence men who "take" the town, Twain clearly presents an example of exploitation of an audience masquerading as entertainment.

18. Lisa Whitney, "In the Shadow of *Uncle Tom's Cabin*: Stowe's Vision of Slavery from the Great Dismal Swamp," *New England Quarterly* 66 (1993): 552–569.

19. See Genesis 32:46–47.

20. For an excellent discussion of the nineteenth-century perception of the dangers of sympathetic identification, see Athena Vrettos, *Somatic Fictions: Imagining Illness in Victorian Culture* (Stanford: Stanford University Press, 1995).

21. Arguably, Twain leaves less room for reader freedom, presenting a deterministic image of reading in the reading of palms and (by extension)

fingerprints. The Twins comment that it is "as if our palms had been covered with print" (127). Luigi's life is written on his hand — as is Tom's fate.

22. *Dred* never sold as well as *Uncle Tom's Cabin*, though the sales figures were respectable: 150,000 in America in the first year; 165,000 in Britain. It went through dozens of editions and was translated in Austria, Bulgaria, Holland, France, Germany, Italy, Poland, and Sweden, with dramatic adaptations in Britain and America in 1856, and Bulgaria in 1948. Under the alternative title *Nina Gordon* it was republished after the war (Boston: Ticknor and Fields, 1866), with one-volume editions in 1867 and 1869, when Twain had newly become acquainted with Stowe. See Margaret Holbrook Hildreth, *Harriet Beecher Stowe: A Bibliography* (Hamden, Conn.: Archon, 1976).

Shaped by Readers:
The Slave Narratives of
Frederick Douglass and
Harriet Jacobs

STEPHEN MATTERSON

The differences between *Narrative of the Life of Frederick Douglass, an American Slave* (1845) and Harriet Jacobs's *Incidents in the Life of a Slave Girl* (1861) seem so substantial as almost to invalidate any grounds for meaningful comparison. The very forms of slavery they describe vary, even though both are family based and involve a small number of slaves. Douglass experienced house slavery in both an urban and a rural setting, worked as a farm slave, and was "let out" to work elsewhere for his owner. Jacobs, under the pseudonym "Linda Brent," presents her experiences as a house slave, but provides far less detail about her working life than Douglass does. Although generically both works belong to the "slave narrative," they again differ substantially. Douglass's narrative is orally driven, whereas Jacobs's is more self-consciously literary, in her use of literary trope, in the invention of Linda Brent as involved first-person narrator, and in direct reference to another literary genre, the romance. Both narratives are counter-genres, but since they work against different models, they vary strikingly in their representation of how slavery threatens to dehumanize the slave. Douglass undoes the terms of autobiography and thereby draws attention to a series of tragic absences in the life of the slave — absences signaled from the very first sentence — but then restores the terms of autobiography and demonstrates his own self-making. Jacobs utilizes the romance narrative in a highly complex way, implying the unattainability of genteel romance for the slave woman but also to some extent destabilizing the conditions of genteel womanhood more generally.

Telling though the differences between the narratives are, they testify primarily to the different aims of the narratives and to the use that Jacobs could make, in a way not readily available to Douglass in 1845, of a developing political communal consciousness. Jacobs's *Incidents* is a text in dialogue with Douglass's *Narrative*; at times she elaborates his text and at times she consciously offers an alternative version of the slave narrative. To claim that Jacobs parodies *Narrative* as a precursor text is an overstatement, but suggestive in recognizing the narratives' intertextual relationship.[1] They differ principally in the forms of antislavery action that they imply, and this difference is rooted in the development of a political language. Perhaps the most significant point of divergence between the two texts is their appearance on either side of the 1848 Seneca Falls Declaration.[2]

Gendering the Narrative

The most obvious and in some respects the most crucial difference is that Douglass presents (perhaps unconsciously) a male narrative of slavery, while Jacobs consciously plays off this perspective and presents a female narrative, a voice in a "soft canon." It may be hyperbolic to speak, as Jenny Franchot does, of "Douglass's attachment to the narrative conventions of the white masculine world" (150), but the two stories do form a fascinating index to the cultural expectations governing the behavior of men and women. Both writers, for instance, emphasize how slavery destroys manly independence and punishes those who try to assert their masculinity. Douglass uses himself, before the fight with Covey, as the example of this unmanning, whereas Jacobs explores the idea in her chapter 4, "The Slave Who Dared to Feel Like a Man," based on her uncle Joseph.[3] Yet Jacobs is much more directly concerned than Douglass with gender divisions within slavery; as her preface makes clear, she explicitly addresses the woman reader and frequently states that the distinctive focus of her narrative is the experience of the female slave. The instances that Douglass gives of cruelty to women slaves function primarily as touchstones for the reader's pity rather than as part of an analysis of the broader effects of slavery on women. Thus, he uses the whipping of his aunt, Hester, as both his and the reader's introduction to the cruel treatment of individual slaves: "the blood-stained gate, the entrance to the hell of slavery."[4]

Confronted by the deprivation of his manhood, Douglass offers a narrative about its ultimate attainment through a form of Emersonian self-reliance, and about how manhood functions as a vital expression of his full humanity. He demonstrates his fitness not only to be considered fully human but, more specifically, by confronting dehumanizing racial stereotyping, to be considered a man. In this respect, his narrative is an already familiar, even canonical one, a form of conversion narrative or a success narrative of becoming and self-fulfilment akin to the *Autobiography* of Benjamin Franklin.[5] A story that begins by pointing out the tragic absence in Douglass's life — the absence of grounding in time — ends with a series of gestures indicating a form of self-fashioning through work, self-ownership, and self-naming.[6] Douglass concludes with the development of his individual political consciousness through his reading of the *Liberator*, and with his speaking at an abolitionist meeting. These achievements do not make up for the absences with which the narrative opened, but the discovery of an individual voice represents for him the significant step to both complete manhood and political involvement.

The gaps in Douglass's narrative that allow it to function as a countergenre to mainstream autobiography are obviously terrible and tragic. The absence of a birth date is felt especially strongly, and Douglass also underscores that family separation was a systematic device to "blunt and destroy the natural affection of the mother for the child" (48). But the narrative actually shows that such absences are made to function positively for Douglass, since he is consequently unhindered in his acts of resistance and eventual flight. That is, his decisions can be taken without regard to the likelihood of reprisals on others. Strikingly, entirely the opposite is true for Jacobs. She indicates that keeping families together was a preferred strategy of the slaveowner, because it curbed the tendency to abscond, and that this restraint functioned especially strongly on slave mothers.[7] Jacobs emphasizes how Linda Brent's desire for freedom is checked by the terror of the consequent surrender of her children — what Vladimir Nabokov a century later called "the lever of love" in a totalitarian state.[8]

Much of Jacobs's narrative is driven by a desire for freedom — especially because of the pressure placed on her by Dr. Flint—

but also by a desire to live up to an ideal of womanhood. Interestingly, while it is often accepted that *Incidents* ironizes the nineteenth-century ideals of womanhood, this claim is usually made by relocating the story into a nonracialized discourse.[9] Perhaps our eagerness to read *Incidents* as a woman's narrative has been at the expense of seeing it as a black woman's narrative. Undoubtedly, the references that Jacobs makes to virtuous domestic womanhood have the cumulative effect of suggesting that the virtues are relative and not absolute, and even that they depend on a comfortable, unchallenged domestic situation. Hence, the appeal for understanding is sometimes made on the assumption that the virtuous reader has never had her virtues tested: "Pity me, and pardon me, O virtuous reader! You never knew what it is to be a slave; to be entirely unprotected by law and custom; to have the laws reduce you to the condition of a chattel, entirely subject to the will of another. You never exhausted your ingenuity in avoiding the snares, and eluding the power of a hated tyrant; you never shuddered at the sound of his footsteps, and trembled within hearing of his voice" (86). But at the same time that Jacobs qualifies her stance, she does maintain the virtues as ideals. This maintenance of the ideals is itself a significant gesture, and one that perhaps, at the end of the twentieth century, we are in danger of failing to appreciate.

During the antebellum period, and indeed for a long time afterwards, there was little expectation that women of color, whether slave or freed, needed to aspire to these ideals. Genovese quotes Mary Boykin Chesnut's diary comment, "Under slavery we live surrounded by prostitutes, yet an abandoned woman is sent out of any decent house. Who thinks any worse of a Negro or mulatto woman for being a thing we can't name?" (426). Ostensibly, the statement seems sympathetic, an admission that what Chesnut calls the "monstrous system" forbids or otherwise makes impossible the cultivation and practice of virtue — a statement mirroring Jacobs's "I feel that the slave woman ought not to be judged by the same standard as others" (86). But the dynamics of Chesnut's observation serve to sustain the female virtues as white virtues. It is "we" who are surrounded by "them"; the virtues are goals beyond the reach of nonwhite women; no colored need apply.

Thus, for her contemporary readers Jacobs's destabilization of the womanly virtues would be less striking than her appropriation of them, her assumption that they are ideals equally available to her and equally relevant to her; as she writes, "I had resolved that I would be virtuous, though I was a slave" (87). Overstating the ironizing of Jacobs's attitude to the virtues is understandable if the narrative is deracialized and Jacobs is seen as a woman more than as a black woman. In a way, this reading is actually a form of tribute to Jacobs, because one explicit aim of *Incidents* is a supraracial woman's movement.[10] But in another way it represents a significant disservice because it ignores the narrative's most radical gesture: Jacobs reformulates the Seneca Falls Declaration to render its terms more clearly applicable to her own situation. The declaration had identified the existence of a double standard between men and women, professing that man "has created a false public sentiment by giving to the world a different code of morals for men and women, by which moral delinquencies which exclude women from society, are not only tolerated, but deemed of little account in man."[11] Jacobs pointedly uses this double standard to apply to the different expectations of white women and women of color, contending that the virtues represent valid aspirations for black women too — however difficult, as Linda Brent's case demonstrates, it might be to fulfil them. In this respect the portrayal of the self-reliant grandmother is clearly intended to demonstrate the fitness of black women for these ideals.[12]

At the same time, in the complex discourse of *Incidents*, Jacobs makes use of the idea that marriage is a variation of slavery. This coupling of the woman's position in marriage with slavery had been central to the Seneca Falls Declaration, with its assertions that the married woman is "civilly dead" and "completely deprived of liberty" (Stanton 104).[13] Jacobs reiterates this binary opposition between marriage and freedom in her celebrated statement, "Reader, my story ends in freedom; not in the usual way, with marriage" (302). Nevertheless, the statement is rather more complex than it may at first appear. It functions partly as a genre reference, since the form of romance that Jacobs has been using as a model would have led the reader to expect marriage as a suitable conclusion; more specifically, it is probably intended as an echo of the "Reader, I married him" of *Jane Eyre*.[14] But again, there is a danger of locating Jacobs only within a tradition that privileges womanhood over black womanhood. That is, there is a tragic element in the statement that we are likely to miss if we see it only as ironic. Of course, freedom is the major goal of *Incidents*, but the statement's tragic dimension lies in its premise that Linda cannot have both freedom and marriage. The narrative has told us why she cannot have both; the nature of her attachment to Sands has compromised the version of womanhood that is suitable for marriage. Furthermore, the statement represents the fullest development of an earlier comment, in which Jacobs writes that the female slave "is not allowed to have any pride of character. It is deemed in her a crime to wish to be virtuous" (49). An additional irony of the statement is that freedom itself has been seriously compromised. The ideal of freedom that Linda had held has not been fulfilled; her freedom comes in a way that she specifically did not want: to be bought by a white woman, in New York (300).

Blackness and the "Loophole of Retreat"

Perhaps in its very form the slave narrative is primarily assimilationist. The ideal of demonstrating civility and full humanity through literacy, application of higher thought, and devotion to Christian principles was a strong motivating force in the abolitionist sponsorship of many narratives. In this respect, the act of writing itself can be as radical a gesture as the subject matter of a narrative and, consequently, Douglass's account of his struggle to literacy is a crucial element of his story. The innately assimilationist drive of the slave narrative was of great significance to ex-slaves in their desire for acceptance, even though it perhaps reached its controversial (and even slightly ludicrous) extreme in Booker T. Washington's 1901 *Up From Slavery*.[15] Although Washington's references to slavery as a sort of moral school seem preposterous, they actually represent only the extreme of a conventional trope in the classic slave narrative, by which comparable (and perhaps even ritualistic) submissive gestures are made to moral, legal, and religious hegemony. Douglass's selection of his name is especially telling in this respect: he accepts the surname suggested by Mr. Johnson, though he insists on the retention of the first name "Frederick" (147). This acceptance seems to strike a neat balance between his sense of established identity and his willingness to assimilate. But the name "Douglass" comes from

Scott's 1810 poem *The Lady of the Lake*. The figure after whom Douglass is named, Lord James of Douglas, is a rebel, an outlaw who comes eventually to be reconciled with the king. Symbolically, then, the name is that of the outlaw who is reformed and who accepts the imposition of outside authority.

Certainly, this stated obedience may have been politic, given the economics of publication, and might well have been essential (even inevitable) as a form of reassurance, given the presumed beliefs of the white middle classes who likely formed the bulk of the narratives' readership. Nevertheless, Douglass and Jacobs are both apologists for themselves as deviants from the standards of nineteenth-century white middle-class American society. In seeking to justify their behavior they are, though in different ways, entreating a form of acceptance from the reader. It was left to W. E. B. Du Bois much later to articulate the concept of the "double consciousness" of the African American, precariously attempting to preserve an African identity that is threatened by the needs of obedience to an American reality.[16] Although the conditions for this double consciousness are apparent in these two narratives, they are muted by the need to demonstrate, for the readers, fitness to be called American. Douglass must offer a rationale for his confrontation with Covey and for his flight. Jacobs must explain Linda Brent's deliberately choosing a liaison with Mr. Sands, and the consequent illegitimacy of her children. Douglass must acknowledge and vindicate his transgression of the Christian principles of obedience and meekness without destabilizing those virtues (a fact that necessitated an appendix as an elaboration of his attitude to Christianity). Jacobs has to do likewise with regard to the feminine virtues that, she assumes, her reader ("O virtuous reader" [86]) cherishes. Jacobs strategically places her reader in the position of judge or jurywoman — an act suggesting how much *Incidents* might owe to the tradition of earlier "confessional" literature.

Yet interesting differences emerge in the forms that these apologies take and in the implications that they have for further action. In his 1845 narrative, Douglass often presents himself as different from the other blacks, holding himself fairly aloof from them. This stance is apparent in several episodes; for example, it resonates in his explanation of how the drunken celebration of the Christmas holiday is a tactic of the master to demonstrate the hollowness of freedom, and in his observation that the "fraud and inhumanity of slavery" is evident in thus engendering in the slave a kind of "disgust" for freedom (115–116). The effect of this observation, however unconscious and even unfortunate it may have been, is to suggest that Douglass is an exception to the other slaves, both in his desperate struggle to become literate and in the informed perspective that he brings to bear on the master-slave relation.[17] There is even a form of denigration of African American traditions, a denigration that may appear gratuitous, but which is central to Douglass's overall demonstration of his obedience to the white hegemony.

This stance of difference is most apparent in the pivotal episode of Sandy Jenkins and the root. Returning to Covey after his flight, Douglass meets Jenkins, a fellow slave, and Jenkins gives him a root that, he says, will protect him from Covey. At first the root seems to work, but soon Covey attacks him. It is at this point that Douglass stands up to Covey's aggression, an act so important that Douglass describes it as "the turning point in my career as a slave," which "revived within me a sense of my own manhood." Adding that "from this time I was never again what might be called fairly whipped" (113), Douglass makes nearly explicit the episode's moral: it is when he relinquishes the superstition of the root and struggles self-reliantly against Covey that he becomes a man. This self-reliance is an extreme example of the form that Douglass's obedience to Americanness takes, and, indeed, he subtly but significantly altered the episode for the 1855 version of his autobiography. The contrast between the two versions suggests just how far Douglass shifted from an implicit denigration of Africanness in the 1845 narrative toward an acknowledgment of an important African religious tradition in the 1855 revision.[18] By the time Jacobs comes to write *Incidents*, she is able, much more than Douglass could in 1845, to suggest the importance to her of an African past.

Strikingly, this African alliance is suggested primarily by absence rather than presence. At a pivotal moment in *Incidents*, as she is considering flight, Brent goes to the woods to visit the graves of her mother and father. While there, she prays and then seems to hear her father's voice exhorting her to freedom (138). The incident is a strange one because, unlike her description of other "incidents," Jacobs withholds an explanation for Brent's actions.

That is, the common ground between author and reader that Jacobs has so carefully established elsewhere is absent here. Linda's going to the graveyard rather than to the meetinghouse is ostensibly explained by the fact that since the Nat Turner revolt the slaves had been forbidden communal worship. Moreover, the expression of piety toward her parents harmonizes with Brent's aim of validating and conforming to the values of her readers. But Jacobs is also suggesting that Brent amasses a particular power at this point by her obedience to an African tradition of appeal to dead ancestors.[19] Much has been made of the phrase "loophole of retreat" (173) that Jacobs uses to describe the space in the grandmother's attic where Linda lives for seven years.[20] However, the narrative of *Incidents* contains *figurative* loopholes of retreat. One of them is the scene in the graveyard, in which Jacobs suggests, but does not elaborate on, an African spiritual tradition. In this way a black identity is being reserved and even suggestively made available to black readers in a narrative expressing compliance with the expectations of conventional Christian thought. Jacobs's withholding an explication of the visit represents a form of resistance, of self-definition as African, in a narrative of ostensible deference to white American values. Thus, in addition to critiquing (white) masculine traditions of self-reliance, Jacobs alters the assimilationist thrust of the "canonical" male slave narrative.

"He Has Compelled Her to Submit to Laws, in the Formation of Which She Has No Voice"

The Seneca Falls Declaration, itself utilizing the discourse made available by abolition, placed special emphasis on the powerlessness of women before the law. As might be expected, both Douglass and Jacobs reflect on the situation of the slave in law, but their striking differences again indicate the influence of the Seneca Falls Declaration. Both provide examples of the slave's virtual nonexistence in legal terms. In some of the most powerful passages in *Narrative*, Douglass describes the murder of a slave named Demby by an overseer called Gore, commenting that "killing a slave, or any colored person, in Talbot county, Maryland, is not treated as a crime, either by the courts or the community" and going on to detail other murders that went unpunished (67–68). It is the absence of law that appalls Douglass, rather than any injustice at the hands of a law. Similarly, when he is in jail after the attempted escape, what is most striking is that no law is applied to the case of the conspirators. In effect, they are released from jail after a form of conspiratorial pragmatism by their owners.

Through these examples Douglass suggests that in juridical terms the outrage of slavery lies in its denial of the slave's right to legal recognition or due process. This suggestion contrasts sharply with *Incidents*, in which Jacobs takes particular issue with the injustice of existing laws rather than with the slave's legal invisibility. Of course, this difference arises in part because Jacobs is writing after the Fugitive Slave Act of 1850, which effectively nullified the freedom Linda Brent had expected after her journey north.[21] Jacobs powerfully articulates the deferment of Linda's freedom because of the act and has her polemic reach a climax with the "sold in New York" section of the narrative (300–301). This part of *Incidents* functions so powerfully because of Jacobs's strategy of bringing slavery closer and closer to the Northern reader; as H. Bruce Franklin has observed, there Jacobs "brings it all home" (25).

However, slavery is brought "home" not only geographically but also legally and morally. The last chapters of *Incidents* contain an appeal that was disallowed by Douglass's view of the law in his *Narrative*. Jacobs sees the necessity of mobilizing public opinion against the law, and she does so, ironically, by appealing to the woman reader who is, she suggests, comparably disenfranchised. Jacobs's phrase about the sale — that it demonstrates how "women were articles of traffic" in mid-nineteenth century New York (300) — draws attention to gender and not to race, as if Brent's condition comes so close to the reader's that it is only the extreme of the condition of all women. Twenty-five years before the publication of *Incidents*, Angelina Grimké had made the same appeal to the disenfranchised: "*No* legislative power is invested in *us*; *we* can do nothing to overthrow the system, even if we wished to do so. To this I reply, I know you do not make the laws, but I also know that *you are the wives and mothers, the sisters and daughters, of those who do,* and if you really suppose *you* can do nothing to overthrow slavery, you are greatly mistaken."[22]

It is in this light that we may need to revise some of the assumptions that have been made about the readership of *Incidents*. It has too readily been assumed that because Jacobs makes use of the romance form, *Incidents* would have been read by romance readers as if it were escapist fiction. Franklin even writes airily of the contrast between "the fictional life of the typical romantic heroine and the actual one of the cozy (perhaps bored) reader" (25). Also, Lydia Maria Child's editorial role for *Incidents* has sometimes been deemed to account for the book's romance elements. This view ignores — to the point of scorn — the radical and polemical nature of much of Child's work, notably her novel *Hobomok* (1824), her essay *Appeal in Favor of that Class of Americans Called Africans* (1833), and her letters to the governor of Virginia (published as *Correspondence* in 1860). It is erroneous, and faintly condescending, to assume that an 1861 reader of *Incidents* (however cozy or even bored) would expect it to be a romantic novel simply because Child's name was connected with it. By 1861 there were certainly plenty of sophisticated, politically informed, and radically minded women readers for whom Child's name was associated with reform and women's rights. Jacobs's polemic against the Fugitive Slave Act depends for its effect on the reader's being informed and, also, prepared to act. It is specifically an appeal to women to view themselves as comparably disenfranchised and, albeit in a less extreme way, similar victims of the law.

Douglass ended his 1845 narrative by assuming his own voice in a public meeting. His private self-fulfilment or self-invention thus necessarily precedes his public, communal action, in a narrative of powerful closure. Jacobs, however, ends *Incidents* with a sense of unattained or partial freedom, with compromise and failure. This partial freedom gestures significantly to the reader (not cozy, not bored) concerning the need for action. The reader must, as it were, fulfill and complete what *Incidents* has left only partially completed, partially fulfilled.

In one regard, these different endings emerge from the different kinds of narrative that precede them. That is, Douglass's masculine self-reliance has been expressed in the relatively independent manner of his escape from slavery, whereas Jacobs emphasized the familial and communal assistance that Linda Brent had received. This need for assistance is communicated to the reader as a form of possible action and involvement, a route into which anger and indignation may be usefully directed. Furthermore, because Jacobs explicitly addresses sexual politics and the issues of power, she succeeds in extending her discourse beyond the particular conditions of slavery. That is, Jacobs has been able to use a public language, mainly developed by women, in which a telling series of parallels might be made between the slave and the freed woman. The appalling injustice represented by slavery is different only in extremity, not in kind, from the situation of white women. Douglass's 1845 narrative presupposes that the only necessary reform is the legal abolition of slavery, whereas Jacobs makes clear the need for possibly extralegal social reform beyond slavery.

NOTES

1. Anne Bradford Warner asserts the parody element in relation to the journey north. Warner, "Carnival Laughter: Resistance in *Incidents*," in *Harriet Jacobs and Incidents in the Life of a Slave Girl*, ed. Deborah M. Garfield and Rafia Zafar (Cambridge: Cambridge University Press, 1996), 222.

2. Douglass attended the Seneca Falls Women's Rights Convention in July 1848, but no speech is recorded. Douglass often spoke on behalf of women's right to franchise and to the same "intellectual culture" as men, though he was not convinced of a wife's right to be joint owner of property, and his relation to the women's movement has been seen as ambiguous. See John W. Blassingame, ed., *The Frederick Douglass Papers*, Series One: Speeches, Debates and Interviews, vol. 2 (New Haven: Yale University Press, 1982), 451; Jenny Franchot, "The Punishment of Esther: Frederick Douglass and the Construction of the Feminine," in *Frederick Douglass: New Literary and Historical Essays*, ed. Eric J. Sundquist (Cambridge: Cambridge University Press, 1990), 151–154.

3. Joseph is called Benjamin in *Incidents*. With regard to this male-female narrative, we should note that Jacobs's brother John published his own narrative, "A True Tale of Slavery," in London a month after *Incidents*. The relation between these two narratives as both corroborative and supplementary has been examined by several critics; see Jennifer Fleischner, *Mastering Slavery: Memory, Family and Identity in Women's Slave Narratives* (New York: New York University Press, 1996); Jacqueline Goldsby, "'I Disguised my Hand': Writing Versions of the Truth in Harriet Jacobs's *Incidents in the Life of a Slave Girl* and John Jacobs's 'A True Tale of Slavery'" in Garfield and Zafar, 11–43; Rafia Zafar, "Introduction: Over-exposed,

Under-exposed," in Garfield and Zafar, 1–10; Jean Fagan Yellin, "Through Her Brother's Eyes: *Incidents* and 'A True Tale,'" in Garfield and Zafar, 44–56.

4. In the preface Jacobs writes: "I do earnestly desire to arouse the women of the North to a realizing sense of the condition of two millions of women at the South, still in bondage, suffering what I suffered, and most of them far worse." Harriet Jacobs, *Incidents in the Life of a Slave Girl* (1861; reprint, New York: Oxford University Press, 1988), 6. Frederick Douglass, *Narrative of the Life of Frederick Douglass, An American Slave* (1845; reprint, Harmondsworth, England: Penguin, 1986), 51. All second citations for these and other sources are in the text.

5. Rafia Zafar, "Franklinian Douglass: The Afro-American as Representative Man," in Sundquist, 99–117.

6. While in slavery, Douglass was named Frederick Bailey. Leaving Baltimore, he changed his name to Stanley, and in New York, to Frederick Johnson. The name Douglass (actually Douglas; see below) was suggested by an abolitionist, Nathan Johnson, in reference to Walter Scott's poem *The Lady of the Lake* (*Narrative*, 146–147).

7. Historians have tended to confirm this view. For example, Eugene Genovese has noted the sharp imbalance between male and female runaways — at least 80 percent were men aged 16–35; like Jacobs, Genovese explained this disparity in terms of the restraint placed on slave mothers. Genovese, *Roll, Jordan, Roll: The World the Slaves Made* (New York: Pantheon, 1974), 648–649.

8. Vladimir Nabokov, introduction to *Bend Sinister* (New York: Time Magazine Books, 1964), xiii.

9. See, for example, H. Bruce Franklin, *Prison Literature in America: The Victim as Criminal and Artist*, expanded ed. (New York: Oxford University Press, 1989), 24–27.

10. Jacobs suggests this ideal in the depiction of Linda's grandmother and her crossracial friendships; such a perspective was consistent with the abolitionist targeting of mothers. Mrs. A. L. Cox, a speaker at the 1837 Anti-Slavery Convention of American women claimed that "there is no class of women to whom the anti-slavery cause makes so direct and powerful an appeal as to *mothers*" (emphasis in original). See John Ernest, "Motherhood Beyond the Gate: Jacobs's Epistemic Challenge in *Incidents in the Life of a Slave Girl*," in Garfield and Zafar, 179.

11. Elizabeth Cady Stanton, "The Seneca Falls Declaration," in *American Culture: An Anthology of Civilization Texts*, ed. Anders Breidlid et al. (Lon-

don: Routledge, 1996), 104. The heading of my final section is drawn from the same page of the declaration.

12. This depiction, a significant act of family piety, was made prominent after the editorial advice of Lydia Maria Child. The extent to which Child's editorial role shaded into authorship has been much debated (see Frances Smith Foster, "Resisting *Incidents*," in Garfield and Zafar, 57–75), but recently critics have tended to accept her statement that she *altered* less than fifty words of Jacobs's text, even though she advised on abridging and reshaping (Bruce Mills, "Lydia Maria Child and the Endings to Harriet Jacobs's *Incidents*," *American Literature* 64.2 [1992]: 264). She did urge Jacobs to revise the narrative so that it concluded with the grandmother and not, as it originally had, with praise for John Brown (see Fleischner, *Mastering Slavery*, 92; Mills, 255). In 1867 Child published excerpts from *Incidents* under the title "The Good Grandmother" (Fleischner, 196 n. 1).

13. The declaration most obviously utilized the language of abolition in its references to the married woman, as, for example, in the phrase regarding how the man becomes "to all intents and purposes, [the wife's] master — the law giving him power to deprive her of her liberty, and to administer chastisement" (104).

14. Charlotte Brontë, *Jane Eyre* (Oxford: Oxford University Press, 1993), 473. *Jane Eyre* itself has recently attracted some attention as a text making use of the discourse of slavery through metaphors of mastery and enslavement. See Carl Plasa, "'Silent Revolt': Slavery and the Politics of Metaphor in *Jane Eyre*," in *The Discourse of Slavery*, ed. Carl Plasa and Betty J. Ring (London: Routledge, 1994), 65–93.

15. In his imposition of an Horatio Alger narrative on his material, Washington virtually gives thanks for slavery's existence. See *Up from Slavery*, ed. William L. Andrews (1901; reprint, New York: Norton, 1996), 13.

16. W. E. B. Du Bois, *The Souls of Black Folk*, in Du Bois, *Writings*, Library of America Series (New York: Literary Classics of the United States, 1986), 356, 504.

17. Douglass and Jacobs contrast significantly in their representation of Christmas. Jacobs writes of the sense of community that Christmas brought to the slaves and of the food involved in their celebrations (179–181). However, she complains of New Year, since that is customarily the beginning of the hiring out period and, consequently, means the separation of slave families: "to the slave mother New Year's day comes laden with peculiar sorrows" (26).

18. See Douglass's additional description of the character of Sandy

Jenkins, in which Jenkins's belief is seen to have a source in African rituals and a significance far beyond that of superstition. Douglass, *My Bondage and My Freedom* (1855; reprint, New York: Dover, 1969), 238, 239.

19. See Jon Hauss, "Perilous Passages in Harriet Jacobs's *Incidents in the Life of a Slave Girl*," in Plasa and Ring, 145.

20. See, for example, Valerie Smith, "'Loopholes of Retreat': Architecture and Ideology in Harriet Jacobs's *Incidents in the Life of a Slave Girl*," in *Reading Black, Reading Feminist*, ed. Henry Louis Gates (Harmondsworth, England: Meridian/Penguin, 1990), 213. In his comparison of Jacobs and Douglass, Donald B. Gibson has usefully reminded us that, historically, the term "loophole" denoted not only a retreat but a means of attacking the enemy. Gibson, "Bondage, Family and the Discourse of Domesticity," in Garfield and Zafar, 170.

21. Douglass also focused on the injustice of the Fugitive Slave Law; see, for instance, his celebrated 1852 speech, "What to the Slave Is the Fourth of July?" (Blassingame, *The Frederick Douglass Papers*, 376).

22. Angelina Grimké, "Appeal to the Christian Women of the South," in *The Heath Anthology of American Literature*, vol. 1, 2d. ed., ed. Paul Lauter et al. (Lexington, Mass.: D. C. Heath, 1994), 1858, emphasis in original.

Genre Matters

Body Politics and the Body Politic in William Wells Brown's *Clotel* and Harriet Wilson's *Our Nig*

R. J. ELLIS

William Wells Brown's *Clotel* is generally regarded as the first published African American novel; Harriet Wilson's *Our Nig* is frequently identified as the first African American novel written by a woman and the first African American novel published in America. While both writers, then, in some sense confront a "soft" canon — the novel is a malleable form for antebellum African Americans — this, of course, does not mean these novels are genreless. Both take as their central character a female, and, though *Our Nig* deals with the plight of an African American servant in a Northern state and *Clotel* with the sufferings of enslaved Southern African American women, both deal with servitude (Frado, the heroine of *Our Nig*, despite living in the "free" North, is a bond-servant until she reaches eighteen). Both also explore the inflammable ambiguities of African American–white sexual relations and the baleful influence of the 1850 Fugitive Slave Act. The two novels that result accordingly draw on the genres of sentimental fiction and abolitionist slave narrative. But in the process they exhibit an uneasy generic hybridity as they construct an alliance between aesthetics and politics.[1] Both Brown and Wilson negotiate with the act of turning, as African Americans, to fiction, but their negotiations turn out differently.

I will focus on the ways in which Brown and Wilson handle the potentials and problems that they encounter when deploying the conventions of the sentimental genre. Critics have responded differently to the presence of the sentimental in antebellum writing about slavery. For Jean Fagan Yellin the sentimental genre is an "inadequate vehicle to express black experience," while Philip Fisher and Jane Tompkins view it as possessing a potent emotional purchase on the reader, making it highly effective in confronting slavery. Fisher, indeed, describes it as "the appropriate form" for depicting "the modest homestead or family farm with its corrosive fact of slavery."[2] This partial disagreement provides me with a starting point for exploring the ways in which Brown and Wilson represent cruelties meted out upon the body. Suffering is central to these two novels, but whereas in Brown's *Clotel* suffering is measured — sentimentally, sensationally, and documentarily — against the body politic, in Wilson's *Our Nig* suffering is measured out physically upon the body — as body politics, with punishment represented as a "political tactic" and the body as "*directly* involved in a political field."[3] As a consequence, though neither novel resides comfortably in the sentimental genre, *Our Nig* fractures generic boundaries more fundamentally than *Clotel*. This distinction can initially be made apparent by setting the two fictions alongside a key text lying behind them both, *Uncle Tom's Cabin*. *Clotel* and *Our Nig* bear an intertextual relationship to Stowe's novel, and both deviate from this intertext; however, they do so in different ways.[4]

Schematizing the central plot bifurcation of *Uncle Tom's Cabin* helps clarify this difference. As George and Eliza Harris escape north, Tom progresses southward, deeper into servitude and suffering. As George and Eliza travel north, their story increasingly engages with the public politics of abolitionism and the solutions posited by those abolitionists who saw the remedy for slavery as residing primarily in political change. The passage of the Fugitive Slave Act was a key defeat for them, but it simultaneously demonstrated that political action could indeed drastically affect slavery's impact in the United States. The bitter irony was that this act resulted in a dramatic *extension* of slavery's impact on the nation. Stowe's novel, as it traces the progress of George and Eliza northward, focuses on these consequences: bounty hunters strive to retake the Harrises during their journey to Canada; Senator and Mrs. Bird debate the act's rectitude; George makes his "Declaration of Independence" in an armed standoff; and, finally, the British colony of Canada is ironically identified as representing the blessed land of freedom for the runaways.

In counterpoint with this political, northward plot line, Tom's involuntary progress south engages with the arguments of those abolitionists who saw a resolution to the issue of slavery residing not in the political arena (since the Constitution itself countenanced slavery) but in the persuasive efficacy of the moral arguments against both slavery (Little Eva's debating with St. Clare) and racism (Miss Ophelia and St. Clare conversing about Ophelia's dread of "touching" Topsy). This ethical and religious abolitionist approach is usually denominated the moral suasionists' position on slavery. It is climactically articulated by Tom's Christlike death ("Ye poor miserable critter [Legree]! . . . I forgive ye, with all my soul!") and underlined by the way Tom secures the salvation of Cassy, Sambo, and Quimbo through his saintly example.[5]

The focus of the political plot strand in *Uncle Tom's Cabin* (centering on Eliza and George) is thus primarily external/public (despite some of the implications of Rachel's kitchen and its potent domestic politics) and may be characterized by its "male" picaresque structure (a series of incidents along a road), while the moral suasionist strand (Tom's story) is primarily internal/domestic and may be characterized by its "female" picaresque structure, transporting its protagonist from domestic setting to domestic setting and from bondage to bondage.[6] Viewed in this way, *Uncle Tom's Cabin*'s intertextual relationship to Brown's *Clotel* might be held to reside partly in its political abolitionist momentum and to Wilson's *Our Nig* partly in its moral suasionist perspective. Importantly, however, the African American novelists' works constitute reconfigurative "swerves" from these respective abolitionist positions, as depicted in both Stowe's best-selling text and the sentimental and abolitionist genres she draws upon. But the reconfigurations contained in *Our Nig* become more fundamentally transgressive than those in *Clotel*.

The Search for "True Liberty": *Clotel*

The central reason *Clotel's* reconfigurations are less pronounced resides in its reliance on stereotypical representations and how these derive from the novel's close dependence on its sources. Brown's final chapter draws emphatic attention to these substantial debts ("Some of the narratives I have derived from other sources").[7] Indeed, one can argue that Brown, through the frequent splicing-in of other people's words and narratives, far from aspiring to the sort of Romantic originality at that time so prized in New England high culture, is pursuing an alternative project. While his reliance on such retelling plainly has something in common with those alternative cultural conventions governing narrative recycling to be found in oral folk traditions,[8] Brown's near-plagiarism also interlaces quite different narrative and stylistic conventions with so little mediation that a complex generic fecundity results: abolitionist documents, sermons, and slave narratives are drawn on as much as popular fiction and far more than oral folk traditions.

To take one key example, in the space of only eighteen pages (190–208) *Clotel*'s narrative borrows from a startling range of modes: sentimental hyperbole when narrating the death of Georgiana ("There sat the Liberator,— pale, feeble, emaciated, with death stamped upon her countenance, surrounded by the sons and daughters of Africa. . . . Peace to her ashes! she fought the fight, obtained the Christian's victory" [190, 192]); a species of "blood sports" review, possibly culled from a New Orleans paper (201–204); a quasi-documentary reproduction of a description of a yellow fever epidemic taken from John R. Beard's biography of Toussaint L'Ouverture (205–206);[9] and finally what can be called "sentimental gothic"— a dark tale of attempted seduction ("the young girl needed no one to tell her of her impending doom. The young maid was immediately removed to his country seat . . . a most singular spot, remote, in a dense forest spreading over the summit of a cliff that rose abruptly to a great height above the sea . . . so grand in . . . the desolate sublimity which reigned around" [208]).

The effect of this generic crisscrossing is disorienting. Though the reader never loses track of the narrative, the novel exhibits a fluctuating resourcefulness that swerves decisively from conventional norms. This transgressiveness is strategic: a repeated departure from and return to the sentimental genre that the novel's multiple plots, overall, inhabit most readily. The effect is to draw, cumulatively, the maximum of emotional power from the established authority invested in a range of popular narrative genres possessing widespread familiarity, recognition, and hence cultural effectiveness. For example, one clear inspirational source for Georgiana's death would be the impact of a pure, saintly female's death — most pertinently, Little Eva's in the best-selling *Uncle Tom's Cabin*. Brown plainly draws on an already stereotypical sensational design to dramatize and reinforce his message. But even in this instance a swerve occurs. Little Eva's death frees no slaves, and St. Clare dies before he changes his will. In contrast, *Clotel*'s Georgiana actually frees her slaves. Brown's modulation presses the reader toward a subtly repositioned sentimental empathy. Then, interpolating a quite different narrative resource, he introduces a short abolitionist-inspired intellectual debate about the need to send the emancipated slaves out of the state and whether Africa is an appropriate destination (191).

Such an unsettling mix of modes and genres constantly shrugs off the impetus of the plot line rather than letting it develop any momentum. The fiction seems constantly uneasy within any one genre, recurrently deserting the sentimental's cumulative power — and so short-circuiting its consensual propensities — but without settling elsewhere. Above all, the sentimental narrative is interrupted by quasi-documentary interpolations, such as illustrative examples of slave abuse culled from newspapers, verbal testimonies, and radical political stump speeches so much a feature of the times.[10] To some extent the effect is to subvert readers' horizons of expectation.[11] However, any such advantage is largely offset by another, constraining, consequence: constantly shifting genres, the text, to achieve at least some stability, leaves characterization almost uniformly one-dimensional, rooted in familiar stereotypes that depend for emotional resonance on their generic conventionality. The force of Brown's pointed deviation from Stowe, Georgiana's deathbed liberation of her slaves, is thus partly dissipated by a predominant sense that this story line, tumbling past in a welter of narrative modes, is already familiar, and that Georgiana is a sentimental type; Brown's careful finesse of Stowe's narrative is somewhat obfuscated by the weight of the generic expectations the story generates.

What holds Brown's narrative together positively is a constant thematic undertow drawing the text back to the politics of abolitionism. Thus, while Brown's representation of Georgiana as a successful deathbed liberator is at least as conventional as Stowe's portrait of Little Eva, the strategies of moral suasion, apparent enough in this representation ("Some were upon their knees at the feet of their benefactress" [190]), are accompanied by a rhetorically dense description of Georgiana's political philosophy certainly absent from Stowe: "it was of a noble cast. It was that all men are by nature equal; that they are wisely and justly endowed by their creator with certain rights, which are irrefragable" (188). This deployment of the cadences of the Declaration of Independence is not, of course, original: the same can be found, though much more obliquely, in *Uncle Tom's Cabin*, when George makes his "declaration of independence" (298). What is different is its omnipresence: the constant recurrence of such explicit political reference in the text, extending (pointedly) to women and white Americans as well as escaped slaves.

I will call such sustained repetition of Jefferson's Declaration of Independence and his name (implicitly invoking his document) *Clotel*'s recurrent "Jeffersonian refrain." For example, in the brief eighteen-page segment of *Clotel* already analyzed, Georgiana's "philosophy" ("true liberty is freedom for all!" [193]) is implicitly linked a few pages later to the reminder that Clotel's nieces, Ellen and Jane, are granddaughters of Jefferson. In this way, the Jeffersonian refrain constantly expands in significance beyond Stowe's limited use. In Brown's novel, it not only carries a resonant political burden, it also has marked socioeconomic implications. When the text stresses that Ellen's and Jane's light color and Jeffersonian lineage increased their monetary value (208), this economic and ideological point reminds us forcibly of two other textual strands. The first, repeatedly weighed by the narrator and discussed only a few pages earlier, when estimating Georgiana's philosophy as she signs manumissions, is the price paid materially (the market value of slaves) as well as ideologically (in terms of reputation) by any Southerner opposing slavery. The second sets up an ironic contrast between use value and commodity value. As Ellen and Jane are, effectively, commodified by the auctioneer to raise their price, this irony is arrestingly plain, and it combines with Brown's recognition that upbringing (family, church, education) works both to sanction their sale and to oppose Georgiana's manumissions (in contrast to George Shelby's act in *Uncle Tom*, where family and religion are arrayed in support of his manumissions [613–617]).

Again, however, *Clotel*'s generic shiftiness intervenes to dissipate the impact of this politicized representation. Ultimately, the powerful depiction of slavery's economic corruption of human rights is all but swamped by the attendant, pervasive accent on the physical attractiveness of Brown's female mulatto characters: Clotel, the illegitimate daughter of Jefferson; Mary, Clotel's daughter (Jefferson's granddaughter); Clotel's sister Althesa and her children, Ellen and Jane (three further descendants of Jefferson); and Clotel's mother, Currer, Jefferson's discarded mistress. All function within the stereotype of the "tragic mulatta," drawing *Clotel* into an uncomfortably close (albeit strategic) liaison with dominant, white sentimental representations of the issue of abolition. (Thus, the mulattas, the novel repeatedly insists, are prone to abuse from both whites and black African Americans — a representation effectively endorsing color lines.) Such stereotyping along white abolitionist lines also invites questions about the extent to which the emphasis on females' sexual abuse functions voyeuristically for the book's white audience, through its insistence on "blood-clotted cowhides" and helpless yet pure young women — though it is crucial to identify the contemporary cultural power of these sentimental (and sensational) icons in moving people to anger and resistance (the sexual politics of the body is complex here). Symptomatically, Brown, like Frederick Douglass, places an account of whipping a female at the start of his introductory narrative, right at *Clotel*'s opening to mobilize this culturally loaded image's sensational power to arouse aversion (18).[12]

The subversive potency possessed by *Clotel* resides not in such conventional appeals to indignation (powerful though they are), but in another, more political source of tension generated by slavery's emotional pain. We have seen how the distress generated by the death of Georgiana and the sale of Althesa's two daughters following the death of their white father (who — again the text shadows Stowe — has failed to free them before dying from yellow fever) is *politicized*: directed toward the hypocrisies inherent in the Declaration of Independence's valuation of freedom on the one hand and the Constitution's preservation of chattel slavery on the other. The pain imposed by these convolutions in the body politic is carefully contrived to writhe upon the page and forms a repeated pattern in *Clotel*.

The novel's "framing" is preparatory in this respect. The title and the opening epigraph both insistently point to underlying political ironies. This title-page framing is deliberately careful (setting aside both the inclusion of an "advertisement" for an earlier work by Brown and the affinities with antecedent slave narrative

CLOTEL;

OR,

THE PRESIDENT'S DAUGHTER:

A Narrative of Slave Life

IN

THE UNITED STATES.

BY

WILLIAM WELLS BROWN,

A FUGITIVE SLAVE, AUTHOR OF "THREE YEARS IN EUROPE."

With a Sketch of the Author's Life.

" WE hold these truths to be self-evident: that all men are created equal; that they
are endowed by their Creator with certain inalienable rights, and that among these are
LIFE, LIBERTY, and the PURSUIT OF HAPPINESS." — *Declaration of American Independence.*

LONDON:
PARTRIDGE & OAKEY, PATERNOSTER ROW;
AND 70, EDGWARE ROAD.

1853.

titles).[13] The quotation from the Declaration of Independence and the use of capitals to highlight the United States' "inalienable rights" conjoin with "The President's Daughter," "THE UNITED STATES," and the repetition of the word "slave" to create an unstable paradoxical formation: slavery is rife, even *Presidential*, in the very America that endlessly vaunts freedom. These broad political references prepare the way for the narrative focus, which constantly shifts away from Clotel (only 40 out of 188 pages directly involve her). Instead the story line divides and subdivides, broadening the narrative's inclusiveness as a representation of the body politic.

The only way *Clotel* could be construed as aptly titled is if we regard Clotel's hurling herself from the Long Bridge in Washington to escape recapture as the narrative's climactic moment. But Clotel's death has to compete with the equally sensational deaths of Ellen and Jane, and the final reunion of Mary with her lover, George. The title's appositeness is better revealed by focusing on the particular site where Clotel dies: on the Potomac, in full view of the White House, thereby directing attention not toward Clotel's story so much as toward her emblematic power as a locus for the political contradictions of slavery in the United States. This links her to the Jeffersonian refrain defined in *Clotel*'s subtitle and renders the book's title wholly apt. This emblematic function is economically underlined by the title of the chapter depicting her suicide, "Death Is Freedom" (chapter 25), which intimately links Clotel's death with the core political element of the Jeffersonian refrain — repeated direct references to the Declaration of Independence, most contingently found in the quotation at the head of chapter 18, "The Liberator."[14]

These persistent swerves from the conventions of the sentimental novel toward a heavily foregrounded, explicitly political emphasis on the paradoxical constitutional ironies established by countenancing slavery in the world's first democracy propel *Clotel* into a propinquity with another conventional narrative mode, rooted in political abolitionist speeches and writing; its intertextual interrogation of Stowe's text in this way becomes fully established. At best, what results is a distancing of the text from sentimental fiction, enabling a deconstruction of the ways in which, in such fiction, slave characters are always already rhetorical structures, bound by representational conventions, and African

American females are doubly bound — by those rhetorical conventions governing the representation of femininity (and female sexuality) and those governing race (black sexuality) — processes within which the mulatta slave is always already discursively constrained. Identifying the text's inevitable problem with establishing any distance from dominant sexual conventions may in turn help account for the abruptness of Brown's digressions into quasi-documentary abolitionist anecdotes. So crudely sudden that they jerk the reader out of the illusionism of the narrative, they potentially compel reflection on its formulaic limitations.[15] In turn references of the omnipresent Jeffersonian refrain to the republic's founding document and "Father" polemically direct such moments of reflection into political channels. But all this is only what happens at best. At worst (and more usually), the narrative collapses such moments back into stereotypical plot devices drawn from sensational fiction. Let me call all this a recurrent "shameless manipulation" of the emotion of shame, rooted in rhetorical and narrative hyperbole, whether political or sentimental discourse is deployed: "Such was the life and such the death of a woman whose virtues and goodness of heart would have done honour to one in a higher station of life, and who, if she had been born in any other land but that of slavery, would have been honoured and loved" (220).

"True Liberty Is Freedom for All": *Our Nig*

Our Nig's narrative also deals with shame, but it never becomes as shamelessly hyperbolic as *Clotel*'s. Instead, it deploys the quite opposite tropes of litotes and ellipsis, which sit uneasily within the story's sentimental frame. Not that these tropes are omnipresent. Indeed, the opening chapter's account of Frado's white mother's "fall" is replete with overblown sentimental rhetoric: "Lonely Mag Smith! See her as she walks with downcast eyes and heavy heart. It was not always thus. She *had* a loving, trusting heart. Early deprived of parental guardianship, far removed from relatives, she was left to guide her tiny boat over life's surges alone."[16] This elaboration, however, soon gives way to the sharply contrasting forensic restraint consistently shown when representing the shameful sufferings of Mag's daughter, the mulatta Frado, at the hands of the Bellmont family, with whom she is left when Mag deserts her: "Seizing Frado, [Mrs. B.] said she would 'cure her of tale bearing,' and, placing the wedge of wood between her teeth, she beat her cruelly with the raw-hide. Aunt Abby heard the blows, and came to see if she could hinder them" (93).

What is remarkable here is the narrative's restraint: the absence of any embellishing comment on this punishment. The wedge of wood has previously been used to prevent Frado from crying out in pain following a whipping. Here, for the first time, the wedge is used to prevent Frado from making any sound *during* a whipping (her jaws are propped so far apart she cannot utter a sound). This narrative moment of silencing cries out for elaboration, yet, in a subtle and restrained device, the narrative instead imposes a silence concisely replicating Frado's silencing. The paragraph following drives this point home; her silencing continues: "Surprised by [Abby's] sudden appearance, Mrs. B. suddenly stopped, but forbade her removing the wood till she gave her permission" (93). Similarly, litotes and ellipsis again predominate in the quiet juxtaposition of this whipping scene with the preceding paragraph, which depicts Mrs. B. refusing to help Susan, Frado, and Abby lift up her ailing son, James: "Mrs. B. was too weak; she did not feel able to lift so much. So the [other] three succeeded in relieving the sufferer" (93). Yet, only a few moments later, Mrs. B. has sufficient strength to whip Frado so vehemently that the sound of the blows attracts Abby's notice. Again, however, the narrative remains silent; the irony inherent in Mrs. B.'s sudden recovery is neither spelled out nor sentimentalized. These narrative silences and restraints thus tropically replicate the constrained silences imposed on Frado, not least by the threat of further beatings should she ever speak out.

There is a cunning dialectical complexity in such powerful understatement, since it contrasts so sharply with the opening chapters and other moments in the text, when Wilson fully lards on lush sentimentality. This disparity is strategic: repeatedly, sentimentalism's characteristic rhetorical hyperbole is deployed when describing the experiences of the white characters in the book (Frado's mother, Mag, for example), whereas Frado's experiences recurrently draw on litotes and ellipses. While not complete, this distribution is pervasive; although sentimentalism seems generically appropriate when narrating white women's stories, Frado's tale requires a different articulation. This arrangement is ironically underscored when James tells Abby how he overheard Frado lamenting her lot — an outburst drawing on sentimental language to add emotional traction to her expression of suffering. Though this articulation stands in contrast to her enforced silences, Frado's silence is broken accidentally and occurs through the intercession of a white man (as reported speech); Frado only gives vent to her feelings when she thinks she is alone (see also Stern, "Excavating Genre," 449).

The subtle tropic dialogue that results is (as was the case with *Clotel*) anticipated by the framing of the title page. Plainly, there are some correlations with Brown's use of irony on his title page, most patently in the juxtaposition of the words "free black" with the words "slavery" and "Nig." But in this instance a further level of complexity is also present, existing in a subtle and understated linguistic reflexivity (again, the figure of litotes predominates): "two-story"; "our nig." This reflexivity subverts expectations, and this subversiveness is replicated in the text. *Our Nig* on one level straightforwardly engages with the arguments against human bondage advanced by moral suasionists when advocating abolition: the predominant setting is the Bellmont family home, and the novel focuses on the cruelty with which Frado is treated and the ways in which the morality of this treatment is negotiated — within the family and in terms of Frado's Christian "progress." Such cruelty is plainly represented as morally reprehensible and unchristian. This conventional moral suasionist discourse, exposing the evils of servitude, is just as radical as persuasion based on overtly political appeals (as found in *Clotel*) — maybe even more so. But alongside this forthright moral suasion Wilson generates a deeper level of subversive complexity. Frado's religious conversion is ambivalent and incomplete: Frado celebrates Mary Bellmont's death, as the text itself observes, with unchristian lack of forgiveness, and, though she assumes "a devout and Christian exterior" (125), she never finally decides whether prayer "is only for whites, not for blacks" (94).[17] The conventional, sentimental conversion narrative is compromised by these instabilities. Even more disturbingly, gender roles are disrupted. It is the *female* Bellmonts who mete out the greatest cruelty rather than proving to be reservoirs of moral probity (and Aunt Abby is ineffectual as an angelic moral influence). The representation of the male Bellmonts

OUR NIG;

OR,

Sketches from the Life of a Free Black,

IN A TWO-STORY WHITE HOUSE, NORTH.

SHOWING THAT SLAVERY'S SHADOWS FALL EVEN THERE.

BY "OUR NIG."

"I know
That care has iron crowns for many brows;
That Calvaries are everywhere, whereon
Virtue is crucified, and nails and spears
Draw guiltless blood; that sorrow sits and drinks
At sweetest hearts, till all their life is dry;
That gentle spirits on the rack of pain
Grow faint or fierce, and pray and curse by turns;
That hell's temptations, clad in heavenly guise
And armed with might, lie evermore in wait
Along life's path, giving assault to all." — HOLLAND.

BOSTON:
PRINTED BY GEO. C. RAND & AVERY.
1859.

as passively unable to prevent Frado's punishment yet striving to exert moral restraint further accentuates this gender inversion.

Such unsettling disturbances decisively subvert dominant sentimental aesthetic conventions. The resulting disruption creates a semiotic space in which a political difference stands revealed: in the words of Wilson's subtitle, "slavery's shadows" can indeed be shown to "fall" on all Northerners, male and female. This revelation is most sharply defined by the establishment of Frado's body as the field of dispute between male and female Bellmonts. The dispute is not conducted in the expected abolitionist sexual terrain, recurrently mapped out as a flat, sadoerotic world, mobilizing moral abhorrence along stereotypical lines that more than flirt with racism's and sexism's conventional demarcations of sexuality and power. Rather, *Our Nig*'s affinities with slave narratives become deeply compromised, as female Northerners torture a "free" female African American with dark sadism. Representationally, these radically divergent gender politics have fundamentally politicized the text. This overt politicization informs any reading of Frado at the woodpile resisting Mrs. Bellmont: Frado is making her declaration of independence from the stereotypical terms of her generic representation. Crucially, this declaration is conveyed most fully not by language (which she uses initially) but by body-language (as she stands silently still): "'Stop!' shouted Frado, 'strike me, and I'll never work a mite more for you;' and throwing down what she had gathered, stood like one who feels the stirring of free and independent thoughts" (103).

The text recurrently acquires its greatest weight through such meaningful moments of half-stated or unstated communication. Up to this point these moments have emphasized pain and enforced stillness; now, Frado offers resistance that implicitly connects with political resistance — in terms of gender, race, and human intercourse. This climax links to the linguistic play in the subtitle's use of the term "White House." The "White House, North" is indeed a "Two-Story" one, and it is a political "Two-Story" of the "White House" that is narrated. But this "Two-Story" is not now the familiar two-story of an emancipated North and a slave-holding South but rather a different national two-story: a *nationwide* combination of ideology and cultural hypocrisy. Abolitionist values may by 1859 have come to dominate the antebellum North (McKitrick, "A Hero of Antislavery," 46), but racist-enforced servitude can persist and will persist unless fiercely resisted.

What I am claiming for Wilson's text is a sophisticated apprehension of the relationship of language, discourse, and ideology, accessed by subtle linguistic and generic modulations, refusing the seductive comforts of sentimentalism.[18] This observation again takes us back to the simply observed but extraordinary semantic self-reflexivity of *Our Nig*'s title page. It alludes (as Brown's did) to the established conventions of slave narrative title pages, but now the comparison is marked by fracturings and subversions at the level of linguistic design. The title page literally circles back on itself, "Our Nig . . . by 'Our Nig.'" This circling in a sense enacts the endless proscriptions placed upon African Americans, but simultaneously this circle is disturbed by a (self-) conscious use of inverted commas, as the pseudonymous author, "Our Nig," disturbingly arrests the "author," holding her inside her "assigned" label and social role. So the narrative, at the woodpile, stops Frado silently still at the very moment she has reached the limit of ideological possibility. No thrilling chase of runaways ensues, but rather an anticlimactic recognition of uncrossable racist boundaries and how these impinge on attempted resistance: Frado can never strike back at Mrs. B., since the ideological prohibition would provoke punishing revenge. The narrative lays this reality before us: Frado and Mrs. B. silently return to the house and take up their stations.

The "two-story" rhetoric underscores the uncrossable status of the color line by predominantly representing the whites' story through one rhetorical trope — sentimental hyperbole — and the African Americans' story through the contrasting tropes of litotes and ellipsis. Crucially, the use of the latter tropes swerves from the usual discursive practice of abolitionist narratives. These narratives, like *Clotel*, characteristically deploy hyperbole, so helping to fuel Southern counterpropaganda, which could controvert the resulting moments of excessive exaggeration and throw doubt upon the veracity of the whole. The lengthy reviews of Stowe in the *Southern Quarterly Review* and *Literary Messenger* are cases in point.[19] These extended rejoinders, rooted in counterpropaganda, are also (damagingly) partly based in fact — a species of mid-nineteenth-century spin doctoring. Furthermore, abolitionist hyperbole, like its sentimental counterpart, draws on stereotypes, which, as we have seen, are saturated by a cloudy relationship to conventional racist sentiments (e.g., concerning sexuality). Wilson's narrative illuminates this proximity disturbingly by refusing to represent Frado as a conventionally sentimentalized mulatta: at times mischievous, never a tragic romance heroine carrying a sexually titillating frisson, she unsettles expectations as much as the text in which she is situated.

Once again, the frame to the novel is important preparation for this disturbing focus: *Our Nig*'s preface implicitly refers to abolitionist hypocrisy by declaring that "what would most provoke shame in our good anti-slavery friends" has been "purposely omitted." This thrust is sharply barbed, not least because evidence suggests that Wilson was indentured to a family with abolitionist sympathies.[20] This suggestion lends an extraordinary piquancy to *Our Nig*'s two-story representations, as does the eventual revelation that Frado's African American lover/husband is a fraud, pretending to be an escaped slave to secure a living off the abolitionist circuit. The text thus offers a concise, ironic recognition of the marginalized position of African Americans within a racist society, and two quite different ways of negotiating with this position (principled resistance or hypocritical accommodation). Such subversive explorations differ distinctly from those found in *Clotel*.

"This, Reader, Is No Fiction": Fact-finding

Cross-reference to *Clotel* helps define the subtlety of Wilson's exploration of racism, for in Brown's autobiographical preface his modes of negotiating around/with racism are far less nuanced. *Clotel*'s preface consists in part of Brown's extraordinary rewriting of his autobiography as a third-person narration. But despite this third-person device there is no sense of narrative distancing: it remains a straightforward "narrative of the life and escape of William Wells Brown," largely adhering to the rhetorical conventions of slave narrative, centered on the proposals of abolitionism — a giving out of the sensational facts.[21] The shift into fiction — the start of the novel, *Clotel* — does not detach from this slave narrative. Instead, the novel at first becomes curiously freighted with documentary detail. Each segment of the hybridized novel (sensational romance/abolitionist document) that results persistently falls back under the purview of the dominant discursive practices of abolitionism. Though the text's polemic against slavery is therefore overt and sustained, its interrogation of deeper-rooted causes, the integument of racism (and sexism) remain underdefined, proscribed, or disabled by constant returns to generic or thematic conformity. Even the seven-page denunciation of "Jim Crow" segregation (176–181) loses much of its potency by offering an uneven mix of dramatization and documentary in depicting the incident and by featuring only a peripheral character, William. William's racist treatment is reduced to mere anecdotal interpolation. Rather than serving as a springboard for a sustained interrogation of United States racism, it remains textually un(re)marked as the narrative presses on with Clotel's family story.

I'd like to propose, then, that Brown's text (the preface and the novel in indivisible combination) ends up as a retelling of abolition's story, in an accretive piling on of repeated narrative detail, ultimately propelled by both its abolitionist-validated sentimental power and its explicit residence within the propositions of the Declaration of Independence. Brown can therefore recurrently round off sections of his narrative patchwork-collage with familiar homilies. When he ends his Jim Crow section with "This, reader, is no fiction" (178), this "closure" (effectively sealing off the representation of Northern racism) resonates with many other such moments in the text, tied to their abolitionist origins: "This reader, is no fiction; if you think so look over the files of the New Orleans newspapers" (148); "This, reader, is an unvarnished narrative of one doomed by the laws of the Southern states to be a slave" (210). This last example is particularly telling, for Brown simply tags this homily onto his (self-confessed) plagiarism of Lydia Maria Child's story, "The Quadroon," thereby crudely pasting on a familiar political message to her short romance (which appends no such didactic sentiment). Such strident insistence on the text's use of the "facts" ironically highlights the presence of the representational stereotypes borne within them, returning *Clotel* to the fold of authoritative (monologic) political abolitionism. It never ventures far from confirming the accepted abolitionist "facts." Perhaps this is why Brown can end his novel with the complementary monologic authority of high sentimentalism: a happy reunion and marriage (albeit in France).

Wilson's text lacks such moments of resolving closure as it probes at deeper contradictions when laying down its politics of the body — namely, the virulent persistence of underlying national systems of racism and gender politics. Wilson's narrative generates a more transgressive analysis than Brown's ultimately abolitionist-endorsed representation of African American maltreatment (though both stand as correctives to Stowe's moral suasionism). Implicitly arraigned in Wilson's preface, abolitionism is dissected in the text, as Northerners sympathetic to Frado's plight stand by in ineffectual complicity. The real contradictions, the significant elements of the composition of racism and sexual politics (and their interaction), can thus become central to the novel's meaning. The body, here the body of Frado, is almost entirely not a site of sensational abolitionist sexuality (desire, rape, breeding) but of pain. She is racked by these hypocrisies — the disease of racism within the body politic: infecting abolitionist discourse, shockingly administered by women, it lays waste her frame. Frado's declaration of independence invokes not that species of sentimental politics leading to successful release but rather a cry of insecure revolt: "I'll never work a mite more for you" (103). Her freedom remains conditional (note the "like" in "she stood like one who feels the stirring of free and independent thoughts"). The "traps slyly laid by the vicious to ensnare her" (129) that Wilson mentions later plainly refer in part to unscrupulous slave hunters' excesses in the post–Fugitive Slave Act North, but these "traps" also refer to ideological snares. Northern white houses' two-story hypocrisies are resolutely laid bare, and "freedom," the Jeffersonian cornerstone, is problematized for the abolitionist Northern reader: Frado becomes "maltreated" by "professed abolitionists." Here, in the novel's closing pages (129), the phrase refers back to the preface's identification of the "shame" that could be provoked among "our good anti-slavery friends," drawing into focus these contradictions.

Gagging the Facts

The novel's endless circlings (*Our Nig* . . . by "Our Nig," "shame . . . in . . . anti-slavery," and "professed abolitionists") formally replicate the circle formed by Frado's forcibly silenced mouth, propped open by a stick or stuffed with rags. This vivid image ironically references a fundamental tactic of antiabolitionists: the so-called gag rules. These gag rules, lasting from 1836 to 1844, were used to prevent the employment of a device favored by political abolitionists seeking to raise the issue of slavery in Washington: petitions requesting the abolition of slavery in the District of Columbia. The petitions were denied a hearing by the gag rules and were instead "laid on the table." The campaign against the gag rules was enormously influential and widely reported in the press.[22] Vicious attacks were made on the virtue of women petitioners who opposed the gag rules; they were scurrilously arraigned by Southern congressmen for so allowing themselves to "be laid on the table" (McKitrick, "A Hero of Antislavery," 50). Ironically, the spread of opposition to the gag rules owed as much to their constraint upon free speech as to their curtailment of debate about abolition (the "fellow-traveler principle").[23] By setting aside an autobiographical reading of Wilson's novel, we can interpret Frado's silencing as a riposte to these gag-rule debates: Frado, a bond-servant in the "free" North, is, ironically, gagged in turn — her suffering denied a hearing. She is bodily laid out, not "on the table" by sexual innuendo (in a representational sense this is the fate of *Clotel*'s mulattas), but on the ground by political violence. Where constitutional gagging once silenced abolitionist protests, now "Nig" is literally gagged by Northern racists (who may, with deep irony, be themselves abolitionists).

While Brown recurrently invokes the Declaration of Independence, returning the debate to parameters within which constitutional authority is implicitly the point at issue, and then lards on the sentimental laced with a sensational erotic frisson, Wilson necessarily goes beyond such an explicitly authorized set of political debates and generic representations to raise one further, more threatening specter: the general cultural gagging of the pervasive racism in America's national culture and society, *inside* the whole body politic.

Perhaps the resulting greater interrogative potency of *Our Nig* explains why this particular novel vanished from view from 1859 to 1983, despite its having been printed by an abolitionist sympathizer who worked closely with Garrison (whose son, at least, possessed *Our Nig*),[24] while *Clotel* remained in fully documented historical view. *Our Nig* trespasses beyond authorized abolitionist parameters in its grimly unsentimental portrait of U.S. racism: "It is impossible to give an impression of the manifest enjoyment of Mrs. B. in these kitchen scenes. It was her favorite exercise to enter the appartment [*sic*] noisily, vociferate orders, give a few sudden blows to quicken Nig's pace, then return to the sitting room with a satisfied expression" (66). This portrait of a harrowing other, "Northern," "free" reality, coldly underlined by Frado's naming as "Nig," symptomatically disappeared from the record for another century. The full retrieval of Frado's pain, her experience of body politics, stands as a disturbing complement to any analysis of abolition's discourses and how these frame Brown's sentimentally tragic mulattas — models fully validated by the North's body politic. In this comparison we can obtain a sharpened sense of what is politic and what is not.[25]

NOTES

1. See Julia Stern, "Excavating Genre in *Our Nig*," *American Literature* 67.3 (1995): 439–446, who argues (unconvincingly, I think) for "*Our Nig*'s essential gothicism" (439).

2. Jean Fagan Yellin, introduction to *Clotel* by William Wells Brown (New York: Arno Press and New York Times, 1969), iv; Jane Tompkins, *Sensational Designs: The Cultural Work of American Fiction, 1790–1860* (New York: Oxford University Press, 1985), 140–141; Philip Fisher, *Hard Facts: Setting and Form in the American Novel* (New York: Oxford University Press, 1985), 10. Yellin and Fisher disagree with Tompkins only partially because they are writing about sentimental novels written by white authors, while Yellin speaks of African Americans.

3. Michel Foucault, *Discipline and Punish: The Birth of the Prison* [*Surveiller et punir: Naissance de la prison*], trans. Alan Sheridan (Harmondsworth, England: Penguin, 1977), 25 ff. In Foucault "the body politic" is viewed as "a set of material elements and techniques that serve as weapons, relays, communication routes and supports for the power and knowledge relations that invest human bodies and subjugate them by turning them into objects of knowledge" (28). My use of the term "body politic[s]" in this essay is certainly cognate, though not identical; I have added to Foucault's idea a simple pun: body politic (with its designed omission of African Americans) / body politics (the politics of the body). For a complementary discussion, see Cynthia J. Davis, "Speaking the Body's Pain: Harriet

Wilson's *Our Nig,*" *African American Review* 27.3 (1993): 391–404. I wish to go further than Davis in proposing that representations of bodily pain introduce emotions that impel toward action: e*motions*.

4. For a discussion of the relationship between *Clotel* and *Uncle Tom's Cabin*, see, for example, Peter A. Dorsey, "De-authorizing Slavery: Realism in Stowe's *Uncle Tom's Cabin* and Brown's *Clotel,*" *ESQ: A Journal of the American Renaissance* 41.4 (1994): 257–287. This deviation seems to me to be a species of clinamen in the sense defined by Bloom, though I pursue a different angle of discussion. Harold Bloom, *The Anxiety of Influence* (London: Oxford University Press, 1973), 19 ff.

"Intertextuality" is used here in the sense proposed by Julia Kristeva, who prefers the term "transposition." Kristeva, *Revolution in Poetic Language* [*La revolution du language poetique*], trans. Margaret Walker (1964; reprint, New York: Columbia University Press, 1984), 59 ff.

5. The divide between moral suasion and political abolitionism is not clear-cut, but these distinctions are useful when exploring basic orientations. See John R. McGivigan, "The Frederick Douglass–Gerrit Smith Friendship and Political Abolitionism," in *Frederick Douglass: New Literary and Historical Essays*, ed. Eric J. Sundquist (Cambridge: Cambridge University Press, 1990), 205–232.

Harriet Beecher Stowe, *Uncle Tom's Cabin or, Life Among the Lowly*, ed. Ann Douglas (1852; reprint, Harmondsworth, England: Penguin, 1981), 584.

6. Eva Figes, *Sex and Subterfuge* (London: Macmillan, 1982), 11 ff.

7. William Wells Brown, *Clotel or, the President's Daughter*, ed. William Edward Farrison (1853; reprint, New York: Carol Publishing, 1989), 245. All second references to this and other sources are cited in the text. The relationship of *Clotel* to Lydia Maria Child's story, "The Quadroons," warrants comment. Child, *Fact and Fiction: A Collection of Stories* (Boston: J. H. Francis, 1846), 61–76. Brown's changes to "The Quadroon" inflect Child's story differently (on this point I disagree with Farrison's contention in his edition of *Clotel* [249 ff.]). A key difference is the particularity of Brown's focus on slavery. Brown inserts a discussion of how Clotel was illegally taught to read, where Child never mentions the literacy of her central character, Rosalie. Whereas in "The Quadroons" Rosalie's mother has never formally been given her freedom, the sexual politics of Brown's version is quite different, a matter of power. Brown reinforces this undermining by ominous rephrasings; for example, where Child writes affirmatively about the love relationship ("ten as happy years as ever blessed the heart of mortals" [63]), Brown offers a far more subdued version: "passed their time

as happily as circumstances would permit" (84; emphasis added)—a change highlighting how Brown's portrait of a master-slave relationship, regular absences by the male lover, and unfulfilled pecuniary promises establish a very different set of political inflections. See also M. Giulia Fabi, "'The Unguarded Expression of the Feelings of Negroes': Gender, Slave Resistance, and William Wells Brown's Revisions of *Clotel*," *African American Review* 27.4 (1993): 639–654.

8. On the relation between African American writing and oral storytelling, see, for example, Bernard Bell, *The Afro-American Novel and Its Tradition* (Amherst: University of Massachusetts Press, 1987); Sterling Stuckey, *Slave Culture: Nationalist Theory and the Foundations of Black America* (Oxford: Oxford University Press, 1987), esp. 22 ff.; and Dorsey, "De-authorizing Slavery," who speaks of a "cultural and communal ownership of stories" (278).

9. John R. Beard, *The Life of Toussaint L'Ouverture, the Negro Patriot of Hayti* (London: Ingram, Cooke, 1853), 214–215. See also Farrison's notes in *Clotel*, 252–253.

10. David Reynolds, *Beneath the American Renaissance: The Subversive Imagination in the Age of Emerson and Melville* (New York: Knopf, 1988), 54–91. A key further source used in *Clotel* is Theodore Dwight Weld and Angelina Grimké, *American Slavery As It Is*, which sold more than 100,000 copies and was consulted by Stowe as well as Brown for documentary details (see Eric L. McKitrick, "A Hero of Antislavery," *New York Review of Books*, 14 November 1996, p. 50). Weld and Grimké, *American Slavery As It Is: Testimony of a Thousand Witnesses* (New York: American Anti-Slavery Society, 1839). As Dorsey observes, "abolitionist orators and writers frequently borrowed accounts from each other" ("De-authorizing Slavery," 258).

11. Hans Robert Jauss, *Toward an Aesthetic of Reception*, trans. Timothy Bahti (Brighton: Harvester, 1982); Susan K. Harris, *Nineteenth-Century American Women Novelists: Interpretative Strategies* (Cambridge: Cambridge University Press, 1990), 13 ff.; Fabi, "The Unguarded Expression."

12. On Douglass's voyeurism, see David Van Leer, "The Anxiety of Ethnicity in Douglass's Narrative," in Sundquist, 118–140; Jenny Franchot, "The Punishment of Esther," in Sundquist, 141–165.

13. See, for example, Geraldine O. Matthews, *Black American Writers, 1773–1949* (Boston: G. K. Hall, 1975), 67–79.

14. The "liberator" proves to be Georgiana, whose acts of manumission are regarded as political—a resistance to religious teaching, family upbringing, education, and economic pressures. Indeed, the novel reflects a deep mistrust of these ideological state apparatuses and the overdeter-

mined unity ("harmony") that they combined to create in the American South. The configuration that results is more potent than that found in Stowe. George Shelby's act of manumission occurs in Stowe's penultimate chapter, entitled "The Liberator." I think the fact that Brown's Georgiana commences her more challenging process of manumission in a chapter also entitled "The Liberator" is pointed (Stowe 613–617; Brown 161–167). See Louis Althusser, *Lenin and Philosophy and Other Essays*, trans. B. Brewster (London: Monthly Review Press, 1971), 127–186, esp. 150.

15. This is essentially Fabi's argument; I take issue with her idea that "the reader experience[s] the powerlessness, the uncertainty, the absurdities that characterize slave life" (642). This claim is too large; the reader does not "experience slave life" but is displaced, disoriented, and disconcerted by a text that is generically unsettled and unsettling.

16. Harriet Wilson, *Our Nig*, ed. Henry Louis Gates (1859; reprint, New York: Vintage, 1983), 1.

17. As Frances Smith Foster observes, "virtually every extant [African American woman's] text was written by a professed Christian." Foster, *Written by Herself: Literary Production by African American Women, 1746–1892* (Bloomington: Indiana University Press, 1993), 2 ff. For example, Jarena Lee's 1836 *Life and Experience* was mainly concerned "to continue her evangelical work" (77).

18. For related analyses, see Claudia Tate, "Allegories of Black Female Desire; or, Rereading Nineteenth-Century Sentimental Narratives of Black Authority," in *Changing Our Own Words: Essays on Criticism, Theory and Writing by Black Women*, ed. Cheryl A. Wall (London: Routledge, 1990), 98–126; Gabrielle Foreman, "The Spoken and the Silenced in *Incidents in the Life of a Slave Girl* and *Our Nig*," *Callaloo: Journal of African American Arts and Letters* 13.2 (1990): 313–324; Beth Maclay Doriani, "Black Womanhood in Nineteenth Century America: Subversion and Self-Construction in Two Women's Autobiographies," *American Quarterly* 43.2 (1991): 199–222.

19. L. S. M. McCord, review of *Uncle Tom's Cabin*, *Southern Quarterly Review*, 7 January 1852, pp. 81–120; George F. Holmes, review of *Uncle Tom's Cabin*, *Southern Literary Messenger* 18 (October 1852): 630–638. For further discussion of the impact of proslavery on the abolitionist debate and the implications for *Our Nig*, see John Ernest, "Economies of Identity: Harriet Wilson's *Our Nig*," *PMLA* 109.3 (1994): 430.

20. Barbara A. White, "'Our Nig' and the She-Devil: New Information about Harriet Wilson and the 'Bellmont' Family," *American Literature* 65.1 (1993): 34.

21. The close similarities between Brown's and Frederick Douglass's

openings, along with the parallelisms of their titles, makes this point economically. My use of "facts" here refers to Garrison's and other abolitionists' injunctions to Douglass to stick to the "facts" and his rejection of this advice. See Douglass, *My Bondage and My Freedom*, ed. William L. Andrews (1855; reprint, Urbana: University of Illinois Press, 1987), 220.

22. Eric L. Miller, *Arguing About Slavery: The Great Battle in the United States Congress* (New York: Knopf, 1996).

23. Stanley Elkins, *Slavery: A Problem in American Institutional Life* (Chicago: University of Chicago Press, 1959), 185 ff.

24. Eric Gardner, "'This Attempt of Their Sister': Harriet Wilson's *Our Nig* from Printer to Readers," *New England Quarterly* 66.2 (1993): 234.

25. For a definition of the "melodramatic and titillating . . . 'tragic octoroon,'" see Jules Zanger, "The 'Tragic Octoroon' in Pre-Civil War Fiction," *American Quarterly* 18 (1966): 63–64. For two complementary accounts of the reason for the "silencing" of *Our Nig* as a published text, see White, "'Our Nig' and the She-Devil," 44–45, and Henry Louis Gates, "Harriet E. Wilson," in *Black Women in America: An Historical Encyclopedia*, vol. 2, ed. D. C. Hine et al. (Bloomington: Indiana University Press, 1993), 1272.

Wild Semantics: Charlotte Perkins Gilman's Feminization of Edgar Allan Poe's Arabesque Aesthetics

GABRIELE RIPPL

When located in the negotiation between "aesthetics" and "politics," women writers too often lose status. Traditional (modernist-inflected) critics have devalued women's writing — and "feminine literary traditions" — on the basis of ostensibly insufficient artfulness and an excessive investment in the political and its alter ego, the sentimental.[1] Yet, as the case of Charlotte Perkins Gilman reveals, even feminist criticism often fails to conceptualize and appreciate the aesthetic merits of such writing, focusing instead too narrowly on Gilman's sexual politics. Aiming to take Gilman seriously on aesthetic grounds and to bridge the division between male and female writers, I will discuss Poe's aesthetic influence — and, in particular, the concept of the arabesque — on Gilman's writing. More specifically, I will outline how Gilman represents and explores culturally "masculine" and "feminine" reading practices — here embodied in the text's internal male and female readers — that function in opposed and hierarchical manner. Gilman's difficult conclusion highlights the dangerous benefits of "feminine," "arabesque" readings. Finally, by connecting the "aesthetic" and the "political" in *The Yellow Wallpaper*, Gilman is — like the collection of essays in hand — "interrogat[ing] the critical opposition between these terms."[2]

Poe, the Grotesque, and the Arabesque

The grotesque and the arabesque figure centrally in many of Edgar Allan Poe's texts.[3] In "Metzengerstein" (1836), "Ligeia" (1838), "The Fall of the House of Usher" (1839), and "The Pit and the Pendulum" (1843) they constitute the theme underlying his meticulous descriptions of ornamental wall decorations. Ornamentation theory defines the arabesque as a design with plant-based — or, alternatively, completely abstract— motifs the elements of which can be infinitely repeated. Because the elements are abstract, they have no semantic value and only acquire meaning through the ornamental syntax. In contrast, the elements of the grotesque are autosemantic and heterogeneous in themselves as well as in comparison with each other (mixed beings consisting of animated, plant-based, and artificial elements); therefore, they cannot be repeated.[4] Since German Romanticism, the term *arabesque* has stood for the self-reflexiveness and self-referentiality of the romantic literary text, for its deceiving twists and turns and re-iterative structures, as well as for its skepticism regarding signs and its renunciation of intentional communication.

Poe's interest in the grotesque and the arabesque goes back to Sir Walter Scott's essay on the German romantic author E. T. A. Hoffmann,[5] which was published in the *Foreign Quarterly Review* in 1827 and reprinted in 1841 in Philadelphia, where Poe lived at the time. Scott exemplifies the romantic confusion of the grotesque and the arabesque, which he uses synonymously. In his view, both terms are negative concepts testifying to an unrestrained, morbid imagination. Subsequently, Poe tried to differentiate the two, making them aesthetic as well as positive psychological concepts. Notably, while Scott reserved the term "arabesque" for painting, Poe applied it for the first time to English and American literature.[6]

In this context, it is evident that when Poe refers to "arabesque figures" that sometimes look like "simple monstrosities" in "Ligeia," he is confusing the arabesque with the grotesque by ascribing a special meaning to the former. Yet his *Tales of the Grotesque and the Arabesque*, published in 1840, attempts to differentiate between them. Two years later, in his essay *The Philosophy of Furniture*, Poe is even more precise than in his literary texts, stating that "In brief — distinct grounds, and vivid circular or cycloid figures, *of no meaning,* are here Median laws. . . . Indeed, whether on carpets, or curtains, or tapestry, or ottoman coverings, all upholstery of this nature should be rigidly Arabesque."[7] Ornaments without inherent meaning, i.e., rigidly arabesque ornaments, are to be preferred to well-known objects of any kind, precisely because they do so much to stimulate the imagination.

Poe's texts embody many characteristics of the arabesque: for example, from the onlooker's point of view and from a different perspective, the arabesques described in "Ligeia" can produce differing meanings precisely because they are polysemic signs.[8] In Renate Lachmann's view, arabesques provoke a metamorphotic, centrifugal semantic, while arabesque texts show a high degree of self-thematization by focusing on descriptions of carpets, wallpapers, calligraphies, and palimpsests.[9] In "Ligeia," the detailed descriptions of the wall and ceiling decorations suggest the changing meaning of the arabesque as well as its elements of playfulness, illusion, and movement, which stimulate the imagination: "The ceiling, of gloomy-looking oak, was excessively lofty, vaulted, and elaborately fretted with the wildest and most grotesque specimen of a semi-Gothic, semi-Druidical device. From out the most central recess of this melancholy vaulting, depended . . . a huge censer . . . with many perforations so contrived that there writhed in and out of them, as if endued with a serpent vitality, a continual succession of parti-coloured fires."[10] Arabesques are also found on the tapestry, which creates a "phantasmagoric" effect:

The material . . . was spotted all over, at irregular intervals, with arabesque figures. . . . But these figures partook of the true character of the arabesque only when regarded from a single point of view. By a contrivance now common . . . they were made changeable in aspect. To one entering the room, they bore the appearance of simple monstrosities; but upon a farther advance, this appearance gradually departed; and step by step, as the visitor moved his station in the chamber, he saw himself surrounded by an endless succession of the ghastly forms. . . . The phantasmagoric effect was vastly heightened by the artificial introduction of a strong continual current of wind behind the draperies — giving a hideous and uneasy animation to the whole. (163)

The curved lines and the repetition of the arabesque pattern create a transitory, fluid effect intensified by the wind and stimulating the onlooker's imagination by challenging customary patterns of perception. I would suggest that Poe proclaims an anticlassical (or anticlassicist) aesthetic agenda, which in the tradition of Western Renaissance ornamentation has been represented by the grotesque and the arabesque: fantasy is preferred to mimesis, sinuous ornamental lines to straight ones, chaos and accident to order, variety to unity.[11] The frequent descriptions of tapestry and furniture, as well as Poe's allusions to the problematic representational power of language, underscore the self-reflexiveness of his texts, with the "serpent vitality" of the tapestry representing a metatextual thematization of his arabesque aesthetic principles. "Serpent vitality" also describes the movement of "Ligeia" as a whole, which performs many conspicuous repetitions (e.g., on the phonetic level and on the level of idioms and character) and therefore resembles the infinite repetition of an arabesque, taking on the qualities of a continuous incantation.

Beyond the Romantic: Behind *The Yellow Wallpaper*

"Ligeia," as well as "Metzengerstein," "The Fall of the House of Usher," and "The Pit and the Pendulum," represents an important pretext of Charlotte Perkins Gilman's *The Yellow Wallpaper*, which obviously refers back to Poe thematically and structurally. To observe a few connections: in both Gilman's story and "The Fall of the House of Usher" we have unreliable narrators; in both there are parallel images — anticipating Gilman's toadstools, Poe highlights the "minute fungi" that "overspread the whole exterior" of the Usher family mansion (*Tales of Mystery and Imagination*, 130). Nature turns into a threatening force in both texts, and both protagonists are influenced by their unanimated surroundings. In "The Pit and the Pendulum," the walls and the ceiling of the prison cell are covered with grotesque monstrosities, and the pit has a "sulphurous light," which in *The Yellow Wallpaper* returns as the sulfurous smell of the wallpaper. And, like Gilman's protagonist, Poe's finds himself on the verge of madness.

My reading of Gilman's story will seek to demonstrate that, by commenting indirectly on Scott's negative assessment of the grotesque — and arabesque — as resulting from a pathological imagination and by helping to make the grotesque a positive and psychological category, Gilman is Poe's successor.[12] Moreover, by introducing a female protagonist and including the category of gender in the debate on ornaments, especially on the arabesque, Gilman articulates in formal terms the sexual politics of her period while differentiating herself from Poe by means of this ongoing aesthetic debate.

Published in the *New England Magazine* in 1892, *The Yellow Wallpaper* fictionalizes Gilman's encounter with the psychiatry of her era.[13] After the birth of her child, a young doctor's wife suffers from nervous exhaustion, which results in psychotic delusions and schizophrenia. The protagonist's obsessive reading of the orange and yellow patterned wallpaper of her sickroom serves to describe not only the interior of the room but also the protagonist's state of mental health: since the wallpaper is clearly a projection, the protagonist's reading may be considered the "transcription" of her psychological state, and the history of this reading becomes the history of her illness. This semiautobiographical text met with a varied reception. The story was rejected by many because its theme was so clearly sexual politics; in a nineteenth-century context, the connection between madness and the protagonist's gender role constituted a scandal.[14] *The Yellow Wallpaper* was praised by some, however, for its precise, realistic description of the onset of mental illness and by others as an exciting ghost and horror story in the tradition of Edgar Allan Poe and the gothic novel: Gilman's romantic and fantastic narrative situates the protagonist in "a colonial mansion, a hereditary estate, I would say a haunted house," which is reminiscent of English country estates and which exudes a certain "ghostliness" (91, 11).

Since its rediscovery in the early 1970s, *The Yellow Wallpaper* has been read from feminist social critical or psychopathological perspectives; the wallpaper has consequently been interpreted as representing woman's morbid social position in the nineteenth century or the protagonist's desires.[15] Yet *The Yellow Wallpaper* exceeds the level of social criticism or a precise account of illness. This aesthetic excess emerges in Gilman's allegorizing her own position as reader and writer. First, she parallels her own situation in her protagonist's, though this twinning involves a fictively autobiographical "I." Second, ostensibly excluded from the writing process, the narrator begins her intensive ongoing reading of the wallpaper, which she records on "dead paper," as she calls her diary (10), thus making the wallpaper a "living text." By composing the secret diary, the protagonist also is writing *The Yellow Wallpaper*, which represents her psychotext, as it were.

These intricate fictional duplications point to the narrative's self-reflexiveness and provide a rationale for my reading, which extrapolates the aesthetic principles that Gilman's story thematizes. I read *The Yellow Wallpaper* as a metatext that takes the constructedness of literary texts as its subject and that demonstrates how readings of such texts are inconclusive, necessarily ending up with a "misreading." The yellow wallpaper described in the story thus functions both as a text metaphor and a structural model for literary texts in general. Since the arabesque wallpaper model points to key concepts in romantic poetics, it also acquires a mise-en-abîme function, given the protagonist's reading: the wallpaper text of *The Yellow Wallpaper* reflects the romantic text. Such a reading, however, ignores the narrative's polymorphous structure, as reflected in the wide range of interpretations in its reception history. Gilman's emphatic textual strategy of self-referentiality, her steady attention to writing and reading, the pronounced inclusion of the reader in the text and its meaning, and, finally, her increasing focus on the problematic nature of language and of the processes of perception, serve to make the text more than a romantic paradigm, instead (or also) assigning it a place in modern literature.[16]

Masculine and Feminine Reading(s)

In *The Yellow Wallpaper* Gilman explicitly makes a connection between writing/reading and mental illness, using the device of the arabesque wallpaper pattern. As Günter Oesterle has shown, the German classicist Karl Philip Moritz had already added anthropological and psychological dimensions to the arabesque as an aesthetic form. Moritz linked "the attempt to create a classical style," implying "purity and clarity of thought," with the problem of subjectivity, which suffers from a surfeit of ideas that create "disorder and confusion."[17] During the Enlightenment and the classicist period, the arabesque (termed by Friedrich Schlegel "the oldest and original form of the human imagination"),[18] which produced "non-sense instead of sense, wild flights of imagination instead of nature and truth,"[19] was denigrated in Germany as a decadent phenomenon and a fall from the heights of classicist standards of beauty. For, in contrast to rationalist aesthetics, the arabesque has diversity taking precedence over unity and the unrestrained, uncontrolled imagination flooding reason — it is, in the words of Moritz, a rejection of the "masculine (sublime) way of thinking."[20] Thus, it is not surprising that in *The Yellow Wallpaper*, the (female) protagonist lacks a unified self precisely because of her hypertrophic, unrestrained imagination, which results in what we might call an arabesque polysemantics, both for herself and her readers.

In this context, the protagonist and her husband represent two diametrically opposed aesthetic philosophies: the rational-realistic one represented by the doctor contrasts with the romantic, amimetic, and antimimetic aesthetic[21] represented by the protagonist's reading (which she ultimately rejects). It is no accident that the opposing configurations of the arabesque and linguistic economy — or romanticism and rational classicism (or realism) — correspond to such antonyms as feminine madness and masculine reason, unreality and reality, and invisibility and visibility. Two different reading models presented in *The Yellow Wallpaper*, which I will characterize briefly, correspond to these two aesthetic philosophies.

First, the story demonstrates the "masculine" reading model embodied in the doctor husband, which is based on clear language, economy, and lucidity; this model takes a linear-teleological approach to reading with a tendency toward hermeneutic standardization and fixation. The narrator suggests that as a reader, the doctor demonstrates an antagonism to imaginative qualities and a total acceptance of empirical facts: "John is practical in the extreme. He has no patience with faith, an intense horror of superstition, and he scoffs openly at any talk of things not to be felt and seen and put down in figures" (9). Slightly later in the narrative, Gilman underscores John's "rational" perspective compared to the narrator's imaginative one: "He laughs at me so about this wall-paper! . . . John has cautioned me not to give way to fancy in the least. He says that with my imaginative power and habit of story-making, a nervous weakness like mine is sure to lead to all manner of excited fancies" (15 ff.). From the very beginning the protagonist detests the wallpaper in her sickroom, but her husband refuses to give in to her desire for new wallpaper.[22] He thus proves to be a bad reader, for he remains completely blind to his patient's steadily deteriorating condition, insisting, "You really are better, dear, whether you can see it or not. I am a doctor, dear, and I know" (23). By assuming a fixed, conventionalized signifier/signified relationship and believing what he sees, the doctor as an empirical-rational reader fails in terms of his inability to interpret correctly her "hysterical" signifiers and to understand the unstable context of meaning produced by his wife.[23] Since he believes there is no reason to suffer, his wife cannot be suffering ("John does not know how much I suffer. He knows there is no reason to suffer, and that satisfies him" [14]). Furthermore, the doctor's interpretation of his patient's condition can easily be applied to hermeneutically uniform and institutionally sanctioned readings: as Shoshana Felman has demonstrated, the mistaken masculine reading of women is paralleled by the mistaken masculine reading of texts.[24]

The second ("feminine") reading model presented in *The Yellow Wallpaper* is characterized by an "arabesque" reading movement, which, rather than proceeding in linear-teleological fashion, moves in undirected and phantasmagorical fashion, and, rather than proceeding from a fixed signifier/signified relationship, assigns polysemantic meaning. Ferdinand de Saussure has defined texts as anagrammatic that have, underneath their manifest, surface level, a second, latent level of meaning.[25] We see this layering figured in Gilman's narrative when the protagonist discovers a subpattern in the wallpaper: "This wallpaper has a kind of subpattern in a different shade, a particularly irritating one, for you can only see it in certain lights, and not clearly then" (18). The protagonist's inconclusive and uncontrolled reading finally results in synesthetic interpretive strategies that involve not only the sense of sight but also touch and hearing. As she follows the labyrinthian ornamental wallpaper pattern, the flat, abstract, two-dimensional pattern becomes a three-dimensional space in the course of the story, ultimately eliminating the distinction between the subject (the reader) and the object (the text to be read), and the woman/reader disappears into the wallpaper/text.

Feminist critics have hypothesized that, in its divergence from representative models and concepts of the monologue and the identical, women's language is polymorphous, a polylogue. In *The Yellow Wallpaper*, the protagonist reads and writes "as a woman,"[26] for her "feminine" reading contrasts with a "masculine" reading that tends toward cooptation and disciplining and is based on the reduction of meaning and the principle of linear causality. She is thus, as it were, a deconstructive feminist, albeit inadvertently. As long as the protagonist has not definitively lost her individuality and identity, her reading provides the arabesque text with a decentralization of potential meaning and a perspectivist semantics; the wallpaper's pattern has a different meaning in different lights: "By daylight she [the woman behind the paper] is subdued, quiet. . . . As soon as it was moonlight and that poor thing began to crawl and shake the pattern, I got up and ran to her help" (26, 32).

The narrative's stylistic economy, with concise, clear sentences and brief, clear paragraphs, provides lucidity for both the narrator and the external reader, so that, at the structural level, *The Yellow Wallpaper* appears to be the simulacrum of an uncoded text. This lucidity contrasts strongly, however, with the protagonist's worsening condition and, at the content level, with her arabesque reading of the baroque, undulating, elusive wallpaper pattern. The contrast between the protagonist's clarity of speech and her imaginative fantasies — and thus the coexistence of insight and delusions — is a symptom of schizophrenia; the dual structure reemerges in the relationship between structure and content. Thus, *The Yellow Wallpaper* might be referred to as a "schizophrenic text," which draws the reader into its interpretive vortex. In Poe's "Ligeia" and "The Fall of the House of Usher," the reader is similarly drawn in due to the unreliability of the protagonist-narrators, who suffer from deceptive visual perceptions, mental disorders, and morbid acuteness of the senses.[27]

But there is a significant difference between Gilman and Poe. Because Gilman attempts not only to present a psychotic-schizophrenic woman and her perceptions but also to represent schizophrenia on the level of language, her narrative is psychologically much more troubling than Poe's stories. The haunting gap between the protagonist's clarity of speech and lucidity on the one hand and her fantastic delusion on the other hand makes *The Yellow Wallpaper*'s psychological insights much more frightening for its readers. At the same time that the narrative embodies the power of nonlinear reading practices, however, *The Yellow Wallpaper* paradoxically views a "hermeneutical" reading of a literary text as a psychotic approach and demonstrates its failure: the protagonist succumbs to her psychosis at the very moment that she *stops* her "arabesque wallpaper reading," assigning one meaning to the wallpaper pattern. In this sense, her own psychotic reading model corresponds to her doctor husband's therapeutic reading: both result in premature interpretations.

The limitations of the linear, "masculine" approach, as well as the pleasurable dangers of an arabesque, "feminine" reading, permeate the narrative. The partially torn and faded wallpaper of her sickroom, which acquires great symbolic meaning both as wallpaper[28] and as *yellow* wallpaper,[29] is described by the protagonist at the beginning: "I never saw a worse paper in my life. One of those sprawling flamboyant patterns committing every artistic sin. It is dull enough to confuse the eye in following, pronounced enough to constantly irritate and provoke study, and when you follow the lame uncertain curves for a little distance they suddenly commit suicide — plunge off at outrageous angles, destroy themselves in unheard of contradictions. The color is repellent, almost revolting; a smoldering unclean yellow, strangely faded by the slow-turning sunlight. It is dull yet lurid orange in some places, a sickly sulphur tint in others" (13). Because the wallpaper pattern adheres to no structural principle and also has a horrible sulfurous "tint," it "irritates" the viewer's senses, representing a source of annoyance "to a normal mind." Although the narrator describes this pattern as a "florid arabesque" (25), the effect of an arabesque is spoiled completely because the ornamental wallpaper is not playful and bright. The objects from organic nature — fungi, toadstools, seaweed — identified by the protagonist heighten her associations with something threatening and uncanny, even satanic,[30] and the protagonist speaks of "waves of optical horror," which the wallpaper pattern arouses.

As in Poe's work, aesthetic modes converge: the arabesque ornaments seem to move, displaying grotesque grimaces and figures depending on the time of day. Sunlight, twilight, and moonlight each create a different effect. By daylight, the laws of symmetry and the repetitiveness of the pattern that characterize the arabesque disappear. This is not a "line of beauty"[31] à la Hogarth, for "ballooning curves and scrolls," which look like "debased

Romanesques," waddle up and down the plain pillars and could at best be treated in the context of an "aesthetics of ugliness."[32] In the evening, however, when the light is weaker, the reader feels that she has discovered symmetry and a law of radiation: meaningless in themselves, the arabesques now become an endless series of grotesques, that is, objects that by definition are meaningful: the protagonist now perceives staring disembodied eyes instead of the usual florid arabesques. The arabesque lines of the wallpaper look like poisonous, twitching mushrooms, which metamorphose in new and uncanny ways: surging seaweed, staring eyes, drooping heads of dead persons and, finally, women crawling around in a locked space.

By introducing the less current term "romanesque" in this description, Gilman invokes another important term in the discussion of ornamental texts. "Romanesque" originally meant "in a Romance language," i.e., literature that has been written in the vernacular (like the romances). In *On the Supernatural in Fictitious Composition*, Sir Walter Scott notes the commonly synonymous use of "romance" and "fictitious composition" (314): "Romanesque," as well as its synonym "romantic," refers to fantastic-irrational, bizarre literary texts, which were discredited by Dr. Johnson as "romantic absurdities and incredible fictions."[33] During the eighteenth century, "romantic" actually came to mean "like a romance" and possessed positive connotations, whereas "romanesque" was used to refer to chimerical, fairy-tale-like, fantastic, and grotesque texts.[34] Because the term "fiction" is obviously connected to Gilman's use of "romanesque," her protagonist, when talking of "debased romanesques," simply means "debased fictions," that is, low genres such as the burlesque or the grotesque (which here names a coarse comic mode of writing that mixes humor with horror) that are produced by a morbid and abnormal imagination.

As the protagonist's illness progresses, the distance between the text/wallpaper and the reader — both internal and external — is eliminated: the narrator believes in the hideous influence of the evil wallpaper, which mocks her by doing backwards somersaults to withdraw from her:

> This paper looks to me as if it *knew* what a vicious influence it had!

There is a recurrent spot where the pattern lolls like a broken neck and two bulbous eyes stare at you upside down. I get positively angry with the impertinence of it and everlastingness. Up and down and sideways they crawl, and these absurd, unblinking eyes are everywhere. There is one place where two breadths didn't match, and the eyes go all up and down the line, one a little higher than the other. (16)

This action only serves to increase the protagonist's obsession with decoding its hieroglyphs. Now every curved line and every scroll represents a message, a symbol; possessing a high degree of association, this method of reading has been described by Aleida Assmann as "gazing," or staring.[35] The protagonist sees her own "gaze" reflected in the wallpaper: two huge rolling eyes stare at her. She is thus definitively denied the self-confirmation provided by "the pleasure of contemplation" postulated by Karl Philip Moritz with regard to ornaments in antiquity;[36] what the protagonist finally envisions is her own frightening loss of self.

The increasingly palimpsestic nature of the wallpaper ultimately leads to an anagrammatic reading: another pattern is discovered by the protagonist under the obtrusive outer wallpaper pattern: "a strange, provoking, formless sort of figure" (18). In a final reading, which involves all her senses, the protagonist sees the wallpaper shake ("The front pattern *does* move — and no wonder! The woman behind shakes it" [30]), hears it scream, and is dirtied by it. Perhaps its worst feature is the smell (28), described as a "peculiar odor" that "in this damp weather . . . is awful . . . a yellow smell" (29). Accompanying the foul odor are "all those strangled heads and bulbous eyes and waddling fungus growths [that] just shriek with derision!" (34). Tearing it off the wall, the protagonist has now solved the wallpaper's riddle: she perceives women who are locked up and emerge from the wallpaper by day to crawl around in the garden. In this reading, *The Yellow Wallpaper* ends with complete identification between the protagonist and her doubles: as the shift in personal pronoun suggests (35), she herself has emerged from the wallpaper, as she uses her body to "write" the arabesque wallpaper pattern on the floor, getting down on all fours and following imaginary lines and herself becoming the wallpaper's "text." These lines transcribe a unidimensional — and finally limited — narrative and interpretive model.

Poe introduced detailed descriptions of grotesques and arabesques (particularly on furniture and tapestry) to provide a metatextual, self-reflexive comment on the romantic text. But while Poe seems to ask his readers to develop an arabesque reading practice to cope with the intricacies of romantic texts, Gilman feminizes this strategy by introducing a female protagonist and then opposing her protagonist's "feminine" reading practice with the "masculine" rational-hermeneutic one. She is thus able to connect the ongoing aesthetic debate with a discussion of the sexual politics of her time. She is especially critical of the confinement of women and the attribution to them of irrationality and overactive imaginations. As this account suggests, Gilman follows Poe in her use of the terms "grotesque" and "arabesque," sometimes confusing them: meaningless arabesques, which are especially prone to stimulate the imagination in twilight or in moonlight, turn into grotesque apparitions with a definite meaning. In contrast to Poe's texts, where a rational explanation for the movement of the tapestry and wallpapers is always provided (in "Ligeia" it is the wind; in "The Pit and the Pendulum" it is the machinery of the Inquisition that causes the wallpaper or decorations to move), in Gilman's story the movement of the wallpaper is produced exclusively by the female protagonist's imagination.

In *The Yellow Wallpaper* the hermeneutic, therapeutic reading method employed by men fails because it is unable to deal with "feminine" text models. But the protagonist's "feminine" reading method also fails; finally a representative of "classicism," she seeks to escape her own painful and powerful reading. She "succeeds" when she suffers a psychosis and gives up her "feminine" model for a "masculine" reading. Finally, the failure of both readers *in* the text indicates what is expected of *us*: an arabesque reading, which does justice to the openness of the literary text, in part by remaining inconclusive. Contextualizing *The Yellow Wallpaper* within a male tradition of writing and reading theory enables us to reintegrate the narrative into the canon of "aesthetic," sublime, and "masculine" texts. Although Gilman's "family" topic simultaneously situates her in the political sphere, her approach to the subject prohibits classifying her story exclusively as feminine writing. By referring to and extending historically male aesthetics while engaging in critical sexual politics, Gilman's work enables critics to close the gap between "masculine" and "feminine" literary traditions.

NOTES

1. For some recent discussions of the relationship between sentimentalism, evaluation, and politics, see Suzanne Clark, *Sentimental Modernism: Women Writers and the Revolution of the Word* (Bloomington: Indiana University Press, 1991); Susan K. Harris, *Nineteenth-Century American Women's Novels: Interpretative Strategies* (New York: Cambridge University Press, 1990); Joanne Dobson, "The American Renaissance Reenvisioned," in *The (Other) American Traditions: Nineteenth-Century Women Writers* (New Brunswick: Rutgers University Press, 1993); Shirley Samuels, ed., *The Culture of Sentiment: Race, Gender, and Sentimentality in Nineteenth-Century America* (New York: Oxford University Press, 1992).

2. Karen Kilcup, "The Conversation of 'The Whole Family': Gender, Politics, and Aesthetics in Literary Tradition," 14.

3. G. R. Thompson, *Poe's Fiction: Romantic Irony* (Madison: University of Wisconsin Press, 1973); Jutta Ernst, *Edgar Allan Poe und die Poetik des Arabesken* (Würzburg: Königshausen und Neumann, 1996).

4. See Günter Irmscher, *Kleine Kunstgeschichte des europäischen Ornaments seit der Frühen Neuzeit (1400–1900)* (Darmstadt: Wiss. Buchgesellschaft, 1984), and Susi Kotzinger, "Arabeske-Groteske: Versuch einer Differenzierung," in *Zeichen zwischen Klartext und Arabeske*, ed. Susi Kotzinger and Gabriele Rippl (Amsterdam: Rodopi, 1994), 219–228.

5. Sir Walter Scott, "On the Supernatural in Fictitious Composition; and Particularly on the Works of Earnest Theodore William Hoffmann," in *On Novelists and Fiction*, ed. I. Williams (London: Routledge & Kegan Paul, 1968), 312–353.

6. Just as Poe applied the term "arabesque" to literature in the British-American context, so did Friedrich Schlegel in the German context in 1800.

7. Edgar Allen Poe, "The Philosophy of Furniture," in *The Works of Edgar Allan Poe*, Tamerlane edition (New York: Leslie Judge Company, 1911), 5:189; emphasis in original.

8. Rosemary Jackson, *Fantasy: The Literature of Subversion* (London: Methuen, 1981).

9. Renate Lachmann, "Dezentrierte Bilder: Die ekstatische Imagination in Bruno Schulz' Prosa," *Wiener Slavistischer Almanach* 31 (1992): 454.

10. Edgar Allan Poe, *Tales of Mystery and Imagination* (London: Dent, 1981), 163. All subsequent references appear in the text.

11. Günter Oesterle, "'Vorbegriffe zu einer Theorie der Ornamente': Kontroverse Formprobleme zwischen Aufklärung, Klassizismus und Romantik am Beispiel der Arabesque," in *Ideal und Wirklichkeit der bildenden Kunst im späten 18. Jahrhundert*, ed. H. Beck, P. C. Bol, and E. Maek-Gérard (Berlin: Mann, 1984), 119–139.

12. Gilman highlights Scott's connection between the free play of imagination and pathology. Her own protagonist has many characteristics in common with Scott's description of E. T. A. Hoffmann. See Scott, 335.

13. Born in Hartford, Connecticut, in 1860, Gilman (1860–1935) grew up in difficult circumstances without a father, who had deserted the family shortly after Charlotte's birth, and with an embittered mother. At the age of twenty-four she married Charles Walter Stetson, a painter. Shortly after the wedding, Gilman began to suffer from depression, which increased a year later, after the birth of her daughter. The neurologist S. Weir Mitchell, who specialized in women's nervous disorders, prescribed bed rest and isolation: writing and painting were proscribed, and reading was limited to a maximum of two hours daily. Once Gilman decided not to continue following Mitchell's instructions and to leave her husband, she began to recover. She earned her money as a journalist and by giving lectures and writing. Her best-known writings include *Women and Economics* (1898) and *The Man-Made World* (1911). She was a committed feminist (but called herself a humanist) and social economist, and her literary works dealt almost exclusively with women's issues. In 1935, when she was diagnosed with cancer at an advanced stage, Gilman committed suicide.

14. Elaine Hedges, epilogue to *The Yellow Wallpaper*, by Charlotte Perkins Gilman, ed. Elaine R. Hedges (New York: Feminist Press, 1973), 39, 41.

15. See Sandra M. Gilbert and Susan Gubar, *The Madwoman in the Attic* (New Haven: Yale University Press, 1979), 90–92. Gilman's heroine suggests "the madwoman in the attic" of Charlotte Brontë's novel *Jane Eyre*, published in 1847. See also John S. Bak, "Escaping the Jaundiced Eye: Foucauldian Panopticism in Charlotte Perkins Gilman's 'The Yellow Wallpaper,'" *Studies in Short Fiction* 31 (1994): 39–46; Jeanette King and Pam Morris, "On Not Reading between the Lines: Models of Reading in 'The Yellow Wallpaper,'" *Studies in Short Fiction* 26.1 (1989): 28.

16. See Barbara Will, "Nervous Systems, 1880–1915," in *American Bodies. Cultural Histories of Physique*, ed. Tim Armstrong (Sheffield: Academic Press, 1996), 92.

17. According to Oesterle, "'The deviant variants of classicist aesthetics

(affluence and poverty) correspond right down to the details to the model of a selection of ideas in Moritz's rational psychology. The problem discussed therein of a 'Ueberfluss(es) von Ideen, welcher Unordnung und Verwirrung verursacht und die Reinigkeit und Klarheit im Denken hemmt', is treated as a formal problem relating to the arabesque" (131). Moritz was not only a theoretician of classicist aesthetics and author of an aesthetics of ornament but also the publisher-editor of the first German journal of psychology, entitled *Gnothi sauton oder Magazin zur Erfahrungsseelenkunde*.

18. F. Schlegel, *Charakteristiken und Kritiken*, vol. 1, quoted in Oesterle, 138.

19. See Oesterle's commentary on Riem (134).

20. Quoted in Oesterle, 136; Oesterle quotes from K. Ph. Moritz's *Einfachheit und Klarheit*. See also Günter Oesterle, "Arabeske und Roman," in *Studien zur Ästhetik und Literaturgeschichte der Kunstperiode*, ed. Dirk Grathoff (Frankfurt am Main: Lang, 1985), 273.

21. See also Richard Feldstein, "Reader, Text, and Ambiguous Referentiality in 'The Yellow Wallpaper,'" in *Feminism and Psychoanalysis*, ed. Richard Feldstein and Judith Roof (Ithaca: Cornell University Press, 1989), 274.

22. Greg Johnson reports that shortly before Emily Dickinson was born, her mother wanted to have new wallpaper. Johnson, *Studies in Short Fiction* 26.4 (1989): 521.

23. Luce Irigaray has shown how the therapeutic system in Freudian psychoanalysis forces women to become malingerers and hysterics. See Irigaray, *Speculum: Spiegel des anderen Geschlechts* (Frankfurt am Main: Suhrkamp, 1980), 69 ff. In Gilman's text, it is ultimately the doctor who is responsible for the protagonist's illness.

24. Shoshana Felman, "Women and Madness: The Critical Phallacy," *Diacritics* 5 (1975): 2–10.

25. See Jean Starobinski, *Wörtern unter Wörter: Die Anagramme von Ferdinand de Saussure* (Frankfurt: Ullstein, 1980), 44 ff.

26. Luce Irigaray has hypothesized that women speak a different language ("parler femme") than men; see Irigaray, "Das Geschlecht, das nicht eins ist," in *Das Geschlecht, das nicht eins ist* (Berlin: Merve, 1979), 22–32. But "reading like a woman" and "writing like a woman" is not necessarily what happens when a woman reads or writes; for a critical reading of Irigaray, see Peggy Kamuf, "Writing Like a Woman," in *Women and Language in Literature and Society*, ed. S. MacConnell-Ginet, R. Borker, and N. Furman (New York: Praeger, 1980), 284–299.

27. See Gabriele Rippl, "E. A. Poe and the Anthropological Turn in Lit-

erary Studies," in *The Anthropological Turn in Literary Studies*, ed. Juergen Schlaeger, *Yearbook of Research in English and American Literature* 12 (1996): 223–242.

28. While in England, Gilman had met William Morris, who sought to revitalize the medieval decorative arts and whose designs included wallpaper. Gilman, *The Living of Charlotte Perkins Gilman: An Autobiography* (Madison: University of Wisconsin Press, 1991), 209.

29. Gilman creates many connotations by using the color yellow. For example, see Susan S. Lanser, "Feminist Criticism, 'The Yellow Wallpaper,' and the Politics of Color in America," *Feminist Studies* 15.2 (1989): 415–441, esp. 425–429. Among other readings, yellow points to the "yellow peril," and thus to the many Asian immigrants in the United States at the turn of the century; it connotes inferiority, foreignness, cowardice, dirt, uselessness, and illness, and it expresses the collective angst of white Americans.

30. This satanic quality is indicated by the sulfurous yellow color and the smell of sulfur that characterizes the wallpaper, the intensity of which increases as the story progresses. Greg Johnson (see above) has worked with other areas of religious imagery. The prisoner of the Spanish Inquisition in Poe's "The Pit and the Pendulum" is also engulfed by a sulfurous smell.

31. William Hogarth, *Analysis of Beauty* (1753; reprint, Hildesheim: Olms, 1974), 38.

32. It is probably no accident that Karl Rosenkranz's *Aesthetik des Haesslichen* had been published in 1853, systematizing ugliness according to amorphousness, incorrectness, and defiguration or deformation, and serving as a pathology of beauty. The connection between the medical and the poetological and aesthetic discourse is interesting. The hidden pattern behind the front pattern discovered by Gilman's protagonist represents an "amorphous figure," which fits Rosenkranz's category of ugliness as amorphousness. Rosenkranz, *Aesthetik des Haesslichen* (Leipzig: Reclam, 1990).

33. See Mario Praz, *Liebe, Tod und Teufel* (München: Hanser, 1988), 38. For the history of the term "romanesque," see Fernand Baldensberger, "'Romantique,' ses analogues et ses équivalents: Tableau synoptique de 1650 à 1810," in *Harvard Studies and Notes in Philology and Literature* 19 (1937): 13–105.

34. See Brande's 1842 *Dictionary of Science*, cited in the *Oxford English Dictionary* entry for "Romanesque." *Oxford English Dictionary*, 2d ed. (Oxford: Clarendon Press, 1989), 14:63.

35. Aleida Assmann, "Die Sprache der Dinge — Der lange Blick und

die wilde Semiose," in *Materialität der Kommunikation*, ed. H. U. Gumbrecht and K. L. Pfeiffer (Frankfurt am Main: Suhrkamp, 1988), 237–251. 36. See Günter Oesterle, *Vorbegriffe*, 128. The reading described as "gazing" by Aleida Assmann does not involve the decoding of signs either, but rather the immediacy of visualization, empathy, and contemplation.

Deepening Hues to Local Color: George Washington Cable and Sarah Barnwell Elliott

ARANZAZU USANDIZAGA

George Washington Cable's and Sarah Barnwell Elliott's often similar literary response to matters of genre and culture in the last decades of the nineteenth century underscores the urgent need for volumes such as *Soft Canons*, for studies investigating the limits of "separate sphere" criticism and challenging the apparently unbridgeable distances between "masculine" and "feminine" literary traditions.[1] When read together, Cable and Elliott's work invites the critic to acknowledge the flexible connections and negotiations between these traditions, and the ways in which they are mutually appropriated and transformed. Myra Jehlen was one of the first critics to suggest reading women's writings in the context of what she defines as the "parent tradition,"[2] that is to say, in relation to canonical male texts. According to Pamela Glenn Menke, Jehlen's model can be improved, because "Jehlen's comparative method suggests cultural perceptions [that] appear to be powerfully arranged around binary oppositions." Although she initially agrees with Jehlen on the "importance of shared textual form," Menke proposes that, when comparing texts by women and men, "the basis for selection [should] rest on additional articulated *moments of similarity* shared by the woman writer and a male author. These shared moments may be historical, racial, ethnic, or ideological."[3]

Jehlen's suggestions provide a useful starting framework in which to discuss Cable and Elliott's writing on the South, for the authors share a similar "textual form," both contributing to the genre of local color or regionalism. But Jehlen's models of comparison must immediately be expanded in order to account for Cable's own complex dialogue with the "parent tradition," as well as Elliott's attempts at transforming it. Their mutual tensions with it result in their shared "moments of similarity," often articulated in formal practices intimately connected to ideology. For example, Cable's changes in narrative perspective in his early work on the South and his dehierarchization of authorial voice dramatically affect accepted social and aesthetic norms. Similarly, Elliott's decision to tell her mulatto heroine's story in "The Heart of It" from the character's perspective forces the reader into an unprecedented process of identification with a black person. As Elaine Sargent Apthorp suggests in her study of women regionalists, "our intimacy with [the characters'] perspectives forces us to feel with them, not merely to evaluate them."[4] Such formal changes are the result of these authors' "moments of similarity" in their perception — and fictionalization — of history, as well as in their understanding of social change and racial conflict.

Though modernism discredited the genre of local color, in the past few years, besides inviting critics to discover the literary and cultural relevance of much forgotten writing in late-nineteenth-century America, canon revision has also encouraged them to reread neglected genres such as local color and regionalism. Many critics believe that local color and regionalism, particularly in the South, tended to provide rhetorical models with which to sublimate regional frustration by projecting falsified memories of the past as well as romanticized illusions of the present. Some recent critics, however, have highlighted the importance of economic and political pressure on local color writing. According to Barbara C. Ewell, the literature of local color and regionalism in the South contributed to disguising the truths about Southern life at the end of the century because "the post-war prosperity of the United States, largely identified with the industrialized Northeast, depended on re-establishing the semi-colonial status of the South, an arrangement that was effectively accomplished after the Civil War." But more important, "local color served to name and *contain* as 'regional' many of the disturbing differences that remained unsolved by the Civil War and its aftermath."[5] This capacity to control and mask the unsolved problems of the times made the genre immensely popular in its initial phase but destroyed it in the long run. Other recent critics who trace the origins and development of American regionalism attribute its failure to account for the true complexities of regional difference to the limitations of the poetics of realism: "Regionalism flourished under the poetics of realism. . . . the romantic yearning for cultural homogeneity is merely replaced by a realist desire to frame regions in a homogeneous, one-world ontology."[6]

Nevertheless, some scholars have recognized local color and regionalism as often innovative and capable of incorporating important political and ideological dimensions, and they have seen the need to take into account the considerable differences among regional writers. In his study of regionalism and class, Richard Brodhead confirms that regionalism "offered freshly found primitive places for the mental resort of the sophisticated . . . and was produced as an upper order's reading at a time of heavy immigration and the anxieties associated with such immigration"; but he also acknowledges that the genre "made the experience of the socially marginalized into a literary asset, and made marginality itself a positive authorial advantage." Marjorie Pryse, Judith Fetterley, and Karen Kilcup have focused on some of these marginal writers and have anthologized the many important and neglected women writers who often wrote subversive versions of local color. Pryse acknowledges that "a critique of hierarchy based on geographical and ideological differences as well as on the confinements of 'woman's sphere' emerges as regionalism's 'essence.'" She insists on the "differences" between regionalist texts, and on how such texts often "challenge hierarchies of cultural value."[7]

Inspired by similar notions of history, Cable and Elliott shared revisionary attitudes toward the South; consequently, they both challenged the genre of local color/regionalism. In different ways, both engage critically in reading the present in relation to the past. Unlike many other regionalists, they look at the past not with the purpose of offering picturesque idealized images but with the intention of understanding and improving the many problems in Southern life. Mary Ellis Gibson reminds us that in American literature "the romance tradition can deny the contingencies of history, the concrete, specific past. . . . At a loss for how to distinguish between history and fiction, American writers have opted to write historical fiction that either openly proclaims or utterly disguises its fictionality."[8] Cable's *The Grandissimes* (1880) may be read as one of the few American historical novels in the European tradition. As Alfred Bendixen observes, "History in *The Grandissimes* is not to be worshipped but confronted and rectified. . . . It was the truth of history to which Cable remained faithful. Cable understood how much Reconstruction had resolved and how much it had failed to resolve." While these words echo Edmund Wilson's early reading of Cable's perspective ("not fundamentally romantic but historical and sociological"),[9] they also apply well to Elliott's writing about the Southern past, obsessed with imagining change and harmony for the future.

Like other Southern regionalist writers such as Grace King, Ruth McEnery Stuart, and Kate Chopin, Cable and Elliott also responded to the radical changes that the century's end was imposing on fiction, changes not only in genre but also in gender, having to do with the emergence of the New Woman as a fictional character. Helen Taylor, Anne Goodwyn Jones, Anna Shannon Elfenbein, and others have discussed the important steps taken by some Southern women regionalists, especially Grace King and Kate Chopin, in the representation of dissenting heroines.[10] Except for her *Jerry* (1891), all of Elliott's nonregional novels are centered on women who cannot adapt to their environment and must seek new models of existence as well as new self-definitions. Elliott, King, Chopin, and Stuart wrote some years after Cable and went further than Cable in challenging the literary representation of women characters, yet their writing may well have been initially encouraged by Cable. For example, Cable's Southern stories provoked King into offering her own version of the South; Elfenbein suggests that King's acknowledged reaction to Cable offered little advantage, for it distracted critics from realizing her true ideas (80). But by the time these Southern women regionalists begun to publish their stories, Cable had left New Orleans, was living in the North, and had ceased to write convincingly about the South. In an article published in 1904 on the many Southern women writers living in New York at the turn of the century, the reporter Julia Tutweiler quotes Elliott as having said: "That winter in New York stands out in many ways. It was then that I renewed my friendship with Mr. Charles Dudley Warner, that I met Mr. Cable."[11] Elliot's single known reference to Cable, this letter invites us to reconsider his regional work as a context for her own.

"Barbaric and Magnetic Beauty":
Rewriting the Southern Lady

Cable scholars have agreed that his early volumes of stories, his novel *The Grandissimes*, and his novella, *Madame Delphine* (1881), the works in which he simultaneously dramatizes white racism and women's oppression, are also his most original and creative. The literary energy found in Cable's best local color work is clearly stimulated by moral passion. A profoundly religious man, he passionately denounces the ideological and cultural limitations he recognizes in the South, and, more specifically, the intense injustice to which both women and African Americans were subject in Louisiana. But, as is well known, Cable was also forced to write during most of his life in order to meet his many financial obligations, and he continued to write about the South long after he had left the region and after having lost the edge, passion, and commitment that dominate his early writing. His early indignation seems to have encouraged his highest literary energy and inspiration, and his best writing is unquestionably regional, not because he provides a colorful and attractive picture of his region, but because to him the local incarnates the ethical dilemmas that define his own youthful questioning moral self. Though Cable had fought in the Confederate army during the Civil War, after years of thoughtful observation and careful historical research he moved toward a passionate conviction that his region needed to change, and he made a remarkable artistic effort in providing models for and examples of possible solutions to the central tensions of Southern life.

Though some critics have judged his work to be "locked into the sentimental, chivalric tradition of heroines" and have argued that "his innovations in fiction do not apply to women characters" (Taylor, 48), I wish to underscore his exceptional awareness of the need to revise the literary representation of women. Cable became intensely immersed in women's culture, and, besides creating many memorable heroines, he was, for example, one of the first to realize the importance of war diaries by women, publishing "The War Diary of a Union Woman in the South" in *Strange True Stories of Louisiana* (1888). In his introduction to this collection Cable explains that the diary was handed to him by "a lady in black." His words to the lady after receiving the manuscript suggest the radical modernity of his concern for women's culture: "Ah! Madam," he tells her, "if you had only done what no woman seems to have seen the importance of doing — written the women's side of that awful war."[12] The manuscript becomes the last "strange true story of Louisiana" in his collection and one of the first published war diaries by a woman.

Many of Cable's most convincing stories deal with the complex struggle between the different cultures of Louisiana — the Spanish, the French Creole, and the Anglo-American — as well as with the wider problems of racial injustice. His most memorable characters, however, are mostly women: "Cable's heroines are in general much more believable and attractive as human beings than his heroes; and the realism with which his heroines are depicted contrasts and occasionally conflicts with the standard romantic situations in which they are cast" (Elfenbein, 29). His well-recorded voyeurism alternates with an intuitive awareness of the reduction and victimization of women, surely stimulated by the awakening of the late nineteenth century to the subject. Elfenbein suggests that his capacity to identify and sympathize with women's destinies was very probably also increased by the example provided by his strong and brave mother, an early widow, and, later, by the suffering of his sisters and his own wife. Yet Cable's overt statements on the woman question tend to be scarce and contradictory,[13] and he expresses his involvement in women's suffering only in his early fiction.

Although some of Cable's recent critics have recognized the originality of his women characters, I wish to take their suggestion one step further and argue that his almost untheorized moral interest in women at the early stage of his literary career contributes importantly to the quality of his writing. The invention of original women characters offers a great challenge to writers in the last decades of the nineteenth century, as writers take up the venture of "writing beyond the ending" to devise plots not centered on romantic love.[14] The question of women's unhappy destinies, both in life and literature, stimulates his revision of the standard fictional treatment of women in late-nineteenth-century fictional writing, as he suggests new paths. His desire to imagine women's destinies in less oppressive and more acceptable moral terms forces him to a highly experimental treatment of the feminine subject. The quality of Cable's art thus becomes essentially dependent on his talent in the creation of unconventional women characters; as soon as he loses interest in the creation of memorable heroines, his fiction decreases dramatically in narrative conviction.

Analyzing and coming to terms with Southern life, Cable begins to experiment both formally and thematically with the emerging genre of Southern regionalism/local color in the stories contained in *Old Creole Days* (1879). In "Jean à Poquelin," one of his best-received early stories, he focuses on the cultural meaning of the different regional dialects, while in "Café des Exilés" he explores possible new functions for the narrative voice and undermines established social positions. In most of these stories he begins to work out possible plots in which to juxtapose and compare Creole and Anglo-American perspectives and in which to introduce his opinions of Southern racial tensions. But in "Belles Demoiselles Plantation" and "Madame Delicieuse," Cable signals his growing uneasiness with accepted notions of Southern femininity. In the first, though the author's main target is the presentation of the dramatic consequences of Southern corruption and racism, he suggests the moral ambiguity of plantation life and the lack of responsibility underlying standard conceptions of Southern womanhood. Critics agree that the uncontrollable natural force of the Mississippi that finally swallows up the idyllic house and gardens — as well as the seven belles that Cable describes with such critical fascination — stands for Cable's symbolic indictment and punishment of a culture of which he disapproved. By naming the plantation "Belles Demoiselles," Cable identifies it and the Southern plantation life it represents with the seven beauties who inhabit it and who represent Southern notions of idealized womanhood. Alice Hall Petry reads the story as a religious allegory of punishment and redemption and suggests that "the placidity of the family . . . belies its origins in embezzlement, arson, lying, miscegenation, and bigamy."[15] The idyllic regional surroundings and search for beauty and pleasure that are the belles' only aim and accomplishment suddenly become tragic when the seven sisters and their colorful paradise violently disappear.

But if Cable denounces the myth of womanhood in plantation society, he also attempts to devise new roles for women in these early stories. In "Madame Delicieuse," for example, he designs a

"Creole coquette" who is also a "pointedly strong, independent woman" (Cleman, 42). Madame Delicieuse becomes the link in "the clash between the old (Creole) order and the new (American) one" (Petry, 132), represented by a Creole father who stands for the old world and a bookish, sedentary son who stands for the new. "Virtuous and generous, but very much acquainted with the ways of the world, and by no means averse to using deceit if the ultimate goal be good" (Rubin, 56), Madame Delicieuse is a very unconventional Southern belle. Petry considers her the story's only problem, "stridently atypical of a Creole belle," a heroine "whose ability to bridge the generation gap strains credulity, and whose character is oddly elusive" (Petry, 136, 135). Her involvement in politics and her manipulative procedures indeed contradict the author's presentation of her otherwise conventional Southern charm and beauty. But Cable's incoherences and tentativeness in the delineation of the character also reflect the author's desire to devise a new heroine for an Americanized Louisiana, and to assign new functions to women in a changing culture. Though retaining some of the Southern belle's features, the author tries to devise a new social and political space for Madame Delicieuse that encroaches — I believe affirmatively — on "masculinity" (Petry, 136). As is the case with Dr. Frowenfeld in *The Grandissimes*, in this story Dr. Mossy is also feminized, a feature that has disturbed many of his critics but that becomes significant in a gendered reading of his work, for it proves Cable's awareness of the possibility of breaking the cultural barriers between gender roles. Madame Delicieuse is allowed to "charmingly" influence life around her by reconciling her lover to his estranged father, and though not allowed to vote — something she complains about in the story — she challenges local politics by writing an article in the newspaper that will seriously affect one of the candidates. In spite of the sentimental ending and Madame's acceptance of feminine conventions, her determination and strength of purpose stand out as promising features that reappear in Cable's best writing.

Cable's concern for the condition of women is intricately connected to his dramatizations of the racial struggle in the South. His most challenging heroines are mostly women of mixed color, so that his feminism can hardly be disengaged from his explorations of racial oppression, as we see in such early women characters as Madame John in "'Tite Poulette," Madame Delphine in *Madame Delphine*, and Palmyre Philosophe in *The Grandissimes*. Both "'Tite Poulette" and *Madame Delphine* dramatize similar conflicts and reflect the deep connections between racial and women's issues in Cable's writing. In both, the innocent and helpless daughters of quadroons whose white male protectors have died fall in love with and are loved by white men who wish to marry them. Given the laws and attitudes toward miscegenation at the time, no woman of mixed blood could aspire to marry a white man. In both stories the quadroon mothers end up renouncing their motherhood and lying about their daughters' white parenthood. In the first, the reader is left uninformed about the actual truth or falsity of Madame John's declaration. In the second, the quadroon is described as intentionally lying about her daughter's parenthood and race, aided by a priest. When, in order to assure their daughters' marriages to the men who love them, the mothers in these two stories declare their daughters to be white, they undertake dangerous initiatives to prevent the tragic destinies that await women of mixed race in Southern society. In both stories, but particularly in *Madame Delphine*, these mothers are turned into rich literary heroines by the complexity and intensity of their feelings in the difficult processes they undergo before defying the inhuman laws that tragically limit the lives of women of mixed color. Cable allows both quadroons to develop a powerful and precise rhetoric in the expression of their heroism when they undertake the tragic sacrifice of renouncing their right to be acknowledged as mothers of their own children.

Though the narratives are written six years apart, and though *Madame Delphine* is the more artistically consistent of the two, both are dominated by powerful mother figures, and in both cases the daughters remain conventional shadows in the background. There is nothing particularly new or challenging in Cable's treatment of the two young women. Both 'Tite Poulette and her lover, Koppig, are inarticulate and conventional (Petry, 100–197; Rubin, 100); and Olive and Vignevielle in *Madame Delphine* are subject to dated processes of narrative idealization (Petry, 24–49; Rubin, 102–103). Cable does not become an innovative artist until he engages in rendering his strong women characters with a kind of heroism that can only take place outside the conventional love plot. Such is the case of the two mothers, who, unlike their daughters, become truly creative and eloquent when they are allowed to invent ways out of their misery, when they can devise the means and the words to escape the injustice to which they are submitted, when they are allowed to act as imaginative characters transforming their world at the cost of their own happiness — and even life itself in the case of Madame Delphine.

Perhaps the best example Cable's writing provides of the potential as well as of the limitations that women characters impose on his art can be found in the women he creates in his finest novel, *The Grandissimes*. There are four women characters: two are of mixed race, two are white; critics agree that the black characters are far more interesting than their white counterparts, who, as in " 'Tite Poulette" and *Madame Delphine*, are mother and daughter (Elfenbein, 47). The two white women inhabit a double love plot, the more sentimental and old-fashioned part of the novel. The two black women represent subversive figures who openly defy white society. Aurora and Clotilde, the white mother and daughter, are defined by their language, and Cable emphasizes their ladylike femininity and their sexual/verbal appeal by having them express themselves half in Creole French and half in English, a tentative rhetoric often interrupted with a meaningless "ha ha ha." Rather than increasing their attractiveness, their almost childish speech proves them hardly capable of rendering a critical understanding of themselves or of their world. But in spite of their weakness, the writer's intuition about the potential in women characters emerges when he allows them, in some sporadic but important moments, to openly question their limited opportunities: "It is not so hard to live . . . but it is hard to be ladies. . . . After all . . . what troubles us is not how to make a living, but how to get a living without making it."[16] Unlike the powerful mothers, Madame John and Madame Delphine, Aurora and Clotilde never dream of breaking out of the awful conventions that reduce women's destinies. In the end Aurora perversely teaches her daughter how to take advantage of women's only power, sexual power: "Clotilde, my beautiful daughter . . . I tell you now, because you don't know, and it is my duty as your mother to tell you — the meanest wickedness a woman can do in all the bad, bad world is to look ugly in bed!" The young widow is allowed to express the disadvantages of marriage for women (288), but in the end mother and daughter are romantically saved by their beauty and their sexuality; in the traditional romantic plot, they both marry the right, rich hero, although, as Charles Swann has noted, "Cable . . . subverts a sentimental narrative by showing what lies behind and generates the feminine surface charm." [17] Neither of the two black women characters marry. Their destiny is far more tragic: the more unconventional Clemence, whose role has been compared to that of the Shakespearean fool,[18] is brutally murdered by a member of the Grandissime family; the other, Palmyre, recognized by many critics as the most memorable character, disappears in France at the end of the novel. According to William Bedford Clark, "Cable has transformed the usually passive heroine of the 'tragic mulatto' tradition — more sinned against than sinning — into a terrifying physical realization of the spirit of righteous wrath." [19] Critics have dealt at length with Palmyre, with her exotic beauty and powerful sensuality, capable of upsetting even as self-controlled a character as the Anglo-American Frowenfeld. Unlike the two white heroines in the novel, Palmyre is not reduced to the charming verbal hesitations of bilingualism; like her self, her speech is straightforward and consistent. Depicted as simultaneously admirable and dangerous in her "barbaric and magnetic beauty," she paradoxically possesses "the purity of true womanhood" (60). Although in part stereotypical, she achieves a mythical dimension by her determined expression of a fierce unhappiness and unyielding rebellion. Her only possible equal in the text is the legendary black hero Bras Coupé, but she is a far more elaborate character. Unlike the white women in the novel, Palmyre refuses to come to terms with the prevailing ideological order; she stands alone, a powerful and menacing figure to the end.

Cable's contradictions in his representation of Palmyre demonstrate his own many personal uncertainties and his weakness for Southern sensuality. Simultaneously fascinated by the mulatto women and critical of white men's attitudes toward them, he defines Palmyre as "sensual, svelte, predatory. . . . the scene in which Joseph Frowenfelf goes to her quarters . . . is full of repressed sexuality" (Rubin, 91). Elfenbein suggests that Palmyre deconstructs Cable's message of peace and possible negotiation between different groups and races (64). Palmyre's unmitigated violence and her desire for revenge — "The lesson she would have taught the giant [Bras Coupé] was Insurrection" (Cable, 184) —

seem to contradict Cable's apparent purposes as well as the comic mood that dominates many parts of the book.[20] But her complexities allow her to grow into a radically new literary character, remarkably independent from available models of women, particularly of colored women, in Southern literature. Cable's initial impulse to investigate the resources of the genre of local color, his daring articulation of racial oppression, and his early challenge to the function of female characters, make him finally the exceptional writer he has recently been recognized to be.

"Dipped in Tears and Blood": Elliott, the Old South, and the New Woman

Sarah Barnwell Elliott is a later regionalist who begun writing about the South after having successfully published many short stories and a female Bildungsroman, *The Felmeres* (1879), and who, besides her regional stories, wrote several other novels well known at the time: *Jerry* (1891), a story about the Gilded Age; *Fortune's Vassall* (1899), a brief female Künstlerroman; and *The Making of Jane* (1901), a long novel also centered in the tensions between independence and marriage, love and professional fulfillment for women at the turn of the century. Reflecting the presence of the New Woman in American culture, Elliott's revisions of women heroines extend the possibilities suggested by Cable in his best regionalist fiction and contribute to the investigation of Southern culture, including racial conflict.

Originally from Beaufort, South Carolina, Elliott was the daughter of an Episcopalian bishop who moved his family to Savannah in 1852. After Bishop Elliott's death in 1866, his family settled in Sewanee, Tennessee, in 1870, where Elliott's father had been one of the founders of the University of the South. Except for a few years in New York, two journeys to Europe, and some months in Texas with her brother Robert, the writer spent most of her life in Sewanee, in close relation with her very intellectual family. Though she was able to attend university at Johns Hopkins only during the summer of 1886 as an extracurricular student, Elliott in 1913 became the first woman to receive an honorary degree from the University of the South, after having become an acclaimed writer and the president of the Tennessee Equal Suffrage Association in 1912. She is still remembered for her liberal views among the older professors of the University of the South. Clara Childs MacKenzie observes that it was Constance Fenimore Woolson, well known for her friendship with Henry James, who in 1887 suggested to Elliott the writing of Southern stories.[21] Because stories about the South had become very popular, Woolson, like other local colorists and short story writers from outside the South, had also worked in this genre. As with Cable's most innovative interpretation of the South, Elliott's version is consistently realistic, critical, and wide in scope; she deals with many aspects of Southern life, including in particular the huge changes that were taking place in the New South. Like Cable, she often provides models of possible social harmony, but, unlike Cable, she has received little critical attention. After publishing an introduction to the author in 1980, MacKenzie collected the writer's Southern stories in *Some Data and Other Stories from Southern Life* (1981). Apart from a few isolated references, the first contemporary critic to have become interested in her regional writing is Nancy A. Walker, who emphasizes Elliott's feeling of displacement in several stories, as well as her strong sense of place, particularly in the stories located in Kingshaven or Deep Haven, Elliott's own lost Yoknapathawpha, the Beaufort tidewater area in her native South Carolina.[22]

Though belonging to two very aristocratic families, Elliott's parents were also learned and liberal, and she had probably acquired a considerable distance from Southern plantation life long before the South was defeated. Like Cable's, Elliott's best Southern stories confirm the writer's simultaneous involvement with and distance from the Old South, her talent for combining deeply felt nostalgia with character analysis and rigorous research into the causes of Southern defeat. The scope of her dramatization of both past and present is broad, and it includes an analysis of tensions in the New South. Writing about situations affecting people of all classes, she explores conflicts related to the practice of justice in the postbellum South and to the difficulties of adapting to the social, economic, and political changes brought about by losing the war.

Critics have privileged Cable's progressive racial attitudes (see Rubin, 19; Elfenbein, 51), but I wish to argue that some of

Elliott's stories are also profoundly concerned with race, and that, though she was never as outspoken about racial matters as Cable was in his essays "The Silent South" (1885) and "The Negro Question" (1890), her response is as radical as his. Writing at a later date, Elliott published her Southern stories when racial relations had worsened — to the point of forcing Cable to leave the South. By this time, state legislation, the famous Black Codes, racial violence, and Jim Crow had precipitated "the collapse of Reconstruction ideals," securing white supremacy in the South and the reenslavement of those freed after the war.[23] Few writers faced the tragedies of racism in this cultural climate; writers of local color tended to evade racial conflicts by depicting African Americans in conventional terms.[24]

In a context of legitimized prejudice, sentimental interpretations of race relations, and only rare and very subdued voices of dissent, Elliott's approach to the matter deserves careful attention. Of the four stories she wrote on racial matters in her collection of Southern stories, only one, "An Incident," was published in her day. None of her personal documents offers reasons, but one feels tempted to hypothesize that publishers might have considered two of the stories, "A Speculation in Futures" and "The Heart of It," too daring in their inquiry into racial conflicts, too skeptical of the accepted arguments in favor of segregation. Elliott's suggestion of the intrinsic superficiality of skin color and her subversive fictionalization of white prejudice, particularly in "The Heart of It," openly challenges common beliefs of her time about race. Only in "Old Ties" can Elliott's representation of racial relations be read as conventional and subject to the "paralyzing contradiction" of white liberal writers. But in this case the author carefully points out at the beginning that she is referring to bygone ways and times, when "the old plantations of the South Eastern coast retained many of their old-time customs, and the bonds between master and man were still tinctured with responsibility on the one hand and dependence on the other, and through all there ran a thread of affection."[25]

Elliott's attitude toward race emerges explicitly in a letter to her mother from Paris in 1907: "Yesterday I saw a very pretty French woman leaning on the arm of a negro man. . . . I was with a Yale Ph.D. . . . to whom I had been explaining the negro problem. I showed him the couple as an object lesson — he did not like it."[26]

Some of Elliott's stories unsentimentally echo the proximity between early feminism and abolitionism.[27] Though she represented the understanding between white women and slaves on the old plantation, Elliott also wrote very critically about the viciousness with which African Americans could be treated both before and after Reconstruction. "An Incident" (1899) dramatizes the actual ways in which white violence is inflicted upon black persons, but, most interestingly, it also explicates the origins of the legendary violence attributed to the African American male in his awareness of a white woman's irrational fear of him and his race. The story opens by dramatically reproducing the postbellum atmosphere saturated by whites' unconscious fear of African Americans: the simultaneous disappearance, during her husband's short absence, of a young white wife and their black hired man in the wild, watery geography of a Southern tidewater village. On the husband's return, his search with the help of his neighbors and the sheriff evokes the usual late-nineteenth-century response of white men to their own fears: the group determines to kill the black man without a trial as soon as they find him. The negro is easily found in a common postbellum site, a nearby abandoned plantation; a member of the search party observes, "Nothin' but niggers have lived there since the war, an' that nigger's there, I'll bet." Though they all believe the black man to be guilty of the white woman's disappearance, the sheriff, who is new in the area, decides the black man is not to die "by Judge Lynch's court" (133) and opposes the threatening townsmen. The sheriff's great skill and quick action in hiding the accused man prevents the townsmen from killing him when they break into the courthouse, and the menace of violence is halted by the arrival of a telegram from the wife, announcing that she is safe. Upon her return, the wife offers a confused description of her reasons for having run away: she had sent the black servant to the woods with a hatchet to make a broom, and, when she went out and encountered him, she became suddenly terrified: "And then — something, I don't know what; I saw him — saw him coming — saw him stealing up behind me — with the hatchet in his hand, and a look — a look! And everybody gone. . . . I was paralyzed . . . *and when he saw me looking he stopped.* The next moment he threw the hatchet at me, and begun to run towards me. The hatchet struck my foot, and the blow roused me, and I sprang into the boat" (146, emphasis added).

The story's ultimate realism lies in its sad ending; though the sheriff and the judge prevent the mob from lynching the black man, he is nevertheless sentenced to life imprisonment. Some years later an older white woman on a missionary visit asks the black convict: "And how did you get such a dreadful sentence?" In his ignorance and simplicity the black man proves to have understood the simple truth: "I ent do much, ma'm; I des scare a white lady" (148). Beyond the story's main purpose in recording the legal treatment received by African Americans in the South after the war and the tensions between the law and the brutal tradition of lynching, what is most innovative in this story is Elliott's definition of white fear as the origin of black violence. Nothing seems to disturb the negro cutting wood until the white woman's gaze makes him conscious of his strange power over her. The moment of horror and madness is triggered by the white woman's consciousness, and, according to records of actual cases of rape at the time (Taylor, 10, 11), the wife's reaction reflects white women's exaggerated and uncontrolled fear of being assaulted and raped by African American men. Elliott's story dares to handle a delicate question, but it goes beyond representing the viciousness of lynching in its subtle understanding of the complex feelings of hatred and fear many whites felt toward African Americans in the South.

Elliott's critical perspective on matters of Southern race relations is reinforced in "A Speculation in Futures" and "The Heart of It," two daring mulatto-centered stories on the subject of miscegenation. Though racial mixing had been initially accepted during the eighteenth century,[28] as the nineteenth century proceeded, legal codes tried to find justification for racial segregation in scientific explanations, and Darwinism was used to confirm blacks' inferiority by locating their evolution at an earlier stage than that of whites. Though such pseudoscientific notions soon began to be questioned, Herbert Spencer's Lamarckian reading of Darwinism helped to fix and reinforce racist convictions and essentialist interpretations of racial difference by analogizing social processes to "biological laws."[29] In relation to mulattos, "The fear of mongrelization . . . pervaded the radical rhetoric about miscegenation. . . . The mulatto was held by some social theorists to be an unnatural hybrid . . . a perversion of the organic development toward higher, more pure racial forms" (Sundquist, 64–66). Miscegenation became a matter of great anxiety to white Southerners, as local Southern laws punishing mixed marriages demonstrate (Elfenbein, 13).

Though miscegenation was a subject "determinately kept out of sight in the South" (Wilson, 563), there are some interesting fictionalizations in Southern literature of its tragic consequences.[30] Like Cable's, Elliott's attitudes toward the subject are contradictory: on the one hand, she devotes two of her most interesting Southern stories to show the irrationality of whites' response to miscegenation; on the other hand, the stories continue to consider miscegenation in conventionally tragic terms and as a source of disgrace. But both stories manage to dramatize whites' ultimately subconscious and uncontrolled fear toward mixture. The seriousness of Elliott's approach in her acknowledgment of the inhumanity and unfairness of irrational rejection can be read as an important step in coming to terms with the South's worst nightmare.

One of the narrative patterns repeated in stories of miscegenation appears in Kate Chopin's "Desirée's Baby" (1892), in which the skin color of a newborn child reveals the unknown racial heritage of one of its parents. In the first of her stories on miscegenation, "A Speculation in Futures," Elliott offers her own version of this pattern, which she augments considerably by focusing on the actual living conditions of what was then considered the tragic mulatto. While Chopin writes a protofeminist story to exemplify the victimization of a young wife by her insensitive and ignorant husband, Elliott is far more interested in the social and personal consequences of miscegenation in the South. The story is divided into two parts. In the first, the author introduces an "old family" living in "an old city" somewhere "in the South-atlantic coast where swamps abound" (27). When the story begins, the discussion of racial inheritance is subtly but immediately introduced by the plantation overseer who is talking to his master, the father of two grown sons, about genetic surprises in horse breeding. By association of ideas, the overseer mentions the loss of a slave, "the best horse-breaker of any of the plantations" (28). The slave has been exchanged for a woman octoroon by the eldest son of the family, a young man educated abroad who has become an abolitionist and plans to secretly marry the octoroon. But before these events are made explicit to his family, father and son discuss slavery, the father voicing the standard beliefs of the dominant race: "I hope for gradual emancipation . . . to free all is to endanger our civilization" (29). What becomes increasingly relevant is the Southern horror of miscegenation: "The lower class of foreign emigrants might intermarry with them — never the Anglo-Saxon, thank God — in this country" (29). When his son lets him know he plans to marry an octoroon, the father's first concern is that his son will "breed a mongrel race . . . a sin against the laws of God — a sin against nature!" (31).

The immediate consequences of Edward's marriage are isolation and disgrace. At the beginning of the second part of the story his mother suggests that within the Southern code only death can expiate the sin of miscegenation. A year later, the family and servants are eagerly expecting the birth of Edward's child, but life has been hard and sad for Edward since his marriage. Unable to sell his plantation, he lives in poverty, and not only have his own mother, father, and brother rejected him, but even his beloved black mammy, Elsie, the slave who brought him up, passionately hates his octoroon wife ("dat white nigger" [33]) and has set a voodoo spell on them. Elsie is the first of the family to see the child when it is born; she reports in loud despair, "De chile is black, m'am" (36). As his mother has suggested, Edward must die in a world that cannot accept his action. He chooses to kill himself in his childhood bed, in the lost space of memory and desire. Like Palmyre Philosophe, Cable's mulatto heroine in *The Grandissimes* (1880), a character who survives only in France, Elliott's Edward also dreams of escaping to Paris: "I shall sell my land, free my Negroes, go to Europe, to Paris — there are no prejudices there!" (31). Though there is indeed a remote hope of a better life in France, the irrational interiorization of hatred toward the black race must necessarily end tragically in the South.

Elliott's analysis of the negro question culminates in another tragic story of miscegenation, "The Heart of It," one of her best, also unpublished in her day. The story evokes once again the Southern scenario of Reconstruction in the lush and sensual world of the impoverished postbellum plantation in an unspecified rural environment. The first innovation in this second story is that it is narrated from the perspective of a young orphan mulatto girl, significantly named Hagar ("an alien . . . an outcast" [122]) by her dead father. The reader discovers in Hagar's monologue that the girl had never questioned her whiteness until a few hours before the beginning of the story when, after informing her aunt (and guardian) that she and her white neighbor were in love and planned to marry, the aunt asserts that they could not because her dead mother was a mulatto, and she carries "one drop of Negro blood" (122). Soon afterward, Hagar runs away in the darkness of a rainy night. In the passionate despair of her discovery, Hagar awakens to the memory of how her aunt often used to talk to her about racial difference, and she realizes for the first time how racial hatred had been subtly and constantly taught to her throughout her childhood. Hagar's memory records her lifelong instinctive and unconfessed antagonism toward her aunt and provides the reader with two incompatible approaches to racial difference: the white woman passionately defining her aversion to the black race as an instinct, and the girl, who had always thought herself white, suddenly realizing she has been perversely taught to hate blacks.

In Hagar's recollection the aunt's insistence in defining her hatred as "Race instinct!" is balanced by her own memory of defining it as "Prejudice" (117), and the story becomes an attempt to redefine the dangerous meanings of the aunt's term. Elliott seems quite certain of the inadequacy of the scientific explanations that tried to justify segregation, and the harsh aunt becomes a clear and passionate symbol of racial hatred, agonizing in her intolerance, in search of the nonexistent argument with which to justify it, since "the only possible answer [to definitions of racial difference] had to be one which claimed some fundamental difference between master and slave . . . [for] all racial arguments ultimately ran counter to the obvious genetic similarities between whites and blacks."[31]

Centering the narrative with Hagar's perspective offers a radical move toward a more complete understanding of prejudice's tragic consequences. Also, since Hagar, though technically black, has always thought, lived, and loved as if she were a white person, the story blurs racial difference and makes social prejudice increasingly difficult to justify. Elliott uses the young girl's sudden obligation to become an Other — to transform her identity from white to black — to explore socially constructed racial boundaries. Hagar's change of perspective allows for her privileged position; she must take into account the feelings of both races: "Never until that moment had she thought of them as having any feeling on the subject of being black" (118). The memory of her long and obsessive observation of blacks' behavior on her aunt's plantation, and of the implied political meanings of their different discourses, mixes in her consciousness with her aunt's unreasonable hatred, making her own discourse highly experimental in the fictional rhetoric of race, for black and white perspectives overlap. The girl remembers Lou, the young educated daughter of an old slave, whose references to "the awfulness of amalgamation" offer a frightening answer to Hagar's own conventionally provoking words on matters of race: "You mean that we are an inferior race . . . we are a little backward . . . it is a great tragedy, an awful tragedy! Yes, and you don't care. . . . But there is an outlet, an outlet to this terrible tragedy, yes, we cross over to you whites! . . . We cross over and you don't know it, ah ah!" (115–116). The story is deeply committed to questioning the arbitrariness of racial boundaries, as well as to evoking the human suffering that they necessitate, for racial intolerance becomes a matter of life and death.

Yet, in spite of its daring, as the story proceeds it reveals the degree to which racism had been insurmountably interiorized, for Hagar accepts the horror of her mixed blood and is ultimately abandoned by the writer, suffering loneliness, lovelessness, and possibly death. Elliott can only imagine her heroine's self-destruction, while the aunt's fierce racism, though subverted, seems finally almost understood, though not justified. Although Elliott may have decided not to publish her stories of miscegenation, to withdraw her lucid inquiry into the true reasons for racial segregation, her simultaneous gesture of speech and silence, of action and withdrawal, occurs in a confusing historical and aesthetic context. With the precedent of Cable's exile, the final uncertainty of Elliott's unpublished stories could be read as a sad act of Realpolitik. Nevertheless, her choice to give voice to a character who is simultaneously "white" and "black" allows her to suggest the tenuous nature of racial difference and the perversity of its social construction.

Finally, Elliott's attitude to the problems of the New South is never submissive, and though she covers a wide variety of important social and political aspects of Southern life, her response is never that of passive recognition and regret. Her stories work intensely to understand Southern cultural problems at the turn of the century and to suggest possible improvements. Like Cable's, her work becomes highly relevant to history and politics, though, of course, in the ways available to the artist as defined by William Gass: "The artist's revolutionary activity is of a different kind [from the politician's]. He is concerned with consciousness, and he makes changes there."[32] Both Cable's and Elliott's writing is clearly concerned with changing readers' consciousness of the many matters that made life in the South difficult, matters such as the nostalgia for old privilege and the survival of traditional ideas of honor and justice. Their best stories challenge the limits of theories of racial difference and initiate an honest analysis of the nature of racial discrimination. Though conditioned by the contradictions suffered by the Southern writer, and perhaps sometimes silenced by fear, their innovative regionalist work recognizes the need for Southern society to transform itself. Above all, their stories deconstruct the idealized nature of the national dream of harmony and integration that many writers and politicians were proposing in their definitions of the South and its relation to the nation at the turn of the century.

NOTES

1. Kilcup, "The Conversation of 'The Whole Family': Gender, Politics, and Aesthetics in Literary Tradition," 1–31 above.

2. Myra Jehlen, "Archimedes and the Paradox of Feminist Criticism," *The Signs Reader*, ed. Elizabeth Abel and Emily K. Abel (Chicago: University of Chicago Press, 1983), 84.

3. Pamela Glenn Menke, "Chopin's Sensual Sea and Cable's Ravished Land: Sexts, Signs, and Gender Narrative," *Cross-Roads* 3.1 (Fall 1994–Winter 1995): 81, emphasis added.

4. Elaine Sargent Apthorp, "Sentiment, Naturalism, and the Female Regionalist," *Legacy* 7.1 (1990): 11.

5. Barbara C. Ewell, "Changing Places: Women, the Old South; or, What Happens When Local Color Becomes Regionalism," *Amerikastudien* 42.2 (1997): 163, 164.

6. David M. Jordan, *New World Regionalism: Literature in the Americas* (Toronto: University of Toronto Press, 1994), 52.

7. Richard H. Brodhead, "Regionalism and the Upper Class," *Rethinking Class: Literary Studies and Social Formations*, ed. Wai Chee Dimock and Michael T. Gilmore (New York: Columbia University Press, 1994), 163,

146, 151; Judith Fetterley and Marjorie Pryse, *American Women Regionalists, 1850–1910* (New York: Norton, 1992); Karen L. Kilcup, ed., *Nineteenth-Century American Women Writers: An Anthology* (Oxford: Blackwell, 1997); Marjorie Pryse, "'Distilling Essences': Regionalism and 'Women's Culture,'" *American Literary Realism* 25.2 (1993): 12; Pryse, "Reading Regionalism: The 'Difference' It Makes," in *Regionalism Reconsidered: New Approaches to the Field*, ed. David Jordan (New York: Garland, 1994).

8. Mary Ellis Gibson, "Southern Women Writers and Literary Tradition," *Mississippi Quarterly* 46.4 (1993): 644–645.

9. Alfred Bendixen, "Cable's *The Grandissimes*: A Literary Pioneer Confronts the Southern Tradition," *Southern Quarterly* 18.4 (1980): 28, 32; Edmund Wilson, *Patriotic Gore: Studies in the Literature of the American Civil War* (Oxford: Oxford University Press, 1966), 557.

10. Helen Taylor, *Gender, Race, and Region in the Writings of Grace King, Ruth McEnery Stuart, and Kate Chopin* (Baton Rouge: Louisiana State University Press, 1989), 83, 165, 159. See also Anne Goodwyn Jones, *Tomorrow Is Another Day: The Woman Writer in the South 1859–1936* (Baton Rouge: Louisiana State University Press, 1981); Anna Shannon Elfenbein, "George Cable: The Stereotype Resurrected," in *Women on the Color Line: Evolving Stereotypes and the Writings of George Washington Cable, Grace King, Kate Chopin* (Charlottesville: University Press of Virginia, 1989); Anne Firor Scott, *The Southern Lady: From Pedestal to Politics* (Charlottesville: University Press of Virginia, 1995).

11. Julia R. Tutweiler, "The Southern Woman in New York," part 1, *Bookman* (February 1904): 634.

12. According to Louis D. Rubin, the lady was Dora Richards Miller. Rubin, *George Washington Cable: The Life and Times of a Southern Heretic* (New York: Pegasus, 1969), 195. George Washington Cable, *Strange True Stories of Louisiana* (1888; reprint, Gretna, La.: Pelican, 1994), 17.

13. See John Cleman, *George Washington Cable Revisited* (New York: Twayne, 1996), 14–15.

14. Rachel Blau DuPlessis, *Writing Beyond the Ending: Narrative Strategies of Twentieth-Century Women's Writing* (Bloomington: Indiana University Press, 1985).

15. Alice Hall Petry, *A Genius in His Way: The Art of Cable's Old Creole Days* (Rutherford, N.J.: Fairleigh Dickinson University Press, 1988), 61.

16. George Washington Cable, *The Grandissimes: A Story of Creole Life* (London: Penguin, 1988) 255.

17. Charles Swann, "The Price of Charm: The Heroines of *The Grandissimes*," *Essays in Poetics* 13.1 (1988): 87.

18. Schöling Tipping, "'The Sinking Plantation-House': Cable's Narrative Method in *The Grandissimes*," *Essays in Poetics* 13.1 (1988): 76.

19. William Bedford Clark, quoted in Elfenbein, *Women on the Color Line*, 48.

20. Donald A. Ringe, "Narrative Voice in Cable's *Grandissimes*," *Southern Quarterly* 18.4 (1980): 13–22; William Bedford Clark, "Humor in Cable's *The Grandissimes*," *Southern Quarterly* 18.4 (1980): 51–59.

21. Clara Childs MacKenzie, *Sarah Barnwell Elliott* (Boston: Twayne, 1980), 42, 84. See Constance Fenimore Woolson's "Rodman the Keeper," "Felipa," and "In the Cotton Country."

22. Nancy A. Walker, "Living with Difference: Nineteenth-Century Southern Women Writers," in *Nineteenth-Century American Women Writers: A Critical Reader*, ed. Karen L. Kilcup (Oxford: Blackwell, 1998), 33–46.

23. Eric J. Sundquist, "Mark Twain and Homer Plessy," in *Mark Twain's Pudd'nhead Wilson: Race, Conflict, and Culture*, ed. Susan Gillman and Forrest G. Robinson (Durham: Duke University Press, 1990), 50.

24. For some examples of other writers' depictions of African Americans, see Grace King, *Monsieur Motte*, "A Crippled Hope," "The Little Convent Girl," and "Bonne Maman"; Kate Chopin, "A Little Free Mulatto," "Desirée's Baby," "La Belle Zoraïde," and "At the 'Cadian Ball." For critics' views of these and other stories, see Taylor, 156; Clara Juncker, "Grace King: Feminist, Southern Style," *Southern Quarterly* 26.3 (1988): 15–30; Myra Jehlen, "The Ties That Bind: Race and Sex in *Pudd'nhead Wilson*," in Gillman and Robinson, 120.

25. Clara Childs MacKenzie, ed. *Some Data and Other Stories of Southern Life*, by Sarah Barnwell Elliott (Bratenahl, Ohio: Seaford, 1981), 149; see 158. All Elliott references are to this volume.

26. Sarah Barnwell Elliott to Charlotte Bull Barnwell, 14 December 1907, Jessie Ball duPont Library, University of the South, Sewanee, Tennessee.

27. Eric Foner, *A Short History of Reconstruction, 1863–1877* (New York: Harper & Row, 1990), 193; see Jones, 29; Taylor, 15.

28. See, for example, William Byrd II, quoted in J. V. Ridgeley, *Nineteenth-Century Southern Literature* (Knoxville: University Press of Kentucky, 1980), 10: "For my part, I must be of opinion . . . that there is but one way of converting these poor infidels . . . and that is charitably to intermarry with them. . . . All nations of men have the same natural dignity, and we all know that very bright talents may be lodged under a very dark skin."

29. Ruth Meyer, "'Ther's somethin' in blood, after all': Late Nineteenth-Century Fiction and the Rhetoric of Race," in *REAL: Yearbook of*

Research in English and American Literature, ed. Winfried Fluck (Tübingen: Gunter Narr Verlag, 1995), 122.

30. James Kinney, *Amalgamation: Race, Sex and Rhetoric in the Nineteenth-Century American Novel* (London: Greenwood Press, 1985).

31. Anthony Pagden, "The Children of Ham: How Slavery Rose and Fell in the New World," review of Robin Blackburn's *The Making of New World Slavery: From the Baroque to the Modern, 1492–1800, Times Literary Supplement*, 2 May 1997, pp. 3, 4.

32. William H. Gass, "The Artist and Society," in *Fictions and the Figures of Life* (New York: Knopf, 1970), 288.

Developing Dialogues

Sister Carrie and *The Awakening*: The Clothed, the Unclothed, and the Woman Undone

JANET BEER

Discussions of Kate Chopin's *The Awakening* (1899) and Theodore Dreiser's *Sister Carrie* (1900) often recount the critical hostility that followed — and even preceded — the publication of the novels. Although the degree and extent to which Kate Chopin was affected by adverse criticism, either personally or professionally, has often been overstated, the almost wholly negative reviews of her novel[1] communicate to the modern reader, one hundred years later, a clear picture of the specific nature of the outrage committed against prevailing morality. Chopin's overstepping of the boundaries of decorum in the presentation of her heroine gave precisely discernible offense to contemporary reviewers.

I intend not to query these critical responses but rather to concur with the essential validity of readings that viewed Chopin's novel as full of disturbing and "unpleasant truths."[2] The novel was deeply disruptive of prevailing social mores, with Chopin's heroine dissident in every way from received notions of womanly propriety. Chopin built into the text an indirect acknowledgment of how few of her 1899 readers would be able to see beyond the breach of bourgeois morality — in Dr. Mandelet's words to the unhappy Edna toward the end of her life: "I am not going to ask for your confidence. I will only say that if ever you felt moved to give it to me, perhaps I might help you. I know I would understand, and I tell you there are not many who would — not many, my dear" (105). Alongside Chopin's picture of the "soul that dares and defies" (61), I want to examine Dreiser's *Sister Carrie*, which received comparable — though not so consistently denunciatory — reviews. Dreiser never tired of talking up his novel as having had a serious brush with censorship before publication,[3] but, I would contend, the text does not, in essentials, present as significant a challenge to the status quo in its picture of womanhood or relations between the sexes as *The Awakening* does. As Donna Campbell observes, "Edna Pontellier follows a path of sensual self-indulgence similar to that of men like Vandover and Theron Ware, and the end of her naturalistic 'degeneration' is the same as theirs: an excess of unexplored possibilities leads to an end of all possibilities, followed by actual or spiritual death."[4] When Edna Pontellier terminates her performance as wife and mother, Kate Chopin issues her most substantial refutation of any statute of limitation upon the proper province of women's writing.

I intend to scrutinize the manner in which Chopin and Dreiser present their heroines as women who can express something of the confusion and anxiety about the situation of woman in American society at the turn into the twentieth century.[5] Although their location in "the" canon — or in competing canons of masculine and feminine writers — has varied over time, these writers problematize matters, ranging from women's sexuality to women at work, that have been oversimplified; both seek to expose women unloosed from the coercive power of essentialism. Edna and Carrie aim to establish an identity at odds with the one by which they are classified — married or fallen woman — and thus, within both texts, the ontology of female stereotype is interrogated and revised. At the heart of any question of identity in this social world is essentialism, and Chopin and Dreiser, in releasing their women from stereotype, challenge received notions of the binary opposition of whore or wife — and indeed, in Chopin's case, the binary opposition of male and female sexuality — and replace them with possibility and multiplicity. Both writers acknowledge, within the fabric of the tale, that they are writing for a society that has very particular notions of what the story of a woman's life should look like, but that such a story is unlikely to express either the contingent or the random. To incorporate within their texts a recognition of the inadequacy of the standard narrative is therefore to critique such narratives.

"I Am Yours Truly": *Sister Carrie*

In *Sister Carrie*, Dreiser supplies his readers with what is, in many ways, a deeply conservative portrait of a woman. However, although an intrinsic part of that conservatism derives from his reliance upon reader familiarity with narratives about the inevitable fate of the fallen woman, he also engages in a dialectic with those narratives that challenges easy assumptions about the destination of the woman who topples from grace and remains unrepentant and, indeed, unpunished. There are a variety of received tales of girls and women at work within the larger narrative sweep of the novel, and the most obvious of these opens the story. As Carrie completes her first train journey, Dreiser tells us that she is approaching not only the great city but the great moral divide in any girl's existence: "Either she falls into saving hands and becomes better, or she rapidly assumes the cosmopolitan standard of virtue and becomes worse. Of an intermediate balance, under the circumstances, there is no possibility."[6] The story seems, therefore, to be closed to other interpretations, for we are offered a narrowly focused moral judgment, not the openness of a tale with the potential for multiple meaning. Carrie's first protector, Drouet, traveling on the same train, is attracted both by the simplicity of this country girl and the concomitant opportunity to make something of her, a desire that she awakens in all those who gaze upon her for any length of time. It becomes obvious, all too soon, that the only "saving hands" extended to Carrie, however, are hands made tired and dull by toil, by mere subsistence, and, most crucially, by an unquestioning adherence to a conventional morality that can express itself only in the clichés of a dream sequence that has Carrie variously falling down mineshafts or into deep water. These are hands that have nothing to offer her except equal or unequal toil. The other beckoning hands are bejeweled and insigniaed, have soft ten-dollar bills to pass from palm to palm, and seduce Carrie with the ease of both acquisition and transfer of assets. The traveling salesman, Drouet, snaps Carrie up as surely as if he had spotted her on sale at a warehouse. She is a doll, a mannequin for him to dress up, for she is "really very pretty. Even then, in her commonplace garb, her figure was evidently not bad and her eyes were large and gentle" (60), and, once he has transformed her, she will pass

out of his hands into another's hands. Carrie never refutes ownership; she merely moves, or is carried, onwards, seemingly following the primrose path to perdition but actually arriving at the
sumptuously appointed "Aladdin's cave" (456) of the Wellington
Hotel, where she is asked to represent fashionable society for its
owners.

A further development in the essentialist narrative critiqued
within the novel has Carrie following the career trajectory of
a prostitute. She comes to the city and is lost, as surely as one of
Paul Dresser's sentimentalized country girls. She falls immediately into the arms of a protector who takes her virginity and continuing sexual favors in return for clothing, shelter, and amusement, and who puts her on show to the man who will be her next
client or protector: "I'll introduce you" (80). She is then stolen
away by this new protector, bundled across state, and indeed, national lines, and is kept by him; she subsequently offers herself on
the open market as an actress, having changed her name, as would
any prostitute on entry into the brothel, and, ultimately, finds ease
and comfort in a friendship with another member of the chorus
line, Lola, mirroring the homosocial relationships many prostitutes form with other women in their trade.[7]

Dreiser's picture of Carrie thus conforms to many conventional conditions and developments in the career of the fallen
woman, but he absolves her of any of the physical consequences
that might be expected to follow from her lifestyle — sexual appetite, pregnancy, sexually transmitted disease — none of these
appear to touch her.[8] Dreiser does not portray her as debased by
her chosen lifestyle, as sordid or predatory, as victim or victimizer,
but as a woman so unaffected by her experiences that she can be
described as "quiet and reserved" (478) when at the height of her
fame as an actress. In this way he incorporates the standard story
of the prostitute's life in his narrative but defuses it by closing
down — indeed, throwing out — the morality that had seemed to
be the only hermeneutic tool on offer at the beginning of Carrie's
journey. The deviant subculture, apparently the location for all
those who operate outside the limits of the accepted moral code,
is mockingly shown to be a place where the woman operates as a
little homemaker, producing rarebits and arranging knickknacks,
or reading European naturalist novels, rocking in her chair, the

model of quiet domesticity rather than a representative of a defiant or degenerate lifestyle.

The secret of Carrie's success — and, most particularly, her successful pass at respectability once she has embarked upon a career as an actress — is that she is contained easily within the structure of specularity offered by her society: she is orectic, concupiscent in the eye of the beholder. In her first professional speaking part, Carrie Madenda, actress, quondam wife, and mistress, extemporizes the line: "I am yours truly" (431) and thereby confirms her part in the narrative as endlessly contingent upon the demands or feelings of another. Carrie embodies specularity: in reflection she gives back to the male onlooker the answer he is always looking for, the picture of his own desire, not hers. Carrie's active choices have to do with seeking paid work, while all her other actions represent mere compliance. On entry to the city she has to negotiate a number of choices that amount to a choice of life: to become a cowed wife like Minnie or one of the girls Drouet points out as worthy of her admiration. In choosing the latter, she redefines herself merely as the woman who is contemplated, observed as deserving of comment. Her destiny as an actress is sealed at that point because she allows herself to be caught and trapped in specularity alone.

Walter Benn Michaels writes, "What you are is what you want, in other words, what you aren't. The ideal that Ames represents to Carrie is thus an ideal of dissatisfaction, of perpetual desire. And, in fact, in *Sister Carrie*, satisfaction itself is never desirable; it is instead the sign of incipient failure, decay, and finally death."[9] While I concur absolutely with Michaels's description of the contiguities of satisfaction in the novel, I would like to delimit severely the extent to which Carrie can actually be considered to be the perpetually hungry "desireful Carrie" (487) that Dreiser tries to persuade us she is. From first to last Carrie is neutralized, rendered passive, as a creature without appetites beyond the basic ones of food and clothing. She is the ideal soft pornographer's model, having internalized exactly what is required of her: she takes on the role assigned, demonstrating the possibility for desire's fulfillment but never exerting any physical preference herself, except, of course, where it is a sensual response to the imprecations of leather and lace: "'My dear,' said the lace collar she secured from Pardridge's,

'I fit you beautifully; don't give me up'" (98). Carrie is the mediated woman — endlessly described in terms of her appeal to other people and always uncertain of her own authenticity — "what is it I have lost?" (88) — unable to see shame in her mirror but always able to be spotted by the man or in the job that will take her to a place of comfort. As Irene Gammel suggests, despite Dreiser's reputation for having radicalized writing about sex, he was actually a firm adherent of the "gender stereotypical seduction theme,"[10] and in his picture of Carrie she is always compliant, taking the initiative only insofar as it reinforces the already overt passion of her admirer.

Carrie understands that in order to get what she wants she must respond as if she were completely yielding to the pleasure of the man; indeed, the imitation of devotion, or sexual excitement (for imitation is all that Carrie is capable of), is what ensures her success as ersatz wife or actress. Her response is, above all, disproportionate to what is on offer, as, with that crucial line, "I am yours truly," she makes herself distinct from the rest of the harem but remains a member of the group, there to display collective sexual availability to the man, to simulate excitement when chosen for sexual favors. Carrie in the harem is again the soft pornographer's model, ready to fake sexual excitement and even fulfillment; the fact that she never conceives a child, despite her two sexual relationships, only serves to confirm that she is designed for male pleasure, not for productive or reproductive purposes. However, Carrie's success in specularity — that is, in reflecting what the male onlooker wants to see — is ultimately, Dreiser never lets us doubt, dependent upon the simultaneous sucking away of power from that male. The most reactionary message in the text is that women such as Carrie are monsters, ball-breaking and insatiable in their expectations of material gain, that Hurstwood made a fatal error when he thought that "in the mild light of Carrie's eye was nothing of the calculation of the mistress. In the diffident manner was nothing of the art of the courtezan" (122).

The story of Carrie's meteoric rise to fame is interwoven with the stations of Hurstwood's humiliating journey toward a death that becomes a martyrdom. Hurstwood stands and looks at the evidence, on advertising hoardings, of her ascent, as he descends into the underworld of homelessness and hunger. The prerogative embedded in the relationship has shifted from the once powerful Hurstwood, the shiny, well-dressed, successful showman, to the governed, the once complicit woman whose demands he aroused but can no longer satisfy. The turning point is marked by Dreiser as Carrie returns home: "When she saw him in bed that night, she knew that it imported failure. Coming on top of a further improvement in her own situation which must now be detailed, and as a destroyer of her hope that he had really roused himself, it was a shock. She could only shake her head in despair" (430). The moment of revelation of his insufficiency in enterprise is made confluent with his insufficiency in bed; indeed, his very presence in the bed means "failure," he is una*roused* whereas she is "on top" and intolerant of his inadequacies. A price is exacted of the man who once invited such as Carrie to perform for him, who took his pleasure on "a junket that was to last ten days" (86) and in New York took "cognizance of the pleasures of the tenderloin." [11] Once his own part in the transaction begins to falter, once he fails to come up to the standards of vigor and enterprise expected by the woman, the end of the relationship is a foregone conclusion.

Carrie is at first nonthreatening to men because she sits or stands where she is placed; Hurstwood has to carry her away by trickery in order to get her to move, and her body language is endlessly precipitate: "She had a chic way of tossing her head on one side, and holding her arms up as if for action — not listlessly. In front of the line this showed up even more effectually" (401). The telling phrase is "as if for action": there is nothing real about Carrie's preparedness for action; she can simulate energy as well as she can simulate attention to the male onlooker. As Amy Kaplan argues: "Although desire in *Sister Carrie* propels constant motion, it also becomes a substitute for actively changing either the social order or the individuals within it. This form of desire contributes to the paradoxical sense of stasis in the text at the times of greatest motion; Carrie is constantly on the move up the social scale — from one city, one man, one job to the next — yet she always seems to end up in the same place, as the final scene suggests: rocking, and dreaming, and longing for more." [12] Carrie is, in particular, sexually inert; she is only active in pursuit of clothes or material comfort. Although she performs various roles as mistress, wife, and actress, these roles, as Kaplan underscores, give the appearance of action but leave her — and others —

untouched in essentials. She performs the drama of class mobility through dressing up and acting up; she likes to work, her dream is "to be rid of idleness and the drag of loneliness — to be doing and rising — to be admired, petted, raised to a state where all was applause, elegance, assumption of dignity" (177). These are, of course, the demands that she makes in return for her compliance, a compliance that is endlessly expectant and therefore exacting, and which, in the end, seals Hurstwood's fate as a man irrelevant to her needs.

Like Kate Chopin, Dreiser is uncritical of his heroine's illicit liaisons, although he does intervene directly to acknowledge at every step of the way the contraventions of his characters against the accepted moral code. Woven into the text — in Minnie's cliché-driven dream of Carrie's fall as well as in Dreiser's direct commentary — is the standard of bourgeois morality breached by Carrie's easy acceptance of money, favors, sexual congress, and bogus or bigamous marriages. Dreiser has an apologetic and often pompous tone in the interpolations that gloss his characters' weakness in the face of temptations both carnal and fiscal: "And whoso is it so noble as to ever avoid evil, and who so wise that he moves ever in the direction of truth?" (91). These special-pleading interruptions in the text serve only, however, to highlight the fact that the most effective means of undermining conventional moral-ity is the portrait of Carrie herself, who, despite living with two different men as their mistress, taking part in a bigamous mar-riage, and working as an actress, passes for respectable and has a fairly chaste notion of what it means to be a "good time" (444) girl. The best argument against easy acceptance of female stereotyping is the final version of Carrie, who wants, at the close, to do good: "Not applause — not even that — but goodness — labor for oth-ers" (486). Dreiser's final irony is that given work, decently paid work from which she derives status and economic independence, the woman is restored to respectability. Carrie becomes a celibate, spurning offers from the stage-door Johnnies who blandish her with tales of great wealth and comfort. No longer interested in being a kept woman, she is given encouragement by Ames to be-come her own woman, although Dreiser tells us plainly that Carrie does not lose her ability to reflect back at the observer that which he wants to see: "[Ames] looked after her sympathetically. What Mrs. Vance had told him about her husband's having disappeared, together with all he felt concerning the moral status of certain kinds of actresses, fled. There was something exceedingly human and unaffected about this woman — something which craved neither money nor praise. He followed to the door — wide awake to her beauty" (487). This new Carrie is not, however, any more authentic than the earlier Carrie; surrendering endlessly to specularity, to the philanthropist's vision as easily as to the soft pornographer's notion of her purpose, her identity is neither stable nor single nor fixed: "She was the old, mournful Carrie — the desireful Carrie, — unsatisfied" (487). Her very capacity to pass for respectable, to pass for tragic heroine, made possible by Hurstwood's banishment to a separate strand of the narrative, emphasizes the folly of trying to contain the woman within a standard tale. Dreiser thus confirms that economic, sexual, and social boundaries can and will be crossed, and that categorization can only lead to the proliferation of performative fictions of identity, fictions that put some on the stage and put others to bed into a sleep from which they will never awaken.

"The Inward Life Which Questions": *The Awakening*

Kate Chopin's Edna Pontellier possesses the only voice in *The Awakening* allowed to acknowledge that her behavior might be construed as at odds with the prevailing morality: "By all the codes which I am acquainted with, I am a devilishly wicked specimen of the sex. But some way I can't convince myself that I am" (79). In contradistinction to Dreiser, Chopin refuses to offer moral prescriptions or judgments to her readers through the authorial voice, leaving Edna, as the author said in her famous "Retraction," free to "[work] out her own damnation."[13] Edna, of course, poses the particular danger to the social order that arises from a woman's having independent financial means. The possession of an inheritance from her mother underscores that she is not forced to perform the role of wife. She need not live in fear of the withdrawal of maintenance, she need not fear a husbandless future for economic reasons; therefore, she fulfills the worst fears of the male-dominated social order: that an economically independent woman will be an uncontrollable woman. This is the really frightening specter in Chopin's novel, not the sexually awakened woman, but the sexually independent woman with a cash base unconstrained by either love or need.

In *The History of Sexuality* Michel Foucault describes the strategic "deployment" of sexuality within the family: "The family is the interchange of sexuality and alliance: it conveys the law and the juridical dimension in the deployment of sexuality; and it conveys the economy of pleasure and the intensity of sensations in the regime of alliance."[14] Edna Pontellier very precisely and deliberately takes her "sexuality" outside the legal and social framework of marriage; indeed, an intrinsic part of her awakening is the recognition that her physical desires cannot be contained within the family unit or, ultimately, in relationship with one man. Chopin shows Edna herself at first bemused by the fact that her newly awakened sexual appetite is indiscriminate, that the first erotically fulfilling encounter of her new life is not with the man with whom she is infatuated and who has been the focus for all her unrequited desire: "She felt as if a mist had been lifted from her eyes, enabling her to look upon and comprehend the significance of life, that monster made up of beauty and brutality. But among the conflicting sensations which assailed her there was neither shame nor remorse. There was a dull pang of regret because it was not the kiss of love which had inflamed her, because it was not love which had held this cup of life to her lips" (80). Edna has been as much a "dupe" (105), as she herself describes it, as other women to the commonly accepted idea of complete romantic fulfillment with one man, whether Robert or one of her earlier fantasy lovers.

Unlike Carrie, Edna does not seek material advantage in taking new sexual partners, for in sleeping with a well-known roué, Alcée Arobin, she is embracing the disreputable, the declassé. Edna seemingly wants to sleep with men who will worsen her financial security and destroy her respectability, men who are marginal in both social and financial circles. She deliberately relinquishes her secure position as married woman in order to seek physical fulfillment. She declassifies herself, shedding her inhibitions, her class and status, her material wealth, and her clothes in order to become more fully herself. She identifies herself with no other woman, taking herself, instead, outside convention, outside society.

Edna Pontellier goes to her death having failed to find a reflection anywhere in her world of the kind of woman she becomes during the course of the narrative. Where specularity was Carrie's route to survival and success, Edna fails to return the image required of her by husband, family, and friends; where Carrie imitates, Edna deviates and initiates. She can find no one who leads the kind of life she wants to lead; having rejected the roles of mother, wife, and artist, there are no models for her to imitate. Carrie is constantly imitative; she copies those girls that Drouet points out to her as stylish and well-presented, and through her contact with him — and the immaculately turned out Hurstwood — she betters her material status, re-dressing herself in the eyes of the world. Edna Pontellier, however, cannot authenticate herself in the eyes of the world, and eventually she gives up, defeated. She dresses down to the raw; she takes off her clothes in order to recodify herself, seeking physical comfort and freedom, seeking a real self in naturalness, in absence of ceremony, in nakedness. She can find no other reflection of herself in the exterior world than the naked man she herself envisions as a part of her imaginative response to Mademoiselle Reisz's playing. The human creature, naked and unadorned and finally ungendered, is her last — and the only possible — point of identification before she swims to her death.

Edna has not been able to discern any likeness in those that surround her to the woman she wants to be, because the only models on offer are the married woman categorized by Chopin as the "mother-women . . . who idolized their children, worshiped their husbands, and esteemed it a holy privilege to efface themselves as individuals and grow wings as ministering angels" (9). Neither Chopin nor Dreiser portrays married love with any zest: the two marriages we see in *Sister Carrie*—Minnie and Sven, Hurstwood and his wife — are either dreary or ill-tempered matches. Chopin does, however, spend a considerable portion of her narrative on her portrait of the Ratignolles: in love and bourgeois contentment, they are compatible, safe, and ultimately dull. What her intimacy with Adèle Ratignolle does for Edna, however, is not to provide her with a role model as perfect wife and mother but to alert her, through the sensual response she makes to her friend, to the indiscriminate and anarchic nature of sexual attraction. Edna regards most of Madame Ratignolle's pursuits with bemused contempt;

she joins in with activities such as dressmaking in order not to appear "unamiable and uninterested" (10), because the real attraction of being in Adèle's company is that Edna is sexually stimulated by her proximity. Madame Ratignolle is described as realizing to perfection ideals of "feminine" beauty in contrast to the "long, clean and symmetrical" (15) lines of Edna's body. Adèle's nearness disturbs Edna's equilibrium: "The excessive physical charm of the Creole had first attracted her, for Edna had a sensuous susceptibility to beauty. Then the candor of the woman's whole existence, which every one might read, and which formed so striking a contrast to her own habitual reserve — this might have furnished a link. Who can tell what metals the gods use in forging the subtle bond which we call sympathy, which we might as well call love" (14–15). The attraction is absolutely sensual, as is Adèle's response to Edna. She is unequal to the challenge of responding to Edna's expressions of confusion about the feelings she is experiencing except with touching and stroking and murmurs of generalized sympathy — *"pauvre chéri"* — and although "the action was at first a little confusing to Edna . . . she soon lent herself to the Creole's gentle caress" (17).

It is a sensual awakening to the pleasures of the flesh in the person of Madame Ratignolle that lends the character of anarchy, of "tumult" (14) to Edna's newly realized sexuality. This is the real center of deviance from the norms of the established sexual and social "regime of alliance," in Foucault's words: Edna's awakening is homoerotic and thus disrupts the structure of power and affiliation in sexual as well as economic and social terms. Every time that Edna responds unconventionally — for example, to Robert's expression of his dream that she will become his wife — by saying that she gives herself where she chooses, that she is no one's possession, she is refuting the precept that says that the woman's sexuality must be neutralized by passivity and compliance and expressed only within the family unit. Edna's conduct throws into flux not only preconceptions of female sexuality but the category of woman in its entirety; in Judith Butler's terms, she takes herself out of the "context of the heterosexual matrix" — to the point of fracture. As Butler notes: "When the constructed status of gender is theorized as radically independent of sex, gender itself becomes a free-floating artifice, with the consequence that *man* and *masculine* might just as easily signify a female body as a male one, and *woman* and *feminine* a male body as easily as a female one." [15] Edna Pontellier's rebellion confutes conjugal, maternal, and social structures of womanliness; she unsexes herself, taking to the streets, walking, talking, eating, drinking, smoking, gambling, forming sexual liaisons in the public spaces of New Orleans.

The home of the married woman, after the return of all the vacationing families to New Orleans, becomes the site of this rebellion, of the subversion of all the modes of behavior denoted as normal. Unlike Carrie, with her pathetic attempts at domesticity while in Drouet's establishment, Edna abjures housekeeping, receiving visitors, marital relations, and mothering, and, in removing herself to the pigeonhouse, endeavors to escape from the pigeonhole to which she has been assigned. She pursues the erotic feelings inspired by one woman in a relationship with another, as she demands from Mademoiselle Reisz the sexual charge provided by her music and that she become the representative of Robert, the desired physical presence. In the pianist's attic rooms Edna surrenders her reserve in full as she allows herself to be swept into sensation by the intensity of the emotional atmosphere as well as by the music. The words exchanged between the two women are passionate and much more closely approximate the teasing, ardent language of lovers than any dialogue between Edna and Robert. Mademoiselle Reisz calls Edna *"ma belle"* and *"ma reine"*; she has a declamatory, histrionic tone as she confronts Edna about the nature of physical attraction and disputes with her about the putative reader of Robert's letters: "'Haven't you begged me for them? Can I refuse you anything? Oh! you cannot deceive me" (77). The two woman enact the struggle toward frank expression of desire, which never happens either between Edna and Arobin or Edna and Robert, and it is because of the passionate nature of their engagement that Edna is ready to respond to Arobin and "the first kiss of her life to which her nature had really responded. It was a flaming torch that kindled desire" (80).

Unlike Carrie, Edna Pontellier refuses to keep still and refuses to fake her emotions. She expresses her newfound sense of self in motion, walking through the city, involving herself in the move between houses, climbing ladders, moving furniture, and performing otherwise unexpected exertions in order to reclaim both her body and her living space. In *The Awakening* Chopin refuses to indulge the cultural predisposition to pathologize any behavioral or sexual deviation from the norm; as Butler notes in discussion of Foucault, "The binary reproduction of sexuality suppresses the subversive multiplicity of a sexuality that disrupts heterosexual, reproductive and medicojuridical hegemonies" (19).[16] Indeed, Chopin makes this refusal even more emphatic by making the only man who has any insight into Edna's true condition a doctor, an elderly family doctor at that, who sees beyond the repressive effects of the stereotypical expectations for women's satisfaction to the frustration and pain of an individual case: "The Doctor . . . knew his fellow-creatures better than most men; knew that inner life which so seldom unfolds itself to unanointed eyes. He was sorry he had accepted Pontellier's invitation. He was growing old, and beginning to need rest and an imperturbed spirit. He did not want the secrets of other lives thrust upon him. 'I hope it isn't Arobin,' he muttered to himself as he walked. 'I hope to heaven it isn't Alcée Arobin'" (68). When the doctor expresses this wish, it is because he recognizes Edna's awakened sexuality, not because he thinks she is especially depraved or debauched; he merely wishes her a better lover than the roué Alcée Arobin, with his practiced, glib charm. In his experience, then, she is actually representative, not exceptional; to Doctor Mandelet the sexually alive woman is a known quantity. This recognition allows Chopin to normalize — albeit in a manner that points to the esoteric nature of the knowledge required — Edna's developing sensuality. Again, it is this very acceptance, this normalization, that would have been one of the most profoundly shocking aspects of the narrative to most of its readers. Women with dissatisfactions, with appetites like Edna's, might not, then, be aberrations or exceptions; such women, women who refuse to be bound by the appearance of conventional morality, are well known to the Doctor in his professional if not in his personal life. In presenting a challenge to the social order, Edna Pontellier fails to externalize a mode of existence that will provide her with a coherent self-definition. From the beginning "she had apprehended instinctively the dual life — that outward existence which conforms, the inward life which questions" (14), but after undermining, even undoing the ontology of her identity as married woman, she has nothing to put in its place except the certainty of total isolation. She has sought to choose her mode of existence, and, as every choice is a recognition of the limits that operate to constrain choice, she finally understands that a life authenticating her newly awakened physical self does not and cannot exist. Finally, to surrender to the close embrace of the sea is her only option.

The crucial difference between Edna and Carrie ultimately inheres in the distinct economic circumstances that condition their lifestyle choices. Chopin launches her heroine from a position of financial independence; Edna is able to see integrity and wholeness in divesting herself of material possessions, loosening and finally discarding her clothes in order "to realize her position in the universe as a human being, and to recognize her relations as an individual to the world within and about her" (14). Carrie clothes herself in a number of conventional attitudes and poses in order to achieve the material independence that is Edna's from the outset; for Carrie, "the voice of want made answer for her" (90). Carrie ends, however, in defiance of stereotype, surrounded with material comfort, unpunished physically or mentally by promiscuity, and distinguished from the chorus line or harem by her autonomy. Carrie has been more the object of desire than the "desireful Carrie": she has been able to convert illicit into the appearance of licit sex, she moves from the pathetic adoption of the (false) married name to the point where her "name is worth . . . repute" (451). Edna makes herself subject to desire and thereby removes herself from any world recognizable to those around her; as she tells Robert, "I give myself where I choose" (102), and her "choosing" to give herself to the sea is the only manner in which she can locate a secure self-identity, unclothed and uncompromised.

NOTES

1. See Emily Toth, *Kate Chopin* (London: Century, 1990), 422–425, for a discussion of the myths and misapprehensions that have grown up around the reception of *The Awakening*. See the selection of reviews published in the Norton Critical Edition of *The Awakening*, ed. Margo Culley, 2d ed. (New York: W. W. Norton, 1994), 161–173.

2. See Culley, ed., *The Awakening*, 164 (review in the 20 May 1899 St. Louis *Post-Dispatch*). All second and subsequent references to this and other sources appear in the text.

3. See Ellen Moers, *Two Dreisers: The Man and the Novelist* (London: Thames and Hudson, 1970), part 3, chapter 2.

4. Donna M. Campbell, *Resisting Regionalism: Gender and Naturalism in*

American Fiction, 1885–1915 (Athens, Ohio: Ohio University Press, 1997). Campbell argues that Edna's career most closely parallels the male protagonists of such naturalist writers as Frank Norris and Harold Frederic (149).

5. For a discussion of American women writers of this period, see Elizabeth Ammons, *Conflicting Stories: American Women Writers at the Turn into the Twentieth Century* (New York: Oxford University Press, 1991). For some other views of the two novels, see Donald Pizer, *New Essays on* Sister Carrie (New York: Cambridge University Press, 1991); David E. E. Sloane, Sister Carrie: *Dreiser's Sociological Tragedy* (New York: Macmillan, 1992); Margit Stange, *Personal Property: Wives, White Slaves, and the Market in Women* (Baltimore: Johns Hopkins University Press, 1998); Cynthia Griffin Wolff, "Un-Utterable Longing: The Discourse of Feminine Sexuality in Kate Chopin's *The Awakening,* in *The Calvinist Roots of the Modern Era,* ed. Aliki Barnstone et al. (Hanover, N.H.: University Press of New England, 1997), 181–197. For a discussion of Chopin's use of historical discourses of homoeroticism, specifically, her use of the emerging stereotype of the lesbian and her connection to the woman artist, see Kathryn Lee Seidel, "Art Is an Unnatural Act: Homoeroticism, Art, and Mademoiselle Reisz in *The Awakening,*" *Mississippi Quarterly* 46.2 (1993): 199–214; for a more theoretical reading of Edna as "lesbian," see Elizabeth LeBlanc, "The Metaphorical Lesbian: Edna Pontellier in *The Awakening,*" *Tulsa Studies in Women's Literature* 15.2 (1996): 289–307. See also Laurie E. George, "Women's Language in *The Awakening,*" in *Approaches to Teaching Chopin's* The Awakening, ed. Bernard Koloski (New York: MLA, 1988); Emily Toth, *Kate Chopin* (New York: William Morrow, 1990), 438. Readers may also wish to consult the following forthcoming volume: Emily Toth, *Kate Chopin: The Centennial Story* (Jackson: University Press of Mississippi, 1999).

6. Theodore Dreiser, *Sister Carrie* [the unexpurgated edition], ed. N. M. Westlake et al. (New York: Viking Penguin, 1981), 3–4.

7. Ruth Rosen, *The Lost Sisterhood: Prostitution in America, 1900–1918* (Baltimore: Johns Hopkins University Press, 1982), 102–103.

8. For a discussion of Dreiser's desexualization of Carrie, see Laura Hapke, *Tales of the Working Girl: Wage-Earning Women in American Literature, 1890–1925* (New York: Twayne, 1992), 78–82.

9. Walter Benn Michaels, "Sister Carrie's Popular Economy," *Critical Inquiry* 7 (1980): 382.

10. Irene Gammel, "Sexualizing the Female Body: Dreiser, Feminism, and Foucault," in *Theodore Dreiser: Beyond Naturalism,* ed. Miriam Gogol (New York: New York University Press, 1995), 31.

11. Dreiser, 316; see Rosen's enumeration of red-light districts in major U.S. cities, including "New York's Bowery, Five Points and Tenderloin" (78–79).

12. Amy Kaplan, *The Social Construction of American Realism* (Chicago: University of Chicago Press, 1988), 149.

13. Culley (78) cites the "Retraction" printed in *Book News* 17 (July 1899): 612.

14. Michel Foucault, *The History of Sexuality*, vol. 1, trans. Robert Hurley (London: Pelican Books, 1981), 108.

15. Judith Butler, *Gender Trouble: Feminism and the Subversion of Identity* (New York: Routledge, 1990), 5–6.

16. See also Marjorie Garber, *Vice Versa: Bisexuality and the Eroticism of Everyday Life* (New York: Simon and Schuster, 1995).

Ladies Prefer Bonds: Edith Wharton, Theodore Dreiser, and the Money Novel

CLAIRE PRESTON

Social conditions as they are just now in our new world, where the sudden possession of money has come without inherited obligations, or any traditional sense of solidarity between the classes, is a vast & absorbing field for the novelist, & I wish a great master could arise to deal with it.[1]

"Undine Spragg," the name of the protagonist of *The Custom of the Country*, glares like a neon sign amid Edith Wharton's more traditional, natural nomenclature. As the book's first phrase, it seems to enter the fictional room like an indiscriminately applied scent, before its owner. The disagreeable ungainliness of the syllable "Spragg" begins with an assailing consonant cluster, plosively suggesting the embouchure of spitting or of disdain, and it ends in a rhyme with "nag," "gag," and "slag." But those initial consonants also recall "sprite," the famous folkloric bearer of the name "Undine."[2] An attempted pronunciation of "sprite," it seems, has swerved disastrously off the tongue. And when to "Spragg" is added "Undine" — hard to know how to pronounce, delicately feminine, probably foreign — we are further disconcerted. Is she "undeen," "undīne," or "oondeen," and on which syllable is the name accented? Her hapless mother calls her "Undie," which may or may not be authoritative. The mystery and instability of pronunciation, the irksome yoking of the adamantine "Spragg" with the sinuous and ethereal "Undine," are also features of the girl herself.

To Ralph Marvell the name suggests the motion of waves and an improbable allusion by the Spragg parents to Montaigne;[3]

Wharton, too, notices Undine's irritating rippling effects and ceaseless posing. What is actually being commemorated in her christening, however, is the successful hair-waving formula invented by her father and patented in the week of her birth, a substance so-called because — as Mrs. Spragg explains — "of *un*doolay . . . the French for crimping."[4] The product is named not for sprites or for aqueous disturbances but for a hairdressing technique; so the daughter, who is named for the chemical. She could as well be called Marcel, or Blondine, or Clairol. By name and by nature, Undine is a product, genetic and commercial, and she roams the novel like a traveling saleswoman. A ruthless, fluctuating self-promoter and self-merchandizer, her name is an exact account of all that she is.

In 1907 the foundation of the Harvard School of Business Studies dismayed Edith Wharton: "[it] plunged me into . . . depth[s] of pessimism. . . . skyscrapers don't symbolize a lifting of the soul. . . . Alas, alas!"[5] In spite of this she herself was engaged at that moment, as were many of her contemporaries, in the creation of a money novel, a novel rich in the culture of business and skyscrapers, *The Custom of the Country*. The American money novel of the period 1870–1930 is, like the study of business, primarily interested in the mechanics of getting rich, which it discovers in the technicalities of finance, commerce, consumption, labor relations, and social mobility. Often it figures such themes in the career of a stratospheric entrepreneur, who might be a thinly veiled portrait of a Vanderbilt, a Morgan, a Yerkes, a Rockefeller, Frick, Belmont, Gould, or Cooke,[6] embodiments of what William Dean Howells called "the American poetry of vivid purpose."[7] Mark Twain's *The Gilded Age* (1873) and Howells's *The Rise of Silas Lapham* (1885) and *A Hazard of New Fortunes* (1890) were the first models in the genre; Frank Norris's *The Octopus* (1901) and *The Pit* (1902), charting railroad battles and wheat wars, derive their texture and surface from the ebb and flow of market transactions; Upton Sinclair was writing *The Metropolis* (1908) and *The Money Changers* (1909), muckraking satires of Wall Street; Theodore Dreiser was establishing the poetics of upward mobility in Frank Cowperwood — in the so-called "Trilogy of Desire," *The Financier* (1912), *The Titan* (1914), and *The Stoic* (posthumous, 1947). Later, Sinclair Lewis's *Babbitt* (1922; dedicated to Wharton) satirized boosterism and salesmanship; Booth Tarkington's *The Plutocrat* (1927) showed the business titan at play;

and John Dos Passos's *USA* trilogy (including *The Big Money* [1936]) was built around high finance and heroic industrial development. Near the end of this era, Fitzgerald's *The Great Gatsby* (1926) evoked the potential tragedy of the self-made man. Both Harvard and the money novelists, in other words, were giving their imprimatur to the art and science of profit.

The "primary" money-novel era of Twain and Howells is, distinctively, morally conservative. *The Gilded Age* imagines financial desire as a kind of malady. Like the heirs in *Bleak House*, everyone in the book is corroded and finally destroyed by the dreams of avarice prompted by the vast but worthless tract of Tennessee land at the center of the story. One young man is prematurely aged, his father loses his wits, his sister dies of heart disease, their patron is publicly humiliated. Silas Lapham, unlike Twain's pipe dreamers, has actually discovered, dug, mixed, manufactured, and marketed his best-selling mineral paint; it is his misguided but admirable refusal to take advantage of business adversaries that brings about his downfall, with a slippery former partner functioning in the Lapham business chronicle like a family curse from a Greek tragedy.

The subsequent development of the money novel — and this may be a symptom of the modernist shift from romance to realism[8] — prefers to leave ethics aside, to allow that avarice and its psychological conditions, unembellished by moral consequences, is itself a fit subject for the novelist. These later novels, especially those by Dreiser and Norris, tend to replicate the addictive rhythm of money operations at the expense of characters, who become bland and null in comparison with the fascinating power they wield. It is a blandness articulated with special power in a related money narrative — what we might call "woman-on-the-make," a genre well known since Defoe but suddenly enjoying an energetic reflorescence at the beginning of the twentieth century. Among these are Dreiser's *Sister Carrie* (1900) and *Jenny Gerhardt* (1911); Robert Grant's *Unleavened Bread* (1900) (perhaps the single most important influence on *The Custom of the Country*);[9] Robert Herrick's *One Woman's Life* (1913); Louis Joseph Vance's *Joan Thursday* (1913); Winston Churchill's *A Modern Chronicle* (1910); and Anita Loos's *Gentlemen Prefer Blondes* (1925). The heroines of these romances are not, of course, tycoons, nor could they be;[10]

instead, they reinvent the dynamic aggrandizing impulses of the upwardly mobile, greedy, financially cunning, traditionally male money figures in forms of personal, sexual, or aesthetic transaction. These novels show that the pathology of the financier is not sex-specific. The female money figure shares the financier's incessant and insatiable appetite for gain, but like him she cannot be satisfied by anything money can buy; she has his enigmatic, or merely vacant, insubstantial quality; and her story, like his, is open ended and unfinished. The pathology is neatly formulated in the motto of Dreiser's Frank Cowperwood: "I satisfy myself"[11] has the grammatical reflexivity of Undine's Spragg's self-absorption. The genre that in 1912 had yielded a Cowperwood, the essential male money figure, had by the same moment discovered his female equivalent in Undine.[12]

Among Wharton's surviving papers from the period 1910–1914 is the outline of a money story in which a panic on the markets provoked by the serious illness of an important financier is supposed to be averted by the secret substitution of his cousin, a near double. The cousin, overwhelmed by the strain of publicity, has a fatal heart attack, and the real financier must be displayed on his sickbed to calm the markets; but the punters, confused and imposed upon, panic anyway. The story's central conceit is an act of substitution that mimics the transactions of commerce, the transactions that Undine herself will promote in her career of upward trading. Wharton ends this note with the tantalizing question, "*Après?*"[13] This "*après?*" might be the watchword of the money novel she did write, the word encapsulating the appetite that impels it and the narrative structure that contains it.

"In America," Paul Bourget wrote, "all men in society have been and still are business men. They were not born to social status; they have achieved it."[14] Dreiser was fascinated by the ability of those known to the chroniclers of wealth as "nature's noblemen" (Howells, *Silas Lapham*, 21) to *achieve*— money, status, possession — by means of their astonishing, imperial appetite and energy for financial acquisition and conquest. In spite of the New York *World*'s conviction that the careers of such men could not be written by any living novelist,[15] hardly any money novel in this period is so abandoned to the minutiae of transaction as *The*

Financier. The descriptions of Cowperwood's complex and arcane share dealings and loan hypothecations, the cunning manipulations of his companies, holding companies, sinking funds, and deposit accounts, have the salaciousness and relentless monotony of pornography. Only Frank Norris and Upton Sinclair pitch transactional energy as fervently: in *The Pit*, the lunacy of the trading floor is electrifyingly poeticized; Sinclair, by contrast, surrenders to the tragic, epic inevitability of Wall Street, "where they fought out the battle of their lives . . . the cruel waste and ruin of it, the wreckage of the blind, haphazard strife."[16] These writers are more ravished by wheeling and dealing, triumph and disaster, in the money arena than by the fruits of finance. Norris's Jadwin buys houses, yachts, and paintings that are pointedly dreary and pompous; Sinclair gleefully burdens his plutocrats with lists and descriptions of their vulgarities. The truth is that their possessions cannot sustain the attention of the financier or his creator for long; only the market unfailingly stimulates and summons him. Notably remote from goods, Dreiser is much more interested in the physical laws of greed, which best demonstrate themselves in financial activity, and he is careful to detach Cowperwood from any profound connection to his collections of art and women; these are rendered clinically, almost insouciantly, because *things* are only the epiphenomena of transaction.

Wharton's entrepreneurial capitalist is a woman whose ferocity of acquisition must partly displace the ferocity of transaction, and her portrait of Undine's possessions is, unlike Dreiser's, rich and enthusiastic. The novel's texture is overburdened not just with deals but with *things*, a plenitude almost as extravagant as Cowperwood's precipices of debt and unlimited leverage, partly because no extravagance of daring or of possession can ever still her appetite, but mainly because Undine herself is unimaginable, incomprehensible, and is only intelligible in her acquisitions.

Navigating new worlds and laying them low with commercial cunning, or through arcane, often abstract, operations in the fiscal arena, the money figure is a kind of frontiersman, that valiant, wily conqueror of the howling American wilderness who arrives (usually solitary) in unsettled territory, a "young giant out of the East"[17] who subdues wild beasts and hostile aboriginals to his will and establishes a state or a city or a family fortune by destroying what he finds in the name of profit and glory. Like him, the financial frontiersman rarely has identifiable roots; any that he has are indistinct, onomastically western — places with names like Apex, Opake, Euphoria, or Deposit. Even if he *has* established mines, oil fields, railroads, and manufacturing empires, this frontiersman immediately heads *east*, not further west, to subjugate the financial landscape of the major metropolises (principally New York) with the cash laboriously acquired. He was modeled on the multitude of Civil War profiteers who converted their earnings into houses, parties, wardrobes, yachts, and art collections, and proceeded to translate their financial success into social prestige; the numbers of millionaires in postwar America increased by an order of magnitude.[18] The social sanctuary simultaneously breached is the domain of the female money figure: Undine is new and heroic, quite unlike the demure daughter of the established elite, vigorously and intrepidly in command of her own material and matrimonial destiny. She too heads east, and, armed with male earnings and her own energy and ambition, she vanquishes the swollen monsters of social exclusivity, as the financier demolishes the barriers erected by its capital.

In twentieth-century money novels, the struggles of the money titans rock New York: "Swift, imperious, terrible, trampling over all opposition . . . Wall Street had reeled in the shock of the conflicts" (Sinclair, 192). The plutocrat is likened to "a passage in Homer, or in some Gothic poem . . . some great scarlet-robed Carthaginian . . . Hamilcar or his gorgeous son Hannibal";[19] his books on banking and credit promise "to unfold the shining secrets that only Midas and Morgan and Maecenas knew";[20] he is an overreacher, "a great personage of the Elizabethan order" (*Titan*, 245), hailed as the Weird Sisters hail Macbeth (*Financier*, 448). "Everything stopped when he raised a finger; everything leaped to life with the fury of obsession when he nodded his head. . . . no Czar, no satrap, no Caesar ever wielded power more resistless" (149).[21]

Even Wharton's Elmer Moffatt recites his business battles with "Homeric volume" (145); his exploits are "like the long triumph of an Asiatic conqueror" (303). Indeed, Moffatt's epic (Ralph Marvell wants to write a book about him) is the mighty underpinning of the more frivolous but narratively primary tale of Undine, a strong obbligato theme of financial ebb and flow in the form of shady land deals, insider trading, bubbles and booms, blackmail, and bought evidence, which is never straight-forwardly — only laconically and indirectly — delivered. Moffatt is a financial magician whose tricks rely on numerical legerde-main, hype, and low cunning rather than on solid investment or production.[22] Neither exact nor public, Moffatt's career and the story of it are like one of those "shadowy destructive monsters beneath the darting small fry of the surface" (*Custom*, 149).

This "epic effrontery" (146) belongs also to Undine Spragg, the social and financial pirate.[23] With her financier's temperament, appetite, and initiative, and her own acquisitive cunning, Undine's character and behavior are replicated by the surface of the novel, Wharton's most energetic and febrile. Like the seventeenth- and eighteenth-century buildings she so admired, with their Vitruvian, Palladian cadences and stately rhythms, her best stories are usu-ally measured, almost architecturally patterned, entirely governed by their design, with scant room for extraneous detail or episode. But *The Custom of the Country* simulates an upward trajectory with no hint of gravity in it, no corresponding downward path. The novel and the career of its protagonist are more like the detested skyscraper than the Italian villa.

Despite this scale there are, perhaps oddly, no epic similes for Undine. Instead, she attracts two other kinds of image: the fluid and liquid (she has the name of a water sprite; she ripples and glit-ters; she is launched into New York society on the profits of the Pure Water Move), and the adversarial, the umbrageous, the bel-licose (she thinks always in terms of "getting even," of dominat-ing, of "running the show"). Constitutionally (even onomasti-cally) in transit and full of fluctuations, Undine is like Curtis Jadwin of *The Pit*, the man unable to sit out the contention in fu-tures, or Frank Cowperwood, who cannot take his eyes off the market even in prison, or in love. Money figures are incapable of rest; and Undine ripples in company, is ceaselessly *mouvementée*; her restlessness is both geographical and social. Even if Undine Spragg Moffatt Marvell de Chelles Moffatt, as she is at the end of the novel, is never actually likened to Tamburlaine, she collects husbands and patronymics the way Tamburlaine collects king-doms, and the litany of her momentary American locales reads like Sherman's march through Georgia — Apex, Deposit, Skog Harbor, Potash Springs, New York City, Dakota — in a progress that uses up a good half of the American continent. Like those conquerors, she leaves behind a trail of social and financial wreckage. Undine arises, like a force of nature, out of the soil of the Midwest, a creature without history or tradition, autochthonous, autonomous, relentless. Hers is a heroic narrative on a par with any Wall Street titan: she rampages through countries and continents, families and neighborhoods, never satisfied, always, like her classical counterparts, looking for new domains to conquer. As Moffatt boasts, "Nobody can stop me now if I want anything" (301), so the object of Undine's gigantic and exhaustless appetites is, "Why, *everything!*" (57). *The Custom of the Country* is the heroic account of getting it.

Although Undine originates in the dismal boomtown of Apex City, to say she is *from* anywhere in particular is too sentimental a reading of her origins, just as it is sentimental to imagine that her name has any traditional or intended symbolic significance. Apex is a name as opportunistic as "Undine," an unmeant booster joke (like the real place in Illinois hopefully called "Hometown"), a place invented every day by shady boomers like Undine's father even as Undine invents herself. But Undine's placelessness is as necessary as it is typical: like the financier, she can only aggregate by ceaseless motion: as stasis is fatal to the stock market, where fortunes are made from transaction on movement in either direction, so Undine is never still. The joke-name "Apex," like "*après?*" is, in other words, perfectly serious after all; Apex is simultaneously everywhere and nowhere: it is only the temporary pinnacle from which Undine surveys a loftier, beckoning eminence. A kind of Faustian ubiquism, "Apex" is the word for everything Undine wants, achieves, and immediately puts behind her: "She had everything she wanted," Undine muses, "but she still felt, at times, that there were other things she might want if she knew about them" (333). This, the most terrifying sentence in the book, is also its most typical.[24] Although Undine deploys her personal capital with the shrewdness of an investor, she is caught up in "a nightmare of perpetually renewable choice and decision. . . . her amusement at any cost and in any quantity that suits her she *will* have, let who will pay."[25]

Like Undine's beauty, Frank Cowperwood's brilliance is apparently coercive, the source of infinite means. The son of a middling bank clerk, he follows a seemingly inexorable upward trajectory in Philadelphia financial circles, always moving on to ever more

arcane operations until, having reached the purest (and most lu-
crative) forms of finance in the abstract arithmetic of discount
bonds, arbitrage, market manipulations, and leveraged buyouts,
rather than the messier transactions involving commodities, real
estate, and stock, he is ruined by the far-reaching consequences of
the Chicago fire of 1871. Bankrupt and in prison for financial im-
proprieties, and friendless for having appropriated the daughter
of a powerful machine politician, on his release he nevertheless
quickly recoups and outstrips his old prosperity in the panic that
follows the Northern Pacific Railroad failure of 1873. In *The Titan*
and *The Stoic* he goes to Chicago and London and founds street
railways, becoming one of the richest men in the United States.

In his analysis of modes of wealth, Thorstein Veblen makes a
distinction between "worthy" and "unworthy" employments,
which he calls, respectively, "exploit" and "industry."[26] Industry
is deemed in the social code of leisure to be the necessary but "unworthy" activity that creates new things out of brute material; it is
associated, primitively, with agriculture or manufacture but could
in a more modern form include certain services. Industry, com-
prising work and effort of all descriptions, is essentially dishonorable. Exploit, by contrast, is the peremptory *seizing* of others'
goods or energies. Exploit is removed from sources or means of
production; it represents instead the higher exercise of force over
others. Exploit, in Veblen's scheme, is "worthier" than industry.

Cowperwood, Moffatt, and Spragg are hard to contain within
these definitions. In Veblen's scheme, the most honorable kind of
wealth is passively, unlaboriously acquired in the form of inherited money. But these three have little or no inherited funds; instead, they commit great energy to acquisition, as if they were industrious, and yet they are nonproductive (they manufacture
nothing, usually provide no goods or services); they specialize —
on Wall Street or Fifth Avenue — in covert and transgressive exploit in the form of the financial killing or the social conquest. If
industry yields "earnings" (a morally loaded word), exploit consists of "takings"; and the vocabulary of finance is violent and
abrupt, with words like "killing," "hit," "takeover," and the "big
steal" evoking its combat. Veblen comments that "in the life of
the barbarian, prowess manifests itself in . . . force and fraud"
(273); exploit in its most refined form is financial deception, the
exemplary behavior that appropriates the possessions of others

with least cost to the predator. Undine, Moffatt, and Cowperwood are, paradoxically, industrious *and* exploitative: without hereditary wealth, they are energetic in the pursuit of money. Cowperwood's exploits, like Moffatt's, are rarefied in numbers and pure cash, away from goods and chattels, particularly in the form of fraud. Undine's power over money is more rarefied still; she has long since abandoned anything like industry (Ralph imagines her as a child having made only foolish items of cork and cigar wrappers) for the imperious grabbing of men, jewels, and transatlantic junkets. Undine's cunning is not the conscious art of the financiers — she cannot, ironically, understand why all her entitlements "come to her as if they had been stolen" (275); nevertheless, with her indistinct but potent sexual allure, she too is a fraudster. She is not interested in sex but in acquisition; she cuts deals with men to whom she never delivers her part of the bargain. Her desirability is snake oil or a junk bond — a false product or at best a high-risk investment. "Everything in Wall Street is stolen," says Upton Sinclair (*Metropolis*, 214); her history, even if she cannot see its resemblance to Moffatt's and Cowperwood's, is a tale of steals rather than of deals.

Undine and Cowperwood share an unreflecting, disturbing boldness, a casual disregard for the subtle social arrangements and obligations that stand in the way of desire. She truculently reflects upon her French husband's devotion to the abstract and immaterial concept of Family, a concept symbolized by needlework — the embroidery carried out by the women of the de Chelles cousinage for the ancestral chateau, and the great Louis Quinze Boucher tapestries, the family's chief hereditary treasure. Their "industrious" behavior (significantly, traditional "women's work") and their familial solidarity (so much nonliquid capital tied up in a relic) are faintly dishonorable, and certainly stupid, because not self-serving, and attract only her scorn. This reaction emblematizes that of the exploiting individual about toil in the service of remote, disembodied, and selfless ideas such as "heritage." Her attempt to have the world-famous tapestries appraised pits exploit against industry, expedience against tradition. It characteristically seeks to put a price tag on what is priceless, invaluable to de Chelles. As an exploiter, she wants to know what the tapestries might be converted into (cash or dresses or central heating) as a way of finding out what can be "got out of" her husband.

But this appraisal represents an act of appetite rather than of imagination, and in this Undine is essentially distinct from her male counterparts. Moffatt does not care about the de Chelles tradition any more than Undine does, but he covets the tapestries as art objects. Undine, by contrast, is outraged, bewildered, or ignorant of everything not already hers or within her horizon of wants; to her the tapestries are merely "old and faded." "Passionately imitative" (14), her desires are uninflected by taste or opinion. Moffatt looks at the tapestries and calculates how much money will buy these priceless objects; Undine looks at them and calculates how much they will yield. Money figures are characterized by their extraordinary appetites: Moffatt, as billionaire railroad emperor, has driven up prices on the international art markets with the volume of his buying. Cowperwood has a collection ranging from the Old Masters to the Pre-Raphaelites. Like Lorelei Lee in the book described by Wharton as "*the* great American novel,"[27] Undine needs only to hear of something unattainable to discover an instant need to own it. As instantly, she will find a man to buy it for her. With inchoate, impatient appetites, these young women do not know what they want until they are confronted with it; they have no long-term outlook; they could never be futures traders.

Elmer Moffatt and Frank Cowperwood, however, are specific embodiments of the inventive acquisitive imagination; they understand the similitude of railroads and Rembrandts,[28] and quickly learn discrimination equivalent to their wallets. They have plans — and patience. Moffatt's rapidly developing taste and discernment are as carefully charted as his business exploits. His personal and ethical grossness and the subtle delicacy of such descriptions (of a crystal, a leather binding, a piece of Phoenician glass) produce a fascinating and unexpected counterpoint typical of the man. His sophistication as a collector, famous for his Persian carpets and Chinese porcelain, is acknowledged in the same breath as his financial skill. Although Cowperwood is rather more detached from his extensively described collections, Dreiser takes care to suggest the discrimination of such acquisitions, which include a portrait of Cesare Borgia, significantly rich with "rumor of his crimes and machinations" (*Titan*, 117). Exploiters are quick learners and use this faculty to get their possessions, like their money, out of the blue. In this respect, Undine qualifies as a money figure only in the ruthlessness of her acquisition; she fails to live up to the exploiter's inventiveness in her imaginative poverty.

In their creative unpredictability Cowperwood, Moffatt, and Undine epitomize the supple cunning, flexibility, and protean potential of the money character, whose very livelihood depends on the ability to take creative advantage of market opportunities, especially to get something for nothing or for as little as possible. As Cowperwood takes advantage of a sudden panic, Undine ripplingly converts herself into the sort of woman likely to attract the man of the moment. In her person Undine combines at once the financier and the funds he wields, agent and medium. "'The American girl,'" said Wharton in *The Buccaneers*, is "the world's highest achievement,"[29] like American steel and wheat; but the young women of that novel are manipulated commodities, the pawns of two mutually beneficial systems (of capital and of honors); in *The Custom of the Country* both systems are at the mercy of the self-commodified Undine. Undine's financial philosophy is summed up by Lorelei Lee in *Gentlemen Prefer Blondes*: "When a girl looks at Mrs. Nash and realizes what Mrs. Nash has got out of gentlemen, it really makes a girl hold her breath" (78). Lorelei and Undine are gold diggers in almost the literal sense of the term: they are excavating to see what can be "got out of" men.

Any number of American financial magicians might provide models for the male money figure. Jay Gould, the so-called "Mephistopheles of Wall Street," wrecked a railroad and left only its "financially lifeless body" (Josephson, *The Robber Barons*, 137). Wrecking railroads and wrecking homes are compared in *The Custom of the Country*; and, indeed, Undine wrecks homes in the way that railroads are wrecked. She makes preemptive strikes by preventing more credible marriages (between, say, Ralph and Harriet Ray, or between de Chelles and some resident of the faubourg). She maneuvers in romantic intrigues as "Mr. Spragg might have . . . at the tensest hour of the Pure Water Move" (168); she loots marriages as Moffatt might loot a corporation. She is an asset stripper; she leaves the debilitated or lifeless corpses of disillusioned men scattered about the social landscape.

Like Cowperwood and Moffatt, Undine makes and forfeits several fortunes — hers in the marriage market, theirs in the stock market. After their first scandalous union and hasty divorce in the

Midwest, Undine and Moffatt trace nearly parallel careers of boom and bust, only occasionally intersecting. At the end of the book, they merge once more. The consistently offensive, transgressive Moffatt once managed to carry away the teenaged Undine to an illicit marriage in Nebraska, a primitive version of the more rarefied financial combat and wealth grabbing in which he later specializes. Moffatt's truly inconceivable riches subsequently defy the principles of social exclusion because those riches, and he, are predatory: there is no art, no property, safe from his purchasing ability, just as there is, apparently, no social ethos proof, or any man secure, against Undine's predations.

But Moffatt is softer than Undine: he is moved by art, by young children; she merely uses them. She successfully "exploits" her own family in the exact Veblenian sense, seizing their wealth for the same reason that she demands her child from them: because she *can*. Like the chateau, tended by ancillary family members, little Paul Marvell is a treasure selflessly nurtured by all his grandparents, even the Spraggs. But selflessness is outside his mother's philosophy: she needs him in order to furbish up her respectability. Undine's ability to exploit her parents is apparently inherited, the nearest thing to "tradition" in the Spragg family. By the time the novel opens, Mr. Spragg, a quondam exploiter and fraudster, is being efficiently despoiled in turn by his even more ruthless daughter, whose genetic inheritance seems to include not only his active business sense but also his taste and talent for "steals."

"What were you going to do about the so-called morals and precepts of the world?" Cowperwood muses. "There were people who believed in some esoteric standard of right. . . . they were never significant, practical men who clung to these fatuous ideals" (*Financier*, 225–226). Cowperwood's amorality is never made to seem reprehensible, because the money novel is necessarily located in the strangely colorless world of abstract monetary operations, a world either divorced entirely from the acquisitive rewards of great wealth or at least emotionally distanced from those rewards. The process of accrual, dealing, and fraud is dense and hypnotic; however, the details of material or social gain, although finely tuned by someone like Dreiser, are strangely remote from the intensity of the trading floor, obligatory and off-hand, rather than essential to our understanding of the financier. The substantial rewards of money dealing cannot, it seems, compete with the fascinating labor that acquires them, and Dreiser's severe naturalism maintains this detachment in its scientific, carefully reportorial neutrality, which mimics in the transparent and unimpassioned account of his possessions the blankness of Cowperwood's personality. Although we are privy to such specificities as his middle name, the layout of his house, and the richness of his silk underwear, the subject of the novel is money and its operations, and thus he is instantiated (but never substantiated) only in his net worth, his stock-holdings, or his possessions. Barely a personality, he is the construction of his money, the physical representation of its abstract and unstable value; like his money, he is a man of quantities but not qualities. An embodiment only of crude desire, he can sustain no further detail; Frank Cowperwood is a character of whom there is ("frankly") nothing to infer. Although the narrative voice of *The Custom of the Country* is rich and intrusive, it is nonetheless distant and superior to Undine herself, whom her creator, like Raymond de Chelles, seems not to recognize as a member of her own species.

Cowperwood is a fascinating cipher: a magnetic personality whose authority and argument seem to seduce men and women alike, he is nonetheless terrifyingly empty. His attitude to all but the principle of self-aggrandizement is offhand: slavery, the West, panics, the sanctity of the home, right and wrong, the theory of evolution do not concern him; such abstrusities are "the toys of clerics, by which they made money." His earliest understanding is of "money as a medium of exchange" (*Financier*, 240, 11); he "subscribes to nothing" and instead can "fit himself in with the odd psychology of almost any individual" (*Titan*, 8, 21). Dreiser concludes *The Financier* with an emblematic essay about *mycteroperca bonaci*, a fish with "an almost unbelievable power of simulation . . . power to deceive" (*Financier*, 447). All self-made fictional financiers — Gatsby, Jadwin, Wharton's own Beaufort and Rosedale — are powerfully enigmatic in this way. Elmer Moffatt is a cipher, a man known by his schemes, tastes, possessions, and exploits, but ultimately mysterious and unaccountable, never viewed from anything but a great distance. When in *The Great Gatsby* Nick Carraway asks of Gatsby, "Who is he?" he is told, "He's just a man named Gatsby" (50). In truth, financiers are like Gatsby, "platonic conceptions of themselves" (95).

But it is Undine who possesses this psychological blankness in highest measure: she is vacant but for her trimmings. Like Frank Cowperwood, she too is a vacuum: although her beauty is painted out in bold strong colors, a beauty able to withstand the strongest, harshest illumination, a beauty not appropriate to the half-tones of Old New York or faubourg interiors, yet like Cowperwood she has no *innate* qualities. Her beauty is her wealth, the currency in which she trades up. When her divorce from Ralph Marvell temporarily relegates her to the society of the unfashionable, "her one desire was to get back an equivalent of the precise value she had lost in ceasing to be [his] wife. Her new visiting-card, bearing her Christian name in place of her husband's, was like the coin of a debased currency testifying to her diminished trading capacity" (205). Articulation more elaborate than this she — and every money figure — lacks: Moffatt is extremely laconic; Cowperwood repudiates all political conviction; beyond a few conventional exclamations of amazement and consternation, Undine herself has nothing to say: when she speaks, she seems to disappear. She has only "deep-seated wants for which her acquired vocabulary had no terms" (302); her linguistic capacity is primitive and unnuanced: she understands simply that "every Wall Street term had its equivalent in the language of Fifth Avenue" (303).[30]

While still a boy Cowperwood is asked by an uncle what he is interested in. "Money!" Frank replies. "The financial mind partakes largely of the thing in which it deals" (*Financier*, 15, 347), says Dreiser, and Cowperwood and Undine are just like money. Undine, who reads little, who has no ideas, who is merely imitative, whose paltry stock of conversation makes her beauty fade from view, masks her emptiness with her dazzling and flickering surface, which is finally recognized by Ralph as "the bareness of a small half-lit place" (86). Scruple-free, unreflective, morally and psychologically empty, such characters make the way clear for a narrative driven by transaction and profit, by event and process, rather than by development of character. Wharton noted that "the novel of situation . . . forces [characters] into the shape which its events impose."[31] Greed or desire becomes their signal and single property.

The Custom of the Country is in a sense an unfinished, and unfinishable, novel, as is Dreiser's narrative: like Tamburlaine, who dies not in battle but in bed, Cowperwood's bathetic failure is not in spectacular financial collapse but in age and Bright's disease. In the last page of *The Custom of the Country*, Undine querulously rages against the rule that prevents her being an ambassador's wife; but there is an inevitability here quite unlike Cowperwood's: by triumphant money logic, Undine *will* become an ambassador's wife. Either she will find a way around the rule, or she will leave Moffatt for an ambassador (with a huge settlement to back her). Indeed, in the original outline of the story, Undine was to ditch Moffatt for the newly made Ambassador Jim Driscoll, son of Moffatt's old employer and enemy.[32] The open-endedness with which Wharton eventually chose to conclude the novel is more frightening; it is an eternity of conquest, "a nightmare of perpetually renewable choice" that other writers found in industry, commerce, and the market.

NOTES

1. Wharton to Dr. Morgan Dix, 5 December 1905, *The Letters of Edith Wharton*, ed. R. W. B. Lewis and Nancy Lewis (New York: Simon and Schuster, 1988), 99. All second and subsequent references to this and other sources are cited in the text.

2. Thomas L. McHaney, "Fouqué's *Undine* and Edith Wharton's *The Custom of the Country*," *Revue de Littérature Comparée* 45 (1971): 180–186.

3. "*Diverse et ondoyant*," from Montaigne's essay "Par divers moyons on arrive á pareille fin" on the theme of unpredictable and erratic behavior. See Montaigne, *The Complete Essays*, trans. M. A. Screech (Harmondsworth: Penguin, 1987), 5.

4. *The Custom of the Country* (1913; reprint, Harmondsworth, England: Penguin, 1987), 48.

5. Edith Wharton to Sally Norton, 23 June 1907, Edith Wharton Archive, in Yale Collection of American Literature, Beinecke Rare Book and Manuscript Library, Yale University (hereafter "Yale").

6. See Matthew Josephson, *The Robber Barons: The Great American Capitalists, 1861–1901*, 2d ed. (New York: Harcourt, Brace and World, 1962); Charles Francis Adams and Henry Adams, *Chapters of Erie and Other Essays* (New York: Henry Holt, 1886); Thomas William Lawson, *Frenzied Finance: The Crime of Amalgamated* (London: William Heinemann, 1906).

7. William Dean Howells, *The Rise of Silas Lapham* (1885; reprint, Oxford: Oxford University Press, 1996), 82.

8. On this distinction, see Walter Benn Michaels, "Romance and Real

Estate," in *The American Renaissance Reconsidered: Selected Papers from the English Institute, 1982–3*, n.s., 9, ed. Walter Benn Michaels and Donald E. Pease (Baltimore: Johns Hopkins University Press, 1985), 156–157.

9. Edith Wharton to Robert Grant, 25 July 1900, Yale.

10. See Elaine Showalter, "*The Custom of the Country*: Spragg and the Art of the Deal," in *The Cambridge Companion to Edith Wharton*, ed. Millicent Bell (Cambridge: Cambridge University Press, 1995), 90.

11. *The Financier* (1912; reprint, New York: New American Library, 1967), 121. Cornelius Vanderbilt's famous *mot* is almost a motto ("What do I care for the law? Haint I got the power?"). Had she the patience for such things, Undine's motto would be "Go steady, Undine!" (17). William Mulholland, the California water-baron whose career may have provided Wharton with details for the Spragg water dealings at Apex, claimed the motto "Take it" (see Mike Davis, *City of Quartz: Excavating the Future in Los Angeles* [London: Verso Press, 1990], 379–382).

12. Dreiser began *The Financier* (1912) in 1911; Wharton began *The Custom of the Country* (1913) in 1907.

13. Wharton, "Donnée Book" (1910–1914), 9 (Yale).

14. Paul Bourget, *Outre-Mer: Impressions of America* (London: T. Fisher Unwin, 1895), 55.

15. New York *World*, 4 February 1906.

16. Upton Sinclair, *The Metropolis* (London: T. Warner Laurie, 1908), 173.

17. Theodore Dreiser, *The Titan* (1914; reprint, London: John Lane/The Bodley Head, 1915), 223.

18. Ray Ginger, *The Age of Excess: The United States from 1877–1914* (New York: Macmillan, 1965), 93.

19. Booth Tarkington, *The Plutocrat* (Garden City, N.Y.: Doubleday, Page, 1927), 112, 342.

20. F. Scott Fitzgerald, *The Great Gatsby* (1926; reprint, Harmondsworth, England: Penguin, 1990), 10.

21. Frank Norris, *The Pit* (1902; reprint, Harmondsworth, England: Penguin, 1994), 302.

22. Moffatt's complex financial career is scattered within the novel, but it is completely coherent if pieced together, which makes Alfred Kazin's opinion surprising: "what a subject lay before Edith Wharton in that world, if only she had been able, or willing, to use it!" ("Two Educations: Edith Wharton and Theodore Dreiser," in *On Native Grounds: An Interpretation of American Literature* [New York: Harcourt, Brace and World, 1942], 79). Stephen Orgel agrees: "The new American world of capitalist enter-

prise is . . . nearly . . . opaque to Wharton" (*The Custom of the Country*, ed. Stephen Orgel [Oxford: Oxford University Press, 1995], x).

23. Cynthia Griffin Wolff dismisses the female money novel: "Horatio Alger's myth in all its manifestations was for men, not for women" (*A Feast of Words: The Triumph of Edith Wharton*, 2d ed. [New York: Oxford University Press, 1995], 221).

24. Silas Lapham — for comparison — is worried that there may be things his money *cannot* buy (149). Undine has no such doubt. Pure appetite, by the era of the modernist money novel, has become equivalent to means.

25. These are Henry James's words about Wharton herself. James to Howard Sturgis (no date given), cited in R. W. B. Lewis, *Edith Wharton: A Biography* (New York: Harper and Row, 1975), 262.

26. Thorstein Veblen, *Theory of the Leisure Class*, ed. John Kenneth Galbraith (1899; reprint, Boston: Houghton Mifflin, 1973), 25.

27. Anita Loos, *Gentlemen Prefer Blondes* (1925; reprint, Harmondsworth, England: Penguin, 1992) 58. See Lewis, ed., *Letters*, 491 n.

28. Josephson, *The Robber Barons* (quoting Henry Frick), 343.

29. Edith Wharton, *The Buccaneers* (1938; reprint, London: Everyman, 1993), 24.

30. Wharton would later transpose this vacancy onto May Welland, the "nice" girl in *The Age of Innocence*, whose transparency is foil for a terrible cunning.

31. *Character and Situation in the Novel*, unpublished ms., Yale, p. 2a.

32. Ms. and notes for *The Custom of the Country*, Yale.

Mining the West:
Bret Harte and
Mary Hallock Foote

JANET FLOYD

The category "Western writing" is a slippery one, and the exercise of forming and reforming a Western canon has become relatively obscure in the larger context of recent critical considerations of regionalism. Yet, even against a background where Western writers' status is liable to shift, Bret Harte occupies a peculiarly insecure position not only in relation to the tradition of frontier narratives traced from Cooper but even within literary histories of Western literature, where his work is rarely described. Mary Hallock Foote has disappeared in a more complex way from "Western writing," in a manner predictable to the feminist literary historian, only to reappear as a quite distinct figure within the various spheres of 1970s historical writing. Here she is constructed as a writer who is, in some absolute sense, in the wrong place. This is certainly the assumption of Rodman W. Paul, whose edition of Foote's unpublished reminiscences, *A Victorian Gentlewoman in the Far West* (1972), has played a major part, along with Caroll Smith-Rosenberg's "Female World of Love and Ritual" (1975), in recovering Foote as, if nothing else, a Victorian middle-class lady occupying the "separate sphere" of 1970s feminist historical and critical discourse. Paul's assumption is that Foote's experience of the West — and apparently, by the same token, her writing — is especially, if not exclusively, mediated through her class identity as it intersects with constraints upon her as a woman: hence, his use of the anachronistic term "gentlewomen," encoding ideas of inappropriate refinement, blinkered vision, and undemocratic values.[1] This approach has been influential, not least because it matches one of the most common assumptions of writing about Anglo women in the West: that middle-class Eastern migrants were so much in the thrall of contemporary ideologies about womanhood as to be unable to take advantage of the relative flexibility of Western society. "No one," as Richard W. Etulain puts it, "would have predicted she would have become a well-known *Western* writer." [2] Yet such assumptions seem to me to have generated a persistent misrepresentation of Foote's writing, and especially of the mining fictions with which I shall primarily be concerned: "In Exile" (1881), *The Led-Horse Claim* (1883), and *John Bodewin's Testimony* (1886).

Interestingly, Foote's own impulse was to separate herself from a tradition she associated with Harte, though this was not an issue of gender difference. She was not, in my reading, much given to positioning herself in relation to other writers of the West. If anything, she seems to have wanted to link herself with British traditions of medievalism, especially Tennysonian Arthurianism and Victorian fantasy (as, for instance, in the underground fairy stories of George MacDonald); or to have wished to respond — this is true of her woodcuts especially — to the New England canon of her day.[3] But this is what she has to say about Harte: "The East continually hears of the recklessness, the bad manners and the immorality of the West just as England hears of all our disgraces, social, financial and national; but who can tell the tale of those quiet lives which are the lifeblood of the country, — its present strength, and its hope for the future? The tourist sees the sensational side of California — its scenery and its society; but it is not all included in the Yo Semite guidebooks and the literature of Bret Harte." [4] Here, at least, in her restatement of the Howellsian realist project in the context of writing about the West, Mary Hallock Foote places herself at odds with Harte's melodramas of social dislocation and societal hypocrisy.

It comes as something of a surprise, then, to find critics of Harte's and Foote's work choosing to understand them in very similar terms, that is, by association with the activity that some of their most important work describes: mining. This association is very striking in Harte criticism: he is a "casual, clever, literary miner," who "exposes" in order to "exploit," who is "lacking in literary conscience" in his use of his surroundings in California, merely scratching at the surface of his subject to turn a quick profit on fictions of cheap "unearned effects."[5] This criticism represents the West as a literary gold mine that Harte exploits without reflection or pause, to turn a quick profit on fictions of "very little flavour of the soil" (Wyatt, xxiii). Aptly, Harte himself is read as soon "exhausted" as a writer. The association works in similar and different ways for Foote. We must, it seems, search underground to find her "hidden excellence":[6] her work must itself be mined conscientiously for value. Although the critical verdict on Foote's "mining" is less vituperative than that upon Harte, the evaluation of her fiction has also become caught up in the perception that — to her work's detriment — she too is engaged in "converting . . . frontier experiences into artistic and literary capital" (Johnson, 9).

This issue extends beyond the accusation of a lack of literary ambition or even integrity. Paul begins his introduction to Foote's reminiscences by questioning whether Foote was "really a Westerner" (3), really the "authentic voice of the West" that her contemporaries believed (2). As with Harte, Foote's 1880s mining fictions are subject to a critique that finds her unable or unwilling to do justice to "the raw, new West" (Paul, 13): sometimes, as in Graulich's work on Foote, this shortcoming is not construed in terms of lack of artistry but rather as the result of her position as an alienated female in a literary space colonized by men; sometimes, as in James Maguire's argument, the problem lies as much in a predilection for literary fashion as in the "flaws of apprenticeship efforts."[7] Further, Foote's work, like Harte's, is regularly evaluated by reference to her interest in selling her work to an Eastern audience. Both are critiqued as Easterners commodifying the West, appropriating its treasures for a metropolitan audience interested in new places to discover.[8] These writers are compromised, their critics seem to argue, by the same squalid economics as those driving the Western mining economy of the late nineteenth century.

The claim for a particular position occupied by Bret Harte and Mary Hallock Foote in relation to literary markets does not, of course, stand up. It is unusual nowadays to find the evaluation of the worth of artists' work conducted on grounds of greater or lesser complicity with the publishing marketplace; but it is, in any case, peculiarly difficult to make such a distinction in the context of the last two decades of the nineteenth century, when the most lofty American editors and writers operated, whether they liked it or not, within a highly specialized and professionalized, not to say cutthroat, publishing scene in which "the written word was . . . a commodity, bought and sold like other articles of commerce."[9] Harte was an early beneficiary and victim of the system within which Howells and Twain, as well as Foote, worked at the height of their careers. His famous financial success of the 1870s certainly did not preclude his being welcomed with open arms by the high cultural establishment of his own day, nor did it prevent his being considered an important and influential figure in American letters, long after his *annus mirabilis* of 1879.[10]

Likewise, Foote's career need not be read primarily as structured by financial considerations. It may be that some of her writing can be understood as produced in response to financial need; Foote describes, in her reminiscences, the "remorseless practicality" that led her to a point where she "made capital out of her children's tears" (Paul, 298). However, this was certainly not always the case. Her writing evolved from and in tandem with a successful career in woodcut illustration of literary texts, well established when Foote went West. From the mid-1860s (more than ten years before first going to California), she was moving within high cultural circles, supported by her close friendship with Helena and Richard Watson Gilder. Almost all her work was published by the *Century Magazine* (where Gilder was de facto, then actual, editor) as a result. Though we may understand Richard Gilder's commissioning of a friend who could produce the type of regionalist writing that precisely reflected his editorial strategy and the magazine's identity during this period,[11] there is no evidence to suggest that either the Gilders or Foote regarded her work as produced with anything but serious literary ambition. And, in any case, Foote's mining fictions seem to have inaugurated a fashion for writing that dealt with the Far West and with mining (Johnson, 61).

Certainly, both Harte and Foote were apt to express an intense awareness of the relationship between their saleability and their subject matter, and of the currency of a certain kind of Western material for Eastern audiences. Harte is often quoted, albeit from a point later in his life, as bemoaning his need to "grind out the old tunes on the old organ and gather up the coppers."[12] Foote wrote of the problem of producing a Western story with a realism consistent with contemporary genteel manners (Paul, 18). Lee

Ann Johnson also quotes Foote's concern that the West was "too much for my pencil" (46). Plainly, both artists had reason to reflect on their effectiveness in working to publishers' demands: Harte because he could not sustain his success once in the East; Foote because, the need for money aside, she struggled to keep a career going during a migrant existence in the Far West. Still, the link that critics have made between their output and an exploitative process of mining seems scarcely consistent with the level of interest they actually express in the financial rewards of their work. More to the point, the connection itself is less than appropriate: it compares formulaic hackwork to a money-making venture that was wildly unpredictable in financial terms. The late-nineteenth-century mining economy was notoriously a gamble.[13]

Further, this critical use of "mining" is itself organized by an assumption that positions the West as an object for Eastern consumption. I shall argue later in this essay that Harte's and Foote's Western narratives do not grant their Eastern readers so complacent a position. But the point I want to make here is that Harte and Foote did not choose to identify themselves either as migrant Eastern writers "mining" the West or as Western writers uncovering rich new veins of experience for an Eastern audience. To read a text like Franklin Walker's *San Francisco's Literary Frontier* is to understand that Harte, though he subsequently regarded writing for Eastern journals such as the *Atlantic Monthly* as the pinnacle of a literary career, operated in California not as at a literary outpost but rather within a complex literary scene with its own preoccupations and stylistic preferences.[14] It is true that Harte and many of his Californian literary contemporaries went east as depression hit San Francisco in the 1870s, but Harte actually spent only six years of his adulthood in the East, trying to establish a literary career, before settling for his last twenty-three years in Europe, where he moved within expatriate literary circles in England. This was not a writer necessarily disposed to work with a model of writing about California that locates that region at the margins of an Eastern American center.

Foote seems at first to follow the conventional strategy of identifying the West as a blank wilderness space, with her references to the West as a "historic vacuum" and her identification of herself as an exile (Paul, 11, 13). Though the publication of "regional" fiction such as Foote's is sometimes understood in terms of Eastern patronage of provincial outsiders of dubious literary ambitions,[15] Foote's relationship with her publisher actually replicated another model of middle-class East-West relations: as her husband got his first professional post in California through relatives, so Foote herself produced her first Western work through the husband of her close friend. And, like her engineering husband's, Foote's working life was spent on the move — not the life of an exile but rather a typical pattern of working in what were, in some ways, colonial provinces in the West. Foote's East consisted of a rural home and a well-established circle of acquaintance to which she returned in 1878–1879, in 1880, and in 1882–1884 (that is, during the period when she wrote "In Exile" and *The Led-Horse Claim*). The West in which she settled was, on each occasion of her return during the same period of the late 1870s and early 1880s, a very different place. New Almaden, Leadville, and Boise occupied very different positions in relation to, say, the culture of San Francisco, the East, or the Midwest. No simple formula of East/West difference need be used here either.

The understanding of Foote as an exile from a highly cultured Victorian center needs, in any case, to be revised in the light of her understanding of that term. Johnson quotes her as arguing, very early in her career, for the artist's need for the freedom of "exile" from the city to develop a "free yet precise way of working" (20). Accordingly, in her early years as an illustrator, she moved backwards and forwards, in and out of the high cultural milieu of New York, in the pattern we recognize from the careers of Sarah Orne Jewett and her circle. When she wrote her mining fictions, Foote continued to operate in a similar way, moving between involvement in the social and professional world of the West and "retreat" to her early home. While writers such as Jewett and Celia Thaxter define the regional space to which they "retreated" by reference to particular states of mind, particular configurations of social behavior, Foote does not make the same kind of distinction. East and West are not, in novels such as *The Led-Horse Claim* and *John Bodewin's Testimony*, clearly differentiated but are simply physically distant from one another, two spaces between which her characters "[rush] back and forth, thousands of miles at a stretch."[16]

Both Foote's and Harte's representations of the mining economy in the late nineteenth century problematize the very idea of the West as a different space. Certainly, we find both writers measuring the distance popularly imagined to exist between East and West in social and cultural terms. Bret Harte's insignia for the *Overland Monthly*, the grizzly standing on the railway line, snarling its hostility to the oncoming train, expresses a hostility to Eastern industrial capitalism as signified by machine technology; a hostility laced with irony, for such technology was making possible both the national distribution of this Western magazine and his own popularity. Meanwhile, Foote's arid West produces a condition of anomie from which her Eastern characters can barely recover. The deracinated hero and heroine in her early story, "In Exile," mourn the loss of their links to the East of their birth: "The East concerns itself very little about us, I can tell you! It can spare us."[17] But if their profound depression is associated with the landscape, it derives, as Etulain points out, from the destructive presence of the works of Eastern investors in the West (11).

By moving back twenty years to the 1850s in his tales, Harte seems, in particular, to play to the nostalgia of his audience for a world where men might test their mettle against the tough challenges of "the frontier," although it may be argued that the portrait of rootless miners and gamblers that he produces is not inaccurate, for the early gold rushes did indeed produce a highly unstructured society in California. Nevertheless, Harte's retrospective project can appear especially suspect when one considers that, by the late 1860s, when he was writing the stories collected in *The Luck of Roaring Camp and Other Stories* (1870), San Francisco was at the heart of a highly sophisticated economy operating in a global context, where miners and mining companies, although physically removed from the urban center, were actually locked into the operations of a city whose financial market rivaled that of New York. While the problems endemic within the mining communities of Harte's fiction are often resolved with a combination of some of nineteenth-century sentimental fiction's more threadbare techniques and the mechanics of Fate, Harte himself had experience (in his work in the Surveyor's Office and the Mint) of how and upon what grounds problems were actually solved in a multimillion-dollar industry.

The point is an obvious one, and it lies at the crux of the critique of Harte's work. Even the figure around whom Harte orga-

nizes some of his best work, the gambler, seems simply to anticipate the obsessive individualism and the preoccupation with male
identity that is played out in the "big country" of the Western
gunslinger, with all the deceptions about the facts of Western history that are associated with the Western. Certainly, we can see, in
such stories as "The Outcasts of Poker Flat" (1870) or "A Passage
in the Life of Mr. John Oakhurst" (1874), how the gambler seems
able to do all the things that industrial capitalism denies its workers; untrapped by routine, with skills that mark him out from the
rest, he works independently, he can make decisions. Harte's
heavily ironic commentary on those who label gambling as a vice
seems, on one level, simply to reinvent the fantasy of the West as
guarded by that grizzly.

David Wyatt interprets gambling in Harte differently, arguing
that it "sadly approximates the connection between effort, merit
and success in the larger culture. . . . Its outcomes are mechanis-
tic, largely a matter of luck" (xxv). This too seems apt. John
Oakhurst fails, after all, to save the "outcasts" from the vagaries
of the weather. The heroine of "A Protegee of Jack Hamlin's"
(1893) experiences a brief sense of freedom under the gambler's
auspices before finding herself deserted and desperate, the victim — albeit unintended — of the gambler's chivalry. But a reading of gambling in Harte's work that moves between the interpretative poles of escapist fantasy and the expression of the
instability of the Gold Rush West misses the implications of
Harte's choice of gambling as a metaphor around which to organize his representation of California.

As recent theoreticians of gambling have argued, the activity of
gambling is neither "analytically distinct from the realm of work
and production" nor does it operate according to universal patterns divorced from the specificities of its cultural context.[18] I
would argue that gambling in Harte can also be understood in just
this way, as commenting very precisely on the assumptions underpinning the social actors of the California rush. Gambling,
both in gaming and in speculation, was regarded from the first
gold rushes as a Californian obsession, while the association between gambling and the working behavior of Californians was a
matter of cliché, especially during the period in which Harte's
fictions are set.[19] Mining itself was notoriously — and with justi-

fication — perceived as gambling by absentee investors of the 1860s and 1870s as well as by the adventurers and the speculators of the prewar period (White, 260).

In Harte, the primacy of the relations of gambling in Californian culture is asserted in scenes such as in "Mrs. Skaggs's Husbands" (1873), where all conventional relations between husband and wife, father and son are erased in activity that is either explicitly or implicitly a gamble:

> "Wot do you say," said Johnson slowly, without looking at his companion, but abstractedly addressing himself to the landscape beyond,— "wot do you say to two straight games for one thousand dollars?"
>
> "Make it five thousand," replied Tommy reflectively also to the landscape, "and I'm in."[20]

Clearly, gambling is not to be considered merely as a vice or as a sign of entrapment. Harte's gambler heroes, in transferring the codes of the gambling table — grace under pressure, scrupulous adherence to established conventions — to their daily life, pursue a course they perceive to be honorable insofar as it operates independently of the rules of the community: Jack Hamlin, for example, protects a young woman threatened by disgrace as he would shield a greenhorn from the results of his inexperience at the gambling table. This, it seems, is the antecedent of the hero of the Western (the genre of which Harte is sometimes cited as progenitor). Yet a comparison of such behavior and its implications with the situation of the Western hero is instructive here. Although he may defy convention, this hero is carefully and delicately differentiated from the outlaw. He uses his skill to protect the whole community and is often subsequently assimilated (if not altogether comfortably) into the norms of modern society, specifically domesticity. Harte's gambler, by contrast, is neither effective in resisting the corrupt hypocrisies of the community nor is he in any sense "rewarded" by domestic happiness.

This is because gambling, as Harte's fictions make clear, does not actually constitute the escape from patterns of behavior dictated by convention that both the gambler and his critics imagine. Certainly, the community is repressive and without scruple in enforcing the bourgeois values of "civilization and refinement" ("Mliss," Collected Works, 2:3). For the developing middle class of

California, the gambler is condemned by his rejection of those Protestant virtues of self-denial, deferred gratification, and fiscal prudence on which they hypocritically insist that their success rests. For all his sense of his own special status, the gambler is actually reenacting the principles by which the wealth of those whom he rejects is actually created. His is American capitalism's special predilection for laissez-faire economics, its rigid categorization of activity, its ideology of separation between sexes, between leisure and work, home and "the world."

As the husband and son of the invisible Mrs. Skaggs play their desultory game of chance against the scene of destruction outside — the father apparently hardly understanding what he is doing, the son trying to keep the old man occupied, both unaware of their relationship — the reader prepares for the obvious point about moral and emotional impoverishment, and the degrading scramble for cash on which gambling and mining rest. It never comes. Full of ironies, this scene has not actually been one of desultory activity, chance, and poor reward, for which the father has made very precise plans. He is merely keeping his cards close to his chest. Harte's fictional West is always in the process of being domesticated, always either becoming assimilated or already taken over by the community-builders, a process organized around Eastern urban values that are subject to Harte's most withering scorn. But Harte's gambler signifies the actual agenda of Western "development," in all its focus on the accumulation of money as well as its self-deceiving sense of its own undomesticated heroism and unincorporated glamour.

The issue that Harte avoided, however, in writing a West defined by gambling and the hypocrisies around it, was the agency of big business in the creation of the West's mining economy. As Donald Worster argues, the East's West was "given birth by modern technology," and that technology was designed and managed by engineers in the pay of large corporations, a scene rather different from that delineated by Harte.[21] What is so particular about Mary Hallock Foote's West is that she makes this matrix of relationships between absentee investors, migrant speculators, and company engineers her subject. She defines the situation of the mining West not in terms of the world of the gambler posing as a social critic but in terms of the situation of the very figure whose responsibility it was to manage, by means of technological innovation and managerial know-how, the extraction of those resources for investors as likely to be Europeans as Easterners.

While Harte locates his discussion of the West in a scene that is only loosely historicized, Foote places her engineer hero in a very precise context. The role of the mining engineer in the 1870s, during which her mining fictions are set, was at a point of transition from a career for the well-educated, reputedly high-minded sons of the Eastern upper middle classes — the so-called "lace-boot brigade" described by Clark C. Spence — to a more specialized profession positioned within more complex organizational structures.[22] This change provided ripe material for a plot organized around conflicts between opposing forces: pastoralism and technology, moral and practical understandings of the process of Western "development," West and East; and Foote's engineers are indeed embroiled within situations of literally competing (mining) claims. But Foote does not choose to schematize her heroes' choices along such well-worn lines. Although the conventional view of engineers was, as Cecilia Tichi argues (98–99), to imagine them as the noble harbingers of rationalism and science, Foote represents them in terms of their actual function: as the agents of the investors, the people who made the mines run. As David F. Noble points out, the work of engineers was, in essence, to maximize profits by keeping down the cost of labor.[23] Foote shared the paternalist opposition of her lace-boot brigade husband and his fellow professionals to labor organizations, as her novel *Coeur D'Alene* (1894) makes clear.[24] She is, however, interested in imagining situations in which an engineer is caught in the complications of competing claims to the contents of the ground. The plots of *The Led-Horse Claim* and *John Bodewin's Testimony* are both organized around the attempt of one claimant to appropriate the most productive seam of a rival. In both cases, the rights and wrongs of the affair appear increasingly arbitrary, and victory is granted, in the end, to the inglorious (and, in the case of *The Led-Horse Claim*, disembodied) outside investor. In both cases, public and private duty are entangled in such a way as to make the process of finding justice (and especially the engineer's agency within that project) hopelessly problematic, and the incorporation of all the lives of the community within the business of making money very evident. So, for example, the plot of *John Bodewin's Testimony* turns upon the engineer-hero's refusal to assert the right of the claim of Mr. Newbold, a Kansas investor, to a piece of land that contains a rich vein, even though he knows that claim to be well founded. This is because Newbold's raffish rival, Colonel Harkins, has earlier protected his sister from the consequences of her husband's desertion. Bodewin cannot make up his mind to fulfill either his professional duty or his personal debt of gratitude.

Foote's compromised heroes are involved in activities that make their explicitly chivalric ideals irrelevant: the strong imperatives of their professional lives continually interrupt their attempts to come to any understanding of the women with whom they fall in love. The revelation at the end of *John Bodewin's Testimony* that the eponymous hero's middle name is Tristram is pointed not so much in its association between the novel's morally sensitive hero and Arthurian idealism, but rather in its Tennysonian reading of the irrelevance of such ideals to a modern imperial nation.

Critics such as James Maguire have argued that Foote's use of romantic plots is at odds with her mining material, but in fact there is no suggestion of private triumph resolving the dissonances of public life.[25] The private space that provides the sanctuary to which the harassed heroes and heroines of romantic fiction routinely retreat does not exist in these narratives, certainly not in the imprisoning vacuum of Cecil's temporary home in *The Led-Horse Claim* or the lodgings where Frances, in "In Exile," fades into despair. More characteristically, figures engage in encounters with one another in more exposed positions, where the destruction brought by mining of the landscape provides a metaphor for a more general context of their lives. Thus, Hilgard is to be found scratching the frozen ground for the ring his aristocratic lady has given him (*Led-Horse Claim*, 157), while John Bodewin's escape into domestic fulfillment — in the only apparently unincorporated space in the novel — takes place in a desert to the sound of the station telegraph machine.[26] In all of Foote's mining fictions, the personal and ecological terms of incorporating the West are intertwined. There is no question here, to use Donald Worster's terms anachronistically, of "calling a toxic dump the land of freedom" (15).

Foote's reading of the process of Western development through narratives of competing claims allows her to critique the rhetoric of progress that underpinned those involved, in every sense, in mining the West. Engineering itself, as a field, drew on the Spencerian social Darwinism of the era, with its assumption that what was destroyed was not useful anyway (Layton, 55). But the literary frame, national and British, within which Foote places her narratives of mining pulls her work away from the tropes of the American literature of Western development. The representation of underground mining as disruptive in *The Led-Horse Claim*, for example, echoes the Romantic critique of scientific rationalism that underpins, to use an example very familiar to Foote, Hawthorne's portrait of Roger Chillingworth in "The Leech and His Patient," a portrait that makes constant reference to mining as devilish in all its dimensions.[27] The response of Cecil as she sits alone in the Led-Horse mine is informed by a Darwinism that sidelines progress in favor of the fear of decay and that concentrates on the terror of shifts and changes so massive and slow as to be impenetrable to human understanding and investigation: "What a mysterious, vast, whispering dome was this! . . . There were far-off, indistinct echoes of life, and sub-animate mutterings, the slow respirations of the rocks, drinking air, and oozing moisture through their sluggish pores, swelling and pushing against their straitening bonds of timber. . . . Left to their own work, the inevitable forces around her would crush together the sides of the dark galleries, and crumble the rough-hewn dome above her head" (*Led-Horse Claim*, 113–114). Here, the miners' work represents a backward, deadly impulse, a "subanimate" compulsion to delve into darkness that is reminiscent of the use of Norse mythology and the märchen tradition in the work of fantasists such as George MacDonald.

Foote's mining fictions take place in a desolate space that is endlessly disputed, the reverse of the regenerative pastoral dream; in losing no opportunity to destabilize literary conventions of East-West relations, Foote also seems to refuse the exceptionalist rhetoric that justified Western "expansion." The plots of both *The Led-Horse Claim* and *John Bodewin's Testimony* are resolved by a West-East movement, the reverse of the convention. Both texts suggest the difficulty of marking out East and West: in the California of "In Exile," "everything is East," and the West itself is "pervaded by the subtle breath of the Orient" (330); the "Eastern" investor who precipitates the disastrous events of *John*

Bodewin's Testimony is from Kansas. In this context, there can be no mapping of East and West in gender terms, no "Eastern sophisticate" or domestic "Western" woman of instinct. All are immigrants, and, in the arid culture of the mining settlement, the female characters are no happier, no more ruined, except perhaps in terms of physical beauty, than their male counterparts.

To return, finally, to the consideration of the question with which this essay began: How do we understand the relative obscurity, on the one hand, of Harte, one of the inventors of the Western, and, on the other, of Foote, the writer unable, in some sense, to write the West or even participate in her life there? Margaret Duckett has argued convincingly in *Mark Twain and Bret Harte* that it was Twain who invented Harte as a mere hack,[28] a reputation that has yet to pass out of conventional critical usage. Foote meanwhile remains the Eastern gentlewoman, neither recoverable as a forgotten Western writer nor available for appropriation into the feminist critical discourse of regionalism.

Both critical fates are interesting, in their different ways, to the student of canon formation, gendered or not. More to the point here, perhaps, is to consider how far critical discussions of Harte's and Foote's work are still locked within readings of Western writing that deal in longstanding assumptions about the West as a special space where behavior is under negotiation — in essence, with the West in its role as the object of fantasy for Eastern Americans. Harte and Foote, who do not engage with this web of discussion, have become largely invisible within this field. Meanwhile, the "new" Western history that is producing an increasingly dominant historical narrative about the West speaks to understandings of the process and context of "development" and of the deceptions located in the terms "frontier" and "West" that are comparable to those that can be read in Harte's and Foote's work. Interestingly, mining is, in many ways, central to their interpretation of the West as industrial, urban, and ecologically in turmoil; Patricia Limerick's *The Legacy of Conquest*, a founding text of new Western history, begins with an arid landscape and the business of mining.[29] Far from "mining" the West for a quick profit and a quiescent audience of armchair tourists, Harte and Foote seem rather to have written a West that we thought we ourselves had uncovered.

1. Rodman W. Paul, ed., *A Victorian Gentlewoman in the Far West: The Reminiscences of Mary Hallock Foote* (San Marino, California: Huntington Library, 1972); Caroll Smith-Rosenberg, "The Female World of Love and Ritual: Relations between Women in Nineteenth-Century America," *Signs* 1 (1975): 1–29.

2. Richard W. Etulain, *Re-Imagining the Modern American West: A Century of Fiction, History and Art* (Tucson: University of Arizona Press, 1996), 10. For discussions of women in the West, see, for example, Lillian Schlissel's "Frontier Families: Crisis in Ideology," in *The American Self, Myth, Ideology and Popular Culture*, ed. Sam Girgus (Albuquerque: University of New Mexico Press, 1981), 155–164. More recent studies of Anglo women in the West, such as Sarah Deutsch's *No Separate Refuge, Culture, Class and Gender on an Anglo-Hispanic Frontier in the American South-West* (New York: Oxford University Press, 1987), and Peggy Pascoe's *Relations of Rescue: The Search for Female Authority in the American West, 1874–1939* (New York: Oxford University Press, 1990), have been less sanguine about the opportunities for any social class but still tend to assert a particularly restricted range, in terms of thought and behavior, among middle-class women.

3. During her early career, Foote illustrated a number of New England texts, such as giftbook editions for Fields, Osgood and Co. of Longfellow's *The Hanging of the Crane* (1874) and Hawthorne's *The Scarlet Letter* (1878), and editions of Whittier's *Hazel-Blossoms* (1875) and *Mabel Martin* (1876).

4. Foote, cited in Helena de Kay Gilder, "Author Illustrators II: Mary Hallock Foote," *Book Buyer* 11 (August 1894): 339–340.

5. These references are found, respectively, in Stanley T. Williams, *The Spanish Background of American Literature* (New Haven: Yale University Press, 1955), 211; David Wyatt, introduction to *Selected Stories and Sketches*, by Bret Harte (Oxford: Oxford University Press, 1995), xvi; John Milton, *The Novel of the American West* (Lincoln: University of Nebraska Press, 1980), 14; Joseph H. Gardner, "Bret Harte and the Dickensian Mode in America," *Canadian Review of American Studies* 2.2 (1971): 91; Wyatt, xiii.

6. Lee Ann Johnson, preface to *Mary Hallock Foote* (Boston: G. K. Hall, 1980), 9.

7. Melody Graulich, "Mary Hallock Foote 1847–1938," *Legacy* 3.2 (1986): 46–48; Graulich, "'O Beautiful for Spacious Guys': An Essay on the 'Legitimate Inclinations of the Sexes,'" in *The Frontier Experience and the American Dream: Essays on American Literature*, ed. David Mogen et al. (College Station: Texas A&M University Press, 1989), 192; James H. Maguire,

"Fictions of the West," in *The Columbia History of the American Novel*, ed. Emory Elliott (New York: Columbia University Press, 1991), 438.

8. The argument is cast in its most sympathetic form in Graulich, "'O Beautiful'"; she argues that Foote was attempting to delineate a female West for an Eastern female audience. But, in essence, this is the same point as Paul's when he argues that her "continued reliance on the Gilders in artistic and professional terms made Foote subject to Eastern tastes" (9).

9. Daniel H. Borus, *Writing Realism: Howells, James and Norris in the Mass Market* (Chapel Hill: University of North Carolina Press, 1989), 24.

10. Margaret Duckett, *Mark Twain and Bret Harte* (Norman: University of Oklahoma Press, 1964), 70–71, 330–332.

11. Arthur John, *The Best Years of the Century: Richard Watson Gilder, Scribner's Monthly and the Century Magazine, 1870–1909* (Urbana: University of Illinois Press, 1981), 63–65.

12. Gary Scharnhorst, *Bret Harte* (New York: Twayne, 1992), ix.

13. Richard White, "It's Your Misfortune and None of My Own," *A New History of the American West* (Norman: University of Oklahoma Press, 1991), 260.

14. Franklin Walker, *San Francisco's Literary Frontier*, 2d ed. (Seattle and London: University of Washington Press, 1969).

15. Richard H. Brodhead, *Cultures of Letters: Scenes of Reading and Writing in Nineteenth-Century America* (Chicago: University of Chicago Press, 1993), 118.

16. Mary Hallock Foote, *The Led-Horse Claim: A Romance of the Mining-Camps* (Boston: Osgood, 1883), 271.

17. Mary Hallock Foote, "In Exile: A Story in Two Parts," *Atlantic Monthly* 48 (August and September, 1881): 326. The full story encompasses 184–192 and 322–330.

18. Jan McMillen, "Understanding Gambling: History, Concepts, and Theories," in *Gambling Cultures: Studies in History and Interpretation*, ed. McMillen (London: Routledge, 1996), 11.

19. John Findlay, *People of Chance: Gambling in American Society from Jamestown to Las Vegas* (New York: Oxford University Press, 1986), 80–86.

20. Francis Bret Harte, *The Complete Writings of Bret Harte, Collected and Revised by the Author* (London: Chatto and Windus, 1914), 3:30.

21. Donald Worster, *Under Western Skies: Nature and History in the American West* (New York: Oxford University Press, 1992), 14; Edwin Layton, *The Revolt of the Engineers: Social Responsibility and the American Engineering Profession* (Cleveland: Case Western Reserve University Press, 1971), 2–4.

22. Clark C. Spence, *Mining Engineers and the American West: The Lace-Boot Brigade, 1849–1933* (New Haven: Yale University Press, 1970).

23. Cecilia Tichi, *Shifting Gears: Technology, Literature, and Culture in Modernist America* (Chapel Hill: University of North Carolina Press, 1987), 98–99; David F. Noble, *America by Design: Science, Technology and the Rise of Corporate Capitalism* (Oxford: Oxford University Press, 1977), 34.

24. Mary Hallock Foote, *Coeur D'Alene* (Boston: Houghton Mifflin, 1894).

25. James Maguire, *Mary Hallock Foote* (Boise, Idaho: Boise State College, 1972), 11, 14.

26. Mary Hallock Foote, *John Bodewin's Testimony* (1886; reprint, London: Frederick Warne, 1887), 188.

27. Nathaniel Hawthorne, *The Complete Writings of Nathaniel Hawthorne* (Boston: Houghton Mifflin, 1900), 6:184.

28. Margaret Duckett, *Mark Twain and Bret Harte* (Norman: University of Oklahoma Press, 1964).

29. Patricia Nelson Limerick, *The Legacy of Conquest: The Unbroken Past of the American West* (New York: Norton, 1987).

My Banker and I
Can Afford to Laugh!
Class and Gender in
Fanny Fern and
Nathaniel Hawthorne

ALISON M. J. EASTON

I shall begin with some familiar words, though I want
to give them a fresh spin: in an 1855 letter to his publisher, William D. Ticknor, Hawthorne vented his spleen on that "d —— d
mob of scribbling women" whose "trash" had highjacked American public taste.[1] Some late-twentieth-century feminist critics
have gleefully seized on this letter as a classic example of literary
men behaving badly, but in defending these women we must
avoid simply reinscribing this bipolar conception of nineteenth-
century literary culture that tends to treat writers of this period as
if they did indeed exclusively inhabit those separate spheres so
cherished in nineteenth-century ideology.[2] Although I can often
share David Leverenz's conclusion that "the two sexes can barely
see each other,"[3] in this essay I will instead investigate the extent
to which the works of Hawthorne and his contemporary, Fanny
Fern, can be seen to inhabit the same world. In particular, I will
suggest that if we situate the authors within the intersections of
class and gender, we can identify the ways in which some of their
writings are indeed explicitly engaged with related aspects of the
same social order.

"Not Merely Silk and Suavity and Surface":
Gender, Class, and Sexuality in Dialogue

By looking more closely at Hawthorne's letters of this period,
we can contextualize his famous remark and show some parallels

as well as oppositions between him and Fern. Those strictures on women writers did not prevent him from immediately going on to read Fern's latest bestseller, *Ruth Hall*, and, just two weeks later, he writes to Ticknor consciously exploring this apparent contradiction:

> In my last, I recollect, I bestowed some vituperation on female authors. I have since been reading "Ruth Hall"; and I must say I enjoyed it a good deal. The woman writes as if the devil was in her; and that is the only condition under which a woman ever writes anything worth reading. Generally, women write like emasculated men, and are only to be distinguished from male authors by greater feebleness and folly; but when they throw off the restraints of decency, and come before the public stark naked, as it were — then their books are sure to possess character and value. Can you tell me anything about this Fanny Fern? If you meet her, I wish you would let her know how much I admire her. (17:307–308)

At first sight this passage appears so mired in gender preconceptions that one is relieved that Fern's carefully maintained anonymity at this stage of her career would have protected her from being given even a gentlemanly summary of its contents. However, we should bear in mind that the author of a self-confessed "h——ll-fired" novel (16:312), *The Scarlet Letter*, might well half approve of the devil as literary muse and startlingly be able to imagine a woman similarly inspired. It is not so difficult either to see broad parallels between Fern's Ruth and Hawthorne's Hester as these characters struggle with their identities as wife/lover, mother, paid worker, and creative artist within various patriarchal structures. Much as Hester — the seamstress — is envisaged at the end of the novel as the counselor of women made unhappy by their relationships with men, so is the ex-seamstress, Ruth, portrayed receiving letters from female readers sharing the problems of their lives.[4]

But this parallel does not immediately help us understand the troubling sexual implications in Hawthorne's praise of a "naked" Fern. Hawthorne himself, qualifying the image with "as it were," seems to have felt his depiction had slipped a little out of hand. But there is a second, later version of this compliment that clarifies Hawthorne's interest: Fern's capacity to strip off the polite coverings of bourgeois existence: "Certainly not an exhibition to please Nat Willis [Fern's brother, whose failure to support her is savagely exposed in *Ruth Hall*] nor one to suit the finikin, this spectacle of Fanny Fern in little more than her bare bones, her heart pulsating visibly and indecently in its cage of ribs. Still, there are ribs and there is a heart. Here is not merely silk and suavity and surface."[5] What Fern and Hawthorne have in common is an intense dislike of what both called "humbug": the hypocrisy and duplicities of the middle class. Fern chose to expose these shortcomings more directly and persistently than Hawthorne, although both authors, as we shall see, had to work in their writings toward some accommodation with the class they inhabited and addressed. Fern's writer-protagonist, Ruth, describes herself as having "the courage to call things by their right names, and the independence to express herself boldly on subjects which to the timid and clique-serving, were tabooed."[6]

Hawthorne, then, is not making the standard complaint against outspoken women writers — that they are "unfeminine." His objection to most other women writers, who do not directly critique their society, seems to be that they have unreflectingly rehearsed the discourses of femininity to service masculine authority. Hawthorne sees Fern as refusing these cultural illusions. In this context, "decency," a key term in both of Hawthorne's comments, is more than sexual; it encapsulates values required to distinguish middle-class from working-class existence and to hide the former's moneyed construction. By expressing these values in terms of gender roles and female sexuality in particular, this class mystified its economic base.

Hawthorne and Fern inevitably tread gingerly in this area because it involves the sexual. Nonetheless, both have a fundamentally economic understanding of the connections between impoverished women, their need to find work, and the concomitant loss of the sexual respectability that defines one as "woman" in middle-class terms. To work for money was to advertise one's lack of a male protector, without whom (such was deemed the threat of masculine sexuality) the female would only with difficulty remain "pure." As Laura Hapke points out, the public debate on the feminine morality of female factory workers early on overshadowed concern for low wages, and appeals on behalf of the seamstress (Fern's choice of occupation, I note, for both herself and her heroine) was made on her construction as a home-working, genteel, and sexually virtuous figure.[7] The fear too lurks in Hawthorne's compliments about *Ruth Hall* and in his relief startlingly expressed to his wife that she had never had to "prostitute [herself] to the public" (17:456–457) as women writers do.

All Fern's novels —*Ruth Hall, Rose Clark, Fanny Ford*—contain this understanding. Ruth is just a glance away from prostitution when she looks out of her lodging-house window on the brothel opposite (furnished like a wealthy home and patronized by "businessmen, substantial-looking family men" [90]); and her first stay in a boardinghouse is introduced to the reader through the voices of two male residents leeringly speculating on whether she is sexually available, like another female worker, the "little milliner" (73). Ruth blushes when, on first attempting to sell her writing, the middle-class editors in the newspaper office fail to rise to their feet when she enters — even with a profession such as authorship, a bourgeois widow who enters the marketplace is automatically declassed and hence debased. Fern herself had to manage the exposure that her writing gave her, enduring slurs on her reputation that left her with few women willing to risk friendship even while she was deeply admired by her readers.[8] Only when she was very rich indeed could she safely, but still defiantly, make the joke in the preface of *Fresh Leaves* that "my banker and I can afford to laugh!" Capitalism goes arm in arm with female middle-class security and pleasure; respectability has only one guarantor, money.

All these observations underline the fragility of that middle-class life. There was, as Michael T. Gilmore points out, no unbroken hegemony in mid-nineteenth-century America. Leverenz comments, "unstable in membership, starkly insecure in prospects, this was a class defining itself far more by its fear of falling into the working class than by its hopes of rising further."[9] Arguably, bourgeois domestic ideology went into overdrive in order to seal those all-too-permeable boundaries. The deep interest in class in the 1840s and 1850s shown by many journalists, politicians, and social commentators further indicates political and moral uneasiness, though some attempts were made to dissipate anticipated conflict by envisaging a harmony of interests.[10] But the 1850s, the decade in which *The House of the Seven Gables, The Blithedale Romance, Fern Leaves from Fanny's Port-Folio, Ruth Hall,* and *Fresh Leaves* all appeared, was a time of social crisis, when class divisions began to be seen without that veil of middle-class values. Christine Stansell argues that this crisis brought a shift from seeing poverty in terms of virtue and vice to a direct concern for material conditions such as housing, public health, and mortality rates. In previous decades evangelical gentlemen and ladies crossed class boundaries to dispense charity to the virtuous poor; now the poor were seen as the product of their environment and feared.[11]

As we shall see, both Fern and Hawthorne knew from personal experience the fragility of that middle-class life and understood it as a construction. Poverty could shake the bourgeois world, exposing its foundation on artificial structures rather than eternal verities. This does not mean that Fern and Hawthorne rejected that world and its values, but they did have a different view of it than many of their contemporaries professed to have. Fern rejects what Amy Schrader Lang calls a "strategy of displacement," typical of women writers, that subsumed class differences into a vision of the harmonious home (130). When Fern does portray such harmony, it is with the full knowledge of the effort it takes and its financial cost. Hawthorne's work at times embraces that vision of the middle-class home with an awareness of the alternatives that made it preferable.

Although Fern and Hawthorne have a similar sense of the fragility of middle-class life, we need to note the differences between them. Fern, without a supportive male network and faced with the inherent difficulties all women of whatever class faced in the search for paid work, fell further than most writers, male or female — right out of the middle class into six months of dire poverty. Precipitated by her need to leave her disastrous, though respectable, marriage, she had to work for less than subsistence wages as a seamstress before her first newspaper article was accepted. So Ruth Hall's position as the destitute widow is entirely typical; unsupported widowhood would place her in the same situation as immigrant and black women who continued to work after marriage and competed for scarce, underpaid employment. Alice Kessler-Harris estimates that in 1860 only 30 percent of women worked for money, and the majority of these were unmarried.[12] Ruth's family's expectation that she should find work suggests profound ignorance of how social conditions were changing in an industrializing America with the new formation of both middle and working classes.

The experience of lower-class work made Fern's vision different from most middle-class women writers who were her contemporaries. Like them, she claims in her writings what Lauren Berlant terms the "sovereignty of subjective knowledge,"[13] but in her case this experiential knowledge made her question views, commonly held by women of her class, that interpret power entirely in terms of gender. Although there must have been a gap between the ideological images of middle-class domesticity and the actuality of these people's lives (no one could have lived that life wholly unconsciously, and Fern's readers clearly enjoyed the way her sketches drew attention to the work that even the wife had to perform to create the calm, pretty world of the bourgeois home),[14] many seem to have chosen at least in public to maintain that illusion. Fern had personally discovered that the base was economic, not moral.

As Gillian Brown argues, Fern makes Ruth transgress that crucial gender boundary between domesticity and the market.[15] Fern herself went on to be the best-paid columnist of her day and to make thousands of dollars from her books, but she seems never to have lost the awareness that her spell of poverty had given her. In article after article, she returns to the question of the material dependency of the middle-class wife and the situation of widows,[16] and a possible sign of its personal importance to her may be found in her decision to publish her most outspoken piece on the lives of laboring women, "The Working-Girls of New York," under her legal name of Sara P. Parton rather than the nom de plume she normally used even in private life.[17] In other pieces too she exposes the complicity between the market and domestic values demonstrated by Gillian Brown. "Where the Money Is Made" also contains her fundamental emphasis on the capacity of experience to transform an understanding of economic realities. She asks what it would be like to take the perfumed, elegant middle-class woman to the commercial workplace where the male members of her family make their money: "I think *that* could be a new experience for my lady."[18]

Hawthorne's situation must, of course, also be construed in terms of class as well as gender. Like many male writers of the period, his background was upper class. Gilmore argues that

Hawthorne "represents a notable instance of antebellum declassing" and describes him as an "impoverished scion of the American patriciate" who was also "on the verge of redefining his social position as a member of the rising professional class." As both T. Walter Herbert and Walter Benn Michaels observe, Jacksonian politics provided him, as a gentleman, with a party with which he could associate without aligning himself with the expanding commercial world of the rising middle class.[19] This Bowdoin College–educated white male fastidiously selected authorship as his preferred profession (with a long apprenticeship financed by his family) but found himself in a changing commercial literary marketplace — the patrician male facing with distaste competitive individualism, gentility reluctantly expected to work for his living (Leverenz, 11–41). For many years, from the time he contemplated marriage, he was faced with insufficient remuneration (though just enough to keep the servant necessary to maintain his status). On three occasions this situation necessitated his taking paid state employment (jobs made available to him as a male member of a still powerful elite). When he lost the Salem Custom House post in 1849, only his family and his wife's secret savings kept him afloat while he wrote *The Scarlet Letter*. A self-proclaimed "citizen of somewhere else" (1:4), he milked his next government post while repeatedly professing himself disenchanted with his country.

Given these anxieties, it is not surprising that throughout Hawthorne's years as consul in Liverpool his comments on contemporary male and female writers are so often embedded in letters meticulously detailing to his financial representative (Ticknor) exactly how much money he is making out of this post. For the first time in his life Hawthorne was affluent, and he marveled at this change. The paragraph that so notoriously attacks those "scribbling women" actually begins:

It seems to be a general opinion that the Consular bill will not pass. If it should, I shall (according to your statement) be at least a good deal better off than when I took the office. Reckoning O'Sullivan's three thousand dollars [money reluctantly lent to a friend], I shall have bagged about $15000; and I shall estimate the Concord place and my copyrights together at $5000 more;— so that you see I have the twenty thousand, after all! I shall spend a year on the Continent, and then decide whether to go back to the Way Side [his house in Concord], or to stay abroad and write books. But I had rather hold this office two years longer; for I have not seen half enough of England, and there is the germ of a new Romance in my mind, which will be all the better for ripening slowly. Besides, America is now wholly given over to a d——d mob of scribbling women. (17:304)

It is important to note that Hawthorne uses some of the same terms to critique his own work; as Evan Carton points out, Hawthorne frequently used "scribbling" to describe his own writing. The fact that male and female writers were both struggling to make a living in the same market may well account for what James D. Wallace calls Hawthorne's "mixture of liberality and vitriol" for his fellow sufferers and competitors.[20] The gendered expression of these critical judgments obscures the economic reality faced by writers of both sexes, even as it points to the differences each would find in their cultural reception.

"Rank Is the Grosser Substance of Wealth": Fictional Translations of Class

I want now to carry these issues of class and gender into a discussion of some fiction of the 1850s by Fern and Hawthorne. In 1851, while Fern was earning seventy-five cents a week sewing, Hawthorne's finances (after *The Scarlet Letter* but with the Liverpool post still in the future) had only partly recovered: "he must keep producing" (2:xvi). *The House of the Seven Gables* was finished in January 1851, and by November he had begun *The Blithedale Romance*. Fern's successes were not far behind, with the first volume of her newspaper pieces published in 1853 and *Ruth Hall* in 1855. All these works are products of an important decade when, as I have indicated, attitudes toward class began to change, and the three novels I discuss here stand out together because they are all explicitly "about" class and the experience of moving between classes, though Fern's and Hawthorne's senses of how classes are constructed are modified by the different gender positions from which they begin.

I start with *The House of the Seven Gables* as Hawthorne's first work to deal explicitly and extensively with class.[21] Crucially, one of the principal images Hawthorne chooses to launch this historicized exploration of shifting class formations is the figure of a woman forced by poverty into paid work outside the home (as we have already seen in *Ruth Hall*, the event most likely to dismantle the bourgeois illusion). This image immediately provokes in the narrator the following meditation on class in America: "In this republican country, amid the fluctuating waves of our social life, somebody is always at the drowning point. The tragedy is enacted with as continual a repetition as that of a popular drama on a holiday, and, nevertheless, is felt as deeply, perhaps as when a hereditary noble sinks below his order. More deeply; since, with us rank is the grosser substance of wealth and a splendid establishment, and has no spiritual existence after the death of these, but dies hopelessly along with them" (2:38). This analysis of an unstable America has jettisoned the standard ideology of democracy as a guarantor of individual prosperity, that notion of a "country where everything is free to the hand that can grasp it" (2:181). Instead, it identifies money, or the lack of it, as the baseline for a distinctively American stratification — indeed, the actual coin in Hepzibah's "cent-shop" is much emphasized. That the novel explores the instabilities of such a system in terms of an English class system suggests that this is the main vocabulary available to Hawthorne to express economic demarcations to a society that ostensibly denies the inevitability of such differences. Holgrave's alternative radicalism is presented as marginal to this society's actual power structures. As Sean Wilentz shows, by the 1850s a shared vision of the American republic had "virtually collapsed and been replaced by new and opposing conceptions of republican politics and the social relations that would best sustain them."[22] The working men in the street, present at both the beginning and end of the novel, clearly know what a cent-shop involves, and Uncle Venner is a reminder of the poorhouse awaiting the destitute elderly. The novel also demonstrates a fundamental similarity between two apparently distinct social systems. Gentility and ancient propertied power do not in decline yield to free democratic opportunity but instead sometimes metamorphose into new corrupt forms of high politics, law, and business. Holgrave, protean worker, has little power and less money.[23]

However, something odd happens to the figure of the working woman. Phoebe stoutly declares, "'I mean to earn my bread'" (74), and asserts that she knows how to do it from her upbringing in that earlier economic order of the New England village. But she doubles as the midcentury middle-class housewife, whose prime characteristic should be her freedom from paid work outside the home. Although this is all too like those middle-class discourses that rendered the work of housekeeping invisible, on closer inspection we find, as Richard Millington illuminatingly argues, a self-conscious use by Hawthorne of those discourses of the domestic and the feminine as well as an awareness of the fragility and narrowness of Phoebe's pretty world. Furthermore, to be both housewife and shopkeeper (the then-shocking image of the private home opened up by economic necessity to the intrusions of commerce) clearly threatens her charm. In having his characters finally retreat to the countryside, Hawthorne refuses to disguise what is happening: like the middle-class love of rural villas, this move represents sheer escapism from the city of industrial capitalism and is possible only with money.[24]

Moreover, since the source of Phoebe's inheritance has been made abundantly clear throughout, one can hardly argue that her presence successfully launders it. Her femininity, though offered as a universal quality transcending social difference, cannot obliterate the classed society of which she is a part. The corrupt, vicious patriarch dies to the narrator's glee — humbug demolished — but his money persists. Furthermore, patriarchal marriage laws will simply pass her wealth over to her ex-radical husband. The marriage proposal is made while the corpse sits, a continuing presence in an adjoining room, and the oddly unromantic negotiations that then ensue between Phoebe and Holgrave make clear the compromises of middle-class life. This text is too sardonic and shifting in its voices to be a mouthpiece of bourgeois ideology.

Before comparing this text with Fern's narrative of a working woman, it is useful to see the direction Hawthorne takes in his next novel, *The Blithedale Romance*. Placed in the context of *The House of the Seven Gables*, *Blithedale* clearly offers another narrative about work, poverty, and class, in which differing positions of women and men are highly revealing of class realities. This time Hawthorne sets himself to imagine a utopian community seeking alternatives to present-day classed society, particularly for the creative artist, but he comes to an even darker conclusion.[25]

Beneath the gender tensions dominating the plot, class is shown still to affect relations both between characters and between Blithedale and the society in which it has set itself. Priscilla and Zenobia are most strongly marked by their class differences: Zenobia, enormously wealthy with a corruptly rich father now reduced to living among the city's poorest; Priscilla, a seamstress, that icon of working-class poverty, whom Zenobia effortlessly identifies and pointedly places socially as below her dressmaker in status. The fact they are half-sisters underlines the differences that financial status, rather than family, can make. Although Old Moodie is wrong in assuming that Zenobia will treat Priscilla as a lady would her servant, Zenobia still expects Silas, the farmer, to bring her fire and water in the morning, for all that they have sat down in the kitchen (not the dining room) the evening before as supposed social equals who will be laboring together. Hollingsworth himself is distinguished from the other Blithedalers — an ex-blacksmith, he is less educated than they. While the "socialism" of the community would render such class distinctions obsolete, it seems that Hollingsworth has every intention of riding roughshod over these intellectuals, provided he is rich enough to do it. Zenobia loses her attractiveness for him when it becomes clear she is not independently wealthy.

Coverdale is surprisingly acute in his understanding of the class games being played, and he comments wryly on the community's attempt to ignore the social stratification still in operation (even while perpetuating traditional gender roles in their new work). It is not only that the servants are unsure how to behave; Coverdale considers that the Blithedalers, dressing down in the worn-out versions of their expensive clothes and under no financial compulsion to stay on the farm (3 : 24), are in fact taking work away from agricultural laborers who need this work to survive. Moreover, while the community is modeled on early republican notions of agricultural life that reject that key concept of midcentury capitalism, "competition" (3 : 19), Silas sees farming in terms of the market (selling wood) and of competing with the market-gardeners who produce food for a growing Boston. Blithedale's illusory classlessness will have no effect on America's economic structures: "where once we toiled with our whole hopeful hearts, the town-paupers, aged, nerveless, and disconsolate, creep sluggishly afield" (3:246). It is merely a part of the suburbs.

The narrative is at pains to clarify the gendered consequences of this situation and to shape them to a disastrous conclusion. *The Blithedale Romance*, though it ends with a marriage, fails to offer even this as a compromised middle-class solution — no middle-class home shelters these people, no children are born. Priscilla, who embodies Hollingsworth's entirely conventional vision of womanhood ("a gentle parasite," observes Coverdale) is made to seem outrageous, even immoral, in her blinkered devotion — another mesmerized performance for a patriarchal egotist. Zenobia, who had expressed her feminism in terms of speaking "her whole heart and her whole mind" (3:120)— an image not unrelated to Hawthorne's vision of Fern — is silenced. She says: "The mistrust and disapproval of the vast bulk of society throttle us, as with two giant hands at our throats! We mumble a few weak words, and leave a thousand better ones unsaid. You let us write a little, it is true, on a limited range of subjects" (3:120). Within Zenobia the more traditional emotional structures of romance intersect with and nearly destroy her feminist principles, and she is condemned both for loving and for being a feminist.

Fern imagines a different trajectory for her female artist-hero. Moreover, Ruth possesses experience of class and gender intersections that clarifies rather than confuses the situation, unlike Coverdale, who cannot sort out sexual feelings that are simultaneously typical of and resistant to middle-class nineteenth-century masculinity — ogling at Zenobia's sensuous body while admiring her political position, and both craving and despising Priscilla's "sexless," conservative femininity.[26] Hawthorne ends his text with impotence; Fern, with appropriated power.

Ruth Hall's subtitle, "A Domestic Tale of the Present Time," seems to announce a limited subject, and at first middle-class life is presented apparently quite conventionally in terms of gender rather than economics and class. Ruth wonders if her husband-to-be will continue loving her. But for a bride even to consider such doubts (and in the novel's second paragraph) is disturbingly to introduce a practical note into the ostensible romance. Blinkered by her upbringing, Ruth is then shown to be asking the wrong question: Harry's affection may compensate for her unloving father and brother, but his death leaves her wholly unprotected against the consequences of that failure of family love in both sets of parents. The domestic idyll is deliberately allowed to flower in Ruth's and the readers' heads, only to wither overnight. Within hours (and a mere chapter) of her husband's dying, we know she is penniless. We have previously been warned (but failed to understand) that there are worse things than a child's death, the topos of ultimate suffering in contemporary women's fiction. The "worse thing" is destitution.

But even before that domestic happiness is shattered, it has been contextualized, if the reader looks closely, in terms of deep structures of money and class. Ruth and Harry have married, as his parents point out, before he is established financially. Theirs is a new, unstable class. Both their fathers started life as poor men. Although the Ellets have chosen to distance themselves from those origins, the Halls, further from new urban life, remain connected to their past: clothing made, bread baked, hard journeys. The Halls still sit with their cook to save heating costs, and they disapprove of the Ellet children, though their own son wears as fancy cravats as Hyacinth. Hyacinth solves the problem by marrying money and by dishonest journalism; Harry for a time makes "a very good business" (31), while Ruth sews curtains and entertains his business associates with unobtrusive cheapness.

Throughout the novel, even in this opening section, the relations between classes are densely represented and finely calibrated. The novel itself is constructed of a collage of voices of all classes.[27] These people are often presented in relation to another section of society. At the upper end we have the rich: hotel visitors are seen partly through the waiters, and the Millets, carefully preserving their status while Ruth does her laundry in their kitchen, are seen from the servants' perspective. We see the Herberts at family tea: their money comes from a ladies clothing store, but they recoil from the idea of a female member of their own class working side by side with their female sweatshop employees, even though starvation threatens her (the historian Stuart Blumin identifies the separation of retail from manufacture as one defining element in the formation of middle-class life) (84–85, 89).

This separation-connection between classes in both work and socializing allows the Herberts to condone their friends' low payment for services from the lower classes, and translates into a squeamish conflation of money, morals, and aesthetics when the ladies, intending to visit Ruth, recoil from the "vulgar" lodging house (81).

The novel also gives us the people who make possible easy middle-class life. We see cooks, housemaids, washerwomen, farm workers, and hackney coach drivers, as well as a wet nurse, nursemaid, dressmaker, tailor, seamstress, landlady, and boardinghouse keeper. Those near the bottom socially are more outspoken about their employers and tend to be more sympathetic to Ruth. These are the Irish and African Americans who are racially prevented from possible assimilation (Fern marks them as different in their speech), and who, as I noted earlier, were the only groups whose married women worked and were therefore debarred, unlike the German family Ruth sees in the tenement opposite, from any semblance of middle-class life. Those who have social ambitions (the dressmaker, the cabbies) tend to toady to the class they aspire to and appear as villains. In this hierarchical, competitive environment, there are few class or gender loyalties (something also true of the Hawthorne novels). Some of Harry's business associates are fleetingly generous; others cheat her. Her middle-class origins win her no breaks with editors of her class; exceptionally, John Walter makes her a decent remuneration, but out of an unusual sense of social justice that is, however, expressed in terms of her "market value" (142). Ruth's family are prepared to let her sink, provided no one of their rank finds out ("decency" indeed).

Ruth, the one who physically and materially moves across classes, does not, however, identify with the working class, though she feels great sympathy for the poorest once she is in their midst. There are lines she will not cross and etiquette she wants to preserve (for example, the ambivalence of the moment when she notices she is writing in her lodging-house room still dressed in her "walking costume" [145]). Yet, for all the "vulgarity" of the boardinghouse keeper, Mrs. Skiddy, whose tale is told at length, Ruth surely resembles her in learning how to flourish without a husband.[28] Whereas Hawthorne's exposure of the contradictions within class/gender ideologies leads to compromise in

Seven Gables and impasse in *Blithedale*, Fern is able to imagine the best of both worlds for her heroine because she keeps her sights so steadily on the financial and, unlike Hawthorne, does not experience a dangerous sexual frisson in taking the covers off bourgeois existence. Like Fern's, Ruth's writing lacks "humbug," yet it is also largely described in terms of work for money, and this money is charted in precise detail up to the point where payment is large enough to restore her class status — a fact Fern thrusts at the reader by printing the image of money on the very page of her text, the bank share certificate that baldly indicates the sum needed to maintain (without a husband) children and a middle-class home. Unlike Hepzibah, Phoebe, Priscilla, and Zenobia, Fern and her alter ego speak out, pleasing both her feminist readers and her banker.[29]

Twentieth-century critics have placed Hawthorne and Fern in entirely different literary traditions; because these traditions have been defined preeminently by gender, the importance of class and the gendering within class have been obscured. It is these complex intersections of class and gender that should command our attention as we draw the writers together. Although both had bourgeois lives by and large, they found themselves at various times at different levels in their class-stratified society. What they had in common was the experience of class *differences*, which gave them understandings that their more securely placed readers either failed to see or (as seems more likely in an economically unstable world) preferred to ignore or interpret in terms of appropriate "decencies." In contrast to many of their readers, Fern and Hawthorne were exiles in this middle class to which they ostensibly belonged and for which they wrote. Fern made much more money than Hawthorne (being an unsupported woman concentrated the mind wonderfully), elbowing her way to the top where no woman was permitted, while Hawthorne felt excluded from the place rightfully his because of class and gender. They would nevertheless have had much to discuss, including the economics of authorship and the pretenses of a classed America. "If you meet her," Hawthorne says to Ticknor, "I wish you would let her know how much I admire her," yet there was probably no way in the discourse of polite middle-class exchange between the sexes that he could have explained to her this admiration.

NOTES

1. Nathaniel Hawthorne, *The Centenary Edition of the Works of Nathaniel Hawthorne*, ed. William Charvat et al., vol. 17, *The Letters, 1853–1856* (Columbus: Ohio State University Press, 1987), 304. All second and subsequent references to this and other sources are included in the text.

2. See Lora Romero, "Domesticity and Fiction," in *The Columbia History of the American Novel*, ed. Emory Elliott (New York: Columbia University Press, 1991), 110–129.

3. David Leverenz, *Manhood and the American Renaissance* (Ithaca: Cornell University Press, 1989), 165.

4. Fern also received many letters. See Joyce W. Warren, *Fanny Fern: An Independent Woman* (New Brunswick, N.J.: Rutgers University Press, 1992), 259–260.

5. From Ethel Parton's manuscript, "Fanny Fern, An Informal Biography," quoted by Warren, *Fanny Fern*, 122.

6. Fanny Fern, *Ruth Hall and Other Writings*, ed. Joyce W. Warren (New Brunswick, N.J.: Rutgers University Press, 1986), 133. See also Linda Grasso, "Anger in the House: Fanny Fern's *Ruth Hall* and the Redrawing of Emotional Boundaries in Mid-Nineteenth-Century America," *Studies in the American Renaissance* (1995): 251–261.

7. Laura Hapke, "Proletarians or True Women? The Female Working-Class Experience and Nineteenth-Century U.S. Authors," *Overhere: A European Journal of American Culture* 17 (1997): 5–27. On sexual respectability and class, see Joyce W. Warren, "Fracturing Gender: Women's Economic Independence," in *Nineteenth-Century American Women Writers: A Critical Reader*, ed. Karen L. Kilcup (Malden, Mass.: Blackwell, 1998), 146–163.

8. See Warren, *Fanny Fern*, 179–188. For Fern's sympathetic presentations of prostitution, see, for example, "First Pure," in *Fresh Leaves* (New York: Mason Brothers, 1857), 79–82, and "Blackwell's Island 3," reprinted in *Ruth Hall and Other Writings*, 306–309.

9. Michael T. Gilmore, "Hawthorne and the Making of the Middle Class," in *Rethinking Class: Literary Studies and Social Formation*, ed. Wai Chee Dimock and Michael T. Gilmore (New York: Columbia University Press, 1994), 216; Leverenz, *Manhood and the American Renaissance*, 78. See also Stuart M. Blumin, *The Emergence of the Middle Class: Social Experience in the American City, 1760–1900* (Cambridge: Cambridge University Press, 1989), especially 231–257; Michael Newbury, "Healthful Employment: Hawthorne, Thoreau, and Middle-Class Fitness," *American Quarterly* 47 (1995): 681–714; Stephen Knadler, "Hawthorne's Genealogy of Madness: *The House of*

the Seven Gables and Disciplinary Individualism," *American Quarterly* 47 (1995): 280–308.

10. Amy Schrader Lang, "Class and the Strategies of Sympathy," in *The Culture of Sympathy: Race, Gender, and Sentimentality*, ed. Shirley Samuels (New York: Oxford University Press, 1992), 128–130.

11. Christine Stansell, *City of Women: Sex and Class in New York, 1789–1860* (New York: Knopf, 1986), 198–203.

12. Alice Kessler-Harris, *Out to Work: A History of Wage-Earning Women in the United States* (New York: Oxford University Press, 1982), 45–72.

13. Lauren Berlant, "The Female Woman: Fanny Fern and the Form of Sentiment," *American Literary History* 3 (1991): 431.

14. See, for example, "Family Jars" and "A Voice from Bedlam," in *Ruth Hall and Other Writings*, 221–223, 319–320.

15. Gillian Brown, *Domestic Individualism: Imagining Self in Nineteenth-Century America* (Berkeley: University of California Press, 1990), 139–141.

16. See Fern, *Fern Leaves from Fanny's Port-Folio* (Auburn, N.Y.: Derby and Miller, 1853).

17. See Warren, *Fanny Fern*, 265–266. Fern's solution was equal pay for equal work.

18. Quoted in Warren, *Fanny Fern*, 264.

19. Gilmore, "Hawthorne and the Making of the Middle Class," 234. Michael T. Gilmore, *American Romanticism and the Marketplace* (Chicago: University of Chicago Press, 1985); T. Walter Herbert, *Dearest Beloved: The Hawthornes and the Making of the Middle-Class Family* (Berkeley: University of California Press, 1993); Walter Benn Michaels, *The Gold Standard and the Logic of Naturalism: American Literature at the Turn of the Century* (Berkeley: University of California Press, 1987). See also Lawrence Buell, *New England Literary Culture: From Revolution through Renaissance* (Cambridge: Cambridge University Press, 1986), 375–392.

20. Evan Carton, The Marble Faun: *Hawthorne's Transformations* (New York: Twayne, 1992), 9; and James D. Wallace, "Hawthorne and the Scribbling Women Reconsidered," *American Literature* 62 (1990): 207.

21. See, however, Nicholas Bromell, "'The Bloody Hand of Labor': Work, Class, and Gender in Three Stories by Hawthorne," *American Quarterly* 42 (1990): 542–564; and the discussion of *The Scarlet Letter* in Gilmore, "Hawthorne and the Making of the Middle Class."

22. Sean Wilentz, *Chants Democratic: New York City and the Rise of the American Working Class, 1788–1850* (New York: Oxford University Press, 1984), 15.

23. For readings of the novel in related terms, see Leverenz, *Manhood*

and the American Renaissance, 90–93; Brown, *Domestic Individualism*, 69–95; Herbert, *Dearest Beloved*, 93–95; Shelley Streeby, "Haunted Houses: George Lippard, Nathaniel Hawthorne, and Middle-Class America," *Criticism* 38 (1996): 443–472. In *Practicing Romance: Narrative Form and Cultural Engagement in Hawthorne's Fiction* (Princeton: Princeton University Press, 1992), Richard Millington provides a particularly fine reading in terms of Hawthorne's deliberate engagement with the center of that culture.

24. See Brown, *Domestic Individualism*, on invisible housekeeping (63–95) and the "country-seat" (71–77); Millington, *Practicing Romance*, on the representation of Phoebe (115–122).

25. Newbury is particularly useful on middle-class unease about the place of manual work and artistic work in the new midcentury capitalist order ("Healthful Employment").

26. See Ken Egan, Jr., "Hawthorne's Anti-Romance: *Blithedale* and Sentimental Culture," *Journal of American Culture* 11 (1988): 45–52.

27. Here I modify Warren's arguments, *Fanny Fern*, 130–131, that Fern was preoccupied with an economics of gender rather than class.

28. See Susan K. Harris, *Nineteenth-Century American Women's Novels: Interpretative Strategies* (Cambridge: Cambridge University Press, 1990), 122. See also Kristie Hamilton, "The Politics of Survival: Sara Parton's *Ruth Hall* and the Literature of Labor," in *Redefining the Political Novel: American Women Writers, 1797–1901*, ed. Sharon M. Harris (Knoxville: University of Tennessee Press, 1995), 86–108.

29. For varying contemporary feminist responses to Fern, see Susan Phinney Conrad, *Perish the Thought: Intellectual Women in Romantic America* (New York: Oxford University Press, 1979), 172–175. For the marketing of Fern's work, see Susan Geary, "The Domestic Novel as a Commercial Commodity: Making a Best Seller in the 1850s," *Papers of the Bibliographical Society of America* 70 (1976): 365–393.

Transforming Traditions

Body/Rituals: The (Homo)Erotics of Death in Elizabeth Stuart Phelps, Rose Terry Cooke, and Edgar Allan Poe

RALPH J. POOLE

We are not free, nor will we be, until this silence
at last is ended and we are invisible no more.
—*Paula Bennett*

In his (in)famous, obsessively quoted statement that the death of a beautiful woman is "unquestionably" the most poetical topic in the world, Edgar Allan Poe also contemplates the adequate narrator of this topic, declaring that "equally it is beyond doubt that the lips best suited for such a topic are those of a bereaved lover."[1] Clearly, what Poe has in mind are the lips of a *male* lover telling the story of the death of his *female* beloved. What if this polarized heterosexual setting were disrupted, if both the lover and the beloved were female? Does Poe's erotics of death or deathly eroticism apply equally to homoerotically charged narratives, or do these tales tell different stories altogether? In the context of such questions, it is appropriate to invoke Bonnie Zimmerman's call for a lesbian "resisting reader" who creates new possibilities and transforms old realities by resisting "heterotexts," rewriting and appropriating them as lesbian texts instead. This is not to say that the lesbian resisting reader is "merely demanding a plot or character study that the writer has not chosen to create. She is picking up on hints and possibilities that the author, consciously or not, has strewn in the text."[2] Such a reading may reveal subtexts of women's bonding and female friendship that lead "to the rewriting of cultural stereotypes and literary conventions by reversing the values attached to the idea of lesbianism" (142). It may also complicate our understanding of such terms as "masculine literary tradition" and "feminine literary tradition."

Pioneering studies by Lillian Faderman and Carroll Smith-Rosenberg argue persuasively that although there was no name for lesbian love in the nineteenth century, there existed an affirmative tradition of romantic friendship between women.[3] Until the end of the century in America, women loving women were not thought to be perverse inverts, a sexological term later attributed to them. While it may be difficult — not to say impossible — to apply current notions of lesbianism to nineteenth-century society and, accordingly, to its literary texts, we must acknowledge the abundance of sources that indicate the existence and, indeed, the common practice of love between women in the presexologist era. As Smith-Rosenberg observes, "The question of female friendships is peculiarly elusive; we know so little or perhaps have forgotten so much. An intriguing and almost alien form of human relationship, they flourished in a different social structure and amidst different sexual norms" (313). However difficult it might seem to grasp the nature of these romantic friendships, the focus of discussion should not be limited to the question of genital contact as the dividing line between heterosexual and homosexual: "whether or not these women expressed themselves genitally there is no doubt that physical excitement and eroticism played an important part in their love."[4] What is at stake here is a questioning of the hetero/homo binary. The opposition between "heterosexual" and "homosexual," like so many other binary constructions, has always been constructed on the foundations of the related oppositional pair "inside" and "outside." As Diana Fuss observes, "Many of the current efforts in lesbian and gay theory have begun the difficult but urgent textual work necessary to call into question the stability and ineradicability of the hetero/homo hierarchy, suggesting that new (and old) sexual possibilities are no longer thinkable in terms of a simple inside/outside dialectic."[5]

Borders are notoriously unstable,[6] and sexual identity may not be so secure after all. Using a vocabulary evoking the male literary tradition of ghost stories (and the female counterparts that I want to look at here), Fuss claims that for heterosexuality there always remains the psychic proximity of its terrifying (homo)sexual other; and, vice versa, homosexuality can never fully escape the insistent social pressures of (hetero)sexual conformity: "Each is *haunted* by the other, but here again it is the other who comes to stand in metonymically for the very occurrence of *haunting* and *ghostly* visitations" (3, emphasis added). The other, in this discourse, is the figure of the homosexual as abject, undead, and — we might add — ghost. Fuss goes as far as to call the emergence of homosexual production a kind of ghostwriting itself: "Paradoxically, the 'ghosting' of homosexuality coincides with its 'birth,' for the historical moment of the first appearance of the homosexual as a 'species' rather than a 'temporary aberration' also marks the moment of the homosexual's disappearance — into the closet" (4). However tempting the implied idea of a homo-writing as ghostwriting might seem for my concern, I will try not to swallow this alluring bait — at least not right away. Instead of inscribing the concept of homophobic closet-writing that Eve Sedgwick so perfectly applies to male writers[7] onto the female-authored ghost stories with which I am concerned (and thus creating another inside/out dichotomy), I shall ponder the idea that every outside is also an alongside, that there may also be something like a borderline writing that collapses fixed boundaries of both gender and sexuality.

Ghost stories are the perfect medium for such a project. They breathe the air of the forbidden and intimate the unspeakable. This is true of most nineteenth-century ghost writings, and especially of Poe's ritualized erotic death scenes celebrated in such famous stories as "Ligeia," "Berenice," "Morella," and "Eleonora."[8] The "unspeakable," however, means different things for different authors. According to David S. Reynolds, Poe "redirects" the vulgarity and inhumanity of the (often female) sensationalists' literature of his time, which, in turn, accounts for a depoliticization and loss of often explosive social implications. Reynolds also speaks of Poe's containment, which produces a moment of control especially obvious in his first-person narrators. Thus, a typical Poe narrator serves as controlling device, for he translates a sensational plot into the overactive workings of his fancy, depriving the story of its subversive potential: "His horror tales feature violence without repulsive gore, criminality without political import, women without sexuality, nightmares without revolutionary suggestions."[9] According to J. Gerald Kennedy — and quite contrary to Reynolds — the narrator of Poe's stories depicting the death of a woman exhibits a perverse impatience. In stories like "Morella" and "Ligeia," death is portrayed as an ambiguous, temporary parting: "In a monstrous parody of the death of the Other, Poe represents the return of the beloved not in spiritual terms but as a ghastly reincarnation tinged with vampirism. Through such supernaturalism, he implies that death is neither an extinction of the self nor admission to a heavenly social club. Rather, it is a condition of spiritual confinement and unrest, a dream world where one acts out the desires and hostilities of an earlier existence."[10]

One easily forgets that Poe's ghostly death scenarios are not always arranged around a strictly heterosexual male-female setting. His three stories from 1844–1845 on the topic of mesmerism, "Mesmeric Revelation," "A Tale of the Ragged Mountains," and especially "The Facts in the Case of M. Valdemar," evolve around a male first-person narrator and a second, mesmerized male in various states of dying. The scandal here hardly lies in any erotic — not even to mention *homo*erotic — implications, but in the articulated assertion of one's own death in utterances such as "I struggled — I gasped — I died" or "Yes;— no; I *have been* sleeping — and now — now —*I am dead.*"[11] In the textual analysis performed by Roland Barthes, this utterance is a scandal in more than one sense. By turning this sentence from the metaphoric back into the literal, it is a scandal (of the structure) of language since "the coupling of the first person (I) and the attribute 'dead' is precisely what is radically impossible: it is the empty point, the blind spot of language structure which the tale will occupy very exactly."[12] The semantic scandal rests in the assertion of two contraries at the same time (Life, Death): "the signifier expresses a signified (Death) which contradicts its utterance." The psychoanalytic scandal, finally, is produced by the effect "that Death, as primordial repressed, erupts directly into language," resulting in a radically traumatic experience of return, an "exploded taboo." Enter psychosis: it is the scandalous return of the literal that leaves the symbolic (as field of neurosis) and opens the space of psychosis where "every symbol ceases, as does every neurosis" (10). Thus, the cause for trouble is not so much the unbelievability of the utterance but the more radical impossibility, its madness. In Poe's "The Facts," the violation of the taboo is sanctioned at the end. M. Valdemar's return does not end happily: he

shrinks and rots, leaving but a "nearly liquid mass of loath-
some — of detestable putrescence" (103).

In a Barthesian rereading of Poe's story, Tracy Ware de-
emphasizes Valdemar's utterance, leading her to a different conclusion: "Poe's readers may feel that there are greater horrors than
the transgression of a paradigmatic opposition." [13] Poe's combination of humor and horror is most apparent in the story's ending; two "monstrous" puns in the narrator's account appear before waking the mesmerized Valdemar: even though it seemed
clear to the narrator that to awaken him would insure "at least his
speedy dissolution," he nevertheless "made an endeavor to re-
compose the patient" (102–103). While "re-compose" may be
read as a pun anticipating Valdemar's imminent decomposition,
"dissolution" can refer to decomposition as well as to death. The
ambiguity of the situation between rebirth and final death is
heightened by the narrator's clinging to a blind confidence in his
scientific powers: "In this attempt I soon saw that I should be successful — or at least I soon fancied that my success would be
complete" (103). Is it a "success" that a person being mesmerized
for seven long months awakens only to "absolutely [rot] away beneath my hands"? In "The Philosophy of Composition," Poe
claims to always have the ending in mind while writing: "Nothing
is more clear than that every plot, worth the name, must be elaborated to its *dénouement* before any thing be attempted with the
pen. It is only with the *dénouement* constantly in view that we can
give a plot its indispensable air of consequence, or causation, by
making the incidents, and especially the tone at all points, tend to
the development of the intention" (31).

What did Poe have constantly in view when he let the narrator
put Valdemar through the horrors of mesmerizing his already
decaying body under the guise of scientific experimentation?
Valdemar is a hybrid character. Not only does he seem to come
from Eastern Europe, presumably Poland, thus marking him as
foreign and strange, he also looks and acts queerly: the effect of a
"violent contrast" between his white whiskers and his black hair
is paralleled by the dissimilarity between "the extreme spareness
of his person," his "markedly nervous" temperament, and an odd
calmness concerning his near death: "his physicians had declared
him in a confirmed phthisis. It was his custom, indeed, to speak

calmly of his approaching dissolution, as of a matter neither to be avoided nor regretted" (96–97). To what end does the narrator's interest in Valdemar's "peculiar constitution" lead? No (homo)-erotics of death appears in the final scene — indeed, if anything, we could call the deathbed scenario between the two men a homophobic disclosure of a possible emotional attachment. In the seven months' state of suspension, Valdemar's cadaverous body is reduced to the "vibratory movement of the tongue" that "rolled violently in the mouth" until finally emitting the scandalous words while the narrator "makes passes" at the victim that he calls mesmeric: "I rapidly made the mesmeric passes, amid ejaculations of 'dead! dead!' absolutely *bursting* from the tongue and not from the lips of the sufferer" (103). A second later, the sufferer suffers no more. Surely, he will not return, as do the numerous female corpses in Poe's texts.[14]

How significantly different are the endings of the stories I want to examine now. In her evaluation of the nineteenth-century female ghost story, Barbara Patrick claims that the disparity between women's works and those of their male counterparts lies in the experiencing of reality. While male writers' ghost stories are more about "what we cannot know (epistemological doubt) or the fact that people frighten themselves with chimeras (psychodrama)," women's supernatural tales "address a world in which things *are* frightening — not least of which are the silencing and marginalization of women."[15] The women's works expose "the true horror of reality" by exploring social evils through the veil of the supernatural. "Just as ghosts speak from a world beyond to the world we know," according to Patrick, "these writers speak from the world of the text to the world of the reader" (74). There is a sharp discrepancy between the evocation of a ghost as a highly antirealistic device and the otherwise often strikingly realistic settings of the stories. As Patrick points out, the presence of a ghost in these tales "drew attention to the horrors of living in patriarchal culture, particularly the oppression of women through domestication, the withholding of power and knowledge from women, and the discounting of women and women's perceptions" (82).

Both Poe's and the women writers' narratives that I discuss here conjure the unsayable. In a tale such as "Valdemar," language, logic, and cultural taboo are broken, allowing the unspeakable to speak and the unbearable sight to be seen; its supernaturalism "intrudes upon the world of reason and experience to deliver the message of mortality" (Kennedy, 63). However, while Poe invokes the haunting fact of mortality, the women writers seek to challenge death, which functions not as a device of horror, but as a means of transcendence and communication. Ghost stories like Rose Terry Cooke's "My Visitation" (1858) and Elizabeth Stuart Phelps's "Since I Died" (1873) explore the taboo region of "the unspeakable," but this region is configured differently than in Poe's work. At the center of both stories is the love of one woman for another; both are tales of love and loss, mystery and death, in which the understanding of supernatural events was left to the imagination of the reader. According to Susan Koppelman, this kind of elision "gave writers the opportunity to allude to the unsayable, or, perhaps, the unpublishable." We can find coded narratives dealing with such matters as incest, infidelity, addiction, and rape. Koppelman adds: "In this same category of stories female characters rebel against the patriarchy, pursue their personal ambitions, achieve success where they are forbidden to even enter, and love women more than they love men."[16]

Popular and successful writers in the New England local color tradition,[17] neither Rose Terry Cooke (1827–1892) nor Elizabeth Stuart Phelps (1844–1911) is generally regarded as a "lesbian (ghost) writer." Cooke's stories are known for their criticism of many married women's experiences; as Emily Toth has observed, "No other New England local colorist felt so vehemently, or observed in print so acutely, the sufferings of women . . . in bad marriages."[18] These tales highlight the domestic violence within a repressive Calvinist society situated in rural, white, predominantly middle-class New England.[19] While a generation younger, Phelps nevertheless belongs to the same tradition of local colorists as Cooke. Her literary career lasted nearly fifty years, from her first published story in 1864 to her death. She published fifty-seven books, including twenty novels and five collections of short stories. During these years, Phelps underwent an astonishing transformation in her attitude toward the possibilities and limits in women's lives. Her early, almost utopian optimism about women's strengths and abilities, much like that of Harriet Beecher Stowe, changed into a thoroughly pessimistic view that Cooke had often expressed and that would later find ambivalent expression in the works of Mary Wilkins Freeman and Edith Wharton. Even more puzzling is the fact that, as Josephine Donovan points out, "Phelps' alteration may be seen as a transition from a fundamentally female-identified position to one that is male-identified. That is, she moved — both personally and in her works — from an attitude where her emotional and ideological identification was primarily with women to one in which that identification was with men. In this sense she may be said to have abandoned women's literary realism . . . in her late works." [20]

Phelps's stories and novels from the mid-1860s to the early 1880s feature strong female friendships across the borders of age, race, and class. For example, in *An Old Maid's Paradise* (1879), a novel that Donovan calls nearly autobiographical, Puella, an independent rural woman, says: "A — MAN!!! . . . What . . . two full-grown women — should want of *a* man." [21] And in *Dr. Zay* (1882), a novel about a woman physician that Donovan claims as "the high-water mark of Phelps's female-identified commitment" (89), an observer comments on the doctor's independence: "Now then! There are women that love women . . . care for 'em, grieve over 'em, worry about 'em, feel a fellow feeling and a kind of duty to 'em, and never forget they're one of 'em, misery and all." [22] In this period Phelps wrote her proleptic "Since I Died" (1873), [23] one of her numerous stories that present erotic or romantic relationships between women that often have gone unnoticed. Here, however, Phelps turns to the tradition of the ghost story and its implicit death scenario: a woman recently dead narrates her experience as she gradually realizes her transformation. In her undead condition she struggles to communicate with her beloved, whom she has left behind sitting at her bedside. Koppelman notes: "The fact that her beloved is a woman almost, but not quite, escapes notice in the reader's fascination with the mystery of this voice from beyond" (45). Phelps's description of the rising consciousness of a newly dead person may be compared with strikingly similar popular contemporary descriptions of "near-death" or "out-of-body" experiences. However, I find much more interesting Koppelman's remark on "the tension between the narrator's desire to experience 'the immensity' that opens before her once she leaves her body and the pull of her beloved's eyes." She also notes that for us it might seem surprising that the editor of Phelps's story, who had turned down Walt Whitman because he considered the poet a threat to the "religious and upright moral tone" of his magazine, had no objection to this story: "He found nothing immoral or irreligious in a story about a recently dead woman torn between her earthly love for another woman and the beckoning deity" (46).

We might ask, is this love so "earthly" after all? The first-person narrator — never explicitly marked as female — addresses a "you" who later is clearly defined as female, in an affirmative rewriting of Poe's deathly homoerotic narratives. The story starts out with the statement "How very still you sit!" directed at the other woman. Sixteen unfinished "if" clauses follow, linguistically marking the unfulfilled and/or unfulfillable desire of the speaker, who waits for a sign of acknowledgment and perhaps of love:

> If the shadow of an eyelash stirred upon your cheek . . . if you should turn and look behind your chair, or lift your face, half lingering and half longing, half loving and half loth, to ponder on the annoyed and thwarted cry which the wind is making, where I stand between it and yourself, against the half-closed window.
> . . . [I]f you named my name; if you held your breath with terror, or sobbed aloud for love, or sprang, or cried —.
> But you only lift your head and look me in the eye.[24]

Horrified that there might be no sign whatsoever, the speaker imagines the impossible: "If I dared step near, or nearer . . . if I dropped an arm as lightly as a snowflake round your shoulder. . . ." Again she breaks off, suggesting that the enigmas of desire manifest a borderland between the person dead but desiring and the other person alive but fixed: "The *fear* which no heart has fathomed, the *fate* which no fancy has faced, the *riddle* which no soul has read, steps between your substance and my soul." The speaker writhes with the effort to speak: "Speech and language *struggle* over me. *Mute articulations* fill the air. . . . Is there an alphabet between us?" (47, emphasis added). What she seeks is to speak the unspeakable, passionate love to which death alone can give voice.

The speaker remembers former times when there was communication. But a closer look reveals that she has been passive all along to the point of numbness: she did not see her own tears, she did not actually articulate her own thoughts. After death, however, she has become strangely active: "Now that I hold your eyes in mine, and you see me not; now when I stretch my hand and you touch me not; now that I cry your name, and you hear it not,—I comprehend you, tender one! A wisdom not of earth was in your words. 'To live, is dying; I will die. To die is life, and you shall live'" (47). While the speaker was still alive, she remained passive and receptive; now that she is dead, she has passed into a realm of action, has gained life. But now she has no one to act upon, although she has entered a new spatial ground, where "I could show you the fairest sight and sweetest that ever blessed your eyes." She finds death, now that she is experiencing it, no "source of distress," a fact, however, that perplexes her: "I am often bewildered here. . . . Here is a mystery" (48). This mystery relates to her paradoxical agency and ability to speak that marks the story's inverse structure as a whole. In contrast to the "de-composition" that we see in Poe, Phelps's narrator acquires in dying a language she lacked in life.

As the narrative concludes, the speaker struggles to retain her connection with the beloved. Addressing her for a last time, a series of questions desperately asks for reassurance: "Would you not know how it has been with me since your perishable eyes beheld my perished face?"(51). Being left with "a matchless, solitary fear," the addressed "you" gains distance and becomes "she": "I slip from her. . . . I lose her." There is only one moment left to tell her the "guarded thing," the "treasured word" that renders all that has been said a lie: "*Death is dumb, for Life is deaf!*" (52). This recognition brings us back to the narrative's beginning. When exactly is it told? Not at the moment of her death, because we know this moment occurred sometime earlier. It must be a state of being that follows the treacherous present tense of the first paragraphs. The speaker uses the "moment to tell her" the agonies of love as camouflage to tell us a quite different story: the mutual understanding between the two women — that living is dying and dying means living — is precisely the paradox that it seems to be. This clever construction of an ambivalent state of being is wrong: as long as life is deaf, death remains dumb. Is this meant to be a pessimistic outlook on romantic friendship? Or, rather, a fierce appeal for a balanced emotional and physical exchange between lovers?

One of the first women in nineteenth-century America who, like Poe, dared to examine the mind's nighttime, Phelps probed the recesses of the unconscious, the supernatural, the other. Her enormously popular novel, *The Gates Ajar* (1868), served the growing interest of a largely female mass audience by treating the unconscious in a comfortable fashion. Phelps's unconscious is spatial, it "consists of intimations of a superior world in the promptings of God and friendly spirits; it is 'other,' but just a step away, 'over there.' Above all, the unconscious is understood as a definite place in which, mostly unknown to consciousness, spiritual activity is continuous."[25] In this formulation, the unconscious is understood as a gate through which spiritual visitors pass. Dreams, memories, prophecies, divinations are thought to visit the space of the unconscious, all of them ghosts calling upon the self-haunted self.

The coexistence of heaven and earth, marked in the spatial metaphors of the unconscious, is clearly discernible in "Since I Died," where the speaker enters a space located between the earthliness of her beloved, whom she is leaving behind, and the heavenliness of the "Presence" coming for her. Seen in this context, the moment of which she speaks at the end, which marks the exact time of her narrative, may be understood as a ritualistic effort to maintain a connection between two lovers parting. It is an unfixed, unstable moment in which death can speak and life can hear, before all has changed and communication no longer will be possible. This single moment tells the story of their love, which establishes the story we read. Thus, there is a circular as well as a linear movement in this story: circular in its mingling of beginning and end that marks the eternity of love; linear in its closure, since the end of the story coincides with the end of their chance for communication. Therefore, even while there is a melancholic undercurrent, the overall message is a positive one: there is time enough to tell the guarded thing, indeed, "Time to whisper a treasured word!" (52).

At first glance, Rose Terry Cooke's early story "My Visitation" seems much more conventionally structured, closer to the Romantic and Gothic tradition than her later "grimly authentic realism" (Donovan, 68). "My Visitation" shares Poe's fascination with darkness, death, ghosts, and vampires, and his concept of death as transformation as he articulates it, for example, in "Mesmeric Revelation": "There are two bodies — the rudimental and the complete, corresponding with the two conditions of the worm and the butterfly. What we call 'death,' is but the painful metamorphosis. Our present incarnation is progressive, preparatory, temporary. Our future is perfected, ultimate, immortal. The ultimate life is the full design."[26] Like Poe's narrators, who are often regarded as unreliable and disturbed,[27] Cooke's narrator, who supposedly tells the story of her passion she feels for another woman, Eleanor, is, according to Elizabeth Ammons, "disturbed." Ammons sees in the story both a "painful journey . . . away from this passionate same-sex attachment to union with a man" and a horror story—"a kind of living nightmare that tips the narrator into madness." For Ammons, the narrative reveals the danger and damage of such an enforced journey into heterosexuality: "Cooke's heroine must renounce her feelings for Eleanor; she must come to see her beloved as a monster and her own passionate love for her as deranged."[28] This interpretation suggests that we should dismiss "My Visitation" as a failed attempt to resist men's power over women in patriarchal culture.

But there is another way to read this story: as a parable of one woman's (Eleanor's) unspeakable betrayal of another woman. The obviously Poe-like narrator presents herself as unreliable from the beginning: "If this story is incoherent—arranged rather for the writer's thought than for the reader's eye—it is because the brain which dictated it reeled with the sharp assaults of memory."[29] It is the story of a visitation: the ghostly visitor is the woman she once loved, as we finally learn. The setting for the first visit is characterized as a melancholic foreshadowing of death. The narrator is ill—like many women of the time, it seems—and the sadness of autumn's solitude bothers her: "I can endure any silence better than this hush of decay, it fills me with preternatural horror; it is as if a tomb opened and breathed out its dank, morbid breath across the murmur of life, to paralyze and to chill" (15). Yet this atmosphere engenders the speakable truth of love between women.

While savoring the fictional world of Charlotte Brontë ("I was deep in *Shirley*; it excited, it affected me; it was always to me like a brief and voluntary brain-fever to read that book"), the narrator senses a presence of "something else I could not see" (15). She then interrupts her narrative (the first of several interruptions) to return to her youth, when she first met Eleanor, falling passionately in love with her at once: "I speak advisedly in the use of that term; no other phrase expresses the blind, irrational, all-enduring devotion I gave to her; no less vivid word belongs to that madness" (16). The love that she calls madness is addressed toward a young girl described as a marble deity, a "Pallas Athena." She sketches their friendship in almost sadomasochistic terms: "If she was kind in speech or act — if she spoke to me caressingly — if she put her warm lips upon my cheek — I was thrilled with joy; . . . and when she fell into some passion, and burned me with bitter words, stinging me into retort by their injustice, their hard cruelty, it was I who repented — I who humiliated myself — I who, with abundant tears, asked her pardon, worked, plead, prayed to obtain it; . . . I was glad to be clay as long as she was queen and deity" (17). The speaker's "worship" earned her the "masculine contempt for spaniels," the contempt of her beloved, who "despised a creature that would endure a blow, mental or physical, without revenging itself; and from her I endured almost any repulse, and forgot it" (18). How very remote this description of friendship and love is from what we know of the romantic friendships described by Carroll Smith-Rosenberg and Lillian Faderman.

The discrepancy becomes even more evident when a man enters the female sphere in Cooke's story, engendering a precarious ménage à trois that seems to signify the narrator's rejection of a lesbian connection. Herman first loves Eleanor before turning his affection toward the speaker, who finally marries him. The speaker, we learn, is not interested in men; she mentions only a brief engagement that she accounts for by her total inexperience. The incident causes a nervous breakdown, however, and at the same time inspires the recognition that "I had loved Eleanor too well. I had always loved her more than that man; and when the episode was over, I discovered in myself that I never could have loved any man as I did her . . . that so long as she lived for me I should neither die nor craze" (19). It is in this period of feebleness that she again meets Herman, whose health is equally weak. Ironically, quite contrary to the ups and downs that characterize the homosocial friendship of the two women, this heterosocial relationship is perfectly balanced and complementary. Where Eleanor's gender was inclined toward the masculine, Herman's tilts toward the feminine. Their similarity is based on the exclusion of Eleanor: "We talked together as few men talk — perhaps no women — . . . but we never spoke of Eleanor" (22). Herman is so unmanly, so desex(ualiz)ed that, accordingly, the narrator is surprised when he asks to marry her. Because of the narcissistic origins of their relationship, she has to admit that "I had but the lesser part of heart to give any man. I loved a woman too well to love or to marry" (22). She does not tell him that besides Eleanor's being the "one present and all-absorbing passion of my soul," she has yet another reason for declining his offer: "I shuddered at the possibility of loving a man so utterly, and then placing myself at his mercy for life. I felt that my safety lay in my freedom from any such tie to Eleanor" (23). This single moment aligns Cooke's story with her other stories highlighting the sufferings of women in bad marriages. Here, however, this hint against wedlock is almost an aside, too unimportant to be pursued.

Instead, a strange incident occurs at this point: upon her return home, the narrator learns of Eleanor's putative deceit, yet we never discover what happened to divide them: "And here must I leave a blank. The forgiveness which stirs me to this record refuses to define for alien eyes what that trouble was" (23). We must suspect, of course, that she feels betrayed because Eleanor loves somebody else. Why else should the narrator speak of "the loss of all that bound to life a lonely, morbid, intense, and excitable woman" (24)? So far, she has believed "that men are liars in spite of education or policy; what was it, then to know this of my ideal — Eleanor?" (24). Painfully, the narrator learns that in her absence Eleanor has married. Although we are to believe that Eleanor's corporeal removal, rather than the marriage itself, brings about the narrator's disturbance, we are left with the latter's unaccountable refusal to forgive her beloved.

What is striking, however, is that shortly after this discovery of Eleanor's marriage the "visitations" begin, as the narrator returns to her story's beginning. The stages of the visitation, which lasts for weeks, move from "a sense of alien life," from hearing "cries from half-free souls," to feeling that "something yearning, restless, pained, and sad regarded me." First asking herself whether this was death, she resolves to "pity a soul that had cast off life yet could not die to life." Gradually, she begins to perceive a shadow, "a shapeless shape," when once again she interrupts her narrative to return to a description of Herman's virtues. Compared to Cooke's other portraits of manly (mis)behavior, it is astonishing that the narrator here speaks of a "beauty indefinable, fired by the sweet vivid smile of the irradiate soul within," of a "most delicate and careful tenderness," of her sense that "what began in gratitude ended in love. . . . Truly, so far as man can do it, he saved my soul alive!" (28–29). Significantly, the narrator depicts a relationship remote from sexuality and passion; their souls, not their bodies, mingle: "In all this I was drawn toward Herman by the strongest tie that can bind one heart to another — a tie that over-arches and outlasts all the fleeting passions of time, for it is the academic link of eternity; . . . there was a relation between us, undying and sure, . . . where there is neither marrying nor giving in marriage"(28). Far from representing a coercive movement toward heterosexuality, this passage underscores the narrator's movement away from erotic connection entirely.

The story climaxes on Christmas Eve. While the narrator and Herman are having a conversation that she conceals from us, she receives notice of Eleanor's death three months earlier, and the final visitation that night reveals the expected: they have been Eleanor's visits all along. This last time, finally, Eleanor, with "an expression of intense longing," pleads "Forgive! forgive!" (30–31). In this melodramatically tinged ending, the narrator forgives her "darling" Eleanor, giving her the freedom to leave her undead state: "I closed my eyes to crush inward the painful tears, and a touch of lips sealed them with sacred and unearthly repose. I look again; *It* had gone forever" (31). Yet she continues to address Eleanor in "that mystic country."

Reaffirming her forgiveness and love "with a truth and faith eternal!" the narrator offers an ambiguous final sentence: "Thee, forever loved, but, ah! not now forever lost?" This could be a plea that Eleanor's soul should be freed from its ghostly wanderings; in this case, the salvation of Eleanor's soul would not mean a parting forever and could instead provide the possibility for their reunification after death. The end could also signify a symbolic merging of Eleanor's physical presence with Herman's spiritual qualities, with Herman providing the realistic and, above all, speakable possibility for unification. Finally, this closing question may represent an appeal for Eleanor's continued presence. Earlier, hearing that Eleanor's last cry was for her, she had said: "If Death is the Spoiler, so is he the Restorer. . . . I remembered only love" (29). The restoration of the love between the two women may transcend the gap between life and death. In all these readings, I believe this story to center on the love between two women. Herman figures as camouflage in this homoerotic setting, providing a safe place from which the narrative can evolve. This returns us to Ammons's argument. The narrator may not be so unreliable after all. What is told is not the narrator's horrific journey into heterosexuality, it is the untold story of Eleanor's unspeakable betrayal and her unexplained death — perhaps, we might consider, *because* of her betrayal.

However great the mysteries surrounding Eleanor's death and her ghostly visitations, as well as the supernatural wanderings of Phelps's (un)dead narrator, death as such is not depicted as horrifying, which returns me to Poe's own death performances. Philippe Ariès claims: "Since death is not the end of the loved one, however bitter the grief of the survivor, death is neither ugly nor fearful. On the contrary, death is beautiful, as the dead body is beautiful."[30] Elisabeth Bronfen reflects extensively on Poe's dictum on the alliance between melancholy, death, poetics, and beauty, and she speaks of a dangerously fluid boundary between the two registers of a body's being perceived or culturally constructed as an animate natural material, on the one hand, and an inanimate aesthetic form, on the other hand: "The equation between femininity and death is such that while in cultural narratives the feminine corpse is treated like an artwork, or the beautiful woman is killed to produce an artwork, conversely, artworks emerge only at the expense of a beautiful woman's death and are treated like feminine corpses."[31] Extrapolating to the homoerotic stories of Cooke and Phelps, I question Bronfen's generalization that "a colloquial understanding of the corpse is that it is not gendered, that it is an anonymous, inanimate body, pure materiality without soul or personality" (64–65).

Moreover, we might ask: Is there melancholy involved in these poetics of death? According to Freud, melancholia is failed mourning, a denial of loss; the inability to accept the beloved's death produces a perpetual rearticulation of the repression. Only with a masculine mourner do we have the specific structural analogy between mourning and art that Bronfen discovers in Poe. Following Sarah Kofman, Bronfen argues that an ambiguous attitude toward loss is inherent in effective art as the work of melancholy. Art mourns beauty, which in turn creates a self-reflexive moment causing art to mourn itself: "The creation of beauty allows us to escape from the elusiveness of the material world into an illusion of eternity (a denial of loss), even as it imposes on us the realisation that beauty is itself elusive, intangible, receding" (64). In his ghost stories, Poe has represented the death of a female body as the ultimate moment of self-reflexivity. The self-reflexivity of Cooke's and Phelps's texts are undeniable. However, do we encounter in their stories an "illusion of eternity," i.e., "a denial of loss"? Does the death of a beautiful woman serve as motive for the creation of art in their work as it did in Poe's? What about Phelps's speaker, who is the dead woman telling her own story? Is there an autoerotic motive at work here that very well might be analogous to Poe's death rituals? This reading would shed a totally different light on "the moment of self-reflexivity, where the text seems to comment on itself and its own process of composition, and so decomposes itself" (71).

Poe's narrators in poems like "Ulalume" and "Annabel Lee" and stories like "Morella," "Berenice," and "Ligeia" seek a continued bond with a departed lover, holding onto an intermediary position that is balanced between a denial or repression and an embrace of death. The speaker acknowledges death as a mystery penetrating the world of the living and uses his poetic inscription to come to terms with the inflicted loss. Like vampires, the beloved ones seek power over their former lovers from the realm of the (un)dead. Poe's male narrators are torn between a longing for death and a will to live, producing a psychic impasse that marks an unfulfilled desire; their longing is either pathologically repeated or poetically sublimated. Viewed from this perspective, Poe's work suggests a gap between the stories of Cooke and Phelps: while Cooke uses this narrative pattern to tell a different story, Phelps transforms the pattern by exchanging the roles of living speaker and dead beloved. Here, the speaker recounts the experience of her own death, and the melancholic cycle is disrupted.

We might still ask, however, why are the women who love women in these texts bodiless ghosts wandering about the margins of worldly existence? Is this ghostly lesbian, if we want to call her that, a vampire, a monster? Marilyn Farwell argues that "Western tradition codes the female body as negative and threatening, a body so excessive in its functions and sexuality that it must be controlled. The lesbian body . . . is an extension of the excessive female body and therefore the ultimate threat to the dominant order."[32] Farwell argues that the lesbian narrative is not necessarily a story by a lesbian about lesbians but "rather a plot that affirms a place for lesbian subjectivity, that narrative space where both lesbian characters and other female characters can be active, desiring agents." Thus, according to its solution, Cooke's story could indeed be called lesbian, since "*Lesbian* is then a place or narrative space that partakes of old definitions of gender and realigns them" (157, emphasis added).

The narrators in both Cooke's and Phelps's stories exhibit a mobility through and across boundaries that in the traditional ghost narrative is clearly marked as male. Unlike Poe's many narrators, in Cooke and Phelps they perform a gender inversion; Poe's dichotomy — lover = subject = I, beloved = object = you — is radically transformed in the erotics of the lesbian ghost story. In Poe's gender system, only males have agency and subjectivity, and thus, the ability to conquer and manipulate the constructed, female opposite. Important in this ideology is the maintenance of the boundaries that define binaries. The "lesbian," however, fits into Julia Kristeva's concept of the abject as that which "disturbs identity, system, order."[33] In Kristeva's theory, the abject is a body that exceeds limits. Similarly, Mikhail Bakhtin's grotesque body is "not a closed, completed unit; it is unfinished, outgrows itself, transgresses its own limits."[34] Farwell asserts that "not only [must] the lesbian hero . . . be the monster but also . . . the monstrous female must be read as lesbian. The lesbian narrative, then, can be defined as a disruptive story in which the female is given subjectivity, not as a substitute man, but as an oversized, monstrous woman — as a lesbian" (166–167). While such a statement may sound excessive, when applied to the erotics of death in the lesbian ghost story, it makes sense. Importantly, not only character images but the narrative system as such becomes the site of transgression. If an author questions the cultural construction of femininity, as Cooke and Phelps do, the narrative in which these transgressive bodies are positioned itself undergoes transformation: "The gender boundaries are rearranged; the narrative positioning of gendered subjects and objects is altered" (167).

Poe's scenario of reincarnation is that of a completed curse. The return of the other dramatizes a loss that haunts the living and destroys the narrator's sense of reason. While estranging him from himself, "[the] ultimate implication of the separation model becomes clear: death makes us strangers to each other" (Kennedy, 57). According to Kennedy, whenever supernaturalism intrudes upon the world of reason in Poe's texts, it is to deliver the message of mortality. Yet we might question this assumption's application to Cooke's and Phelps's texts, where I would claim that supernaturalism as the return of the dead (Cooke) or as life beyond death (Phelps) discloses the precise opposite: a manifestation of immortality. While in Poe, the uncanny "shatters the illusion of one's control over the flow of existence" (Kennedy, 63), here it does not produce a disruption. Instead, in Cooke and Phelps, the disruption has taken place somewhere in the past, and it is the experience of death that initiates an end to the threat of dissolution. Thus, whereas the female bodies in Poe dissolve into vampirically coded ghosts haunting the autoerotically prone narrator from beyond, the abjected lesbian body articulates the homoerotics of her longing by resorting to channels of communication that are silent, invisible, yet strangely — "ghostly" — coded prophesies of future fulfillment.

NOTES

1. Edgar Allan Poe, "Philosophy of Composition," in *The Works of Edgar Allan Poe*, ed. Edmund C. Stedman and George E. Woodberry (New York: Colonial, 1903), 6:39. All second and subsequent references to this and other sources are cited in the text.

2. Bonnie Zimmerman, "Perverse Reading: The Lesbian Appropriation of Literature," in *Sexual Practice, Textual Theory: Lesbian Cultural Criticism*, ed. Susan J. Wolfe and Julia Penelope (Cambridge, England: Blackwell, 1993), 144.

3. Lillian Faderman, *Surpassing the Love of Men: Romantic Friendship and Love between Women from the Renaissance to the Present* (1981; reprint, London: Women's Press, 1991); see especially chapter 2, "The Nineteenth Century," 145–294. Carroll Smith-Rosenberg, "The Female World of Love and Ritual: Relations between Women in Nineteenth-Century America," in *A Heritage of Her Own: Toward a New Social History of American Women*, ed. Nancy F. Cott and Elizabeth H. Pleck (New York: Simon and Schuster, 1979), 311–342.

4. Sheila Jeffreys, *The Spinster and Her Enemies: Feminism and Sexuality 1880–1930* (London: Pandora, 1985), 104.

5. Diana Fuss, "inside/out," in *Inside/Out: Lesbian Theories, Gay Theories*, ed. Diana Fuss (New York: Routledge, 1991), 1. See also Marjorie Garber,

Vice Versa: Bisexuality and the Eroticism of Everyday Life (New York: Simon and Schuster, 1995).

6. See Gloria Anzaldúa, *Borderlands/La Frontera: The New Mestiza* (San Francisco: Aunt Lute, 1987).

7. See Eve Kosofsky Sedgwick's *Between Men: English Literature and Male Homosocial Desire* (New York: Columbia University Press, 1985) and *Epistemology of the Closet* (Berkeley: University of California Press, 1990).

8. For discussions of Poe's erotic ghost stories, see, for example, Grace McEntee, "Remembering Ligeia," *Studies in American Fiction* 20.1 (1992): 75–83; Yaohua Shi, "The Enigmatic Ligeia/'Ligeia,'" *Studies in Short Fiction* 28.4 (1991): 485–496; Joseph Andriano, "Archetypal Projection in 'Ligeia': A Post-Jungian Reading," *Poe Studies* 19.2 (1986): 27–31; Terence J. Matheson, "The Multiple Murders in 'Ligeia': A New Look at Poe's Narrator," *Canadian Review of American Studies* 13.3 (1982): 279–289; Maurice J. Bennett, "'The Madness of Art': Poe's 'Ligeia' as Metafiction," *Poe Studies* 14.1 (1981): 1–6; Jacqueline Doyle, "(Dis)Figuring Woman: Edgar Allan Poe's 'Berenice,'" *Poe Studies* 26.1–2 (1993): 13–21; Jules Zanger, "Poe's 'Berenice': Philosophical Fantasy and Its Pitfalls," in *The Scope of the Fantastic: Theory, Technique, Major Authors*, ed. Robert A. Collins and Howard D. Pearce (Westport, Conn.: Greenwood, 1985), 135–142; Hal Blythe and Charlie Sweet, "Poe's Satiric Use of Vampirism in 'Berenice,'" *Poe Studies* 14.2 (1981): 23–24; Curtis Fukuchi, "Repression and Guilt in Poe's 'Morella,'" *Studies in Short Fiction* 24.2 (1987): 149–154; Benjamin Franklin Fisher IV, "'Eleonora': Poe and Madness," in *Poe and His Times: The Artist and His Milieu*, ed. Benjamin Franklin Fisher IV (Baltimore: Edgar Allan Poe Society, 1990), 178–188.

9. David S. Reynolds, *Beneath the American Renaissance: The Subversive Imagination in the Age of Emerson and Melville* (New York: Knopf, 1988), 230.

10. J. Gerald Kennedy, "Phantasms of Death in Poe's Fiction," in *The Haunted Dusk: American Supernatural Fiction, 1820–1920*, ed. Howard Kerr et al. (Athens: University of Georgia Press, 1983), 54. See also Steven E. Kagle, "The Corpse Within Us," in Fisher, 103–112; E. F. Bleiler, "Edgar Allan Poe," in *Supernatural Fiction Writers: Fantasy and Horror*, vol. 2, ed. E. F. Bleiler (New York: Scribner's, 1985), 697–705.

11. Edgar Allan Poe, "A Tale of the Ragged Mountains," in *Complete Tales and Poems* (New York: Vintage, 1975), 684, 101; original emphasis.

12. Roland Barthes, "Textual Analysis of a Tale by Edgar Poe," *Poe Studies* 10 (1977): 10.

13. Tracy Ware, "The 'Salutary Discomfort' in the Case of M. Valdemar," *Studies in Short Fiction* 31.3 (1994): 478.

14. For biographical contexts for "Valdemar," see Richard Kopley,

"Poe's *Pym*-esque 'A Tale of the Ragged Mountains,'" in Fisher, 167–177; Clive Bloom, "The 'Humunculus': Marie Bonaparte's, *The Life and Work of Edgar Allan Poe* and Poe's 'The Facts in the Case of M. Valdemar,'" in *The 'Occult' Experience and the New Criticism: Daemonism, Sexuality and the Hidden in Literature* (Sussex: Harvester, 1986), 27–55.

15. Barbara Patrick, "Lady Terrorists: Nineteenth-Century American Women Writers and the Ghost Story," in *American Women Short Story Writers*, ed. Julie Brown (New York: Garland, 1995), 74.

16. Susan Koppelman, introduction to *Two Friends, and Other Nineteenth-Century Lesbian Stories by American Women Writers* (New York: Meridian, 1994), 9, 10. See also David G. Hartwell, "Notes on the Evolution of Horror Literature," *New York Review of Science Fiction* 39 (1991): 1, 10–13; Alfred Bendixen, introduction to *Haunted Women: The Best Supernatural Tales by American Women Writers* (New York: Ungar, 1987), 1–2.

17. For a revaluation of Cooke, see Susan Allen Toth, "'The Rarest and Most Peculiar Grape': Versions of the New England Woman in Nineteenth-Century Local Color Literature," in *Regionalism and the Female Imagination*, ed. Emily Toth (New York: Human Sciences Press, 1985), 15–28; Susan Allen Toth, "Rose Terry Cooke," *American Literary Realism* 4 (1971): 170–176; Cheryl Walker, "Legacy Profile: Rose Terry Cooke," *Legacy* 9.2 (1992): 143–150; Cheryl Walker, "American Women Poets Revisited," in *Nineteenth-Century American Women Writers: A Critical Reader*, ed. Karen L. Kilcup (Malden, Mass.: Blackwell, 1998), 231–244. For a discussion of Phelps, see Lori Duin Kelly, *The Life and Works of Elizabeth Stuart Phelps, Victorian Feminist Writer* (Troy: Whitston, 1983); Carol Farley Kessler, *Elizabeth Stuart Phelps* (Boston: Twayne, 1982), and "The Heavenly Utopia of Elizabeth Stuart Phelps," in *Women and Utopia*, ed. Marleen Barr and Nicholas D. Smith (Lanham, Maryland: University Press of America, 1983), 85–95. For an interpretation of mutual influences between female regionalists such as Cooke, Phelps, and Rebecca Harding Davis, see Sharon M. Harris, *Rebecca Harding Davis and American Realism* (Philadelphia: University of Pennsylvania Press, 1991). For a more general discussion of regionalism, see Judith Fetterley and Marjorie Pryse, introduction to *American Women Regionalists, 1850–1910* (New York: Norton, 1992); for a discussion of women writers at the end of the century, see Elizabeth Ammons, *Conflicting Stories: American Women Writers at the Turn into the Twentieth Century* (New York: Oxford University Press, 1991).

18. Toth, "'The Rarest and Most Peculiar Grape,'" 22. Van Wyck Brooks provides an early critique of Cooke in *New England: Indian Summer* (New York: Dutton, 1950), 89–90.

19. See Sherry Lee Linkon, "Fiction as Political Discourse: Rose Terry Cooke's Antisuffrage Short Stories," in *American Women Short Story Writers*, ed. Julie Brown (New York: Garland, 1995), 17–31; Katherine Kleitz, "Essence of New England: The Portraits of Rose Terry Cooke," *American Transcendental Quarterly* 47–48 (1980): 129–139.

20. Josephine Donovan, *New England Local Color Literature: A Women's Tradition* (New York: Frederick Ungar, 1983), 82.

21. Phelps, *An Old Maid's Paradise* (Boston: Houghton Mifflin, 1885), 85; cited in Donovan, 88.

22. Phelps, *Dr. Zay* (Boston: Houghton Mifflin, 1882), 88; cited in Donovan, 89. For a further discussion, see also Rosemary Garland Thomson, "Benevolent Maternalism and Physically Disabled Figures: Dilemmas of Female Embodiment in Stowe, Davis, and Phelps," *American Literature* 68.3 (1996): 555–582; Susan Albertine, "Breaking the Silent Partnership: Businesswomen in Popular Fiction," *American Literature* 62.2 (1990): 238–261.

23. "Since I Died" was first published in *Scribner's Monthly Magazine* in February 1873 and later collected in Phelps's fifth and last volume of short stories, *Sealed Orders* (1879).

24. Elizabeth Stuart Phelps, "Since I Died," in *Two Friends: And Other Nineteenth-Century Lesbian Stories by American Women Writers*, ed. Susan Koppelman (New York: Meridian, 1994), 46.

25. Jay Martin, "Ghostly Rentals, Ghostly Purchases: Haunted Imaginations in James, Twain, and Bellamy," in *The Haunted Dusk: American Supernatural Fiction, 1820–1920*, ed. Howard Kerr et al. (Athens: University of Georgia Press, 1983), 125.

26. Poe, "Mesmeric Revelation," in *Complete Tales and Poems* (New York: Vintage, 1975), 93. See, however, Kennedy, who claims that Poe's visionary texts "project a false transcendence, a phantasmic existence after death, conceptually embedded in a cosmos of matter and energy, a system that culminates in irreversible dissolution: entropy" ("Phantasms of Death in Poe's Fiction," 60).

27. See David Punter, *The Literature of Terror: A History of Gothic Fictions from 1765 to the Present Day* (London: Longman, 1980), 203.

28. Elizabeth Ammons, introduction to *How Celia Changed Her Mind and Selected Stories,* by Rose Terry Cooke (New Brunswick, N.J.: Rutgers University Press, 1986), xxviii–xxix. Besides Ammons, who perceives Cooke as coming out of "the same mid-century fascination with evil and darkness which produced Poe, Melville, Spofford, and Stowe" (xxvi), Fred Lewis Pattee, in *The Development of the American Short Story* (New York: Harper &

Brothers, 1923), acknowledges that Cooke took up the "short-story technique, as Poe had set it forth" (176).

29. Rose Terry Cooke, "My Visitation," in Ammons, 14. "My Visitation" was first published in *Harper's* 17 (July 1858) but was not reprinted by Cooke in any of her four collections.

30. Philippe Ariès, *The Hour of Our Death* (New York: Knopf, 1981), 43.

31. Elisabeth Bronfen, *Over Her Dead Body: Death, Femininity and the Aesthetic* (Manchester: Manchester University Press, 1992), 72–73. For a further gender-oriented discussion of Poe, see Joan Dayan, "Poe's Women: A Feminist Poe?" *Poe Studies* 26.1–2 (1993): 1–12; Leland S. Person, Jr., "Poe's Fiction: Women and the Subversion of Masculine Form," in *Aesthetic Headaches: Women and a Masculine Poetics in Poe, Melville, and Hawthorne* (Athens: University of Georgia Press, 1988), 19–47.

32. Marilyn R. Farwell, "The Lesbian Narrative: The Pursuit of the Inedible by the Unspeakable," in *Professions of Desire: Lesbian and Gay Studies in Literature*, ed. George E. Haggarty and Bonnie Zimmerman (New York: MLA, 1995), 157–158.

33. Julia Kristeva, *Powers of Horror: An Essay on Abjection* (New York: Columbia University Press, 1982), 4.

34. Mikhail Bakhtin, *Rabelais and His World* (Cambridge: MIT Press, 1968), 26.

The Five Million Women of My Race: Negotiations of Gender in W. E. B. Du Bois and Anna Julia Cooper

HANNA WALLINGER

The extent of gender differences in education in late-nineteenth-century America is well illustrated by the following two quotations, one by the foremost African American leader, W. E. B. Du Bois, and the other by the much less known Anna Julia Cooper, an African American teacher, historian, and writer of genuine distinction. With characteristic fervor, presenting the truth to us partly as it was and partly as he wanted us to see it, Du Bois writes about his application to Harvard in 1888: "I willed and lo! I was walking beneath the elms of Harvard — the name of allurement, the college of my youngest, wildest visions! I needed money; scholarships and prizes fell into my lap — not all I wanted or strove for, but all I needed to keep me in school. Commencement came, and standing before governor, president, and grave gowned men, I told them certain truths, waving my arms and breathing fast! They applauded with what may have seemed to many as uncalled-for fervor, but I walked home on pink clouds of glory! I asked for a fellowship and got it."[1] It is noteworthy that a black American could say at that time that "money, scholarships and prizes" fell into his lap. No doubt Du Bois deserved them and more. There is equally no doubt that this famed intellectual had to work harder than white men of comparable endowments and suffered more setbacks and frustrations than the average white intellectual; "the road to and through Harvard was not so easy in reality" as Du Bois claimed.[2] Yet Du Bois's "pink clouds of glory," however insubstantial they may have been, proved nothing short of unachievable for his contemporary, the equally gifted Cooper.

Du Bois's senior by ten years, Cooper early entered St. Augustine Normal and Collegiate School in her hometown Raleigh, North Carolina, where it did not take her long to reach the limits of education granted to young black girls and women. It was soon clear that she could scarcely find enough material for her eager intellectual appetite: "I had devoured what was put before me, and, like Oliver Twist, was looking around to ask for more. I constantly felt (as I suppose many an ambitious girl has felt) a thumping from within unanswered by any beckoning from without."[3] She bitterly laments the unequal treatment of young male and female pupils she encountered when she made it known that she would like to attend Greek classes: "A boy, however meager his equipment and shallow his pretensions, had only to declare a floating intention to study theology and he could get all the support, encouragement and stimulus he needed, be absolved from work and invested beforehand with all the dignity of his far away office. While a self-supporting girl had to struggle on by teaching in the summer and working after school hours to keep up with her board bills, and actually to fight her way against positive discouragements to the higher education; till one such girl one day flared out and told the principal 'that the only mission opening before a girl in his school was to marry one of those candidates.' He said he didn't know but it was" (77). While Du Bois could at least hope to soar one day on pink clouds of glory, Cooper learned the lesson that would repeat itself over and over during her long lifetime: as a woman, she would have to struggle to get the support necessary to encourage her mentally and, above all, financially; as a black woman, she would have to wrestle with the additional burden of racial inequality. Her ambition constantly met with incredulity and dismay, "as if," she says in her characteristically humorous voice, "a brass button on one of those candidate's coats had propounded a new method for squaring the circle or trisecting the arc" (78). One of her constant pleas was grounded in general observation and personal experience: "To be plain, I mean let money be raised and scholarships be founded in our colleges and universities for self-supporting, worthy young women, to offset and balance the aid that can always be found for boys who will take theology" (79).

To pair W. E. B. Du Bois and Anna Julia Cooper may seem odd because of the great fame of the one and considerable neglect of the other, falling along gender lines in a predictable way. So why undertake a project whose result is determined by the choice of its subject? My purpose is to open a dialogue that never took place, to explore connections that existed or most probably existed, and to enter into negotiations of gender and canonicity that may explain Cooper's publishing silence after her early book, *A Voice from the South* (1892), and shed light on Du Bois's attitude toward women. I argue that Du Bois was a very typical late Victorian intellectual African American whose attitude toward women was dictated by the general custom of his times, while Cooper was his intellectual equal but had to suffer under the general restrictions that her age imposed upon women. This is no novel argument, but one upon which much of the feminist scholarship of recent years has been based.[4] Yet in many individual cases remarkable connections remain unrecognized because a scholarship filling in gaps and silences, reconstructing lives and histories, and revising prevalent notions even in a period of "postfeminism" is still (or perhaps even more) urgently needed. Not only does much feminine literary tradition remain unwritten, its links with various forms of masculine tradition remain obscure.

Although both Du Bois and Cooper lived well into the middle of our century, their lives and careers were largely molded by the sociohistorical and cultural forces of the late nineteenth and early twentieth centuries. This period is marked by the influx of immigrants and an increase in population and size of urban areas, the "closing" of the continental frontier, progress in sciences and in technology, and the beginning of advertising and consumerism. It was a time of intense sociopolitical strife for nonwhite Americans. For the African American population the end of Reconstruction led to various movements toward disenfranchisement, the new black codes, the "grandfather clause," the formation of various Klan groups, lynching, segregation, and the Jim Crow laws. As Thomas F. Gossett has observed, the period can be characterized by the low educational standard of the Negro and high levels of crime, disease, and poverty, all of which were usually explained as being "the inevitable result of [the Negro's] heredity."[5] At the same time, however, as Elizabeth Ammons points out, this era "saw women gain the vote, earn unprecedented percentages of college degrees, enter the professions in unheard-of numbers, lower the birthrate, raise the divorce rate, and stop the sale of liquor" (16). Hazel Carby argues that "these were the years of the first flowering of black women's autonomous organizations and a period of intense intellectual activity and productivity" (7). The claim to power of women and ethnic minorities, with its parallel development of a middle class that was not exclusively dominated by white and male standards, led to a concurrent need by white men to live up to and defend the standards of an idealized masculinity. In *Manliness and Civilization*, Gail Bederman writes about the connections, variations, and interplays between white supremacy, male power, civilized manliness, and middle-class nationhood when these are challenged by so-called primitive masculinity, militant feminism, and African American resistance. All these historical forces engendered a subliminal discourse about race, class, and gender that Du Bois and Cooper could not avoid.

Du Bois's career has become legendary, much discussed, and well researched. His educational beliefs stand for an elitist rule by the intellectually excellent; his "Talented Tenth" were supposed to lead in a society governed by excellence and not by color alone. Coupled with this is a clear belief in upper-class authority, the authority of the "exceptional men" or an "aristocracy of talent and character." Du Bois asks: "Was there ever a nation on God's fair earth civilized from the bottom upward?" and answers: "Never; it is, ever was, and ever will be from the top downward that culture filters."[6] His idea about the black colleges is typical of his times: "The function of the Negro college, then, is clear: it must maintain the standards of popular education, it must seek the social regeneration of the Negro, and it must help in the solution of problems of race contact and co-operation. And finally, beyond all this, it must develop men."[7] The Du Boisian intellectual would be college educated, of middle-class, mostly Northern descent, morally impeccable, a natural leader, and a public role model.

Cooper, equally Victorian in upbringing, although still born in slavery (her father was most probably her mother's white master) sees the role of education in a different light. Time and again she emphasizes women's contribution to the civilized world: "Since the idea of order and subordination succumbed to barbarian brawn and brutality in the fifteenth century, the civilized world has been like a child brought up by his father. It has needed the great mother heart to teach it to be pitiful, to love mercy, to succor the weak and care for the lowly" (51). For Cooper the key observation of the late nineteenth century is that "a 'mothering' influence from some source is leavening the nation" (59). She repeatedly underscores her belief that "the feminine factor can have its proper effect only through woman's development and education so that she may fitly and intelligently stamp her force on the forces of her day, and add her modicum to the riches of the world's thought" (61). Cooper, whose life purpose it was to teach the disadvantaged,[8] rails at "the idea that women may stand on pedestals or live in doll houses (if they happen to have them) but they must not furrow their brows with thought or attempt to help men tug at the great questions of the world" (75). The reader feels a personal bitterness, well concealed under the modest stance of the educated woman, when she writes: "The three R's, a little music and a good deal of dancing, a first rate dress-maker and a bottle of magnolia balm, are quite enough generally to render charming any woman possessed of tact and the capacity for worshipping masculinity" (75).

Certainly, "the three R's" were not sufficient for Cooper. Born Anna Julia Hayward in 1858 near Raleigh, North Carolina, she was educated at nearby St. Augustine Normal School, where she had her problems with the "boys who would take theology." After she married one of these boys, the Reverend George Cooper, and became a widow after only two years of marriage, Cooper completed her B.A. and M.A. at Oberlin College. She then started work as a teacher, later becoming principal, at the M Street High School for black youth in Washington, D.C. (later named Dunbar High School). After a near lifetime as teacher, scholar, and public spokeswoman, she began to study in Paris for her Ph.D. in 1924 at the age of sixty-six. While on sick leave from M Street High School, she completed her residency requirement in Paris, having to rush home so that she would not lose her job and retirement benefits. At that time Cooper had to cope with her teaching, her extensive research, and her role as mother of five adopted grand-nieces and -nephews. In the spring of 1925 Cooper defended her thesis in French in Paris — quite an excruciating experience, as she wrote in her fragmentary, unpublished autobiographical essay.[9] At the same time this was certainly her moment of triumph, in which she could prove to the world the black woman's intellectual worth. Leona Gabel interprets her efforts in the following way: "The Sorbonne experience was at once a triumph and an ordeal; her doctorate was the dream of a lifetime achieved after many years and in the face of great odds. It may have compensated somewhat for the humiliation inflicted upon her as a principal in 1906." Gabel also mentions "the unyielding, unsympathetic attitude of the school authorities and certain of her colleagues regarding her leave of absence" (65, 66). Her experience attests to the fact that education for an intelligent black woman could be achieved only against the greatest odds and was fraught with much more anxiety and stress than in the case of someone like Du Bois.

The gendered possibilities of education at this time are best illustrated by the fact that Du Bois received his B.A. from Fisk in 1888 (at age twenty), a second B.A. from Harvard in 1890 (at twenty-two), his M.A. from Harvard in 1892 (at twenty-four), his Ph.D. in history from Harvard in 1895 (at twenty-seven), and was a professor of economics and history at Atlanta University when Anna Julia Cooper was dismissed from her post as principal of M Street High School in 1906. The reasons for this dismissal, which destroyed her career to a large degree, may have been, as Mary Helen Washington summarizes: "(1) refusing to use a textbook authorized by the Board; (2) being too sympathetic to weak and unqualified students; (3) not being able to maintain discipline (2 students had been caught drinking); and (4) not maintaining a 'proper spirit of unity and loyalty.'"[10] To all evidence, Cooper was caught in the general controversy over the respective values of vocational training and college education for black youth instigated by the clashing opinions of Booker T. Washington and Du Bois. Cooper, herself well read in the classics, always took pride in sending a number of her M Street graduates to prestigious universities. Being accused of a lack of the "proper spirit of unity and loyalty" meant, at that time, that she was not conforming to the more powerful "Tuskegee Machine"; she was eventually replaced by a Tuskegee man. Responding to a questionnaire many years later, Cooper wrote about this instance of insubordination: "For which unpardonable 'sin' against racial supremacy said principal suffers to this day the punishment of the damned from both the white masters and the colored understrappers."[11] Like many other black female intellectuals (such as Ida Wells-Barnett, Josephine St. Pierre Ruffin, Mary Terrell, Lugenia Hope, or Jessie Redmon Fauset [Lewis, 289]), she endorsed the Du Bois side in the controversy, obviously with an enthusiasm that put her own career at risk. Although she was called back to M Street, she never became principal again and later even had to fight (unsuccessfully) for a better professional rating that would bring her an increase in wages (Hutchinson, 148 ff.; Gabel, 46–59).

In different ways, of course, both Du Bois's and Cooper's careers are exceptional. Du Bois received the publicity he deserved and suffered under inevitable frustrations, becoming in many eyes "a dangerous racial malcontent," as Lewis calls him. "Over and again he would have to recast ambitious plans to fit frail budgets, take the leavings of research projects he should have been asked to design or direct, and persevere against heartbreaking odds in order to complete seminal work to which major white foundations, universities, or learned journals gave only cursory notice" (Lewis, 362). Cooper's public life, however, cannot be reconstructed in full. Mary Helen Washington surmises that she was more given to solitary studies in the libraries than to well-publicized public appearances, which would account for her relative lack of fame.[12] It took nearly a hundred years for her major work to be republished in the Schomburg series. Her biographer, Leona C. Gabel, observes that "the career of Dr. Cooper presented itself as a story in search of an author, a tale waiting to be told" (3).

The remarkable collection of essays in *A Voice from the South* (1892) ranges in topic from the treatment of women in contemporary and past society to religion, the development of races, literature, and the place of the Negro in the United States of her period. All the essays are scholarly and argumentative, with occasional glimpses at the author's personal experience, and reveal a strong sense of irony and a deep concern for and knowledge of the subject.[13] Elizabeth Alexander says that Cooper wrote "out of the impulse to present a unified, serviceable vision of a future for African-Americans as well as out of a simultaneous resistance to a static, monolithic view of what it was to be black, and, specifically, to be a black woman."[14] Since from a late-twentieth-century point of view these essays are as interesting as Du Bois's on comparable topics, their neglect in literary and intellectual history has to be seen as symptomatic of the treatment of African American women in public life generally. Mary Helen Washington comes to the conclusion that "the intellectual discourse of black women of the 1890s, and particularly Cooper's embryonic black feminist analysis, was ignored because it was by and about women and therefore thought not to be significantly about the race as writings by and about men" (xxviii).

Today's interested scholars and students have the advantage of reading two of Cooper's essays ("Our Raison D'être" and "Woman Versus the Indian") alongside selections from Du Bois's *The Souls of Black Folk* ("Of Our Spiritual Strivings," "Of Mr. Booker T. Washington and Others," and "Of the Sorrow Songs") and from Booker T. Washington's *Up from Slavery*, all included in the second edition of the *Heath Anthology of American Literature*. They thus benefit from an access to materials, enabling comparative analysis that has been difficult in the past hundred years. With a century's added knowledge and the development of African American feminist thought, Cooper is now being recognized as a direct forerunner and early role model for the present generation of black women writers, scholars, and educators. One of the few remarks comparing Cooper and Du Bois comes in a footnote to Cornel West's essay about Du Bois in *The Future of the Race*, in which he calls *A Voice from the South* "the first major work of a black woman of letters in the U.S."[15] and then briefly comments on how the opening of *A Voice*—with its powerful metaphor of crying—is echoed in the beginning of Du Bois's *The Souls of Black Folk*. And recently Kevin J. Gaines has placed a sustained treatment of Cooper next to an analysis of Du Bois's *The Philadelphia Negro*. In *Uplifting the Race: Black Leadership, Politics, and Culture in the Twentieth Century*, Gaines addresses Cooper's "Western ethnocentrism, her staunch religious piety, and a late-Victorian bourgeois sensibility distrustful of social democracy" and treats her as a "social commentator on a wide array of national questions, which besides gender, included controversies over race, labor, and African American and American cultural identity." In an effort to lift Cooper out of what he calls the "artificial limits" of critical consideration as a black feminist intellectual, he sees her as a "southern, nativist apologist for antilabor views."[16]

Much like her contemporaries Fannie Barrier Williams, Ida Wells-Barnett, and Pauline Elizabeth Hopkins (to name only a few), Cooper suffers under a paradox: as an educated woman she deems herself entitled to the attention due a middle-class lady, but as a black woman she is automatically regarded as poor and uneducated. As Elizabeth Ammons says, "turn-of-the-century women writers found themselves, often in deep, subtle ways, emotionally stranded between worlds," and, she continues, "pleasing this power block [white editors, reviewers, and readers] while remaining rooted in one's community and true to one's own artistic vision . . . represented the almost intolerably schizophrenic challenge faced by turn-of-the-century writers in general who were people of color" (10, 11). In "Woman Versus the Indian," Cooper mocks the white women's movement, when its leaders see it endangered by a colored woman taking classes under its wings, by calling it "this immaculate assembly for propagating liberal and progressive ideas and disseminating a broad and humanizing culture" (82). When she says, "we assume to be leaders of thought and guardians of society" (84), the "we" includes all women. But when she talks about the excruciating "feeling of slighted womanhood" (90) when as a colored woman she travels in the American South, her assertion that "our women are to be credited largely as teachers and moulders of public sentiment" (95) becomes a fierce indictment of the white American woman's responsibility for prejudice and discrimination. Her travels become the yardstick by which she measures racial inequality; good manners evident in the treatment of women regardless of race and class are the proof of a great civilization. So while most of her contemporaries would claim that America has reached the acme of civilization, Cooper here calls for "*apostles of anti-barbarism*" (96) to end discrimination. Her view is informed by a deep sense of the Christian duty of charity: only when "women," the "Indian," and the "Negro" (her terms) have their rights will America be taught "the secret of universal courtesy which is after all nothing but the art, the science, and the religion of regarding one's neighbour as one's self, and to do for him as we would, were conditions swapped, that he do for us" (117).

Despite the scant knowledge we have about Du Bois's and Cooper's direct contacts, it is clear that they were both aware of each other's work and had actually met. Cooper taught at Wilberforce from 1884 to 1885; Du Bois, from 1894 to 1896. Both of them attended the 1900 Pan African Conference in London and both delivered speeches there. Leona Gabel discusses a tour of the Paris Exposition that Cooper, Du Bois, and a group of African American men and women undertook in the wake of the

1900 conference. Cooper and Du Bois were also good friends of Mrs. and Dr. Alexander Crummell, in whose house Cooper lived for some time in 1887 (Gabel, 33). Around 1900 Du Bois also applied for the position of superintendent for the colored schools in Washington, D.C., where Cooper was a teacher. In the winter of 1902–1903, about the time that Cooper became principal of M Street High School, Du Bois addressed the school. And there are various letters from Cooper to Du Bois, urging him to write a response to a racist book or asking why a congress that Cooper obviously wanted to attend should have to take place during school term.[17] Washington laments Du Bois's lack of response: "I cannot imagine Du Bois being similarly faithful to Anna Cooper, offering to publicize her work, or being willing to hawk 10,000 copies of one of her speeches on women's equality, nor can I imagine that any of the male intelligentsia would have been distraught at not being able to attend the annual meetings of the colored women's clubs" (xli). When Du Bois quotes Cooper's "only the black woman can say 'when and where I enter,'" which appears originally in one of the essays of *A Voice from the South*, in his "Damnation of Women," he does not acknowledge his debt to Cooper. She was the only woman to enter the prestigious Negro Academy, but, as Linda Hutchinson notes, "there is no evidence to suggest that any of her writings were published under the auspices of the American Negro Academy; even so, there is no question but that she was respected by the members of the academy for her scholarship" (110). These individual incidents may seem minor, but they certainly added to Cooper's sense of frustration. In her usual restrained manner, she voices this fact in a handwritten answer to the question, "Have you a 'racial philosophy' that can be briefly stated?" She writes: "I am as sensitive to handicaps as those who are always whining about them & the whips & stings of prejudice, whether of color or sex, find me neither too calloused to suffer, nor too ignorant to know what is due me. Our own men as a group have not inherited traditions of chivalry (one sided as it may be among white men) & we women are generally left to do our race battling alone except for empty compliments now & then."[18]

In general, Du Bois's attitude toward "the five million women of [his] race" is ambiguous and seems to be more determined by his gender than by his race; as Lewis concludes: "One of the most vociferous male feminists of the early twentieth century (his essay 'The Damnation of Women' can still quicken pulses), Du Bois often fell somewhat short of his principles in his most intimate dealings with women."[19] His statements about women can be easily compared to similar ones by Cooper. Here, now, is the beginning of a dialogue that never took place:

> WEBD: Yet the world must heed these daughters of sorrow, from the primal black All-Mother of men down through the ghostly throng of mighty womanhood, who walked in the mysterious dawn of Asia and Africa. ("Damnation," 300) [20]
>
> AJC (*agrees*): [the civilized world] has needed the great mother-heart to teach it to be pitiful, to love mercy, to succor the weak and care for the lowly. (51)

Cooper and Du Bois shared common ideas about the roles and spheres of women and men, the development of civilization, and woman's suffrage. They believed in a lofty and idealized vision of the "primal black All-Mother of men" and "the great mother-heart." Cooper firmly subscribes to the Victorian view of woman as the morally superior being. Du Bois's panegyric to the primal force of black womanhood occurs regularly in his works. In his 1928 novel, *Dark Princess*, he calls the protagonist's mother "Kali, the Black One; Wife of Siva, Mother of the World."[21] In this interesting fictional attempt to drive home his lesson of the need for black solidarity, Du Bois contrasts Sara Andrews, a very realistic career woman who is presented as harsh, ambitious, and above all passionless, with Kautilya, the ravishingly beautiful Indian princess. His glorification of the black woman as exemplified by the mother and Kautilya provides a necessary corrective to the predominant image of the black woman as immoral. Yet, as in *Dark Princess*, it also belongs to the realm of romanticized, otherworldly existence, thus obfuscating the view of the real-life situation of African American women and preventing possible solutions to their problems.

In real life, Du Bois also seems to have fallen somehow short of his own ideals. Lewis mentions that Ida Wells-Barnett's name was left out of the original list of the Committee of Forty that preceded the organization of the NAACP. The reason for this, according to Lewis, was that Du Bois "resented her frank independence": "Wells-Barnett was a woman of unrestrained outspokenness who seldom acknowledged the gender etiquette of her day when fighting for a cause. She may have presumed a good deal on Du Bois's large ego." Another incident is Du Bois's failure to properly acknowledge Isabel Eaton's more than incidental contribution to *The Philadelphia Negro* (Lewis, *Biography of a Race*, 396, 397; 191 ff.). In spite of these omissions, the Du Bois-Cooper dialogue might well have continued:

> WEBD: The uplift of women is, next to the problem of the color line and the peace movement, our greatest modern cause. ("Damnation," 309)
>
> AJC (*reminds him of the church*): Will not the aid of the church be given to prepare our girls in head, heart, and hand for the duties and responsibilities that await the intelligent wife, the Christian mother, the earnest, virtuous, helpful woman, at once both the lever and the fulcrum for uplifting the race. (45)
>
> WEBD (*appeasing*): I instinctively feel and know that it is the five million women of my race who really count. ("Damnation," 308)

Cooper's and Du Bois's linking the uplift of women to the uplift of the race was not an exception.[22] To Du Bois's list of the greatest modern causes — the uplift of women, the problem of the color line, and the peace movement — Cooper characteristically adds the powerful agent of Christianity as the basis of every improvement. In her essays she emphasizes again and again that, for her, God is the prime mover; that the power of a firm belief delivered the Southern Negro from slavery; and that agnosticism entails insecurity, danger, and loneliness, while religious faith provides love, security, and community.

Both writers actively endorsed women's suffrage, which they thought would help to end legal and political discrimination. Like most of his contemporaries, Du Bois invokes the famous women of the past to disclaim any notion that women might be of the "weaker sex": "The sex of Judith, Candace, Queen Elizabeth, Sojourner Truth and Jane Addams was the merest incident of human function and not a mark of weakness and inferiority" ("Suffrage," in *W. E. B. Du Bois: A Reader*, 298). In a curious and strenuous statement, Cooper, in turn, feels driven to invoke her powers of irony to argue for suffrage: "The great burly black man, ignorant and gross and depraved, is allowed to vote; while the franchise is withheld from the intelligent and refined, the pure-minded and lofty souled white woman." Cooper follows this statement against the white woman's movement by pleading for a common cause that should unite all women: "Why should woman become plaintiff in a suit versus the Indian, or the Negro or any other race or class?" Her argument is broad and inclusive: "Is not woman's cause broader, and deeper, and grander, than a blue stocking debate or an aristocratic pink tea?" (123) As always, Cooper finds the right metaphor:

> AJC: We might as well expect to grow trees from leaves as hope to build up a civilization or a manhood without taking into consideration our women and the home life made by them, which must be the root and ground of the whole matter. (78)
> WEBD (*vociferous male feminist*): The actual work of the world to-day depends more largely upon women than upon men. ("Suffrage," 297)
> AJC (*reminding him of his own duties*): the problem, I trow, now rests with the man as to how he can so develop his God-given powers as to reach the ideal of a generation of women who demand the noblest, grandest and best achievements of which he is capable. (70 ff.)

When Du Bois, the trained sociologist, claims that the actual work of today depends more upon women than upon men, his argument is well founded on statistical data about the wage-earning capacity of black women.[23] Cooper's metaphor about the trees and the leaves, however, sets the argument in the even larger context of civilization building. As a trained historian, Cooper was certainly aware of the common historical debates of her time about the origins of the races and the development of civilization. The importance she places upon the home life provided by educated and caring women may sound Victorian in its origin. By applying it, as she does, to the African American family removed from slavery only by little more than a generation, this argument becomes a fervent and often-repeated cry for the value of the black home. From a black woman's point of view, Cooper cannot conceal her bitterness about the role of black men falling short in their "noblest, grandest and best achievements" when these should benefit their proper home life. The roles of men and women in marriage engender further conversation:

> WEBD (*typical man of his age*): That the average woman is spiritually different from the average man is undoubtedly just as true as the fact that the average white man differs from the average Negro. ("Suffrage," 297 ff.)
>
> AJC: (*agrees*): All I claim is that there is a feminine as well as a masculine side to truth. . . . That as the man is more noble in reason, so the woman is more quick in sympathy. (60)
>
> WEBD: A woman is as much a thinking, feeling, acting person after marriage as before. She has opinions and she has a right to have them and she has a right to express them. ("Suffrage," 298)
>
> AJC: Women . . . can think as well as feel, and . . . feel none the less because they think. (50)

Du Bois himself was probably not Cooper's ideal model of father, husband, and friend. After confessing that he "was literally frightened into marriage before [he] was able to support a family," Du Bois says his marriage "was not an absolutely ideal union, but it was happier than most."[24] As he sees it, it suffered from one "fundamental drawback of modern American marriage" because his "main work was out in the world and not at home" (280, 281). While he praises the importance of home, he seems to have been no great homemaker himself. At more than ninety years of age, he carefully voices his lament about the effects of a constrained, closely circumscribed female upbringing such as his wife's: "I have often wondered if her limitations to a few women friends, and they chiefly housekeepers; and if her lack of contact with men, because of her conventional upbringing and her surroundings — if this did not make her life unnecessarily narrow and confined" (282). His argument that the modern woman "is as much a thinking, feeling, acting person after marriage as before" reads patronizingly to a modern feminist, but it was certainly not a commonly held belief at his time. Yet it seems that his own conservative surroundings did not prepare him to accept and actively endorse the really independent colored woman. His treatment of

Sara Andrews in *Dark Princess*, which goes hand in hand with a bitter charge against what he sees as the fake values of the black middle class, may prove this point. Lewis also hints at Du Bois's various extramarital affairs, but what they might suggest about his attitude to women is open to dispute (Lewis, *Biography of a Race*, 346–347, 450–451, 464).

I mention all this background not to impute weakness of character to a great man, but to show that even a seer could be insensitive to the needs of women very close to him. There is no extant evidence that Anna Julia Cooper was ever encouraged, helped, or promoted by Du Bois. While Du Bois made his career out in the world and not at home, Cooper must have concluded early on that a full-scale public career would not support her. She needed her job as a teacher so that she would have financial security. And at the age of fifty she acted upon her own ideals of the importance of home for colored youth and became a homemaker for her adopted family. In "The Status of Woman in America" she puts "the happiness of home" on an equal footing with "the righteousness of the country" (133).

Neither Cooper nor Du Bois could deny the differences between men and women. Du Bois equates the spiritual difference between the sexes with the difference between the races.[25] And Cooper claims a masculine as well as a feminine side to truth but quickly goes on to say that "these are related not as inferior and superior, not as better and worse, not as weaker and stronger, but as complements — complements in one necessary and symmetric whole" (60). In the next sentence she qualifies man's alleged capacity for more noble reason by calling him "indefatigable in pursuit of abstract truth" (123). Woman's sympathy is needed for the advocacy of the weak. And that is why every woman has to be educated and trained, which leads Cooper's argument back full circle to the concern basic to most of her essays: "the feminine factor can have its proper effect only through woman's development and education so that she may fitly and intelligently stamp her force on the forces of her day, and add her modicum to the riches of the world's thought" (61). Du Bois agrees to this in principle:

> WEBD: I have always felt like bowing myself before them in all
> abasement, searching to bring some tribute to these long-
> suffering victims, these burdened sisters of mine, whom the

world, the wise, white world, loves to affront and ridicule and wantonly to insult. ("Damnation," 311 ff.)

AJC: We need men who can let their interest and gallantry extend outside the circle of their aesthetic appreciation; men who can be a father, a brother, a friend to every weak, struggling, unshielded girl. (32)

The lamentable fact that Cooper never wrote anything again comparable to *A Voice from the South* cannot be blamed on Du Bois, of course. But the lack of encouragement that she shared with many other women of her age resulted in her failing to take such a forceful public stand on issues of gender, class, and race again. Du Bois's "bowing" before "these burdened sisters of mine" is a metaphorical bow after all, and Cooper's call for men "who can be a father, a brother, a friend to every weak, struggling, unshielded girl" went unheeded more often than not. I would argue that historical writing offered Cooper much safer ground, one that would not endanger her position as a teacher. It is especially remarkable that her best-known public appearances (the World Congress in Chicago in 1893, the Pan African Conference in London in 1900) came before she was dismissed as principal of M Street. One can hardly claim that Cooper fell silent after 1892. She undertook considerable historical research, edited *The Life and Writings of the Grimké Family* (1951), wrote numerous shorter articles, letters to the editor, and some poems. Her own voice could always be heard by those who cared to listen: first as a teacher and lecturer, later as president of Frelinghuysen University. She remained active till her death at the age of a hundred and five.

Both lives and careers offer a glimpse of the gendered possibilities for African Americans at the turn of the century. Du Bois achieved visibility in spite of his being a programmatic black thinker who challenged the white establishment. Partly because of the Victorian values that he shared with his contemporaries, he could move into this male establishment. Paradoxically, Cooper shared many of his values, but they were judged liberal because they came from a woman and concerned mainly the role of women. At that time the world was not structured for a woman to articulate these ideas successfully. As a result, this voice of a black woman from the South has barely been heard.

NOTES

1. W. E. B. Du Bois, *Darkwater: Voices from within the Veil* (1920; New York: Schocken, 1972), 15. All second and subsequent references to this and other sources are cited in the text.

2. David Levering Lewis, *W. E. B. Du Bois: Biography of a Race, 1868–1919* (New York: Holt, 1993), 81.

3. Anna Julia Cooper, *A Voice from the South* (1892; New York: Oxford University Press, 1988), 76.

4. The list of studies that discuss African American women writers from a wide variety of angles or include a discussion of them is increasing. The books I found most helpful are Elizabeth Ammons's *Conflicting Stories: American Women Writers at the Turn into the Twentieth Century* (New York: Oxford University Press, 1991); Gail Bederman's *Manliness and Civilization: A Cultural History of Gender and Race in the United States, 1880–1917* (Chicago: University of Chicago Press, 1995); Dickson D. Bruce's *Black American Writing from the Nadir: The Evolution of a Literary Tradition, 1877–1915* (Baton Rouge: Louisiana State University Press, 1989); Hazel V. Carby's *Reconstructing Womanhood: The Emergence of the Afro-American Woman Novelist* (New York: Oxford University Press, 1987); Barbara Christian's *Black Women Novelists: The Development of a Tradition, 1892–1965* (Westport: Greenwood, 1980); Ann DuCille's *The Coupling Convention: Sex, Text, and Tradition in Black Women's Fiction* (New York: Oxford University Press, 1993); Francis Smith Foster's *Written by Herself: Literary Production by African American Women Writers, 1746–1892* (Bloomington: Indiana University Press, 1993); Paula Giddings's *When and Where I Enter: The Impact of Black Women on Race and Sex in America* (New York: Bantam, 1984); Bert James Loewenberg and Ruth Bogan's collection, *Black Women in Nineteenth-Century American Life: Their Words, Their Thoughts, Their Feelings* (University Park: Pennsylvania State University Press, 1976); Claudia Tate's *Domestic Allegories of Political Desire: The Black Heroine's Text at the Turn of the Century* (New York: Oxford University Press, 1992); Carol McAlpine Watson's *Prologue: The Novels of Black American Women, 1891–1965* (Westport: Greenwood, 1985).

5. Thomas F. Gossett, *Race: The History of an Idea in America* (Dallas: Southern Methodist University Press, 1963), 286. Additional useful studies of race relations in the late nineteenth and early twentieth centuries include August Meier's *Negro Thought in America, 1880–1915: Racial Ideologies in the Age of Booker T. Washington* (Ann Arbor: University of Michigan Press, 1963); George M. Fredrickson's *The Black Image in the White Mind: The Debate on Afro-American Character and Destiny 1817–1914* (New York: Harper, 1971) and his later *Black Liberation: A Comparative History of Black Ideologies*

in the United States and South Africa (New York: Oxford University Press, 1995); and Eric J. Sundquist's *To Wake the Nations: Race in the Making of American Literature* (Cambridge: Harvard University Press, Belknap Press, 1993).

6. W. E. B. Du Bois, "The Talented Tenth," in *W. E. B. Du Bois: A Reader*, ed. Andrew Paschal (New York: Collier, 1971), 31, 36.

7. W. E. B. Du Bois, *The Souls of Black Folk* (1903; reprint, New York: Dover, 1994), 66.

8. See "Survey of Racial Attitudes of Negro Students," for a study published in 1932 by Dr. Charles S. Johnson, Moorland-Spingarn Research Center, Howard University, answer to question 58.

9. Cooper, "The Third Step," Moorland-Spingarn Research Center, Howard University. Most biographical data is taken from Louise Daniel Hutchinson, *Anna Julia Cooper: A Voice from the South* (Washington, D.C.: Smithsonian, 1981), and Leona C. Gabel, *From Slavery to the Sorbonne and Beyond: The Life and Writings of Anna J. Cooper* (Northampton, Mass.: Smith College, 1982). I want to thank Paul Williams for sending me a copy of his "National Register of Historic Places Registration Form" (NPS Form 10–900, OMB No. 1024–0018), which includes a biographical sketch about Cooper. Williams has successfully registered the Edwin P. Goodwin House, the former site of Frelinghuysen University (1800 Vermont Ave. NW, Washington, D.C.), where Cooper was president, as a historic place.

10. Mary Helen Washington, introduction to *A Voice from the South*, xxxv.

11. See Survey of Racial Attitudes, Cooper's answer to question 46.

12. Mary Helen Washington, "Anna Julia Cooper: The Black Feminist Voice of the 1890s," *Legacy* 4.2 (1987): 3.

13. Todd Vogel offers an excellent analysis of Cooper's use of classical rhetoric and deductive logic; see "The Master's Tools Revisited: Foundation Work in Anna Julia Cooper," in *Criticism and the Color Line: Desegregating American Literary Studies*, ed. Henry B. Wonham (New Brunswick, N.J.: Rutgers University Press, 1996), 158–170.

14. Elizabeth Alexander, "'We Must Be about Our Father's Business': Anna Julia Cooper and the In-Corporation of the Nineteenth-Century African-American Woman Intellectual," *Signs* 20.2 (1995): 341.

15. Cornel West, "Black Strivings in a Twilight Civilization," in *The Future of the Race*, ed. Henry Louis Gates, Jr., and Cornel West (New York: Knopf, 1996), 191.

16. Kevin J. Gaines, *Uplifting the Race: Black Leadership, Politics, and Culture in the Twentieth Century* (Chapel Hill: University of North Carolina Press, 1996), 129. In a recent article, Joy James argues that Du Bois's

nonfictional writings "minimize black female agency" and that "profeminism permitted Du Bois to include women in democratic struggles; paternalism allowed him to naturalize the male intellectual" (143, 157). James, "The Profeminist Politics of W. E. B. Du Bois with Respect to Anna Julia Cooper and Ida B. Wells Barnett," in *W. E. B. Du Bois on Race and Culture*, ed. Bernard W. Bell et al. (New York: Routledge, 1996).

17. This exchange, which stimulated this project, is analyzed by Gabel (xii–xiii), Hutchinson (180–182), and Washington (xli).

18. Survey of Racial Attitudes, answer to question 68.

19. David Levering Lewis, introduction to *W. E. B. Du Bois: A Reader*, ed. David Levering Lewis (New York: Holt, 1995), 2.

20. These quotations should be read in their proper contexts and can be found in Du Bois, "The Damnation of Women" and "Woman Suffrage," both of which are reprinted in Lewis, ed., *W. E. B. Du Bois: A Reader*, and in Cooper's *A Voice from the South*.

21. W. E. B. Du Bois, *Dark Princess: A Romance* (Jackson: University Press of Missisippi, 1995), 220.

22. See Gaines's study for a detailed analysis of uplift ideology (esp. chap. 1, 1–17) and Giddings's study for the most helpful information about the roles of black women, especially her chapter on the women's club movement (95–117).

23. See Gaines's analysis of Du Bois's *The Philadelphia Negro*, 152–178.

24. W. E. B. Du Bois, *The Autobiography of W. E. B. Du Bois: A Soliloquy on Viewing My Life from the Last Decade of Its First Century* (New York: International Publishers, 1968), 280.

25. An analysis of Du Bois's concept of the races goes beyond the scope of this paper; see Anthony Appiah, "The Uncompleted Argument: Du Bois and the Illusion of Race" in *"Race," Writing, and Difference*, ed. Henry Louis Gates, Jr. (Chicago: University of Chicago Press, 1986), 21–37; see also Arnold Rampersad, *The Art and Imagination of W. E. B. Du Bois* (Cambridge: Harvard University Press, 1976).

Woman Thinking: Margaret Fuller, Ralph Waldo Emerson, and the American Scholar

LINDSEY TRAUB

When Margaret Fuller, scholar, journalist, feminist, and critic, was drowned in a shipwreck off Fire Island, New York, in July 1850, Ralph Waldo Emerson wrote in his journal: "If nature availed in America to give birth to such as she, freedom & honour & letters & art too were safe in this new world."[1] Yet, a generation later, her awesome reputation for originality and brilliance had ossified into a legend of eccentricity and egotism. The acclaimed role model for an influential generation of New England women had become the subject of a cautionary tale. There is even now no complete edition of her writing; and her letters, collected with great difficulty, have been available in full only since 1988. The apparent distortion and eclipse of a such a figure raises some uncomfortable questions about the selective process of literary survival and demonstrates the vulnerability of the prematurely dead to their literary executors — or, in Fuller's case, her undertakers.

Nathaniel Hawthorne's portrait of Zenobia-cum-Fuller in *The Blithedale Romance* and his spiteful remarks in the *Roman Notebooks* are notorious, but more subtle and more interesting is the role of Ralph Waldo Emerson, her intimate friend, correspondent, and, crucially, her first joint-biographer, in shaping her literary future. For the response to her death of Margaret Fuller's closest associates was not to collect and publish her writing as a freestanding body of work. That might have stabilized her volatile reputation and demonstrated beyond the reach of mythmaking her contribution to the development of American letters. Instead, three close and longtime friends, James Freeman Clarke, Ralph Waldo

Emerson, and William Henry Channing, collected her letters, journals, books and articles, with personal recollections from a wide range of friends on both sides of the Atlantic, and published *Memoirs of Margaret Fuller Ossoli* in 1852. The book divides her life into periods, illustrating each with her own writing, introduced and accompanied by commentary from the three editors respectively. But the treatment of Margaret Fuller and her papers, even by nineteenth-century standards of editorial practice that valued privacy above accuracy, has made modern scholars groan with horror. Robert N. Hudspeth, in the introduction to his Herculean achievement as editor of her letters, gives graphic detail of the damage done to the raw materials of the *Memoirs* and to the image of Margaret Fuller that the finished book conveys: "Channing, Clarke, and Emerson so bowderlized and manipulated their evidence as to ruin a splendid book. The *Memoirs of Margaret Fuller Ossoli* is a mess. . . . The sad evidence of the physical abuse still exists: letters have whole paragraphs blotted by gobs of purple ink; other letters are cut into halves or quarters; editorial changes are written over Fuller's writing."[2]

The effect of their work was to fix Fuller in the character of friend and confidante and to control and regulate her posthumous representation through the filter of their inscribed editorship. The title of the book they published is ambiguous — biography masquerading as autobiography. For while most of the text is Fuller's own writing, she is not the author of her memoirs. These are the editors' memoirs of her: a selection of extracts, divorced from their sources and effectively recontextualized, offered as a privileged view of a private person without proper recognition of her established public career. The biographers' obvious respect for their subject did not prevent this act of appropriation, signaling their fundamental, if unconscious, disregard for her existence as an author in her own right. By 1903 Henry James, whose father had been her friend and who had admired what he knew of her in his youth, could write with nostalgic interest about Fuller as the "Margaret-ghost," who "left nothing behind her, her written utterance being nought."[3]

So why the insistence on the private nature of someone whose chosen role was, as a journalist and critic, so essentially and so successfully public? Why the need to mediate between Fuller and a notional "public" before which her friends blushingly brought her at an admitted cost to their own privacy, when she already had one of her own? James Freeman Clarke, who does justice to his admiration for her intellectual gifts and her contribution to his own development, creates this confessional context in the opening of his early section of the *Memoirs*: "The difficulty which we all feel in describing our past intercourse with Margaret Fuller, is, that the intercourse was so intimate, and the friendship so personal, that it is like making a confession to the public of our most interior selves."[4]

In contrast, Emerson's testimonial does not confess its personal investment in this direct way; instead, we feel this investment through its disavowal. Unlike Clarke's and Channing's general approbation of their subject, Emerson frequently appears to belittle and deprecate her. Yet his reminiscences and critical judgments in the *Memoirs* are belied by the evidence of his own journals and the private correspondence between himself and Fuller. The immediate effect of this public belittlement on the reader in possession of the private record is a disappointing sense of betrayal of what had been a rich and productive friendship. But the betrayal was of more than simply a personal relationship. The qualities in Fuller that Emerson appears to have admired during her lifetime were characteristic of his emerging portrait of an ideal of conduct in the moral, intellectual, and cultural life of America. The clearest version of this ideal was drawn as early as 1837 in "The American Scholar" and never effaced, though Emerson continued to reflect upon the significance of this figure for the rest of his life.[5] Fuller's life and words give evidence of her own struggle with her mind, temperament, and circumstances toward such an ideal, whose achievement became gradually clearer, in the integration of her life and work as she approached maturity. But in the premature closure of that life and work, after fleetingly acknowledging her role to himself once again, Emerson appears to have begun rewriting in public what he had expressed in private. Perhaps it was literally inconceivable to him that he might have known "Woman Thinking."

Ralph Waldo Emerson met Margaret Fuller in July 1836, when she came as the guest of his wife, Lidian, to stay for three weeks at their home in Concord. The visit had a prehistory of roughly two years, during which Fuller's interest in the ascendant Emerson had become increasingly urgent. Through the repeated recommendations of such mutual friends as Clarke, Henry Hedge, Harriet Martineau, and Elizabeth Peabody, Emerson was eventually persuaded that here was someone well worth his attention. His own interest had been kindled by reading her translation of Goethe's *Tasso*, helpfully provided by Hedge and accompanied by well-deserved praise of her scholarship in German literature.

The visit was a success and established Fuller as a regular and welcome guest. She stimulated and entertained the household, engaging all its serious-minded members, sometimes in spite of themselves. Yet they had much in common. Indeed, Sarah Clarke had told her brother James, in attempting to describe Lidian Emerson before her marriage, "She is full of sensibility, yet as independent in her mind as — who shall I say? Margaret Fuller." With Emerson himself the intellectual core of the friendship was established surprisingly quickly, and during her stay he read to her from the manuscript of *Nature*, which he was to publish two months later. From that point, virtually until the time of her death, the two held a remarkable correspondence that tested the boundaries of intellectual and emotional compatibility.[6] They also wrote about each other in their respective journals and in letters to mutual friends. Throughout the years of their friendship Emerson's life remained rooted in Concord, sustaining and sustained by his family and friends. He was to produce much of his best and most influential work during that time and to enlarge his reputation at home and abroad. Fuller's life was another story entirely.

Sarah Margaret Fuller was born in Cambridgeport, Massachusetts, on 23 May 1810, the first child of Timothy Fuller and Margarett Crane Fuller. Her father, a Jeffersonian lawyer who served in both the state legislature and Washington, undertook to give his daughter a full classical education, as if she were a boy. Finding her precocious, he pressed ahead with an astonishingly demanding program of study with the young child, who performed prodigious academic feats to gratify him. By the age of six she was reading and reciting Virgil and Plutarch. At eight she discovered Shakespeare for herself, as a recreation, and went on to explore her father's extensive library. In her late teens, emerging enthusiastically into Boston society, Fuller found it difficult to reconcile the demands of her intellectual training to be rigorous and candid with those of the drawing room to be pliant and docile. But she found scope for both social and intellectual activity among the lively younger generation of Boston-Cambridge intellectual families that flourished around the university. Unable to join her male friends at Harvard, she set herself an ambitious program of study that included Epicetus, Petrarch, Tasso, Milton, Racine, Dante, Ariosto, and Manzoni. Meanwhile, she continued to run the household of six younger children for her ailing mother and play hostess for her politically ambitious father. Studying German opened up the world of German romanticism to her, and she was soon reading Schiller, Novalis, and Tieck, and translating Goethe.

In 1833 Timothy Fuller removed his family to a farm in Groton, abandoning politics for a disastrous domestic experiment. Until he died of cholera three years later, the family suffered severe physical and social privation, and his brilliant daughter was condemned to grueling menial work in looking after them all. It nearly killed her, but it did not prevent her from reading and translating. While preparing her younger brothers for Harvard, she began to submit short articles on literary topics to journals, with modest success but increasing confidence and skill. To help support the rest of family on her father's death, she took a job as Bronson Alcott's assistant in his experimental Temple School in Boston, teaching languages and recording his Socratic conversations with the children.

Meanwhile, the rising star of the New England intellectual firmament, Ralph Waldo Emerson, attracted her powerfully. With no conventional higher education, no obvious career or goal, but with a formidable intellectual drive, she often longed for a mentor who could offer her understanding and stimulation while she continued the struggle to answer her own questions, on the way to "self-trust": "My mind often burns with thoughts on these subjects and I long to pour out my soul to some person of superior calmness and strength and fortunate in more accurate knowledge. I should feel such a quieting reaction. But generally I think it is best I should go through these conflicts alone. The process will be slower, more irksome, more distressing, but the result will be all my own and I shall feel greater confidence in it."[7] In the event,

Emerson filled this role for her, finding her challenging, embarrassing, and irresistible, and Margaret Fuller took her place in the center of American Renaissance intellectual life.

In 1839 the emergent transcendentalist circle proposed a journal, *The Dial,* to publish and share their interests. Margaret Fuller was prevailed upon to edit it from 1840 to 1842, the difficult first two years of its four-year life, providing far too much of the material — in the chronic absence of work from the other members — for her own good. She learned much, however, about critical discrimination and the discipline of regular composition, and she was forced to experiment with a range of genres. Her best work was her literary criticism, which also led her out into wider cultural considerations where her critical mind bore radical fruit. Then followed the years of her acknowledged achievement: the "Conversations" for Boston women from 1839 to 1844; her travel in the West and the publication of *Summer in the Lakes* (1844); her removal to New York to write a regular critical column in Horace Greeley's *Tribune* and the publication of *Woman in the Nineteenth Century* (1845).

She had written more than 250 pieces for the *Tribune* when she accepted an invitation to tour Europe with friends, financing herself by returning dispatches to Greeley. Leaving in 1846, she visited Britain, France, and finally Italy, where she met and fell in love with a young nobleman, Giovanni Ossoli, ten years her junior, on the eve of the Roman revolution. In the midst of the revolution in Rome, in 1848, she gave birth to a son and, when the city fell, escaped with partner and baby to Florence. They started their journey home to America in the spring of 1850, but their ship was wrecked off Fire Island in a storm and all three were drowned. Throughout her adventures, Fuller had maintained an unbroken correspondence with her family and friends, and returned her dispatches to Greeley. She had, however, told them nothing of her relations with Ossoli, and when she announced the birth of her son he was already a year old. The reaction of her circle to this news delights the imagination. The reaction to her death was all the more complex and, ultimately, decisive.

Emerson announced the event to himself in his journal with a certain simplicity characteristic of his entries on some other major occasions (such as his marriage and the death of his beloved son, Waldo): "On Friday, 19 July, Margaret Fuller dies on the rocks of Fire Island Beach within sight of & within <400 yards> 60 rods of the shore" (*JMN*, 11:256). The rest of this entry and those that follow reveal the constituent elements and the gradual development of Emerson's response to this tragic news. With careful reading of these entries we see how Emerson's final representation of Fuller in the *Memoirs* took shape. Here is the rest of this initial extract: "To the last her country proves inhospitable to her; brave, eloquent, subtle, accomplished, devoted, constant soul! If nature availed in America to give birth to many such as she, freedom & and honour & letters & art too were safe in this new world. She bound in the belt of her sympathy & friendship all whom I know & love, Elizabeth, Caroline, Ward, the Channings, Ellen Hooper, Charles K. N., Hedge, & Sarah Clarke. She knew more select people than any other person did & her death will interest more" (*JMN*, 11:256).

Here three distinct ideas follow each other: first, that Margaret was somehow anomalous in America; second, that she was a magnificent person who set a unique example in her moral, intellectual, and artistic life; and, third, that she possessed a quality and range of friendships that coincided exactly with Emerson's own. This passage has the air of a spontaneous tribute, for certain notes in it were very soon to be modified, as if upon reflection. He says, for example, not "*at* the last," as if Margaret were rejected uncharacteristically by her native land in her hour of need, but "*to* the last," as if it had always been so. As if in defiance of this inhospitality, his estimate of her stature is unstinting in its recognition of her gifts, her high standards, and her integrity, above all, in the service of the nation's cultural life. In the realm of personal relationships, the powerfully sustaining quality of her friendship and its closeness to himself springs to mind first, with the image of all those he values most, who will lose her with him — "all whom I know and love."

The subsequent half-dozen entries in the journal return to these ideas separately and very gradually explore and modify them. The next comment, on the same page, is about her artistic taste and is prefaced by "yet" — on second thought. He says that her taste was idiosyncratic, not universal, but at least "genuine." This is followed, after a gap, by: "She had a wonderful power of inspiring confidence & drawing out of people their last secret," which sounds not a little sinister in someone celebrated for her friendships. He then reveals that there were some people, "the timorous," as he calls them, who were anxious about how she would be "received," with her curious marriage and a child — but he had complete faith in her power to triumph over circumstance and gossip and successfully take the lead in the education of women, who were only waiting for her to begin. But, returning to the subject of her aesthetic side, Emerson muses again, a little ambiguously, upon the quality of her critical faculty, with the suggestion that for all its insight it was fundamentally subjective (*JMN*, 11:256–257).

Then comes the most startling note of all; after a single entry on another topic, Emerson begins again, without preamble: "I have lost in her my audience" (*JMN*, 11:258). This is the simple and complex extent of his loss. In this candid recognition of the service Fuller performed for him, Emerson acknowledges that she was a mind, even *the* mind, that appreciated his own, perhaps his ideal reader. Beneath the superficial egotism of the remark lies something of crucial importance, something that affected other American writers and that Hawthorne identified in his preface to *The Scarlet Letter*: "as thoughts are frozen and utterance benumbed, unless the speaker stand in some true relation to his audience — it may be pardonable to imagine a friend, a kind and apprehensive, though not the closest friend, is listening to our talk."[8] Fuller had stood in just such a relation to Emerson and his circle, and that "true relation" was necessarily both sympathetic and critical, combining rigor and intellectual independence with interest and respect. Such friends are rare. But the sparsity of the critical audience — as distinct from an enthusiastic readership — was more than just a personal disadvantage to Emerson and Hawthorne. It hindered the practice of criticism in America and thereby the growth of national literary maturity. Fuller had gradually, painstakingly, developed the skill and authority to adopt a serious critical role in the public domain. But perhaps therein lay the fatal ambiguity that surrounded the space left by her sudden removal.

For Hawthorne's prescription curiously warns that this vital "audience" should not be "the closest friend," as if the critic and the confidante, far from being complementary, are in practice incompatible. Indeed, to return to Emerson's journal, immediately after his insight into his loss as a writer, Emerson reverts once again to the apparently more disturbing implications of his loss of Fuller's much valued gift for intimacy. What starts as an accolade disintegrates into a nervous confession: "She poured a stream of amber over the endless store of private anecdotes, of bosom histories which her wonderful persuasion drew out of all to her. When I heard that a trunk of her correspondence had been found and opened, I felt what a panic would strike all her friends, for it was as if a clever reporter had got underneath a confessional & agreed to report all that transpired there in Wall street" (*JMN*, 11:258). Letters are, of course, uniquely focused in terms of audience. Emerson relished Fuller's letters to him, and she encouraged him to make her his trusted interlocutor. A private dialogue was established, creating its own context. But once the original recipient was absent, in fact dead, the pact of confidence was broken, and the trusted addressee suddenly appeared, potentially, little better than an eavesdropper. By dying unexpectedly, in possession of his letters, Fuller had abruptly discontinued her interactive relationship with Emerson. Suddenly, she appears in another guise altogether — "the clever reporter."

Yet, for all its startling injustice, this image is not accidental. For some time before her death Fuller had indeed been listened to, in the very public character of a "clever reporter" for the *Tribune*. She had become celebrated and notorious for *Woman in the Nineteenth Century* and for her outspoken articles on social questions as well as literary topics. In her adventures in Europe she had pushed her boat out beyond the reach of her friends — with dubious and ultimately tragic results. To retrieve the situation and recover the original, personal Fuller, complete with her confidences, Emerson endorses Channing's suggestion that a biography should be written called "Margaret and her Friends." He reassures himself that Elizabeth Hoar and Almira Barlow testify to Fuller's absolute fidelity and discretion. Finally, he concurs with Mrs. Barlow that "the death seems to her a fit & and good conclusion to the life. Her life was romantic & exceptional: so let her death be; it sets the seal on her marriage, avoids all questions of Society, all of employment, poverty & old age, and besides was undoubtedly predetermined when the world was created" (*JMN*, 11:259). So much for "the timorous," who had been so roundly repudiated on the previous page. In the end, he concludes, Margaret's integrity was formidable, but she was perhaps her own worst enemy: "She was perhaps impatient of complacency in people who thought they had claims, & stated them with an air. For such she had no mercy. But though not agreeable, it was just. And so her enemies were made" (*JMN*, 11:260).

And so the *Memoirs of Margaret Fuller Ossoli* were begun. In compiling his own section of the *Memoirs*, Emerson opened a separate notebook and began to collect anecdotes and quotations from his own memoranda and journal entries about her. But today's readers quickly see that there are some surprising omissions and that the selected conclusions published in the *Memoirs* are not always as "just" as he observed her own judgments to have been. To read Emerson's letters to Fuller and journal entries about her is to be aware of his enormous admiration, the perplexity she sometimes created in him, and his sense of her ability to inspire. In 1841, for example, during one of Fuller's visits, a rumination on the "Madonnas and Magdalens of the Athenaeum" continues: "12 October. I would that I could, I know afar off that I cannot give the lights and shades, the hopes and outlooks that come to me in these strange, cold-warm, attractive-repelling conversations with Margaret, whom I always admire, most revere when I nearest see, and sometimes love, yet whom I freeze, & who freezes me to silence, when we seem to promise to come nearest. Yet perhaps my old motto holds true here also[:] 'And the more falls I get, move faster on'" (*JMN*, 8:109).

In 1843 an entry of several paragraphs shows no reservations: Emerson composes an extraordinary paean of praise, entitled "Margaret," so full of wondering admiration that it requires extended quotation to do it justice.

MARGARET

A pure and purifying mind, self-purifying also, full of faith in men, & inspiring it. Unable to find any companion great enough to receive the rich effusions of her thought, so that her riches are still unknown & seem unknowable. It is a great joy to find that we have underrated our friend, that he or she is more excellent than we thought. [How indigent must] All natures seem poor beside one so rich as this, which pours a stream of amber over all objects clean & unclean that lie in [the] its path, and makes that comely and presentable which was mean in itself. We are taught by her [bounty] plenty how [narrow &] lifeless and outward we were, what poor Laplanders burrowing under the snows of prudence & pedantry.

Attempting to find words for Fuller's stature and her powerful effect on him, Emerson continues: "Beside her friendship, [all] other friendships seem trade, and by the firmness with which she treads her upward path, all mortals are convinced that another road exists than that which their feet know. . . . She rose before me at times into heroical & and godlike regions, and I could remember no superior women, but thought of Ceres, Minerva, Proserpine, and the august ideal forms of the Foreworld" (*JMN*, 13: 368–369).

He explores and generously celebrates his conviction of Fuller's uniqueness, her as-yet-unmeasured potential, her moral courage and vision that questioned a surrounding "prudence and pedantry" in others, and the certainty of further development in her life and work, so that "there is no form that does not await her beck,— dramatic, lyric, epic, passionate, pictorial, humorous." Though her speech as yet outshines her writing, he continues that the writing has "great sincerity, force, & fluency." Here, triumphantly, he has no doubt about her critical acumen and the intellectual freshness of her opinions: "What method, what exquisite judgement, as well as energy, in the selection of her words, what character and wisdom they convey! You cannot predict her opinion . . . she talks never narrowly or hostilely nor betrays, like all the rest, under a thin garb of new words, the old droning cast-iron opinions or notions of many years standing." In his references to the "Laplanders" and "all the rest," Emerson reiterates his observation that Margaret Fuller was *different*: she was original and independent in ways that were admirable because of her rigorous intellectual honesty and moral integrity. But the key to it all was the achievement of harmony between life and thought which he seems to identify as her special quality: "She < is superior to all>/excels/other intellectual persons in this, that her sentiments are more blended with her life; so the expression of them has greater steadiness and greater clearness" (*JMN*, 13:368–369). From the author of "The American Scholar" (1837), surely there could be no higher praise.

Inexplicably, none of this passage appears in the *Memoirs* in 1850. Nevertheless, a composite and interestingly modified quotation from this private accolade had already appeared in the essay "Manners," published in 1844, the year Fuller completed *Woman in the Nineteenth Century.* "Manners" contains a paragraph on the place of "Woman," in which Emerson states his belief in the superiority of American Woman, her "inspiring and musical" nature, and (as Fuller herself advocates in her book) her right to whatever her nature judges best for her. To amplify his assertion, but without naming names, he detaches some phrases from his private portrait of Fuller in 1843 and blends them into this new context. But the extraction process appears to have defused the powerful sense of exemplary and autonomous activity in the individual who inspired the words in the original passage. What emerges is a generalized, inspirational image of "Woman," entirely conventional in its adulatory vagueness: "The wonderful generosity of her sentiments raises her into heroical and godlike regions, and verifies the picture of Minerva, Juno, or Polymnia; and, by the firmness with which she treads her upward path, she convinces the coarsest calculators that another road exists, than that which their feet know."

This passage continues with some ecstatic and self-revelatory warbling about the effect of certain extraordinary women on "us" (whoever that might be — his editorial self? his readers, male and female?): "women who fill our vase with wine and roses to the brim." But the conclusion sounds curiously familiar and characteristic of one woman in particular, as a submerged connection to earlier self-questioning in the journal reveals: "We say things we never thought to have said; for once our habitual reserve vanished and left us at large; we were children playing with children in a wide field of flowers."[9] Published in such close proximity to *Woman in the Nineteenth Century*, these androcentric effusions seem to illustrate and confirm the very need for radical, self-critical reassessment of familiar assumptions about men and women as Self and Other, which Fuller's book so lucidly identified.

Whatever local transformations Emerson may have made of what was, after all, his own private material, it is still difficult to understand the prevailing deprecation in the *Memoirs* of Fuller's aesthetic and critical abilities. For it is not only his own journals' testimony to her talent that belies his subsequent dismissals but the evidence of Fuller's published work. However, Emerson makes almost no mention of the public prominence of Fuller's writing beyond mentioning her hard-working editorship of the *Dial* and referring to the topics of a few of her articles, with a passing reference to *Summer in the Lakes* as an "agreeable narrative." Under the heading "Criticism," he quotes only from her correspondence, mostly to himself, introducing the material rather ungraciously as her "habit of sending to her correspondents, in lieu of letters, sheets of criticism on her current readings . . . private folios, never intended for the press." Although the letters, he concludes, "are full of probity, talent, wit, friendship, charity and high aspiration . . . they are tainted with a mysticism. . . . In our noble Margaret, her personal feeling colours all her judgement of persons, of books, of pictures, and even the laws of the world" (*Memoirs* 2:15).

Not only does the most cursory reading of Fuller's letters show this comment to be outrageous, it is followed by an extraordinarily revealing remark that must have given offense to many of his readers: "This is easily felt in ordinary women, and a large deduction is civilly made on the spot by whosoever replies to their remark." Clever and literate Margaret Fuller, however, could paradoxically waste a serious man's time by wrapping up her nonsense in pretentious verbiage: "But when the speaker has such brilliant talent and literature as Margaret, she gives so many fine names to these merely sensuous and subjective phantasms, that the hearer is long imposed upon" (*Memoirs*, 2:64–65).

Such perfidy toward an admired intellectual companion is even more surprising when compared to an interestingly parallel passage in the next section of the *Memoirs*, written by William Henry Channing, which precisely reverses Emerson's version. Describing Fuller's contribution to the meetings of the transcendentalists, Channing recalls with pride and pleasure the quality of her mind: "Her critical yet aspiring intellect filled her with longing for germs of positive affirmation in place of the chaff of thrice-sifted negation. . . . strong common-sense saved her from becoming visionary." Far from "imposing" herself upon "the hearer" who might, as Emerson also claimed, be ready to perform the chivalry of indulgence toward women who spoke their minds, Fuller was "acknowledged as peer of the realm, in this new world of thought. Men — her superiors in years, fame and social position, — treated her more with the frankness due from equal to equal, than the half-condescending deference with which scholars are wont to adapt themselves to women." They behaved, in other words, as if "scholars" and "women" were not mutually exclusive groups. Channing concludes: "It was evident that they prized her verdict, respected her criticism, feared her rebuke and looked to her as an umpire" (*Memoirs*, 2:190–191). Perhaps it is reasonable to suppose that Emerson was among them.

Indeed, the voice that emerges from Fuller's public writing seems one of increasing confidence and authority. One of her most famous critical reviews, that of Longfellow's poems in 1845, is a case in point. But it also, notoriously, elicited not only respect as criticism but fear as a "rebuke." Poe claimed that "the review did her infinite credit; it was frank, candid, independent — in even ludicrous contrast to the usual mere glorifications of the day," and he called it "one of the very few reviews of Longfellow's poems, ever published in America, of which the critics have not had abundant reason to be ashamed."[10] But there were those, including the poet himself, who never forgave her for passages like this: "Mr. Longfellow has been accused of plagiarism. We have been surprised that anyone should have been anxious to fasten special charges of this kind upon him, when we supposed it so obvious that the greater part of his mental stores were derived from the works of others. He has no style of his own growing out of his own experiences and observation of nature. Nature with him, whether human or external, is always seen through the windows of literature."[11]

Such urbanity is not only the product of an intelligent and confident wit; it arises as well from a wide and rigorously discriminating understanding of literature. Fuller recognizes an imitation and demands something else — language that bursts its way directly from individual apprehension of experience, not, as she so vividly describes it, "seen through the windows of literature." She goes on to demonstrate and analyze exactly what she finds objectionable:

> Then take this other stanza from a man whose mind *should* have grown up in familiarity with the American *genius loci*.
> "Therefore at Pentecost, which brings
> The spring clothed like a bride,

When nestling buds unfold their wings,
And bishop's caps have golden rings,
Musing upon many things,
I sought the woodlands wide."
Musing upon many things — ay! and upon many books too, or
we should have nothing of Pentecost or bishop's caps with
their golden rings. For ourselves, we have not the least idea
what bishop's caps are;— are they flowers?— or what? Truly,
the schoolmaster was abroad in the woodlands that day! As to
the conceit of the wings on the buds, it is a false image, because
one that cannot be carried out. Such will not be found in the
poems of poets; with such the imagination is all compact, and
their works are not dead mosaics, with substance inserted
merely because pretty, but living growths, homogeneous and
satisfactory throughout." (*Papers on Literature and Art*, 156)

This organic, Romantic view of poetry and the integrity of the
imagination of course parallels Emerson's own, but the connection goes further than that. An important element in Fuller's rejection of Longfellow's verse is that it is borrowed from books
and that it does not arise out of American experience. The American poet is not creating out of a harmony with his American surroundings, he is pretending to respond to natural forms that
patently are not available to him. Pseudopoetry, it will not do.
Failing to contribute to American literature, it exemplifies, as
Fuller precisely indicates, something that Emerson had objected
to eight years before in "The American Scholar": American cultural dependency on "the learning of other lands . . . the sere remains of foreign harvests." He then declared: "We will walk on
our own feet; we will work with our own hands; we will speak with
our own minds" (*Essays and Lectures*, 71).

In "The American Scholar" Emerson could have been writing
Margaret Fuller a prescription for her own life and practice, for in
a number of ways she lived out his ideal. She was incontestably a
major scholar in the breadth of her reading, her mastery of a number of languages, and her influential translation and commentary
on the literature of other countries and ages. But the use she made
of her scholarship most convincingly qualifies Margaret Fuller for
the title. Her achievement was not to acquire "sere remains" but
to attempt, as Emerson had demanded "the scholar" should do,

"to take up into [herself] all the ability of the time, all the contributions of the past, all the hopes of the future." First, she knew and engaged with the work of the best minds of her generation — as they readily acknowledged. Second, what she learned from the great minds of the past she applied to the work of the present, in discriminating quality and setting standards for an American literature in her literary journalism. Finally, as Emerson's journal suggests, she contributed to the national life of the future by joining thought and action in her books, *Summer in the Lakes* and *Woman in the Nineteenth Century*, and in her "Conversations" for women, which Emerson himself had admired, recording in his journal in 1843: "her sentiments are more blended with her life; so the expression of them has greater steadiness and greater clearness."

In "The American Scholar," Emerson had claimed that "drudgery, calamity, exasperation, want, are instructors in eloquence and wisdom. The true scholar grudges every opportunity of action passed by, as a loss of power. It is the raw material out of which the intellect moulds her splendid products. A strange process too, this, by which experience is converted into thought, as a mulberry leaf is converted into satin" (60). Margaret Fuller had experienced such "instructors," and their effect was profound. Drudgery and calamity had attended her struggle for the survival of her family and her own intellect in rural poverty before and after their father's death. Exasperation and want had been both physical and mental, as she worked to educate herself in the face of exclusion from the university and to establish herself among her intellectual peers. But above all, what she learned from this experience she attempted to apply to the condition of her female peers, women whose education left them short of intellectual satisfaction and the training to let them be what Emerson would have his scholar be, "free and brave": "Free even to the definition of freedom, 'without any hindrance that does not arise out of his own constitution.' Brave; for fear is a thing, which a scholar by his very function puts behind him. Fear always springs from ignorance" (65).

Fuller knew that the hindrance to women's freedom did not "arise out of [their] own constitution" but out of social construction, as she argued in *Woman in the Nineteenth Century*. She further understood that the stultification of their intellectual development was the most pernicious, leaving them ill equipped to secure their freedom and fearful through consciousness of their own ignorance. In 1840 she transformed this knowledge into action by initiating her Conversations, an unusual "product" of the intellect and experience, but one of lasting importance in American life. Her ideas were made explicit to her friend Sophia Ripley, cofounder of Brook Farm, in letter of 1839: "The advantages of such a weekly meeting might be great enough to repay the trouble of attendance if they consisted only in supplying a point of union to well-educated and thinking women in a city which, with great pretensions to refinement, boasts at present nothing of the kind and where I have heard many of mature age wish for some stimulus and cheer, and these people for a place where they could state their doubts and difficulties with hope of gaining aid from the experience or aspirations of others."[12]

In this physical and mental space, there could be an active coalition of women who are not only "educated" but — and the distinction is crucial — also "thinking." Fuller continues: "But my own ambition goes much farther. Thus to pass in review the departments of thought and knowledge and endeavour to place them on due relation to one another in our minds. To systematize thought and give a precision in which our sex are so deficient, chiefly, I think because they have so few inducements to test and classify what they receive. To ascertain what pursuits are best suited to us in our time and state of society, and how we may make use of our means for building up the life of thought upon the life of action" (*Letters*, 2:87). To infer a system and inherent relationships in knowledge and thought, to search for appropriate activities in an inherently mutable or provisional "state of society" is to use the language of New England transcendentalism and reform. But to make the attempt specifically as a woman encouraging women — and with the insight and the candor to identify their intellectual disadvantage and its cause — was to press hard on the implications of the ideals expressed in that self-consciously radical milieu. It was to have radical consequences for the future too, when distinguished pupils like Julia Ward Howe became the leaders of the women's movement in postbellum America. Furthermore, in her conclusion, Fuller measures the stature of her ideal and incidentally describes the achievement of her own extraordinary life. She wants her students to think, and to choose, for themselves; confident of their "means," that through self-trust and self-culture, they will be free to integrate the "life of thought" and the "life of action."

In the *Memoirs*, Emerson reproduced most of this letter as part of the introduction to a section dedicated to "Conversations in Boston," which also recalls her editorship of the *Dial*, and quotes at length a record of the Conversations by an unnamed participant. Curiously, however, he prefaces this chapter of her life with an avowal of Fuller's willing subscription to the prevailing female norm, in a carefully prepared context of feminine propriety, which notes but does not endorse the very "revolution" Fuller was to embody. There is not much of dramatic interest, he says, before 1840, and any "events" of "her bright and blameless years" are private. They are enough, however, to make the sensitive biographer feel his responsibility to both subject and readers — especially since the subject is female: "In reciting the story of an affectionate and passionate woman, the voice lowers itself to a whisper, and becomes inaudible." What ever can she have been up to? Enough, clearly to elicit a reminder to curious readers of how happy and well-disposed women do not seek publicity in professional life, enfranchisement, or artistic achievement: "A woman in our society finds her safety and happiness in exclusions and privacies. She congratulates herself when she is not called to the market, to the courts, to the polls, to the stage, or to the orchestra. Only the most extraordinary genius can make the career of the artist secure and agreeable to her" (*Memoirs*, 2:124).

One is forced, apparently, to acknowledge the *status quo*: "Prescriptions almost invincible the female lecturer or professor of any science must encounter; and except on points where the charities which are left to women as their legitimate province interpose against the ferocity of laws, with us a female politician is unknown." Though possibly, on reflection, it should not be so in America and may be changing: "Perhaps this fact, which so dangerously narrows the career of a woman, accuses the tardiness of our civility, and many signs show that a revolution is already on foot." But whatever the rights and wrongs of woman's estate, rest assured, Margaret Fuller was not the wrong sort: "Margaret had no love of notoriety, or taste for eccentricity, to goad her, and no weak fear of either. Willingly she was confined to the usual circles and methods of female talent. She had no false shame. Any task that called out her powers was good and desirable. She wished to live by her strength. She could converse, and teach, and write. She took classes of pupils at her own house." (*Memoirs*, 2:124–125). But of course it was exactly this kind of attitude or expectation that Fuller worked so hard to analyze, articulate, and dispel. Emerson turns her effort back on itself by attributing such internalized attitudes to Fuller herself, as if he were somehow protecting her reputation from misunderstanding. Her action in holding the Conversations was precisely not a matter of eccentricity or egocentricity. Fuller hoped to establish that for women to use their minds seriously and effectively was not only *not* eccentric but entirely natural and healthy to their "constitution."

The Conversations were always oversubscribed, but not because the women found "their safety and happiness in exclusions and privacies" in Emerson's sense. The privacy of the meetings, secured by the exclusion of men, gave the participants a unique and welcome opportunity to speak their minds and spread their wings intellectually without submitting to what Fuller called the "large deduction . . . civilly made on spot by whosoever replies to their remark" or "the half-condescending deference with which scholars are wont to adapt themselves to women." Fuller made her requirements very clear, and they were not in the service of perpetuating an essentialist view of the "feminine" mind, as her friend Sarah Clarke reported: "One lady was insisting upon her sex's privilege to judge things by her feelings, and to care not for the intellectual view of the matter. 'I am made so,' says she, 'and I cannot help it.' 'Yes,' says Margaret, gazing full upon her, 'but who are you? Were you an accomplished human being, were you all that a human being is capable of becoming, you might perhaps have the right to say, "I *like* it therefore it is good" — but, if you are not all that, your judgement must be partial and unjust if it is guided by your feelings alone.'" [13]

The same intellectual honesty and determination to work for active improvement also emerges in Fuller's approach to the *Dial* editorship. Writing to William Henry Channing in March 1840, she expressed first her doubts and then her hopes for the new venture: "I have myself a great deal written, but as I read it over scarce a word seems pertinent to the place or time. . . . How much those of us who have been formed by the European mind have to unlearn and lay aside, if we would act here. I would fain do something worthily that belonged to the country where I was born, but most times I fear it may not be. . . . I am sure we cannot show high culture, and I doubt about vigorous thought. But I hope we shall show free action as far as it goes and a high aim" (*Letters*, 2:125–126).

After the success of the Conversations and the sweated labor of producing the *Dial*, Margaret Fuller was increasingly able to integrate what she knew from active experience into what she wrote for publication. In 1844 her eventful journey through the West with Sarah Clarke became her first book, *Summer in the Lakes*. In contrast to Emerson's tepid and brief description of the book as "an agreeable narrative," Edgar Allan Poe warmly praised its evocation of the magnificence of the scenery through its effects on the perceiver — "subjective" in a laudable sense. Yet the book's most impressive achievement is the clear-sighted and deeply disquieting observations it offers of the effects of colonization on the frontier — both on the indigenous population and the character and activities of the newcomers. *Summer in the Lakes* is not a verbal watercolor from a lady traveler's album but a thought-provoking report by a highly intelligent American on her country's potential for natural beauty and human corruption.

It was, however, one thing to decry the plight of the Native Americans and the desolate settlers in Wisconsin and Michigan and quite another to champion the New York prostitutes of Sing Sing prison, as Fuller went on to do in preparing *Woman in the Nineteenth Century* later in the same year. In this book, an expanded and updated version of an earlier *Dial* article, the slightly bookish scholar turns lucid activist before the reader's eyes. As Annette Kolodny has scrupulously demonstrated, Fuller made inventive and highly conscious use of considerable rhetorical resources to deploy her ideas.[14] After reviewing the annals of world cultural history citing examples of remarkable women, Fuller turned the clarity of her critical mind to bear on the contemporary state of American society and the possibilities for its future. Above all, she brought the human and social implications of transcendentalism, self-reliance, and the notional superiority of American womanhood under close scrutiny. If, as Emerson promised at the conclusion of "The American Scholar," "a nation of men shall for the first time exist, because each believes himself inspired by the divine soul which also inspires all men," then some urgent revision of ideas about women was called for.

Men, Fuller argued, have rightly striven through the centuries, with moments of success, to reach the ideal state of man. This is also true of women, but not only have they not developed as far, their backwardness now impedes the perfection of man himself. This should not happen in America, dedicated as it is to liberty, but it will as long as men regard woman as made for man and not as essentially God's creature. Men's insistence on mediation affects and obstructs all their relations with women: religious, civil, literary, familial, marital, and sexual; they have decided on the "true" nature of women and regard all deviation from the norm they have devised as "unnatural," regardless of the rich and varied examples of history. But if the right of women to the widest possible development were sincerely recognized as *inherent* in their humanity, in their direct descent from God, not *conceded* as if some other humans beings had it to bestow, they would discover the occupations and behavior that befit each individually, as men do. Her cry "Let them be sea captains if they will!" became one of her most famous lines. Women would then cease from their present profound dependence on men — a form of idolatry — and the true nature of each sex could be fully realized.

Fuller was unequivocal about the historic failure of Christianity to liberate women, and of American Christianity in particular, which also tolerated slavery and the slow genocide of the indigenous population. She drew a parallel between slaves and women in their impotence before the law, and identified the circular thinking of gender prejudice, whereby women are refused education on the pretext of their delicate and emotional nature and then find that nature deprecated as self-evidently ineducable. She pointed out that such scruples did not prevent the exploitation of women as laborers, slaves, and prostitutes. Denouncing the injustice of the legal system and the abuses of marriage, she deplored the powerlessness and ignorance of women who still assumed that marriage was their only goal. However, she did not by any means assume that the experience of marriage and motherhood could not be fulfilling and admirable; it was simply that it was nonsense to pretend that they constituted women's sole function. She noted, wryly, how for all the blandishments of chivalry, men never ex-

pressed a wish to be women themselves, and they praised successful exceptions to their limited model of womanhood as "manly."
Men, she concluded, are imperfect and hence insecure and uncertain, not naturally ungenerous or vicious. If they would only recognize the dual aspects of every human being — Apollo and
Diana — men and women could both draw nearer to perfection.

Margaret Fuller was not, it is clear, "willingly . . . confined to the
usual circles and methods of female talent," as Emerson told his
readers after her death. She deliberately and dramatically followed
her own prescription. While participating in the Roman republican struggle, she exhorted her American compatriots, in the
columns of the New York *Tribune,* not to stand by and allow imperial powers to crush the fight for independence from feudalism
by the people of Rome. As a scholar and a woman she also wrote
a history of the revolution and gave birth to a baby.

The conclusion was perhaps there to be drawn: here was the
American Scholar in person. In the moment of lucid praise that
Emerson accorded her in his journal when he recorded her death,
he seems to come close to it: "If nature availed in America to give
birth to many such as she, freedom & honour & letters & art too
were safe in this new world." But the journal here, as ever, reveals
its nature as a protected space, on the boundary between private
and public, where thought can be rehearsed. As a textual form,
it lies between the inherent privacy of intimate letters, where
communication with an absent correspondent could only otherwise be carried on by telepathy, and a finished work offered for
publication. Since thought can be carried on undetected in the
complete privacy of the mind, the commission of a soliloquy to
paper — an internal discourse externalized in the form of a journal — is necessarily, however ingenuously, an act of publicity.
Journals yield a continuum from one-line memos of momentous
events to rehearsals or glosses for later public utterance. The
keeper of a journal may not wish others to read it, but he or she is
willing to take the risk in order to render his or her thoughts, or
what purport to be such thoughts, visible.

Perhaps this paradox represents the source of the discrepancy
between the private and the public representation of Margaret
Fuller by Ralph Waldo Emerson. In the development of his response to Fuller's death, Emerson may have striven to protect the
precious but precarious hinterland of his public work — that ver-

bal performance that bespoke the man. For his published work, with its proclamation of creative self-trust, did emerge from a background of private journals, letters, and discussions that often faced self-doubt and a variety of other emotions and possibilities characteristically transcended (or inadmissible) in the finished product. For Emerson, Margaret Fuller was a crucial inhabitant of that hinterland; she was the "audience" of the preambles and contradictions, the provisional as well as the inadmissible. Like his journals, she was part of the privileged but liminal area of rehearsal and experimentation. But, increasingly, her own all-too-public activities were directly transformed into her own writing as ideas, opinions, observations, and exhortations. Her last, heroic adventures took self-reliance and the integration of belief, feeling, and action beyond his reach. What must have seemed to him the glaring publicity in which she lived out her passions and dilemmas lit up the personal sphere that his writing strove to transcend in order to rhapsodize the pursuit of fearless action and self-reliance. The *Memoirs* were a missed opportunity to recognize what she embodied; but it may have been too difficult for Emerson to describe or expose the contribution of such a figure to his own inner life. Fluidity and freedom were recommended in his public writing by a man of profound self-discipline and periambient control. Perhaps Margaret Fuller was just too messy and empirical to be integrated into the process through which *he* believed he had related thought and action, in seeing *himself* as the American Scholar.

So Emerson's representation of the dizzy, ill-favored, self-important bluestocking, who was an acquired taste and a rather too intimate friend, prevailed. It was not until the doughty Thomas Wentworth Higginson published his neglected biography of Fuller in 1884 that a critical light was shed on the *Memoirs*. Higginson, himself an observant contemporary, explicitly questions the book's effect and the editors' judgment: "I cannot resist the opinion that the prevalent tone of the *Memoirs* leaves her a little too much in the clouds, gives us too little of that vigorous executive side which was always prominent in her aspirations for herself, and which was visible to all after she reached Italy."[15] He considers that the book overemphasizes and misinterprets her goal of "self-culture" as egotism, when in fact she sought "not merely self-culture but a career of mingled thought and action such as she finally found" (4). Self-culture, it has to be said, was a central aspiration in the transcendentalist program. But as with so much that Fuller did, the goal looked different when attempted by a woman who took the exhortation seriously and with an assumption of natural equality. The nature and direction of the growth of the self, the moral obligation to attend to it, and the activities involved in that attention were revealed to be, after all, underpinned by a gendered, double conception of the self, in which one was defined and the other self-creating. Fuller's analysis of this position in *Woman in the Nineteenth Century* renders some of Emerson's ruminations on self-reliance and the inner life somewhat less than universal.

Higginson, however, had no doubt about Margaret Fuller's talent, achievement, and contribution to American letters. He recalled that at a time when it was extremely difficult for a woman to become a professional writer, she maintained a vigorously independent stance and honed her prose under the demands of writing for the press. He actively celebrated the public character of her work while admiring her personal triumphs. As a woman "she shared in great deeds, she was the counsellor of great men, she had a husband who was a lover and she had a child" (314). But it was also as a remarkable woman that "she kept higher laws than she broke. In that epoch of strife, that I well remember . . . she held the critical sway of the most powerful American journal with unimpaired dignity and courage" (217). In 1884 he felt able to conclude, as her original biographers had not, "She seems to me to have been, in her average work, the best literary critic that America has yet seen" (290). To Higginson it seemed particularly appropriate to praise her in this role. Perhaps he, after all, was prepared to conceive of the American Scholar not only as Man, but as Woman Thinking.

NOTES

1. Ralph Waldo Emerson, *The Journals and Miscellaneous Notebooks of Ralph Waldo Emerson*, ed. William H. Gilman et al. (Cambridge: Harvard University Press, 1960–1964), 11:256. Hereafter cited in the text as *JMN*. All second and subsequent references to this and other sources are in the text.

2. Robert N. Hudspeth, introduction to *The Letters of Margaret Fuller*, ed. Robert N. Hudspeth, 5 vols. (Ithaca: Cornell University Press, 1983–1988), 1:61, 63.

3. Henry James, *William Wetmore Story and His Friends* (London: Thames and Hudson, 1903), 1:127–128.

4. [James Freeman Clarke, Ralph Waldo Emerson, and William Henry Channing, eds.], *Memoirs of Margaret Fuller Ossoli*, 3 vols. (London: Richard Bentley, 1852), 1:73.

5. Merton M. Sealts, *Emerson on the Scholar* (Columbia: University of Missouri Press, 1992).

6. See Christina Zwarg, *Feminist Conversations: Fuller, Emerson and the Play of Reading* (Ithaca: Cornell University Press, 1995).

7. Fuller to F. Henry Hedge, 1 February 1835, *Letters*, 1:224.

8. Nathaniel Hawthorne, "The Custom House," in *The Scarlet Letter* (Harmondsworth, England: Penguin, 1970), 35.

9. Ralph Waldo Emerson, "Manners," in *Essays: Second Series*, from *Ralph Waldo Emerson: Essays and Lectures* (New York: Library of America, 1983), 529–530.

10. Edgar Allan Poe, "The Literati of New York City: Sarah Margaret Fuller," *Edgar Allan Poe: Essays and Reviews* (New York: Library of America, 1984), 1172.

11. Margaret Fuller, *Papers on Literature and Art* (London: Wiley and Putnam, 1846), 2:154.

12. Fuller to Sophia Ripley, 27 August 1839, in *Letters*, 2:86–87

13. Fuller to Sarah Clarke, 14 December 1839, from Sarah Clarke, *Letters of a Sister*, quoted in *Letters*, 2:89 n. 1.

14. Annette Kolodny, "Inventing a Feminist Discourse: Rhetoric and Resistence in Margaret Fuller's Woman in the Nineteenth Century," in Karen L. Kilcup, *Nineteenth-Century American Women Writers: A Critical Reader* (Malden, Mass.: Blackwell, 1998), 206–230.

15. Thomas Wentworth Higginson, *Margaret Fuller Ossoli* (Boston: Houghton Mifflin, 1884), 5.

How Conscious Could Consciousness Grow? Emily Dickinson and William James

SUSAN MANNING

In 1890, in a monumental textbook that became a classic work in the emerging discipline of academic psychology, William James attempted the near-paradoxical task of describing the elusive, transient characteristics of consciousness as these present themselves to mental analysis. His writing gestured eloquently to the difficulty of rendering the quality of awareness: taking, as he put it, "a general view of the wonderful stream of our consciousness," he noted a "different pace" about some of its parts: "Like a bird's life, it seems to be made of an alternation of flights and perchings. The rhythm of language expresses this, where every thought is expressed in a sentence, and every sentence closed by a period. The resting places are usually occupied by sensorial imaginations of some sort, whose peculiarity is that they can be held before the mind for an indefinite time, and contemplated without changing; the places of flight are filled with thoughts of relations, static or dynamic, that for the most part obtain between the matters contemplated in the periods of comparative rest." Calling the resting places the "substantive parts" and the places of flight the "transitive parts" of the stream of thought, James identified the function of the latter as connectives for the substantive conclusions. His interest was caught by the extreme difficulty of "see[ing] the transitive parts for what they really are." If they are but flights to a conclusion, he continued, then "stopping them to look at them before the conclusion is reached is really annihilating them. Whilst if we wait till the conclusion *be* reached, it so exceeds them in vigor and stability that it quite eclipses and swallows them up in its glare. Let anyone try to cut a thought across in the middle and get a look at its section, and he will see how difficult the introspective observation of the transitive tracts is."[1]

James's striking analogy between the shape and rhythm of language as the image of thought's processes and the life of a bird, alternately soaring and perching, carries an embedded allegorical figure at least as old as English literature: in the Venerable Bede's eighth-century church history, the journey of a human soul through life is likened to the brief passage of a lone sparrow through a lighted banquet hall; darkness surrounds both its entry and its departure. What we know of it is the portion that is illuminated to our conscious observation.[2] The lyricism of the image is inflected by a submerged melancholy: the bird's life in a sentence, fleeting and transient. In James's description, the sentence becomes not only a model for the operation of consciousness but an image of the rhythm and boundedness of a life. To catch the texture of its flight is, momentarily, to hold off the engulfing, eclipsing, inevitable end.

Approximately thirty years earlier, Emily Dickinson had written more elliptically of the bird's flight:

> Out of sight? What of that?
> See the bird — reach it!
> Curve by Curve — Sweep by Sweep —
> Round the Steep Air —
> Danger! What is that to Her?
> Better 'tis to fail — there —
> Than debate — here —[3]

and, in another poem:

> She staked her Feathers — Gained an Arc —
> Debated — rose again —
> This time — beyond the estimate
> Of Envy, or of Men — (P 798)

Danger and heroism lie in her soaring ascent "beyond the estimate" of men. "Staked" has a compressed urgency reminiscent of Hopkins's religious intensity. Her metaphysical swoops against gravity's laws are apprehended not by sight but by imagination. It is not the personal pronoun alone that hints that the bird's arc on the steep sweep of moving air is — again traditionally — a figure for poetic flight. In her poetry, birds most characteristically *sing*, and their song, like their flight, lies beyond the realms of criticism:

Why Birds, a Summer morning
Before the quick of Day
Should stab my ravished spirit
With Dirks of Melody
Is part of an inquiry
That will receive reply
When Flesh and Spirit sunder
In Death's Immediately — (P 1420)

The "Sylvan Punctuation" (P 1483), as another poem has it, is "oblique" to sense and "transitive" (P 1265); more sharply, it *stabs* — the realizations of consciousness are piercing and confer reality on mere existence.[4] Crucially, "Death's Immediately" is an adverbial interruptus: immanent in the wings, it never arrives in the poem, whose sentence does not end. "When" remains a final point never reached.

This obliqueness takes Dickinson's own writing outside James's "rhythm of language," where "every thought is expressed in a sentence, and every sentence closed by a period." So her emblematic birds become themselves riddles of language, sections cut through sentences:

A Route of Evanescence
With a revolving Wheel —
A Resonance of Emerald —
A Rush of Cochineal —
And every Blossom on the Bush
Adjusts its tumbled Head —
The mail from Tunis, probably,
An easy Morning's Ride — (P 1463)

Dickinson's poetry constantly essays the impossible adventure of fixing perpetual motion, which she dramatizes in the elusiveness of the hummingbird to definition. These bird poems exemplify — before the fact — James's inquiry into the processes of consciousness, the sensation of sentience. Their method is precisely to "cut a thought across in the middle"; sense does not pass sequentially through the sentence, as William James represents it, moving inevitably toward a substantively eclipsing end, but resides rather in the pulsating relation of words and dashes that themselves embody the thought-in-action.[5] Dickinson's poetic consciousness refuses to be bounded by the decorum of the sentence, rounded and finished with a period.[6] The transitive, disjunctive aspects of consciousness to which James first drew the attention of academic psychology were the very substance of her poetry thirty years before.

As a prelude to considering the kinds of reward that might lie in pursuing the comparison, there is a clear question as to what sort of literary genealogy is at work. Is this more than a fortuitous verbal conjunction between the language of a reclusive poet and that of a popular academic philosopher, psychologist, and theologian? The connection between Emily Dickinson and William James proposed here is one of confluence rather than influence: I am interested in exploring the literary consequences of certain structures of thought — the kinds of subject, treatment, possibility, limitation that tend to predominate under the influence of powerfully ingrained ways of thinking. A rather particular understanding of the nature of language and its relationship to experience, and a preoccupation with charting the movements of consciousness, seem to have been congenial — perhaps even inevitable — to writers brought up in a post-Calvinist culture whose characteristic thought structures remained powerfully predetermined — well beyond the reach of actual theocratic domination — by the absolutes of double predestination and its paradoxical imperative of self-abasing, self-reliant introspection.

A single intellectual tradition lies behind the common concern of James and Dickinson with language, consciousness, and the experiential grain of reality. Dickinson points to this inheritance herself in her famous phrase "see[ing] New Englandly" (P 285): the legacy of Puritanism preoccupied all its beneficiaries with the nature and processes of consciousness. As a working simplification, we may say that the emphasis on predestination in Calvinist theology undervalued the *quality* of a person's living while prescribing undeviating self-scrutiny to ascertain the already-settled end. The structure of thinking outlived the teleology and engendered in reaction the powerful secularized Scottish epistemology of David Hume, the repercussions of whose work proved formative for eighteenth- and nineteenth-century American culture as it too entered a post-Calvinist phase.[7] Hume's *A Treatise of Human Nature* (1739–1740) for the first time advanced a theory of the self not (as Shaftesbury and his successors had defined it) in relation to others but known through introspection alone: "when I enter most intimately into what I call *myself*, I always stumble on some particular perception or other, of heat or cold, light or shade, love or hatred, pain or pleasure. I never can catch *myself* at any time without a perception, and never can observe any thing but the perception. . . . [Mankind is] nothing but a bundle or collection of different perceptions, which succeed each other with an inconceivable rapidity, and are in perpetual flux and movement."[8] His rigorous skepticism was tamed by the Common Sense philosophy of his Scottish successors, who nonetheless retained his preoccupation with investigating the movements of mind: "Reflection, Consciousness, or Internal Sensation is that faculty whereby we attend to our own thoughts, and to those various operations, which the mind performs without the aid of bodily organs," as James Beattie put it in an influential essay.[9]

William James's phrase "the stream of consciousness" is in fact borrowed from Thomas Reid's *Essay on the Intellectual Powers of Man*.[10] From Reid and his successors, too, James would have drawn that interest in the structure of language as a means of understanding the shape of consciousness that was characteristic of the Common Sense transfer of emphasis from the Word of God to words of men as the locus of meaning. It was an axiom with Reid that "the very language of mankind, with regard to the operations of our minds, is analogical," and, more fully, "the various operations of the understanding, will, and passions, which are common to mankind, have various forms of speech corresponding to them in all languages, which are the signs of them and by which they are expressed. A due attention to the signs may in many cases give considerable light to the things signified by them" (38, 40). Reid's essays conduct a running dialogue between the structure of language and the principles of perception. Where the Word of God conferred the fixities and unalterable doom of predestination — focused, that is, on *ends*— human words told of process, continuity, the experience of living rather than the point toward which it tended. The self is found in the flow of experience from one sensation to another, and identity becomes essentially a set of memories having coherence in change, just as objects have a kind of permanence even as they alter through time.[11]

In America, Scottish Common Sense thought permeated the colleges, schools, and popular culture. Emerson's pervasive preoccupation with "consciousness" derived from this intellectual patrimony; it is what we would call self-consciousness: the mind's awareness of its own activities, its interest in the processes registered on the inner stage. His most extensive discussion comes in "Experience," whose Calvinist antecedence is explicit: "Dream delivers us to dream, and there is no end to illusion. Life is a train of moods like a string of beads, and as we pass through them they prove to be many-colored lenses which paint the world their own hue, and each shows only what lies in its focus. . . . It is very unhappy, but too late to be helped, the discovery we have made that we exist. That discovery is called the Fall of Man. Ever afterwards we suspect our instruments" (*Essays, Second Series*, 3 : 5 3 − 5 4, 76 − 77). Consciousness is the product of experience, the postlapsarian consequence of the Fall into Knowledge. Without the external guarantee of final meaning provided by faith, human beings are, literally, on their own with evanescent processes, inhabitants not of the material world but of the "glimmering," "darkling" world of the mind.[12] Meaning is what we make rather than what we find. Self-consciousness is the only free action for the individual in a Calvinistic universe.[13] Such freedom blesses and curses in a breath.

To derive this inheritance helps to define the issue I want to pursue. More powerful than social position or divisions of gender, the shared inheritance of post-Calvinist empiricism made introspection the natural mode of literary experience for both Dickinson and James, as for their contemporaries. It also, however, endowed them with a preoccupation with, and a vocabulary for, absolutes and finalities —*endings*— without furnishing them with a framework of belief in which ending, loss, or death could make sense — really *be* a finality, by achieving meaning. Instead, both find themselves irrevocably embarked on the adventure of consciousness, that secularized form of Puritan introspection that post-Calvinist cultures raised to an art form. In very different ways, their writing expands immeasurably our capacity to articulate the experience of "living in" consciousness, moment by moment. Finally, though, the writing of Dickinson and James — for

all their different modes and unequal fullnesses of expression —
returns to the same dilemma: obsessed with a teleological view-
point, it is unable to realize an ending — "For I have but the
power to kill, / Without — the power to die —" (P 754), as Dickinson breaks off one of her most memorable poems.

William James fits much more readily, much more *connectedly*,
into this tradition than Dickinson does.[14] The distant affinity of
even his most public textbook pronouncements with the tradition
of Puritan conversion narratives is everywhere evident; we find it,
for example, in the emphasis in *Principles* on the primacy of "personally owned thoughts": "The only states of consciousness that
we naturally deal with are found in personal consciousnesses,
minds, selves, concrete particular I's and you's. Each of these
minds keeps its own thoughts to itself. There is no giving or bar-
tering between them. . . . Absolute insulation, irreducible pluralism, is the law.[15] This is a fragmenting vision, an awareness of human separateness that seems to refer directly back to Emerson's
"An innavigable sea washes with silent waves between us and the
things we aim at and converse with" ("Experience," *Essays, Second
Series*, 3:52).

For both writers isolation is the condition of consciousness,
but it is a fully "written out" condition, whose discursive ampli-
tude may often appear to belie its declared position: "It seems as
if the elementary psychic fact were not *thought* or *this thought* or *that
thought* but *my thought*, every thought being *owned*. Neither contem-
poraneity nor proximity in space, nor similarity of quality or content are able to fuse thoughts together which are sundered by this
barrier of belonging to different minds. The breaches between
such thoughts are the most absolute breaches in nature" (*Principles, Works*, 9:221). In such a passage, confidence in communi-
cability (that is, the real possibility of a reading community) mitigates any tendency to solipsism or isolation that the psychological
analysis, abstractly viewed, may suggest. *Principles* is a colloquium
of voices as much as it is a compendium of theories; the author is
at home in the company of his peers, like- (or unlike-) minded authorities.[16] This context itself mitigates the starkness of individual
isolated consciousnesses.

Emerson's silent waves may also, though, be the transitive
parts of experience, flowing between and silently connecting the
substantives of which we are most immediately aware and for

which we have a developed vocabulary. James laments the "absence of a special vocabulary for subjective facts [that] hinders the study of all but the very coarsest of them" (*Principles, Works,* 9:194). In a passage reminiscent of Reid, he points to a hole in our experience of experience left by empirical descriptions of consciousness:

> Empiricist writers are very fond of emphasizing one great set of delusions which language inflicts on the mind. Whenever we have made a word, they say, to denote a certain group of phenomena, we are prone to suppose a substantive entity existing beyond the phenomena, of which the word shall be the name. But the *lack* of a word quite as often leads to the directly opposite error. We are then prone to suppose that no entity can be there; and so we come to overlook phenomena whose existence would be patent to us all, had we only grown up to hear it familiarly recognized in speech. It is hard to focus attention on the nameless, and so there results a certain vacuousness in the descriptive parts of most psychologies.

"Namelessness," as he put it, "is compatible with existence. There are innumerable consciousnesses of emptiness" (*Principles, Works,* 9:243).

Independently of intellectual psychology — and indeed largely in advance of its formal articulation as a masculine "science" of study — Dickinson's poetry attempts to supply this failure in language's ability to convey the inner surface of a thought, not by coining new words, but by exploiting the very vacancy to which James points in despair. Her defiant linguistic minimalism replaces an articulated grammatical flow inevitably resting in the substantives of knowledge, with a separated series of hermetic perceptions along the way. Widening the gaps between words, her writing emphasizes the experiential reality of the entities that have no name: "I found the words to every thought / I ever had — but One," she writes, apparently despairing of the expressivity of language:

> To Races — nurtured in the Dark —
> How would your own — begin?
> Can Blaze be shown in Cochineal —
> Or Noon — in Mazarin? (P 581)

In Dickinson's fascicle the variant "phrase" is given for "words" in the poem's first line; the alternative possibility provided by the manuscript makes it clear that what is at issue is *connected* words, the meeting points of one and another, that imply the availability, transferability, of sense or meaning.

Unlike the prolifically published William James, Dickinson "did not print";[17] she chose privacy for her writing, apparently, when publication was available. The decision was connected with her punctuation, which was also deliberate and functional. Mid-nineteenth-century women were not trained to command the "copious" language of public eloquence: "notions of decorum subtly worked to justify women's exclusion from the public sphere."[18] Propriety and civility also worked to construct a unified, articulated "self" that displayed consistency; Dickinson's poetry unwrites this self too. In this sense, her chosen privacy and lack of pointing are also her poetic subject: her poems are like journals of the passing moments, as these register, in multiply varying forms, on the interior surface of consciousness.

"Consciousness is the only home of which we *now* know," she wrote to Maria Whitney early in 1879 (*Letters*, 2:634). Her poetry, isolated and defiantly insular as it presents itself, transposes latterday New England Puritanism and transcendentalism into a thoroughly current concern that is necessarily mediated by the obliquity of its relation to a "connected" tradition of thought (analogized in James's comfortingly rhythmical and closed sentences). In her poetry, consciousness is a home that sometimes appears to be a house without a door.

> This Consciousness that is aware
> Of Neighbors and the Sun
> Will be the one aware of Death
> And that itself alone
>
> Is traversing the interval
> Experience between
> And most profound experiment
> Appointed unto Men —
>
> How adequate unto itself
> Its properties shall be

Itself unto itself and none
Shall make discovery.

Adventure most unto itself
The Soul condemned to be —
Attended by a single Hound
Its own identity. (P 822)

Consciousness can only be accounted for through consciousness;
its activities in the first two stanzas are controlled by the verb
"is aware." That awareness is, first, of the world, second, of death,
and third — most extensively — of its own "adventures." Consciousness is at once both subject and object to itself, self-
transcending but self-limiting, and, finally, self-pursuing: a heavy
metrical weight falls on "condemned" in the last stanza, so that
the attentive "Hound" comes to comprehend not only faithful-
ness but the assistant at an impending blood sport. The processes
of consciousness-as-self-consciousness take the form not of an
articulated flow or flight but of self-confrontation, an inner interrogation that establishes a "society" of divided oneness within, an
encounter that is always, at least potentially, a kind of Puritan psy-
chomachia, a battle that can end only with the defeat of both antagonists. "Ourself within ourself, concealed — / Should startle
most —" (P 670).

This is where Dickinson seems to have little patience with the
associative softenings of Common Sense–mediated Calvinism
that would provide William James with a jumping-off point. Her
poetic interest in the transitive aspects of utterance is, paradoxically, a disjunctive, not a connecting, power; her aim is apparently
not to supply the interstices that would complete the stream of
thought and image the shape of a life in a satisfying sentence
rounded with a stop, but rather to keep alive the *process* to the
point of rupture. Dickinson's canon is an unyielding one and plays
deliberately around the borders of reprobation; the poetry registers with peculiar acuteness the disruptions of human experience
at the edges of forbidden inquiry:

Me from Myself — to banish —
Had I Art —
Impregnable my Fortress
Unto all Heart —

> But since Myself — assault Me —
> How have I peace
> Except by subjugating
> Consciousness?
>
> And since We're mutual Monarch
> How this be
> Except by Abdication —
> Me — of Me? (P 642)

This meditation on inner division is like a compressed version of Edgar Allan Poe's story "William Wilson," or, perhaps more appropriately, in the context of his prose poem *Eureka*, it exploits what that work calls a "rupture through uniformity" without making the "effort at equilibrium" that would resolve its dialectic.[19] The transcendent has disappeared as an agent of resolution from her verse.

To look at it another way, Dickinson's poems intransigently *interiorize*, in advance, William James's melancholic observation in a psychological context: "One great splitting of the whole universe into two halves is made by each of us; and for each of us almost all of the interest attaches to one of the halves. . . . When I say that we all call the two halves by the same names, and that those names are '*me*' and '*not-me*' respectively, it will at once be seen what I mean" (*Principles, Works*, 9:278). But the splitting may be fatal to the song, as it never is to James's exposition:

> Split the Lark — and you'll find the Music —
> Bulb after Bulb, in Silver rolled —
> Scantily dealt to the Summer Morning
> Saved for your Ear when Lutes be old.
>
> Loose the Flood — you shall find it patent —
> Gush after Gush, reserved for you —
> Scarlet Experiment! Sceptic Thomas!
> Now, do you doubt your Bird was true? (P 861)

This literalized, somatized dissection of the singing bird becomes, symbolically, self-murder, a violent internal investigation that assassinates possibility with knowledge.[20] In this poem the biblical allusion is provocatively, rather than reassuringly, placed; Dickinson's own scepticism frames even the conversion of doubting

Thomas. The mind anatomizes loss as a severed bodily connection. The end is imaged as amputation rather than closure, the ultimate amputation being that of the divine limb that seemed to connect the Calvinist self with assurance of immortality:

> Those — dying then,
> Knew where they went —
> They went to God's Right Hand —
> That Hand is amputated now
> And God cannot be found —
>
> The abdication of Belief
> Makes the Behavior small —
> Better an ignis fatuus
> Than no illume at all — (P 1551)

This poem perhaps distills more of her characteristic poetic concerns than any other. It dramatizes the loss of faith as a decisive somatized severance that leaves behind a self at once glorified and diminished. Without the shaping structure, the wholeness of a divine plan that would at once sustain the poetic utterance and provide the sense of an ending, the poem breaks off, a line early, with a near-despairing wish for sustaining illusion. But severance does not provide release. Her poetry epitomizes how "cutting a thought across in the middle" may be, at best, invasive surgery, at worst gratuitous violence, a disconnection of sense.

In other poems the poet herself seems to be the surgeon, bringing about that dissociation of before and after in consciousness that enables us to catch the process in the act, in the arrested moment of perception. There is an extraordinary scorn for the quiddity of the object of the mind's analysis:

> She dealt her pretty words like Blades —
> How glittering they shone —
> And every One unbared a Nerve
> Or wantoned with a Bone — (P 479)

In this decapitated universe God is the ultimate amputee; if God has lost an arm, humanity has lost its Head. Faith, like a lost limb, leaves only an absent-present trace across the consciousness of her verse. Numbness is its major emotional characteristic:

A Drowsiness — diffuses —
A dimness like a Fog
Envelops Consciousness —
As Mists — obliterate a Crag.

The Surgeon — does not blanch — at pain —
His Habit — is severe —
But tell him that it ceased to feel —
The Creature lying there —

And he will tell you — skill is late —
A mightier than He —
Has ministered before Him —
There's no Vitality. (P 396) [21]

In a poem like this, Dickinson's anatomical separation, both emotional and grammatical, of the physiological from the psychological sensation literally disembodies the feeling from its source. A human subject becomes objectified under analysis to a (slightly distasteful) "Creature." The reader is given all the ingredients of emotional anguish, but in pieces, like a disassembled jigsaw puzzle, and without license to connect, or to connect with, them. More crucially, the images of the poet as singing bird and as surgeon seem to have no point of contact with one another; it is as though Dickinson's poetic voice feels equally able to adopt a "masculine" or a "feminine" stance, but without any confidence that each may speak to the other.

Despite her exploitation of the possibilities of the submissive "little Emilie" stance, I would agree with Robert Weisbuch that, characteristically, Dickinson is more interested in "how the emotion is 'done' in consciousness than in its specific origin" or than in the emotion's specific outcome or ending. [22] She shares with James an overwhelming interest in process, but in her writing the *dangerousness* of this activity is never in doubt. Each poem displays the experience of the lapsed, transitive states of consciousness that comprise the bulk of felt life; severed syntax images its constant trembling on the verge of cessation, as far as this can be represented in the living mind. The death of consciousness comes as a derangement, literally an unraveling or dishevelment, of the chains of association that constitute its sensed continuity:

I felt a Cleaving in my Mind —
As if my Brain had split —
I tried to match it — Seam by Seam —
But could not make them fit.

The thought behind, I strove to Join
Unto the thought before —
But Sequence ravelled out of Sound
Like Balls — upon a Floor. (P 937)

Her fractured grammatical and poetic forms look intently at the shape of arrested emotion. Mind/seam, join/sound are dissonant rhymes that will not "fit," with just a possibility of symmetry and closure hinted at in the unusually (for her) perfect rhymes of the alternate lines. The poem enforces its hatchet job with a kind of gothic aura appropriated from Brockden Brown or Fenimore Cooper's scalping Indians; it is also, however, disconcertingly domestic. The effect is analogous to what the psychoanalytic theorist Wilfrid Bion has called an "attack on linking": thought to feeling, intention to expression — a separating vision of words deliberately isolating themselves from their affects.[23] A moment of terrifying portentousness becomes the object of interested — and disinterested — contemplation. The implied pun links the balls of yarn with the nonconsecutive narrative of thought.[24] The gendered, almost homely, image perhaps suggests a feminine vision not constrained to the consistent self-articulation required of public discourse; at any rate, it seems to describe how the impulses of consciousness toward continuity are foiled by the disjunctive insufficiencies of language. The attack on syntactical linking becomes — to paraphrase Bion — a "destructive attack on verbal thought itself" (94).

This is the crucial difference between her description of consciousness and James's: although the inquiries of both remain urgently in the domain of consciousness, the thrust of *his* account is as biased toward continuity as hers is toward disruption: "*Within each personal consciousness,*" he writes, "*thought is sensibly continuous,* . . . without breach, crack, or division. . . . The only breaches that can well be conceived to occur within the limits of a single mind would either be *interruptions, time*-gaps during which the consciousness went out altogether to come into existence again at a later moment; or they would be breaks in the *quality*, or content, of a thought, so abrupt that the segment that followed had no connection whatever with the one before" (*Principles, Works*, 9:231).[25] Against these possibilities he asserts categorically that "the changes from one moment to another in the quality of consciousness are never absolutely abrupt." Dickinson knew otherwise. Her poetry finds itself repeatedly at the breaches, cracks, and divisions of consciousness, for it is here that the mind's awareness of itself is most acute. Grief is represented graphically as a rent or "notch" in the mind's illusion of continuity; it becomes "a trope for experience because the self's relation to experience, like its relation to grief, is oblique, angled, contingent, dissociated."[26]

Loss is so constitutive that it becomes inseparable from experience. As Dickinson writes in a late prose fragment, "are not all Facts Dreams as soon as we put them behind us?"[27] Looking into the space where the lost thing was is to encounter an experience that can only be of loss. The space is not empty; but by definition the thing that filled or should fill it is not there, cannot be recovered. Emerson's grief for his lost son eludes him; there is no place for it in a transcendentalist universe: "I cannot get it nearer to me," he laments in "Experience" (*Essays, Second Series*, 3:52). With typical aphoristic compression, Dickinson's tiny quatrain compels acknowledgement of the complete interfusion of bliss and loss, gain and pain. It is one her few lyrics that ends, having completed its thought, in a period:

> Of so divine a Loss
> We enter but the Gain,
> Indemnity for Loneliness,
> That such a Bliss has been. (P 1179)

Paradoxically, loss may be the condition of possession, as Emerson had obliquely sighted: "There are moods in which we court suffering, in the hope that here, at least, we shall find reality, sharp peaks and edges of truth." Ordinary experience is unable to give us an acute sense of reality, "for contact with which, we would even pay the costly price of sons and lovers" ("Experience," *Essays, Second Series*, 3:52). Not until we lose something do we fully realize its consequence to ourselves.

The converse also turns out to be true. To see something clearly is, in effect, to lose it, because possession is based on an illusion of ownership, the mind's illusion that it can control the continuing existence of its objects, that vigilant self-recording can secure the self against rupture:

> Perception of an object costs
> Precise the Object's loss —
> Perception in itself a Gain
> Replying to its Price —
>
> The Object Absolute — is nought —
> Perception sets it fair
> And then upbraids a Perfectness
> That situates so far — (P 1071)

Here is the crux for an introspective process with no externally assured sense of an ending. The specter of loss is the constant absent-presence at the continuing feast of consciousness in the lighted banquet hall; it haunts because it cannot be realized. Cadences of loss are caught again by James in the first volume of the *Principles*; transience of emotion, no less than of objects, is the condition of existence: "From one year to another we see things in new lights. What was unreal has grown real, and what was exciting is insipid. The friends we used to care the world for are shrunken to shadows" (*Works*, 9: 227–228).

The continuance of consciousness is therefore a tragic fact in life: because consciousness is characteristically longer lived than the objects of its attention, its experience, unrelentingly, must be of loss. So long lived, in fact, that it is all we know of eternity. In Dickinson's poems, questions are so deeply embedded in statements of faith that they become the very fabric of expression:

> To know just how He suffered — would be dear —
> To know if any Human eyes were near
> To whom He could entrust His wavering gaze —
> Until it settled broad — on Paradise —
>
> .   .   .   .
>
> Was He afraid — or tranquil —
> Might He know
> How Conscious Consciousness — could grow —
> Till Love that was — and Love too best to be —
> Meet — and the Junction be Eternity (P 622)

This whole poem is cast in a kind of wondering subjunctive; the desire of "yawning Consciousness" — consciousness perhaps without object to focus its awareness — to *know*, creates a moment vertiginous with possibility. Already, however, the last stanza suggests that knowledge — supposing we *could* have it, of the final moment, would provide but one more temporary object for the limitless expansion of consciousness's inquiries. The apparent resolution in "Eternity" — the final word, in every sense — seems to me a consciously forced and empty one: when thought, inquiry, and awareness itself have expanded to their infinite uttermost, it must be eternity, for it can be nothing else; but the poetic gesture is flaccid through lack of felt content.

To James the failures of memory are the very condition of experience: "The stream of thought flows on; but most of its segments fall into the bottomless abyss of oblivion" (*Principles, Works*, 9:605). Consciousness without memory is cut loose from its own sense of continuity, set adrift on a meaningless undirected presentness devoid of perspective and texture, "unpunctuated." Such potentially tragic moments of insight occur repeatedly in James's writing, only to have the momentum of the prose carry the thought forward into its next phase before the feeling of loss can be realized by the mind. Restlessly discursive, James's exposition of consciousness can no more stay within its periods than Dickinson's suggestions contain themselves within her amputated syntax. When memory dies, however, the substantives fail language soonest: "proper names are what go first, and at all times proper names are harder to recollect than those of general properties and classes of things. . . . adjectives, conjunctions, prepositions, and the cardinal verbs, those words, in short, which form the grammatical framework of all our speech, are the very last to decay" (*Principles, Works*, 9:643).[28] The skeleton of thought remains when the flesh that individualized and personalized it has decayed to oblivion. As with a belief system (Calvinism), the structure survives its content. In this sense, the final withering of consciousness is merely a terminal example of what goes on all through time.

In *Principles* James describes this sense of absent-presence in the context of searching our minds for a word we cannot recall. He describes the consciousness of forgetting a name as "a gap that is intensely active. A sort of wraith of the name is in it, beckoning us in a given direction, making us at moments tingle with the sense of our closeness, and then letting us sink back without the longed-for term" (*Works*, 9:243). "The feeling of an absence," as he puts it, "is *toto coelo* different from the absence of a feeling." Gaps in consciousness have a kind of spectral presence (the Calvinistic aura here is not fortuitous). The missing signifier registers itself like an amputated limb on the mind: "it tingles, it trembles on the verge, but does not come" (9:634; see 685). As with Dickinson, the image of loss carries with it a hint of mutilation. "Every degree of consciousness," he writes, "seems represented in the sense of the missing extremity" (9:749 n. 25). Dickinson brings absence right into the texture of her verse. Empty spaces are lost substantives, as well as vacancies where meaning "should" be.

> To fill a Gap
> Insert the Thing that caused it —
> Block it up
> With Other — and 'twill yawn the more —
> You cannot solder an Abyss
> With Air. (P 546)

The silence that follows the bird's song is not a simple void but a positive absence: "And Place was where the Presence was / Circumference between —" (P 1084).

The absence, the thing that is not there, is like the unconscious and is a reminder of death. Part of the ability of words to signify involves the signifier's inbuilt capacity to signify its own absence, to signal its canceled presence. The sense of being alive involves the consciousness of not being dead; consciousness itself is predicated on the state of not-consciousness. The case is made more complicated — and more agonizing — because the painfully absent-present gap or space or difference is not visible:

> Heavenly Hurt, it gives us —
> We can find no scar,
> But internal difference,
> Where the Meanings, are — (P 258)

Psychically, we are originally weightless; we attach ourselves to others and to things, which in turn tell us where we are and even who we are.[29] But the things beyond fail. The cruel amputation of that which held us in our place can happen in an instant without visible effect. "That something which I fancied was part of me, which could not be torn away without tearing me, nor enlarged without enriching me, falls off from me and leaves no scar. It was caducous" ("Experience," *Essays, Second Series*, 3 : 53). The term is used of organs or parts of things that fall away naturally when they have served their purpose: like the placenta or leaves on a tree. Nothing is *essential* to the self but its own consciousness.

For James even the notion of crisis had a function of connectiveness, as a kind of hinge between past and future. His autobiographical notes record many such moments, when, as he put it, his "feelings came to a sort of crisis," the effect of which "gave me such an unspeakable disgust for the dead drifting of my own life for some time past." [30] True to a secularized version of the Puritan conversion narrative, he invariably used such moments to form resolutions of self-improvement. No matter how often the reformation failed to materialize in his life, apparently, James held to the structural model that promised continuity through change. Dickinson inherited the same Calvinist model of psychic development through crisis but experienced it as definitively disjunctive:

Crisis is a Hair
Toward which the forces creep
Past which forces retrograde
If it come in sleep

To suspend the Breath
Is the most we can
Ignorant is it Life or Death
Nicely balancing.

Let an instant push
Or an Atom press
Or a Circle hesitate
In Circumference

It — may jolt the Hand
That adjusts the Hair
That secures Eternity
From presenting — Here — (P 889)

A crisis of consciousness turns itself inside out to become consciousness of crisis, a thinking rather than a feeling state that reduces the continuities of memory and imagination to a focus at a point of suspended awareness. The embedded grammatical structure of the final stanza gives the word "Eternity" a more conditional specific gravity than in the earlier poem; there is no slippage into a pseudopiety here that might endanger the poem's provisionality. Anguish expands consciousness, as does grief, but beyond a certain extremity the mind attempts to empty itself of consciousness — itself, paradoxically, an intensely intellectual activity, as Dickinson, like James, observed: " 'Tis a dangerous moment for any one when the meaning goes out of things and Life stands straight — and punctual — and yet no content[s] [signal] come[s]. Yet such moments are. If we survive them they expand us, if we do not, but that is Death, whose if is everlasting."[31]

Such a "lived in" consciousness (the phrase is James's brother Henry's, from his late essay "Is There a Life after Death?") is so preoccupied with its processes that it cannot articulate its own ending.[32] Emerson's idealist solution (toward which Henry James's essay seems, surprisingly, to gesture) to the post-Calvinist, post-Humean dilemma of the continuance and significance of introspective selfhood in a universe bereft of the numinous is to make the self itself transcendent. He expands the processes of consciousness, the infinite connectedness of the transitive moments, to encompass all the objects it conceives: "the solid-seeming block of matter has been pervaded and dissolved by a thought."[33] His idealism is modified in different directions by Dickinson and by William James, neither of whom could accept its implicit denial of the material. Dickinson represents consciousness as riddled with gaps and absences, moment-by-moment losses that prefigure the ultimate loss that can never be realized, because it is of itself. Almost every poem dramatizes the slippages and privation of connected meaning; many explicitly predict the end of knowing. None can make this ending "stick" or signify. In June 1878 she wrote to Mrs. Holland, "I suppose there are depths in every Consciousness, from which we cannot rescue ourselves — to which none can go with us — which represent to us mortally — the Adventure of Death — How unspeakably sweet and solemn — that whatever awaits us of Doom or Home, we are mentally permanent. 'It is finished' can never be said of us" (*Letters*, 2:612). Because the experience of consciousness is its only subject, and because consciousness outlives all its objects — indeed, cannot end, except with death, which it can conceptualize but cannot experience from within — this writing cannot comprehend ending:

Forever — is composed of Nows —
'Tis not a different time —
Except for Infiniteness —
And Latitude of Home — (P 624)

For William James experience-as-consciousness has no "sharp peaks and edges," such as Emerson sought, that would help to define and delimit its reality. There is fear as well as scientific positivism in his assertion that "we must turn our backs upon our winged concepts altogether, and bury ourselves in the thickness of those passing moments over the surface of which they fly, and on particular points of which they occasionally rest and perch."[34] The tendency of his thought, as I have suggested, is away from endings and ruptures, and seeks a larger connectedness; all James's work shows a continuity within the development from psychology to philosophy and theology. His conviction — in the context of psychology in 1890 — that "changes from one moment to another in the quality of consciousness are never absolutely abrupt" became a philosophical and then a theological belief in a larger connectedness of consciousnesses, which (though founded on physiological and materialist researches and far from idealist) might not improperly be denominated immortality. Interestingly, it is envisaged as a kind of leaking of consciousness into everything around it:

My present field of consciousness is a centre surrounded by a fringe that shades insensibly into a subconscious more. I use three separate terms here to describe this fact; but I might as well use three hundred, for the fact is all shades and no boundaries. . . . our *full* self is the whole field, with all those indefinitely radiating subconscious possibilities of increase that we can only feel without conceiving, and can hardly begin to analyze. . . . the actual in it is continuously one with possibles not yet in our present sight. And just as we are co-conscious of our own momentary margin, may not we ourselves form the margin of some more really central self in things which is co-conscious with the whole of us? May not you and I be confluent in a higher consciousness?[35]

By the end of *The Varieties of Religious Experience* (1902), notwithstanding his continuing "inability to accept either popular Christianity or scholastic theism," James was able to assert as a "fact" that *"the conscious person is continuous with a wider self through which saving experiences come,"* and to conclude that "the whole drift of my education goes to persuade me that the world of our present consciousness is only one out of many worlds of consciousness that exist" (*Works*, 15:410, 405, 408; emphasis in original). He accepted that this was a religious belief, albeit of a modified kind.

A preoccupation with loss that cannot accommodate a sense of an ending predisposes both Dickinson and James to reconstruct their own versions of what Dickinson calls the "Colossal substance" (P 306) of immortality in the absence of divinity. The different forms that the perhaps similarly motivated resistance to ending takes in Dickinson's and James's writing correspond to their characteristic forms of writing. James's prose fullness reaches toward a larger and larger connectedness for consciousness until it envisages an immortality of selfhoods in the absence of deity, while Dickinson draws "Immortality" into God's vacant seat in a famous poem:

> Because I could not stop for Death —
> He kindly stopped for me —
> The Carriage held just Ourselves —
> And Immortality — (P 712)

"'This World is not Conclusion," she confidently begins a poem, only to end it with a characteristically truncated and gnawingly unsatisfied movement of consciousness: "Narcotics cannot still the Tooth / That nibbles at the soul —" (P 501). The paradox is that the idea of immortality can only come from within consciousness, and yet it is an idea predicated on the death of consciousness, on something larger and other than itself. Though we might have an idea of it from elsewhere, and certainly a wish or need for it as an idea, *experience* of continuity through time, interruption, and (others') deaths comes ineluctably from within consciousness.

Following the "abdication of Belief" (however one may understand the phrase), what I have been calling post-Calvinist writing holds off the end with a focus on introspective processes. Of Dickinson's poetry in particular, it is fair to say that there are no "others," only absent-presences in the mind of the speaker. This is in no way a biographical judgment; it is, as I have been suggesting, a consequence of the way her thought structures its relation to otherness. The only relationship is an internal one — self within or behind the self — so that the processes of consciousness become the primary location for knowledge of identity and value, the nearest thing available to an absolute. Cultures (and individuals) that place more weight on mediated relationships with others, or on an idea of "society," face the crisis of faith differently. Here, the idea of otherness-in-relationship may be a stay against chaos. Individual ties fail or are subject to loss, but each relationship increases the capacity for further relationships, and so meaning can be located transpersonally where it is not available transcendentally. Endings can, painfully, be comprehended as final without being apocalyptic. "Capacity to terminate — is a specific Grace," Dickinson writes (P 1196). All her poetry, like all James's prose, works to postpone a reality that is imagined as self-murder. It is as though, if the bird should cease to sing on its solitary flight, the banquet hall itself would instantly disappear.

NOTES

1. William James, *Principles of Psychology*, 3 vols., in *The Works of William James*, 19 vols., ed. Frederick H. Burkhardt et al. (Cambridge: Harvard University Press, 1975–1988), 9:236–237. Second and subsequent references to this and other sources appear in the text.

2. The Venerable Bede, *The History of the English Church and People*, trans. Leo Sherley-Price (Harmondsworth, England: Penguin, 1960), 124–125.

3. Emily Dickinson, *The Poems of Emily Dickinson*, ed. Thomas H. Johnson, 3 vols. (Cambridge: Harvard University Press, 1955), Poem 703. Subsequent references to Dickinson's poems are cited as "P."

4. Behind both Dickinson and James lurks Emerson: "all language is vehicular and transitive, and is good, as ferries and horses are, for conveyance, not as farms and houses are, for homestead." "The Poet," in *Essays, Second Series*, Riverside edition, *Complete Works of Emerson* (Boston: Houghton Mifflin, 1885), 3:37.

5. In 1911 Flournoy described James's view that "psychic facts must be observed in their integrity, as individual pulsations of the continuous 'stream of consciousness.'" See Gay Wilson Allen, *William James: A Biography* (London: Rupert Hart-Davis, 1976), 497. More than a hundred years before, William Blake had used the image to evoke a time-defeating sense

of poetic creativity; see *Milton*, Plates 28.62–29.3, in *The Poetry and Prose of William Blake*, ed. David V. Erdman (1965; reprint, Garden City, N.Y.: Doubleday, 1970), 126.

6. See David Porter, *The Art of Emily Dickinson's Early Poetry* (Cambridge: Harvard University Press, 1966); Sharon Cameron, *Choosing Not Choosing: Dickinson's Fascicles* (Chicago: University of Chicago Press, 1992).

7. This is a highly compressed summary of a complex and much-investigated subject. For fuller discussions of the intellectual links between Scotland and America and the shared influence of Calvinism on both cultures, see, for example, Terence Martin, *The Instructed Vision: Scottish Common Sense Philosophy and the Origins of American Fiction* (Bloomington: Indiana University Press, 1961); Douglas Sloan, *The Scottish Enlightenment and the American College Ideal* (New York: Teachers College Press, 1971); Andrew Hook, *Scotland and America: A Study of Cultural Relations 1750–1835* (Glasgow: Blackie & Son, 1975); Garry Wills, *Inventing America: Jefferson's Declaration of Independence* (New York: Doubleday, 1978); J. David Hoeveler, Jr., *James McCosh and the Scottish Intellectual Tradition: From Glasgow to Princeton* (Princeton: Princeton University Press, 1981); Susan Manning, *The Puritan-Provincial Vision: Scottish and American Literature in the Nineteenth Century* (Cambridge: Cambridge University Press, 1990); Richard B. Sher and Jeffrey R. Smitten, eds., *Scotland and America in the Age of Enlightenment* (Edinburgh: Edinburgh University Press, 1990).

8. David Hume, *A Treatise of Human Nature*, ed. L. A. Selby-Bigge, 2d ed., text revised by Peter Nidditch (Oxford: Clarendon Press, 1978), 252. See also Stephen D. Cox, *"The Stranger Within Thee": Concepts of the Self in Late Eighteenth-Century Literature* (Pittsburgh: University of Pittsburgh Press, 1980).

9. James Beattie, "Of Memory and Imagination," in *Dissertations Moral and Critical: The Works of James Beattie*, ed. Roger Robinson, 10 vols. (Bristol: Routledge/Thoemmes Press, 1996), 5:1. Beattie describes our understanding of memory as working in the service of our destination of immortality: by knowing this aspect of human nature, we see in ourselves reflections of divine nature. Beattie's *Theory of Language* demonstrates his interest in the relationship between principles of grammar and the structure of the human mind, and in the connection between words and thoughts.

10. Thomas Reid, *Essays on the Intellectual Powers of Man*, ed. A. D. Woozley (1940; reprint, Charlottesville, Va.: Lincoln-Rembrandt, n.d.), 214.

11. See Elizabeth Flower, "Some Interesting Connections between the

Common Sense Realists and the Pragmatists, especially James," in *Two Centuries of Philosophy in America*, ed. Peter Caws (n.p.: Blackwell Publishers, 1980), 102.

12. Emerson, "The Transcendentalist," from *Nature, Addresses and Lectures*, in *Complete Works*, 1:314.

13. See E. Miller Budick, *Emily Dickinson and the Life of Language: A Study in Symbolic Poetics* (Baton Rouge: Louisiana State University Press, 1985), 219.

14. See, for example, the continuities traced by Frederic J. Carpenter, "William James and Emerson," *American Literature* 11 (1939): 39–57, and Richard Poirier, *Poetry and Pragmatism* (Cambridge: Harvard University Press, 1992).

15. *Principles, Works*, 9:221. See also Ross Posnock, *The Trial of Curiosity: Henry James, William James, and the Challenge of Modernity* (New York: Oxford University Press, 1991), 20.

16. See Frederick J. Ruf, *The Creation of Chaos: William James and the Stylistic Making of a Disorderly World* (Albany: State University of New York Press, 1991), 96.

17. Dickinson to T. W. Higginson, *The Letters of Emily Dickinson*, ed. Thomas H. Johnson, 3 vols. (Cambridge: Harvard University Press, 1958), 2:450.

18. Kenneth Cmiel, *Democratic Eloquence: The Fight over Popular Speech in Nineteenth-Century America* (Berkeley: University of California Press, 1990), 30.

19. Edgar Allan Poe, *Eureka*, in *Edgar Allan Poe: Poetry and Tales*, Library of America (Cambridge: Cambridge University Press, 1984), 1310.

20. Interestingly, there is a veiled suggestion in James's writing that he may have experienced the forced choice of vocation as a similar annihilation of the individual's unforced freedom to "sing"; in a lecture delivered to the Harvard Natural History Society in 1880 and subsequently published as "Great Men and their Environment" in *The Will to Believe* (*Works*, 6:171), he describes with considerable animus how a young man, having finalized his choice, "may sometimes doubt whether the self he murdered in that decisive hour might not have been the better of the two."

21. Suggesting some of the more questionable implications of "cutting a thought across in the middle," George Santayana's description of James's investigations into the nature of religious experience makes a suggestive comparison. See *Selected Critical Writing of George Santayana*, ed. Norman Henfrey, 2 vols. (Cambridge: Cambridge University Press, 1968), 1:300–301.

22. Robert Weisbuch, *Emily Dickinson's Poetry* (Chicago: University of Chicago Press, 1975), 106.

23. Wilfrid Bion, *Second Thoughts* (London: W. Heinemann, 1967), 93–109.

24. Daniel Hoffman, "Emily Dickinson: The Heft of Cathedral Tunes," *Hudson Review* 50.2 (1997): 217.

25. James here seems to be echoing Beattie on the disruptions of memory during sleep or as a consequence of "sudden and violent actions" (Beattie, "Of Memory and Imagination," 5:12).

26. Sharon Cameron, "Representing Grief: Emerson's 'Experience,'" *Representations* 15 (1986): 29.

27. Emily Dickinson, Prose Fragment, *Letters*, 3:915. It is a thought that seems to contain a reminiscence of Emerson's "Dream delivers us to dream, and there is no end to illusion" (see above, page 311).

28. In Scottish historical linguistics (Beattie, for example), nouns come first in the development of language.

29. See John J. McDermott, *Streams of Experience: Reflections on the History and Philosophy of American Culture* (Amherst: University of Massachusetts Press, 1986), 57.

30. Quoted from a notebook in Howard M. Feinstein, *Becoming William James* (Ithaca: Cornell University Press, 1984), 308.

31. Emily Dickinson, prose fragment, in *Letters*, 3:919. In "Human Immortality," William James paraphrases Gustav Fechner's influential "threshold" theory of consciousness to indicate the background to his own theory of thought processes (*Essays in Religion and Morality*, in *Works*, 11:90).

32. Henry James, cited in F. O. Matthiessen, *The James Family* (New York: Knopf, 1947), 609.

33. Emerson, "Nature," from *Nature, Addresses and Lectures*, in *Complete Works*, 1:60. This is an oversimplification of Emerson's position, which was never unequivocally idealist, and which become more skeptical, but — as the reference to Henry James suggests — it remained a temptation to many American writers, including, at moments, both Dickinson and William James.

34. William James, "Bergson and His Critique of Intellectualism," from *A Pluralistic Universe*, in *Works*, 4:112.

35. James, "The Continuity of Human Experience," from *A Pluralistic Universe*, in *Works*, 4:130–131.

Contributors

Janet Beer is professor and head of the department of English at the Manchester Metropolitan University. Her publications include *Edith Wharton: Traveller in the Land of Letters* (1990) and *Kate Chopin, Edith Wharton, and Charlotte Perkins Gilman: Studies in Short Fiction* (1997). She is currently working on a literary life of Edith Wharton and coediting a collection of essays entitled *International Episodes: Anglo-American Exchanges.*

Alison M. J. Easton is senior lecturer of American literature and women's studies at Lancaster University and was codirector of its Centre for Women's Studies from 1991 to 1994. Her most recent work includes *The Making of the Hawthorne Subject* (1996) and the new Penguin edition of Sarah Orne Jewett's *The Country of the Pointed Firs* (1996).

R. J. (Dick) Ellis is professor and head of English at Nottingham Trent University. He has published on Frederick Douglass, Mark Twain, William Faulkner, Alice Walker, Lawrence Ferlinghetti, and Kathy Acker, among others. The coeditor of *Science Fiction Roots and Branches: Contemporary Critical Approaches* (1990) and one of the editors of the *European Journal of American Culture,*

he has completed an edition of Harriet E. Wilson's *Our Nig.*

M. Giulia Fabi is assistant professor of American literature at the University of Bologna. She has published essays on William Wells Brown, Frank J. Webb, Sutton Griggs, Frances Harper, A. E. Johnson, Henry James, Edward Bellamy, Alice Walker, and African American feminist criticism. The editor of a series of Italian translations of African American novels, she is completing a book on the trope of "passing" in early African American fiction.

Janet Floyd is senior lecturer in American studies at King Alfred's College, Winchester. Her research interests lie in the writing of the domestic in North America, and she is completing a book on the writing of housework in North American emigrant autobiography. She has also edited, with Inga Bryden, a forthcoming collection of essays, *Domestic Space: Reading the Nineteenth-Century Interior in Britain and America.*

Karen L. Kilcup is associate professor of American literature at the University of North Carolina at Greensboro. The recipient of a U.S. national distinguished teacher award, she has many publications in American women's writing; her work includes *Nineteenth-Century American Women Writers: An Anthology* (1997), *Nineteenth-Century American Women Writers: A Critical Reader* (1998), *Robert Frost and Feminine Literary Tradition* (1998), *Jewett and Her Contemporaries: Reshaping the Canon* (1999), and *Native American Women Writers 1824–1924: An Anthology* (2000). In 1995, while at the University of Hull, England, she founded the International Nineteenth-Century American Women Writers Research Group.

Susan Manning holds the Grierson Chair of English and American literature at the University of Edinburgh. In addition to her book, *The Puritan Provincial Vision* (1990), on Scottish and American writers, she has published essays on eighteenth- and nineteenth-century American writers and is particularly interested in the relationship between literature and philosophy. A recent article pursues relationships between Emily Dickinson and Georgia O'Keeffe as American women artists misunderstood by their primarily male first reviewers, an argument she is developing further in a new book, currently entitled *Fragments of Union*.

Stephen Matterson is senior lecturer of American literature and a fellow at Trinity College, University of Dublin. The joint editor of the *Journal of the Irish Association of American*

Studies, he has published work on a variety of American writers, including *Berryman and Lowell: The Art of Losing* (1988) and the Penguin edition of Melville's *The Confidence-Man* (1990).

Judie Newman is professor of English, American, and postcolonial literature at the University of Newcastle and a past president of the British Association of American Studies. Her publications include *The Ballistic Bard: Postcolonial Fictions* (1995), *Nadine Gordimer* (1988), and editions of Stowe's *Dred: A Tale of the Great Dismal Swamp* (1992, 1998).

Susanne Opfermann is professor of American studies at the Johann Wolfgang Goethe-Universität in Frankfurt. Specializing in gender and ethnic studies, she has published several articles and two books in the field, including *Diskurs, Geschlecht, und Literatur: Amerikanische Autorinnen des 19. Jahrhunderts* (*Discourse, Gender, and Literature: American Women Writers of the Nineteenth Century*) (1996).

Ralph J. Poole teaches American literature and gender studies at the University of Munich. The coeditor of an anthology on serial killers (1997), he is completing a book entitled *Cannibal (P)Acts: Literary Anthropophagy as Social Ritual*. His publications include essays on queer theory and gender studies, vampirism, Asian American drama, pornography, Kathy Acker, Harold Brodkey, Marianne Moore, and

Elfriede Jelinek, as well as *Performing Bodies: Transgressions of Gender-Boundaries in the Theatre of the Avant-Garde* (1996).

Claire Preston is fellow in English and American literature, Sidney Sussex College, Cambridge, and Newton Trust lecturer in the faculty of English. In addition to major work in the Renaissance, she has published essays on such American writers as Wharton and Dreiser. Her book, *Edith Wharton's Social Register*, will be published in 1999.

Gabriele Rippl is lecturer of English and American literature at the University of Konstanz. Her research interests include feminist literary theory, women's writing of the early modern period, and literature and anthropoligy. Recent publications include *Life-Texts: Seventeenth-century Englishwomen's Literary Self-Fashionings* (1998), *Collectors, Bibliophiles, Eccentrics* (1998, with A. Assman and M. Gomille), and *"Indescribably Female": Feminist Anthropological Texts* (1993).

Lindsey Traub is vice president of Lucy Cavendish College, University of Cambridge, where she is also lecturer and director of studies in English. Her research interests lie mainly in American and British nineteenth-century writing, and she has published work on Henry James, Margaret Fuller, and other American women writers.

Aranzazu Usandizaga is lecturer in American and English literature at the Universidad Autónoma de Barcelona. Her publications include *Teatro y política: el movimiento dramático Irlandes* (1985) and *Amor y literatura: la búsqueda literaria de la identidad femenina* (1993).

Hanna Wallinger is assistant professor of American studies at the University of Salzburg. Her publications include *Daughters of Restlessness: Women's Literature at the End of the Millennium* (1998, with Sabine Coelsch-Foisner and Gerhild Reisner) and essays on African American literature.

Index

Gammel, Irene, 172

Garber, Marjorie, 183 n.16, 257–58 n.5

Gardner, Eric, 122 n.24

Gardner, Joseph H., 216 n.5

Garrison, William Lloyd, 117, 122 n.21

Gass, William, 161

Gates, Henry Louis, Jr., 122 n.25

Geary, Susan, 236 n.29

Genovese, Eugene, 94 n.7

George, Laurie E., 182 n.5

Gibson, Donald B., 96 n.20

Gibson, Mary Ellis, 143

Giddings, Paula, 278 n.4, 280 n.22

Gilbert, Sandra M., 23 n.30, 137 n.15

Gilder, Helena de Kay, 216 n.4

Gilder, Richard Watson, 205

Gilman, Charlotte Perkins, 15–16, 123–140

Gilmore, Michael T., 222, 224–25

Gillman, Susan, 80 n.16

Ginger, Ray, 200 n.18

Goethe, Johann Wolfgang von, 284, 285

Goldsby, Jacqueline, 93 n.3

Gossett, Thomas F., 264

Grant, Robert, 186

Grasso, Linda, 234 n.6

Graulich, Melody, 204, 217 n.8

Greeley, Horace, 286

Grimké, Angelina, 96 n.22

Gubar, Susan, 23 n.30, 137 n.15

Guillory, John, 18 n.1

Griswold, Rufus, 1, 2, 3, 4

Halleck, Fitz-Greene, 3

Hamilton, Kristie, 236 n.28

Hapke, Laura, 182 n.8, 221–22

Harper, Frances E. W., 24 n.33, 48–66

Harper's Bazaar, 7

Harris, Sharon M., 259 n.17

Harris, Susan K., 19 n.5, 120 n.11, 136 n.1, 236 n.28

Harte, Bret, 16, 23 n.29, 202–18

Hartwell, David G., 259 n.16

Haselstein, Ulla, 38

Hauss, Jon, 96 n.19

Hawthorne, Nathaniel, 3, 6, 17, 214, 216 n.3, 219–36, 281, 288

Hedge, Henry, 284, 287

Hedges, Elaine, 65 n.23, 137 n.14

Hemingway, Ernest, 23 n.31

Herbert, T. Walter, 225

Higginson, Thomas Wentworth, 6, 303, 304

Higgonet, Margaret R., 47 n.29

Hildreth, Margaret Holbrook, 81 n.22

Hoeveler, J. David, Jr., 329 n.7

Hoffman, Daniel, 331 n.24

Hoffman, E. T. A., 124, 136 n.12

Hogarth, William, 132

Holmes, George F., 121 n.19

Hook, Andrew, 329 n.7

Hope, Lugenia, 267

Hopkins, Gerard Manley, 307

Hopkins, Pauline Elizabeth, 9, 13, 269

Howe, Julia Ward, 297

Howe, Lawrence, 79 n.2

Howells, William Dean, 3, 7–14, 23 n.23, 48–66, 185, 186, 187, 201 n.24, 203, 205

Hudspeth, Robert N., 282

Hume, David, 309–10

Hutchinson, Linda, 271

Hutchinson, Louise Daniel, 279 n.9